BASTARD SONS

BASTARD SONS

AN EXAMINATION OF CANADA'S
AIRBORNE EXPERIENCE
1942-1995

LIEUTENANT-COLONEL BERND HORN

Vanwell Publishing Limited
St. Catharines, Ontario

Copyright© 2001 by Bernd Horn. All rights reserved. No part of this book may be reproduced or utilized in any form or by any means, electronic or mechanical, including photocopying and recording, or by any information storage and retrieval system, without permission in writing from the publisher.

Vanwell Publishing acknowledges the financial support of the Government of Canada through the Book Publishing Industry Development Program for our publishing activities.

Design: Linda Moroz-Irvine
Cover: Linda Moroz-Irvine

Vanwell Publishing Limited
1 Northrup Crescent
P.O. Box 2131
St. Catharines, Ontario L2R 7S2
sales@vanwell.com
phone 905-937-3100
fax 905-937-1760

Printed in Canada

National Library of Canada Cataloguing in Publication Data

Horn, Bernd, 1959-
        Bastard sons : an examination of Canada's airborne experience, 1942-1995

Includes bibliographical references and index.
ISBN 1-55125-078-0

       1. Canada—Armed Forces—Airborne troops—History. I. Title.

UD485.C3H667 2001   356'.166'0971   C2001-902229-8

TABLE OF CONTENTS

Foreword vii
Preface ix
Acknowledgements xii
Regimental Commanders
Commanding Officers of the
Canadian Airborne Regiment xiii
Introduction 15

PART I ROOTS

CHAPTER 1   Reluctant Beginnings 25
The Establishment of a Canadian Airborne Capability 1942-1945

CHAPTER 2   A Question of Threat 43
The Defence of Canada and the Need for Airborne Forces, 1935-1945

CHAPTER 3   Political Expediency 69
Paratroopers as the Guardians of the Canadian North, 1946-1967

CHAPTER 4   Winds of Change 98
Embracing the Concepts of Rapid Reaction Forces and Strategic Mobility, 1964-1968

PART II THE CANADIAN AIRBORNE REGIMENT

CHAPTER 5   The Great Adventure 119
The Establishment of the Canadian Airborne Regiment, 1968

CHAPTER 6   The Long Kiss Goodnight 143
The Canadian Airborne Regiment in the Seventies

CHAPTER 7   Descent into Darkness 161
The Continuing Degradation of the Airborne's Unique Status in the Eighties

CHAPTER 8   Toward the Abyss 185
The Canadian Airborne Regiment and Somalia, 1990-1993

CHAPTER 9   An Absence of Honour 217
The Disbandment of the Canadian Airborne Regiment, 1993-1995

PART III IN THE SHADOW OF PEGASUS: A POSTSCRIPT

CHAPTER 10   A Question of Survival 249
Canada's Airborne Capability After Disbandment, 1995-1999

CHAPTER 11   Conclusion 263

List of Abbreviations 282
Index 285
The Author 288

This book is dedicated to my wife, Kim.

F O R E W O R D

What manner of men are these who wear the Maroon Beret?

These are the opening words of Field Marshal Sir Bernard Law Montgomery's tribute to paratroopers at the close of the Second World War. He went on to answer the question in his own inimitable way:

...they have that infectious optimism and that offensive eagerness that comes from physical wellbeing. They have "jumped" from the air and by so doing have conquered fear....They have shown themselves to be as tenacious in defence as they are courageous in attack. They are in fact, men apart—"every man an Emperor."

Perhaps it is accolades such as Monty's which give to paratroopers that mystic, heroic quality which is so prevalent among airborne warriors. Perhaps it is the aggressive, hard-nosed way in which "sky soldiers" will tackle any job that stays in public perception. Perhaps "elite" springs to mind with the image of men stepping into space through rushing aircraft doors, laden with their body's own weight in equipment, to an uncertain landing. Perhaps too it is nothing more than an intense, personal, common bond of comradeship and trust forged between men who have "jumped" as their way of soldiering. Whatever it is, once acquired, it is always present.

Recently there have been a number of publications—personal, sociological, sensational, anecdotal and judicial—which have made pubic some aspects of the Canadian airborne experience. No doubt the Somalia incident in 1993 focussed much attention not only on the Canadian Airborne Regiment but also on the Canadian Armed Forces generally. It provided the fledgling Liberal government with an opportunity to bring the military to heel and to apply devastating personnel and budget cuts with very little regard for the loss of capability which the imposed changes have wrought. The disbandment of the Airborne Regiment was a travesty that signalled the beginning of a steep decline in military affairs. It had, however, attraction for politicians and bureaucrats. It was a chance to reassign resources and save money. The army, in particular, was dealt with savagely and continues to be undermanned, underequipped and overextended.

Bernd Horn brings us through the whole of the Canadian airborne experience by tracing a detailed and thoroughly researched history from tentative wartime beginnings to the present. Canadian interest in and understanding of airborne forces has never been well developed. That may, in part, be due to the placement of our wartime units (1st Canadian Parachute Battalion and elements of First Special Service Force) in British and American combat formations and hence under foreign operational command. They were, in a sense, orphan units. The records shows, however, that they were highly regarded by their fighting comrades and were courageous, effective units which brought honour and glory to Canada.

This very readable book adds a credible, essential and balanced view of how we got into airborne operations, traces the development of our capability over the years and suggests an outlook for the future. It highlights the question of a viable, credible operational role for our own airborne forces and how that problem has affected the support and determination of our capability in this field. Some of the author's conclusions about incidents, moves, changes of structure, command relationships, selection of personnel, personalities, training and operational deployments will not agree with those of some readers. That being said, he has raised important issues in a scholarly way, analyzed and recorded them in a manner not available in any other single publication.

Bernd Horn has done a masterful job in presenting the Canadian Airborne story. It is told by a professional who has been "under the canopy" and reflects knowledge, sensitivity, and affection. Proud, passionate and peerless were Canadian paratroopers. We shall be the poorer for their passing. As a member of the larger "airborne family," I feel most honoured to have been able to contribute this foreword and also to thank the author on behalf of all "Jumpers" for telling our story.

"Airborne! Prends Garde!"
Major-General (retired) Herbert C. Pitts, MC, CD

P R E F A C E

Who are we in maroon, warriors from the sky so universally recognized but so often misunderstood, uniquely skilled, robust and fearless soldiers so admired but so often reviled and maligned, modern centurions so able and willing to serve but so often marginalized, men who wear the nation's uniform with respect and honour but whose political, social and military membership is so often questioned or denied. All of us who stood so proudly, yet felt so wronged on that quiet Petawawa parade square, the afternoon of 5 March 1995 asked, in our own way, these very types of questions in our silence. We, the last of a great Regiment understood Montgomery's words "they are in fact men apart—every man an emperor" and we indeed appreciate the full message of Lieutenant-Colonel Bernd Horn's book *Bastard Sons*.

The pages that follow present not only one of the best summaries of the Canadian military's relatively brief but proud fifty-seven years of airborne experience but more importantly offer a very well reasoned and thoroughly researched analysis of why the retention of Canada's airborne capability presented such a difficult challenge for the political and military establishments of the day. In breaking down our airborne history into five distinct periods including: the establishment of a wartime parachute capability from 1942-1945, immediate post WWII capability in the form of a Special Air Service Company from 1946-1948, a brigade-group-based Mobile Striking Force and battalion-based Defence of Canada Force from 1948-1967, the Canadian Airborne Regiment from 1968-1995, and the re-creation of decentralized regimental parachute companies from 1995 to the present, Horn describes the awkwardness, hesitation and uncertainty of our transition from one period to another. He emphasizes in a detailed and precise manner the underlying themes that placed Canada's development and commitment to airborne capability on such uncertain ground. Convincingly, his thesis argues that the lack of a clearly defined, credible and enduring role for the use of airborne forces fundamentally undermined any long term and substantive political and military support for such capability. This was apparent in time of war when our senior political and military leadership struggled with the decision of whether to follow the British and American development of airborne forces and, if so, were such forces to be justified by a home defence requirement or, as they eventually became, as part of a spearhead for Allied operations in Western Europe. Equally it was apparent throughout the post WWII period that little or no consensus could be achieved on the role and requirement for such forces as the Mobile Striking Force and the Defence of Canada Force. These structures were born in such hesitancy and with such lack of conviction that they were really nothing more than paper tigers with no supporting doctrinal basis, no agreed upon training focus and little or no dedicated equipment. The arrival of the Canadian Airborne Regiment, whose overall footprint seemed to correct the hollowness and lack of commitment of previous structures still, as the author so aptly argues, failed to camouflage the continual uncertainty over role and need. Its collapse, although dramatic and supremely controversial, was in Horn's view the preordained destiny of yet another airborne structure built without an accepted role.

Even as we crossed the boundary into a new millennium, almost sixty years from the launch of the 1st Canadian Parachute Battalion, we clearly see Horn's thesis being acted out again. The mere existence of our three disconnected regimental parachute companies is being challenged as the Army tries to justify their existence. What is the role of such companies in today's era of the so-called "standardized wheel borne medium weight army"? How can they be supported and maintained in the shadow of a significant Army deficit? A familiar tapestry of argument and discussion that again threatens to disenfranchise those remaining few who wear the maroon beret making them, like those who came before, Horn's "bastard sons."

As the last Commander of the Canadian Airborne Regiment and as a PPCLI infantry officer who reaped the benefit of three airborne tours of duty spanning three decades of service, I have lived Canada's uneasy embrace of the airborne experience. I have felt that schizophrenic existence of soldiering with the most resilient, energized, skilled and committed warriors this country has produced while at the same time knowing these same soldiers have had to routinely justify their very existence. Why is it that being airborne raises such controversy and demands such scrutiny? Is it because we serve a society that is frequently out of touch and ill at ease with its own military heritage and thus the lightening rod connotation of a maroon warrior elite is simply too much to bear? Is it because there is a political environment which finds it easier to consult, deliberate and follow and thus is not anxious to embrace a rapid deployment capability that will force early commitment and therefore leadership? Is it because there is a natural animosity within certain military circles to any organization that projects elitism and exclusivity? Is it because we operate within a military that so values a managerial approach of only addressing the so-called "must dos" that support of anything specialized simply does not enter into the equation? Or, is it simply a question of too little money and too few resources? The author asks and addresses many of these same fundamental questions. His conclusion is that such factors have all impacted on our rocky airborne experience. Above all though, he concludes that it is that lack of attachment to a well defined and lasting role that has made it impossible for Canada to embrace an airborne capability.

Perhaps as we reflect on Horn's study of airborne capability and the past and current struggle over its role and retention, we should reflect on the historical record of such forces. From a Canadian perspective we should remember the airborne successes of WWII in Normandy and in Northwest Europe. We should also recollect those achievements in Montreal during the FLQ Crisis in 1970, in Cyprus during the Turkish invasion of 1974, at the Montreal Olympic Games in 1976, in Somalia in 1993 and finally in Rwanda in 1994. In addition, we should also reflect more broadly on the effect of the maroon beret presence in contemporary international conflict such as the Falklands War in 1982, Grenada in 1983, Panama in 1989, the Gulf War in 1990-1991, Kosovo in 1999, and most recently Sierra Leone. In all of these cases, and in many unmentioned, we see on the one hand an enormous variance in mission and environmental employment and on the other a similarity of requirement. A requirement to have available a ready, mobile force of highly trained warriors, who through their pride and determination, physical and mental toughness and "can-do" confidence, bring to bear a real and psychological operational presence that can guarantee an unmatched quality of performance and success. For those who try to pigeonhole the airborne requirement through a restrictive analysis of existing and potential threat; who judge its necessity through a management process of counting dollars and cents; or who view the requirement through a lens of jealousy, resentment, fear, distrust, tribalism or simple personal failure to "hook up on the anchor line cable"; it is wise to ask this question: In a rapidly changing world, where the unpredictable shape of conflict will continue to be the order of the day, can our country further risk its beliefs, honour and very existence by excluding a rapidly deployable capability whose identity naturally harnesses some of the most versatile, committed and inspired soldiers our nation has to offer? Although the answer to this question is obvious to those of us who have worn the maroon beret it should be pondered by that wider audience who should and must take the time to read this excellent book.

    Peter G. Kenward
    Colonel
    Last Commanding Officer, The Canadian Airborne Regiment

ACKNOWLEDGEMENTS

As with any project of this magnitude, this book could not have been completed without the assistance, encouragement and support of many people. I wish to begin by noting my deepest gratitude to Dr. Ronald Haycock, Dean of Arts at the Royal Military College in Kingston. His advice, guidance and tutelage proved invaluable and created an unparalleled learning experience. Furthermore, his patience and impressive ability to bring discipline to a very emotional subject underscores his stature as a remarkable scholar and educator. Similarly, I must also thank Dr. Jane Errington, also of RMC, for her advice and more importantly for her infectious passion for history.

I wish also to acknowledge my debt to all those who took the time to respond to my queries and share their experiences and thoughts with me. Understandably, the list is too long to identify everyone; however, I do want to mention specific individuals who went that extra mile to provide me with assistance in an effort to set the record straight. Specifically, I wish to convey my special thanks to Major Anthony Balasevicius, Colonel (retired) Mike Barr, Brigadier-General (retired) Ernie Beno, Bob Firlotte, Colonel (retired) Ian Fraser, Major-General (retired) J.M.R. Gaudreau, Colonel Peter Kenward, Major-General (retired) Herb Pitts, and Major-General (retired) R.I. Stewart.

I am also indebted to the staffs of the National Archives (NAC), DND Directorate of History and Heritage and the Canadian Airborne Forces Museum (CAFM). In this vein, I wish to recognize the special assistance of Michel Wyczynski (NAC), Denis Lavoie (CAFM) and Mike Broxham (CAFM).

In addition, I must also acknowledge the outstanding effort of Angela Dobler and her staff for turning the original manuscript into a polished final product. As always, any errors remain my own.

Last, but by no means least, I wish to thank my wife, without whose encouragement, support and tolerance, I could never have completed this project, much less a demanding career in the Canadian Forces.

REGIMENTAL COMMANDERS

CANADIAN AIRBORNE REGIMENT

1968-1969	Colonel D.H. Rochester
1969-1971	Colonel R.G. Therriault
1971-1973	Colonel H.C. Pitts
1973-1975	Colonel G.H. Lessard
1975-1977	Colonel I.S. Fraser
1977-1978	Colonel J.J. Painchaud
1978-1980	Colonel K.R. Foster
1980-1982	Colonel R.L. Cowling
1982-1985	Colonel I.C. Douglas
1985-1987	Colonel J.M.R. Gaudreau
1987-1990	Colonel M.J.R. Houghton
1990-1992	Colonel W.M. Holmes

COMMANDING OFFICERS

1992-1992	Lieutenant-Colonel P.R. Morneault
1992-1993	Lieutenant-Colonel D.C.A. Mathieu
1993-1995	Lieutenant-Colonel P.G. Kenward

COLONELS OF THE REGIMENT

1971-76	Lieutenant-General S.C. Waters
1976-82	Brigadier-General D.E. Holmes
1982-86	Major-General H.C. Pitts
1986-89	Brigadier-General R.G. Therriault
1989-94	Lieutenant-Colonel G.F. Eadie
1994-95	Lieutenant-General K.R. Foster

I do not express the above view with the object of directing criticism on officers...but as a matter of historical record, when this operation can be examined in all its aspects, I feel under an obligation to express my frank opinion.

Lieutenant-General G.G. Simonds
GOC Canadian Forces in the Netherlands
21 January 1946

INTRODUCTION

In early 1995 the Canadian Airborne Regiment was suddenly and unexpectedly disbanded by the prime minister. Publicly, the reasons were its disciplinary problems and the tragic and brutal killing of the Somali teenager, Shidane Arone, by some of the Regiment's members while serving in Somalia two years earlier. Most Canadians continue to believe that these were the causes of the Regiment's disbandment. At best, they were only the immediate manifestations of chronic problems that had plagued the Airborne and its predecessors since their inception almost 53 years previously. This book uncovers and analyzes these complex factors.

Put briefly, the Canadian attitude to airborne forces has always been schizophrenic and driven by political purpose rather than by doctrine and operational necessity. The failure to properly identify a consistent and pervasive role for airborne forces led to a roller coaster existence, dependent on the personalities in power and political expedients of the day. This approach ultimately led to the demise of the Canadian Airborne Regiment (Cdn AB Regt). However, this book is not meant to deal exclusively with the Airborne Regiment, but rather the entirety of the Canadian airborne experience from July 1942 to March 1995.

Key to this discussion is the fact that the Canadian military and political leadership have never believed that airborne forces represented a credible national requirement. Canadian paratroopers, with the exception of 1 Canadian Parachute Battalion which was attached to the 6th British Airborne Division during the Second World War, have never been used for their original purpose. Airborne forces are specifically organized, equipped and trained for delivery by airdrop or air-landing into an area to seize objectives or conduct special operations.[1] Their greatest strength is that they provide a rapid reaction and strategic power projection capability. Although important to great powers such as Britain, France, the former Soviet Union and the United States, as well as some middle-power countries, airborne forces have never been important to Canada. For many reasons speed of action or deployment has rarely been demanded by Canadian governments. For them the time required to ready one's forces is an excellent means to allow an ill-defined but potentially explosive situation to crystallize, if not dissipate. Furthermore, it takes fewer resources to follow a beaten path than it does to break trail.

Over the half century covered by this study the Canadian airborne experience continually demonstrates that reality. The Canadian political and military leadership has repeatedly taken an irresolute approach to the requirement for airborne forces. During the early years of the Second World War the decision to establish a Canadian parachute capability was initially rejected because no viable role for these special troops was visualized. However, the political and military leadership later accepted the idea, but with the caveat that it be kept at a very low and decentralized level. During the Second World War the growing British interest in airborne forces provided the catalyst for the establishment of a Canadian parachute battalion, which later served with distinction during the conflict, but was quickly disbanded at the end of the war.

The postwar era was similarly fraught with hesitation and indecision with regard to the Canadian debate on airborne forces. The mercurial change in technology during the Second World War, particularly jet aircraft and nuclear weapons, shattered the dependence of many nations on geography for security. For Canada, this predicament was exacerbated by the emergence of two rival superpowers which sandwiched the Dominion between them. Of even greater concern, was the realization that the Americans viewed Canada as an exposed flank. American apprehension for the security of the North was matched only by Ottawa's concern over Canadian sovereignty, especially in the northern reaches. To keep the Americans out of Canada's North, the federal government realized it must show not only the intent, but also the capability to guard the back door. An ill-defined threat to the north, a paranoid giant to the south, and a tight-fisted government which traditionally held the military in disdain, created the quintessential marriage of convenience.

The Canadian government quickly perceived airborne forces as a political solution to their dilemma. To politicians, paratroopers represented a convenient, viable force capable of responding to any hostile incursion into the Arctic that threatened Canada, or more importantly the United States. However, for the government, an airborne element also represented an inexpensive means of safeguarding the nation's sovereignty.

And so in the immediate post war period, the reconstitution of an airborne force, now called the Mobile Striking Force (MSF), was rooted in this political reality. Official DND statements described the MSF as a "coiled-spring" of lethality. The truth, however, was substantially different. In the acid test of the real world it became evident that the Mobile Striking Force was a "paper tiger."

The Army leadership consciously maintained this state of affairs. Perhaps realizing that the government was supportive of airborne forces, not for the sake of their operational effectiveness but rather for the perceived capability that paratroopers represented, some in the Army leadership who were themselves not enthusiastic about parachute troops began to redirect the MSF from its original mandate. Throughout its existence, the MSF was chronically starved of qualified manpower, supporting aircraft, and training exercises. Furthermore, its units were habitually confronted with different priorities, ones which were not ideally suited to the efficient use of airborne forces. Activities such as preparing recruits for the Korean conflict or conducting all-arms combined training for the NATO European battlefield consistently took precedence over the stated purpose of the MSF, which was "the Defence of Canada."

By the early 1950s military and political indifference to Canada's airborne forces became even more evident with the changing threat to the North. The Inter-Continental Ballistic Missile (ICBM) radically transformed the nature of the menace to North America. The eclipse of the manned bomber threat over the polar icecap changed the importance of the Canadian North for the United States to merely a question of strategic depth. Predictably, American interest in the Canadian Arctic swiftly dissipated. Canadian activity and concern in the North died almost as quickly.

The effect on the nation's airborne forces of this techno-strategic shift was immense. Already neglected and starved, the airborne capability went into a hiatus in the form of decentralized parachute companies. These were maintained only within the various infantry regiments. The skill was being kept alive, but just barely.

This reorganization from airborne battalions to jump companies in 1958, represented the official demise of the MSF. Collectively, the respective parachute sub-units were now designated the Defence of Canada Force (DCF) to underline their "special" role. The continued charade of maintaining a force of paratroops was simply a function of the existing joint security arrangements between Canada and the United States for the defence of North America. For Canada, airborne forces remained the sop to keep the Americans appeased. For many in the government and in the conventional circles of the military the façade of existence was what mattered. Their ability to respond to a threat, which was largely chimerical in any case, was not deemed important. For them airborne forces represented a classic political expedient.

But, as the northern threat to Canada receded, a new menace emerged elsewhere in the world. The late fifties and early sixties witnessed an international explosion of nationalistic movements and political unrest. "Brush-fire" conflicts, insurgencies, and wars of national liberation flared up around the globe. The concept of rapid deployable forces under United Nations (UN) auspices captured the imagination of the Canadian government which was still euphoric about its international role newly won through its diplomatic and military success in the 1956 Suez Crisis. Four years later, the emergency in the Belgian Congo reinforced the apparent need for international forces that could deploy quickly to avert the potential escalation of regional conflicts into superpower confrontations.

At the same time, as a result of the changing international security environment, the Americans embarked on a program to better address the spectrum of conflict with which they were now faced. The Americans realized that their existing force structure was not adequate to deal with limited wars in distant lands. Therefore, the Pentagon now stressed greater strategic mobility, the expansion of special forces to deal with the proliferation of guerilla style conflict, and the development of an airmobile capability.

The Canadian political and military leadership followed suit. By 1964, the blueprint for a revitalized Canadian Army was based on the concept of a truly mobile force capable of quick reaction and global reach. Instrumental to this force was an airborne element that could provide the country with a strategic reserve capable of rapid, worldwide deployment.

In 1968, this showcase unit became known as the Canadian Airborne Regiment. Although its creation was characterized by great passion and high ideals from some soldiers and politicians, by the late 1970s it suffered from the same ailment as its predecessors. The larger military establishment and the Army in particular, never fully accepted the designated role given to the Canadian Airborne Regiment. The paratroopers' mandate was as elusive as it was inclusive. There existed a wide variance in its stated purpose. Military briefings and official DND press releases described the unit's role as everything from an international fire-brigade, a national strategic reserve, a stop-gap to buy time for heavier mechanized reinforcements to deploy to Europe, to a UN ready force. As an afterthought, political and military planners also claimed that the Canadian Airborne Regiment was ideally suited for Defence of Canada Operations (DCO). The fact that each one of the Airborne's multiplicity of roles was mutually exclusive was simply ignored by nearly everyone.

In the end, the inability to fully rationalize the role, structure, and relevance of the Canadian Airborne Regiment led to its eventual demise. During the seventies the Canadian Airborne Regiment's existence was marked by changing priorities in both relevance and role. It went from an independent formation tasked as the national strategic reserve to simply another conventional unit within an existing brigade. It became the target of continual malevolent debate within the Army, and the hostage to the individual impulses of those in power. As a result, its strength, both in terms of manpower and organizational integrity, was insidiously whittled away.

By the 1980s, the lack of a clear, credible and accepted requirement for Canadian airborne forces proved a difficult obstacle to overcome. As Canada's role in the world turned away from Europe and toward different foreign policy goals, the Canadian Armed Forces underwent a crisis of self-definition. This was manifested by shrinking budgets and declining manpower levels. The Airborne Regiment found it difficult to convince its political and military masters of its relevance. Furthermore, the more its advocates attempted to prove its utility, by assigning it new tasks or reinitiating old ones, the more they highlighted its greatest weakness. *It had no credible or consistent role that made it indispensable*. The eventual erosion of organizational status and support was paralleled by a decrease in postings to the Regiment of the vital experienced leaders and soldiers from the other regiments intended to feed the Canadian Airborne Regiment with talent. The end result was nothing less than the ruin of the Regiment itself.

The disbandment of the Canadian Airborne Regiment in 1995 was significant in the context of the national airborne experience. The airborne capability in Canada became once again nothing but a hologram. The decentralized parachute capability, housed once more within the framework of parachute companies of the Light Infantry Battalions (LIBs), is but a mere shell. The rekindled "jump companies" provide nothing more than the façade of a parachute option. Clearly they do not represent a viable airborne force. They symbolize only an attempt to keep the individual, but not collective, skill alive until some new situation requires such capabilities.

But the absence of a clear and prevalent role for paratroopers in the Canadian context was not the only impediment to the acceptance of airborne forces. Sometimes conventional military minds spurn the distinct, special or unique. Military practice and tradition enshrine the notion of uniformity. Resistance to the concept of an elite, as the Airborne Regiment was often called, is prevalent not only in the military but also in society at large. Canadians, at least in theory, like to think of themselves as just and egalitarian. Moreover, they do not abide special status.

The debacle in Somalia, in 1993, and the disbandment of the Canadian Airborne Regiment less than two years later shattered this image. Public disclosures of disreputable behaviour attributed to Canadian paratroopers seemed to yield a glimpse of a distinct and maverick organization within the nation's military. Unfortunately, the notoriety surrounding the revelations served more to obscure than to promote a complete understanding of Canada's airborne forces. Public statements did nothing to clear up the perception. Messages from official sources, as well as those from the media, were often contradictory. It was unclear whether these special soldiers represented the Army's best or its worst.

Throughout their existence our nation's paratroopers have paradoxically been depicted as both the "pick of the Army" and as "ill-disciplined rogues." They have been extolled both as Canada's pride and as her shame. Consensus has only been reached on the opinion that the Airborne was different. It appears that no one, particularly within the military establishment itself, wanted to clarify whether or not the nation's airborne forces did indeed represent a unique Canadian military elite.

The status of airborne forces worldwide has always been heavily shrouded in emotion and unique warrior imagery. Since their inception, all paratroopers, no matter what country, have been cloaked in an aura of invincibility that captured the imagination of the public at large. Initially, during the Second World War, the government and military carefully nurtured this image for propaganda purposes. As a result, a portentous and very distinctive concept referred to as the "airborne mystique" emerged. It was universally applied to all airborne forces and was often credited with providing tangible strength to those who wore the distinguishing Maroon Beret.[2] The allure is as mesmerizing today as it was during the growth of airborne forces during the Second World War.

Not surprisingly, the Canadian paratroopers quickly perceived themselves as a warrior caste distinct from the other elements within the combat arms. They forged a camaraderie that developed into a tightly knit fraternity, welcoming fellow "jumpers" from all nations but treating their non-airborne compatriots with aloofness and sometimes disdain. This behaviour often created enemies in the military. Membership in this fraternity was not limited to serving paratroopers. It also extended to those former serving airborne soldiers and officers, who after doing time in an airborne unit, filled other positions within the Canadian Armed Forces at large. This created a small "Airborne Family" which could attempt to exert its influence in support of the airborne cause at all levels of command and throughout the entire military institution.

But more disturbing than the establishment of a distinct clique was the adoption of an indulgent elitism. There is no doubt that the paratroopers within the respective Canadian airborne organizations, for the most part, believed they were elite. There was a wide acceptance of this status by those outside of the organizations as well.[3] This was largely a function of the reputation the paratroopers had earned for their physical prowess, their notoriously demanding and tough exercises, their right to wear a special insignia and uniform, the perceived preferential treatment by the chain of command, and of course, the basic element of parachuting. The implicit and explicit elite status accorded to the paratroopers by some elements of the Army, particularly by some of its senior leaders, created a great deal of dissatisfaction and animosity among other soldiers and officers in the conventional units. This is no surprise. It is generally understood that elitism is not readily accepted in Canadian society.

The perceived elitism of Canada's paratroopers became part of their undoing. It generated an arrogance within the paratroopers and the Airborne Family. They became contemptuous and dismissive of those outside the fraternity. This bred resentment from those on the outside; it also bred a reactive, sometimes ill-defined effort to emasculate the airborne lobby within the Army. But the entire debate over the airborne as a distinct military elite highlighted a fundamental problem within the Canadian Armed Forces. There was a definite lack of understanding of what the term "elite" actually meant.

It is not difficult to understand why the concept of an elite always generates enmity. In its purest form it represents "the choice or most carefully selected part of a group."[4] Sociologists and political scientists have tended to define elites as a cohesive minority that holds the power of decision-making in any given group or society. They further note that the chief strength of a given elite is its autonomy and cohesiveness, which are born from an exclusiveness that is protected by rigorous entrance standards. Elites are extremely homogeneous and self-perpetuating.[5] In short, the term connotes a select minority within a group or society which holds special status and privilege.

Traditionally this meant those who held political, administrative and economic power within a society.[6] Simply put, "elites are the 'decision-makers' of the society whose power is not subject to control by any other body in society."[7] This includes leadership positions of special interest groups. Those who lead such organizations are also designated as "elites" as differentiated by the "non-decision-making" mass of their members.[8]

Furthermore, elites (or ruling minorities) are usually so constituted that the individuals comprising them are distinguished from the masses of the governed by certain qualities of material, intellectual or even moral superiority; or else they are the heirs of individuals who possessed such qualities.[9] This includes for some the interpretation that elites can also be elite because they are the "sole source of values in the society or constitute the integrating force in the community without which it may fall apart."[10]

Although the central tenets of elitism, namely autonomy and exclusivity have not changed, the make-up of elites in society has. The new elites are now defined as those who control the international flow of money and information, preside over philanthropic foundations and institutions of higher learning, manage the instruments of cultural production and thus set the terms of public debate. The new elites are "far more cosmopolitan...restless and migratory, than their predecessors."[11]

However, in the case of military elites the issue does not necessarily centre around cultural, economic or political power. The whole question of what constitutes a military elite is not at all clear. The term is often misused because of a wide and varied application, as well as a lack of understanding. The famous writer, James Jones, stated that "an elite unit is only elite when the majority of its members consider themselves already dead."[12] Richard Szafranski, a military analyst with the Toffler Associates, believes that "elite" means people and forces selected, organized, trained and equipped to rapidly adapt to, and even shape, changing or unforeseen circumstances."[13] Roger Beaumont, author and former military policeman, characterizes military elites as those organizations that are relatively free from ordinary administration and discipline, and entry into these units is often through surviving an ordeal, a "rite of passage" requiring tolerance of pain or danger, and subsequent dedication to a hazardous role.[14] These varied interpretations merely scratch the surface.

Eliot Cohen, a Harvard University scholar, developed specific criteria to define elite military units. He states, "First, a unit becomes elite when it is perpetually assigned special or unusual missions: in particular, missions that are—or seem to be—extremely hazardous. For this reason airborne units have long been considered elite since parachuting is a particularly dangerous way of going into battle." Cohen's second criterion is based on the premise that elite units conduct missions which "require only a few men who must meet high standards of training and physical toughness, particularly the latter." Finally, he maintains that "an elite unit becomes elite only when it achieves a reputation—justified or not—for bravura and success."[15]

For the strategist Colin Gray the designation "elite" pertained directly to the standard of selection and not to the activity that soldiers were selected to perform.[16] Conversely, military historian Douglas Porch utilized conventional measures of performance to determine elite status. As a result, he relied on such benchmarks as "battlefield achievement, military proficiency, or specialized military functions."[17] Similarly Eric Morris, another military historian, defined units as elite by virtue of the fact that "they were required to demonstrate a prowess and military skill of a higher standard than more conventional battalions."[18] Numerous other military analysts, researchers and scholars have applied a comparable approach, namely, the designation of elite was applied simply because individuals and units were not representative of their conventional brethren by virtue of the quality or type of personnel, training or mission.[19]

The latter emphasis on discernable differences between the special units and their conventional brethren became the core of the Canadian military's understanding of elite status. Many senior commanders defined and treated the Canadian paratroopers as elite, at least prior to the Somalia debacle, based on the higher levels of fitness, distinctive uniform and the parachuting requirement. Colonel Painchaud, a former Airborne Regimental Commander, was representative of many when he explained, "the airborne soldier is the elite of the Canadian Army. He must be in top shape compared to any other soldier, in physical fitness and shooting and weapon handling."[20] As already mentioned, the paratroopers themselves, as well as most soldiers on the outside, held similar convictions.

But this perception of what constitutes an elite is simplistic and incorrect. Its criterion is somewhat contrived and misleading. Being different and performing a unique task is far from being a de facto "elite." Therefore, for the purpose of this analysis the designation of a military elite, relying heavily on Cohen's definition, is based on selection, specifically, the rigorous screening processes which maintain extremely high standards of mental and physical ability and fitness, professional experience and skill levels, maturity, and motivation. Furthermore, the term military elite also implies the designation of an exclusive and specific special mission or role (either conventional or unconventional or both) that is actually exercised. Finally, it entails a recognized reputation for excellence (based on the level of training, expertise and professionalism of the group or on its success in operations). Considering these criteria, it becomes evident that not all units with unique characteristics warrant elite status. They may demonstrate different skill sets than a conventional unit; however, they do not necessarily represent an individual, qualitative superiority over the latter.

The persistent debate over the elite status of Canada's paratroopers and their relevance in the national context highlight their paradoxical existence. They have always exemplified the best qualities found in our nation's soldiers. They have continually been volunteers who demonstrated courage, professionalism, selflessness, and tenacity. Collectively, the airborne units developed a reputation for unsurpassed performance and toughness. Yet, both the paratroopers and their organizations have rarely been popular or widely accepted by the political or military leadership. Canada's airborne forces have been largely ignored as much as they have been inward-looking, and so their existence has been rooted in controversy and doubt. The nation's paratroopers, throughout their existence, remained orphans.

To uncover and analyse the complex factors that led to the constant marginalization of Canada's airborne capability throughout its fifty-seven-year history, this book is organized chronologically. It examines each of the five distinct airborne periods: the establishment of a parachute capability 1942-1945, the immediate postwar period 1946-1948, the Mobile Striking Force and Defence of Canada Force 1948-1967, the Canadian Airborne Regiment 1968-1995, and the recreation of the decentralised parachute companies after the disbandment of the Canadian Airborne Regiment in 1995.

The last period is important even though the story of the Canadian Airborne Regiment reaches its denouement with the killings in 1993 and the destruction of the Regiment in 1995. But as the reader will discover, the history of paratroopers in Canada did not end with these seminal events. There is a continuation which is both a postscript for airborne forces and a plan for their future. While it may seem an anti-climax, the last two chapters are necessary as both a continuance and as a conclusion.

And so, throughout the five distinct periods the book will trace several themes which by 1995, culminated in the disbandment of the Canadian Airborne Regiment and the return to decentralized parachute companies. It postulates that such an end was predictable—if not inevitable. The lack of a credible and pervasive role, the use of airborne forces solely as a political expedient, internal competition within the military for scarce resources, the reliance on those in power for the continued wellbeing of airborne units, and the persistent animosity between the airborne fraternity and those on the "outside" are all consistent themes which thread themselves throughout the five periods.

The evidence used to support the text consists of interviews with individuals representing the entire fifty-seven years of the Canadian airborne experience. It is also highly dependent on the use of the personal papers and memoirs of many of these individuals, government documents, and published sources. Although the general literature on airborne forces is large there is a lack of Canadian secondary literature in this area. As a result, this work relies mainly on primary sources. What little secondary Canadian literature exists projects a pervasive, often sensational mythology that fails to address the fundamental causes of the airborne's historically weak foundation. The accepted Canadian airborne history portrays an image devoid of the real and long-term organizational or structural turmoil that steadily undermined the fate of the parachute organizations. The majority of the works are journalistic or popular in nature. Many of them are extremely laudatory works in the genre of unit histories. The small segment of academic study which exists, namely the work of David Charters (*Armed Forces and Political Purpose: Airborne Forces and the Canadian Army*, 1984); David Bercuson (*Significant Incident*, 1996); and Donna Winslow (*The Canadian Airborne Regiment in Somalia: A Socio-cultural Inquiry*, 1997), address specific issues and are professionally narrow. Predictably, their analysis builds on incumbent interpretations.

Charters' focus is primarily concerned with the use of airborne forces in relation to modern conflict and Canadian defence policy in the context of the mid-1980s. Bercuson's analysis is dramatically different. He believes the Canadian Army is in a present-day crisis. To explain the causes of this situation, Bercuson utilizes the example of the Canadian Airborne Regiment and the incidents in Somalia. He describes these as symptomatic of the larger problems caused by deep budget cuts, political indecision, careerism and bureaucratization of the high command. His study is focussed more on the Canadian military in general than it is on the nation's airborne forces.

In both studies the examination of the entire Canadian airborne experience is superficial. Although both authors, within their respective time frames, identify the persistent struggle for resources and the recognized absence of a pervasive role for Canada's paratroopers, they fail to address the deep-rooted causes of these issues.

Winslow's scholarly foray into the nation's airborne forces is even more narrow. Her focus is specifically on military culture, particularly that of the paratroopers and how it affected their behaviour in Somalia. Her examination of Canadian airborne history covers a mere two pages and is exceedingly cursory. Not surprisingly, it is built exclusively on prevailing interpretations.

This book is the first in-depth assessment of the entire Canadian airborne experience. As a result, as already noted, it is heavily dependent on primary sources. Therefore, in addition to its comprehensive nature the value of this work is that it also pioneers the scholarly analytical debate in regards to the entire contextual phenomena of the airborne forces in Canada, including the nature of elitism and its impact on the paratroopers. As such, this examination presents a revision and maturation of the prevailing perceptions of Canadian airborne forces.

Notes for Introduction

1. NATO Military Agency for Standardization, *Land Force Tactical Doctrine ATP-35(A)*, March 1984, 8-2; Canada, *CFP 310(1) Airborne, Vol 1, The Canadian Airborne Regiment*, June 1974, 4-5; and Tom Clancy, *Airborne* (New York: Berkley Books, 1997), 2. The three primary missions for airborne forces are: Seize and Hold Operations, Area Interdiction Operations to prevent or hinder enemy operations in a specific area; and Airborne Raids.

2. The Maroon Beret denotes service in an airborne unit in most NATO countries. This practise does not necessarily apply globally. For instance, Russian airborne forces wear blue berets. However, the maroon beret, in accordance with the context it is used, connotes service in any airborne unit.

3. Force Mobile Command (FMC). *A Report on Disciplinary Infractions and Antisocial Behaviour within FMC with Particular Reference to the Special Service Force and the Canadian Airborne Regiment* (Hereafter *Hewson Report*), Ottawa: FMC Study, September 1985, 23-27; Board of Inquiry Canadian Airborne Regiment Battle Group, *Report of Commission* (hereafter BOI—Cdn AB Regt BG), *Phase I, Vol XI*, 19 July 1993, K-1/9; and Donna Winslow, *The Canadian Airborne Regiment in Somalia: A Socio-cultural Inquiry* (Ottawa: Commission of Inquiry into the Deployment of Canadian Forces to Somalia, 1997), 126-135.

4. David Guralnik, ed., *Webster's New World Dictionary* (Nashville: The Southwestern Company, 1972), 244.

5. John Porter, *The Vertical Mosaic—An Analysis of Social Class and Power in Canada* (Toronto: U of Toronto Press, 1965), 27 & 207; Robert Putnam, *The Comparative Study of Political Elites* (Englewood Cliffs, N.J.: Prentice-Hall, 1976), 4; Geraint Parry, *Political Elites* (New York: Praeger Publishers, 1969), 30-32; Sylvie Guillaume, ed., *Les Elites Fins de Siècles—XIX-XX Siècles* (Editions de la Maison des Sciences de L'Homme D'Aquitaine, 1992), 27; and M.S. Whittington and Glen Williams, eds., *Canadian Politics in the 1990s*, 3rd edition (Scarborough: Nelson Canada, 1990), 182.

6. Hervé Bentégeant, *Les Nouveau Rois de France ou La Trahison des Élites* (Paris: Éditions Ramsay, 1998), 19.

7. Parry, 13.

8. Leo V. Panitch, "Elites, Classes, and Power in Canada," in *Canadian Politics in the 1990s, 3rd edition,* 182. Power is seen in this view in terms of relations among elites.

9. Moshe M. Czudnowski, ed., *Political Elites and Social Change—Studies of Elite Roles and Attitudes* (Northern Illinois University Press, 1983), 221.

10. Parry, 13.

11. Christopher Lasch, *The Revolt of the Elites and the Betrayal of Democracy* (New York: W.W. Norton & Company, 1995), 3, 5, 25-26. See also Guillaume, 112-113. In accordance with this study, an elite must fulfill two conditions. First, it must be recognized by the respective "local society" as an elite (by definition the author states that the elite is of small composition). This aspect is symbolic in nature. The second requirement is that the elite must have control and power over the cultural infrastructure of the society.

12. Douglas Porch, "The French Foreign Legion: The Mystique of Elitism," *Elite Formations in War and Peace,* A. Hamish Ion, and Keith Neilson eds., (Wesport: Praeger, 1996), 131.

13. Richard Szafranski, "Neocortical Warfare? The Acme of Skill," in *In Athena's Camp,* John Arquilla and David Ronfeldt, eds. (New York: Rand, 1999), 408.

14. Roger A. Beaumont, *Military Elites* (London: Robert Hale and Company, 1974), 2-3.

15. Eliot A. Cohen, *Commandos and Politicians* (Cambridge: Center for International Affairs, Harvard University, 1978), 17.

16. Colin S. Gray, *Explorations in Strategy* (London: Greenwood Press, 1996), 158. Military analyst and author Roger Beaumont noted that elite units were characterised by voluntary membership, relatively high physical and mental standards for admission, distinctive uniforms and insignia, and a link to a past heroic tradition. The selection criteria is an especially important one. The quality of personnel within an elite is evident in the following sampling of selection ratios. The current U.S. SOF attrition rate is approximately 79%. General H.H. Shelton, "Quality People: Selecting and Developing Members of U.S. SOF," *Special Warfare,* Vol 11, No. 2, Spring 1998, 3. Delta Force, the U.S. anti-terrorist unit accepted 23% of the volunteers from its first selection, a mere 8% from its second, and only 22% from its third course. What makes these numbers even more impressive is the fact that most volunteers came from other SOF units such as the Rangers, Green Berets and airborne units. Colonel C.A. Beckwith, *Delta Force* (New York: Dell Publishing Co., 1985), 123 & 137; and Leroy Thompson, *The Rescuers. The World's Top Anti-Terrorist Units* (London: A David & Charles Military Book, 1986), 127-

128. The statistics for SAS acceptance range between a low of 5% (Philip Warner, *The Special Air Service* (London: William Kimber, 1971, 33) to an average of less than 20%. See Mark Lloyd, *Special Forces: The Changing Face of Warfare* (New York: Arms and Armour Press, 1996), 134; and Michael Asher, *Shoot to Kill: A Soldier's Journey Through Violence* (London: Viking, 1990), 205. Only 15% of candidates passed the Selous Scouts selection course. Peter Stiff, *Selous Scouts: Top Secret War* (Alberton, South Africa: Galago Publishing Inc., 1982), 137.

17. Porch, "The French Foreign Legion: The Mystique of Elitism," 117.

18. Eric Morris, *Churchill's Private Armies* (London: Hutchinson, 1986), xiii.

19. See D.R. Segal, Jesse Harris, J.M. Rothberg, and D.H. Marlowe, "Paratroopers as Peacekeepers," *Armed Forces and Society*, Volume 10, No. 4, Summer 1984, 489; and Winslow, 128-138. Gideon Aran stated that "Jumping can be viewed as a test which allows those who pass it to join an exclusive club, to be initiated into an elite group." Gideon Aran, "Parachuting," *American Journal of Sociology,* Vol 80, No. 1, 150.

20. Dick Brown, "Hanging Tough," *Quest*, May 1978, 12. See Also Commission of Inquiry into the Development of Canadian Forces to Somalia, *Information Legacy: A Compendium of Source Material from the Commission of Inquiry* (hereafter *Information Legacy*), [CD-ROM], 1998, Hearing Transcripts, Vol 36, 22 January 1996, testimony of Lieutenant-Colonel Morneault, 6898.

CHAPTER ONE

RELUCTANT BEGINNINGS
The Establishment of a Canadian Airborne Capability 1942-1945

I have watched with interest the organization here of such special units as Commandos, Ski Battalions and Paratroops. The cycle is always the same—initial enthusiasm which is very high, drawing good officers and men from regular units, distracting and unsettling others, and upsetting the units' organization. With a prolonged period spent in awaiting employment, the enthusiasm evaporates...In consequence I do not advocate the establishment of any separate Paratroops in the Canadian Forces.

Lieutenant-General A.G.L. McNaughton, 19 August 1941[1]

This comment made in 1941 by one of Canada's most famous generals points out the beginning of the fundamental problem which half a century later killed the Canadian Airborne Regiment concept. This statement by Lieutenant-General McNaughton in the desperate early days of World War II was symptomatic of the initial Canadian response to the airborne idea. It did not auger well. In order to understand this, one must briefly examine the theory and history of the airborne concept before the war.

It is virtual heresy, when discussing the evolution of airborne forces, not to mention one of the first visionary statements about them. In 1784, Benjamin Franklin foresaw the potential capability of delivering a force from the heavens and he actually postulated the question, "Where is the Prince who can afford so to cover his country with troops for its defence, as that ten thousand men descending from the clouds might not, in many places, do an infinite deal of mischief before a force could be brought together to repel them?"[2]

Colonel William Mitchell took these musings one step further during World War I. He proposed an iconoclastic scheme to overcome the deadlock of trench warfare and the slaughter of the fixed linear front. He recommended that the men of the 1st US Infantry Division (Big Red One) be armed with individual parachutes and a great number of machine guns. He further asserted that his great force of bombardment airplanes could then drop this group behind enemy lines. Mitchell believed that the parachute infantry could then "attack the Germans from the rear, aided by an attack from our army on the front." The entire endeavour, he insisted, would be supported by the totality of the American Air Force.[3]

Remarkably, Mitchell's superiors approved the innovative plan. However, the armistice was implemented prior to the realization of Mitchell's new concept. His vision, surprisingly, did not die. The inter-war years witnessed numerous experiments throughout Europe with parachute troops. Nevertheless, the 'West,' notably Great Britain and the United States, dismissed airborne forces as inconsequential. Initially, only the Russians established and maintained a serious airborne program.[4]

Soviet military thinkers, based on the lessons learned from the First World War and the subsequent Russian Revolution realized the importance of manoeuvre, speed and surprise. Consequently, they embraced a belief in bold, aggressive action and an ideology that inherently endorsed the offensive. Soviet strategists understood that airborne forces necessitated the enemy to fight both to his front and rear simultaneously.[5] As such, airborne forces became an integral element of their offensive doctrine and the notion of "Deep Battle" was firmly established.

By 1936, the Soviets had refined their theory of "Deep Battle" in both conceptual terms and by practising in field exercises. Red Army Field Regulations, published that same year, reflected the doctrinal entrenchment. "Major units of parachute forces," it stated, "provide an effective means of disrupting the enemy's command and control and logistics. In conjunction with frontal attack, they may play a decisive part in achieving complete destruction of the enemy on a given axis."[6] The Soviet developments, however, were lost in the turmoil of the Stalinist purges which eliminated the innovators that had moved the concept of airborne warfare so far.

Even so, the momentum was not lost. During the thirties the Germans studied the Russian advancements and expanded and improved the theory and practise of airborne operations. General Kurt Student believed deeply in the potency of the paratrooper.[7] He claimed that airborne troops were pivotal to modern battle because they made "third dimensional warfare" possible. "An adversary," Student insisted, "could never be sure of a stable front because paratroops could simply jump in and attack it from the rear where and when they decided."[8] He labelled this technique, "vertical envelopment," borrowing both the concept and the term from the earlier Soviet experimentation.

General Student realized that airborne warfare derived much of its success from the psychological shock of a sudden attack from the sky. As a result he emphasized the necessity to "pounce down and take over before the foe knows what is going on."[9] Student discerned that the surprise and shock action of paratroopers dropping into an area, which was considered safe, "instilled panic in the defender prior to the first shot being fired."[10]

Yet airborne ideas did not figure largely in the thinking of military people to the west of Russia and Germany. However, in 1939, the lethargy, cloaked in a mantle of slow study and experimentation, was shattered by the outbreak of war in Europe. In England, Air Chief Marshal Sir John Slessor recalled that the "bold and brutal" German airborne operations in Norway and the Low Countries in the spring of 1940, deeply impressed everyone, notably Prime Minister Winston Churchill.[11] These events became the catalyst for action.

As early as 6 June 1940, Churchill assailed his staff with proposals to develop a corps "of parachute troops on a scale of equal to five thousand."[12] Winston Churchill, himself an accomplished adventurer, journalist and soldier, held a heroic and romantic image of war. His concept of conflict was irretrievably moulded during the South African War of 1899-1902. To Churchill, the offensive was all that mattered. He believed that audacity and willpower constituted the only sound approach to the conduct of war.[13] General Archibald Wavell wrote, "He [Churchill] always accused commanders of organizing 'all tail and no teeth.'"[14] Similarly, General Alan Brooke recalled:

> He [Churchill] is like a child that has set its mind on some forbidden toy. It is no good explaining that it will cut his fingers or burn him. The more you explain, the more fixed he becomes in his idea.[15]

It took such an extraordinary character as Churchill to drive the conventional British thinkers out of their mould. He became the stimulus for the establishment of paratroopers in the British Army. However, it was not an easy task. Lieutenant-General Frederick 'Boy' Browning, an alacritous advocate for the establishment of British airborne forces, recalled, "Very early we came to certain definite conclusions which we have kept before us ever since and for which we may rightly say we have fought many a stout battle against the doubters and unbelievers: it is always the same with anything new and there is nothing curious about that."[16]

The vehement resistance to establishing airborne forces from the majority of Churchill's military commanders necessitated the prime minister's continual prodding for progress reports to ensure headway was being made. In fact, the opposition was initially so deep-rooted that Churchill suggested to Anthony Eden, the British Secretary of State for War, that a case should be made of "one or two" of the reluctant officers to set an example for the others.[17] Nonetheless, his adversaries met with limited success. They convinced the prime minister to be satisfied, in the beginning at any case, with a parachute corps of five hundred men instead of the five thousand he wanted.[18]

As we have seen from the words of Lieutenant-General McNaughton, Canadian soldiers saw little need for such airborne innovation. Not surprisingly, the Canadian record is similar to the British. After all, Canada was Britain's senior dominion and her soldiers followed British doctrine closely. Prior to the commencement of hostilities in 1939, there had been no effort, either conceptually or in practise, in Canada to investigate an airborne capability. The idea of developing a Canadian parachute force was first raised by Colonel E.L.M. Burns, in August 1940, upon his return from England.

Colonel Burns was recognized as a soldier of great ability and intellect, although one virtually without personality.[19] During the interwar years he was a prolific writer and actively participated in the academic debate on mechanization and the character of modern war. Despite his progressive ideas, Burns never contemplated the employment of paratroopers or the use of air power to transport infantry tactically.[20] However, he did share J.F.C. Fuller's notion of "motor guerilla" to conduct raids on the enemy's headquarters and lines of communications (the "brains and nerves" of an opponent's army).[21] In short, he appreciated the concept of "Deep Battle."

Moreover, Burns's mental flexibility made him sensitive to parachute troops when the war broke out. The successful utilization of German paratroopers in April / May 1940 revealed for him a viable tool to strike at an enemy's command and logistical facilities. Burns believed that "the successes obtained by the Germans with air-borne troops seem to show that this will become a regular method of warfare."[22]

Of equal significance to Burns's thinking was the subsequent parachute scare which erupted in Europe in the aftermath of the German aerial onslaught. By the early summer of 1940, the German *Fallschirmjäger*, by virtue of their stunning accomplishments in the Low Countries, were quickly perceived by the military and general public as invincible. This created a wave of paranoia that infected the still unoccupied territories in Europe, as well as in Britain. One contemporary account asserted that, "One thing is certain: there was a parachute obsession everywhere. Everybody saw them being dropped, everybody was suspect, and even Allied officers and men, sometimes bearing important orders, were arrested by the French military authorities."[23] As the remnants of the British Expeditionary Force (BEF) and the 1st Canadian Infantry Division hastily retreated to England, the threat of an imminent invasion loomed large. "Invasion," conceded Burns in his memoirs, "seemed fearfully close in those days."[24]

Even the ever-fiery and optimistic British prime minister was not immune to the wave of anxiety that swept through England. Churchill estimated the expected scale of airborne attack at approximately 30,000 paratroopers.[25] In Britain, troop dispositions were tailored to counter the envisioned airborne invasion and vast amounts of scarce material were invested to this aim. The government adopted a policy to safeguard the country by ordering all open spaces (meaning virtually every park and playing field) all over Britain to be seeded with long spiked poles, concrete blocks and other obstacles which would impede paratroopers.[26]

The Canadian Expeditionary Force (CEF) in England, now tasked with the defence of the British Isles, was also very conscious of the parachute menace. Canada's Overseas Commander, Lieutenant-General McNaughton, stated that "invasion was a real threat," and that the Canadians were in essence, "a mobile reserve with a 360 degree front."[27] He affirmed that they would have to operate anywhere in Great Britain to meet seaborne or airborne attacks.

This chaotic and desperate environment deeply influenced Colonel Burns, when in July 1940 he returned to Canada at the direction of Major-General H.D.G. Crerar, who himself was recalled to take over the position of Chief of the General Staff (CGS). Burns was appointed Assistant Deputy CGS. As such, the CGS tasked him with various special assignments concerning the organization and development of the Canadian Army. An all-out effort then commenced. "With the fall of France," recounted Burns in his memoirs, "the limits which had been imposed by the previous cautious policy of Mr. Mackenzie King's government were set aside, and the question now was: how much could we do within the limits of Canada's manpower and political situation to build up and train and equip those formations needed for the task?"[28] Burns's fertile mind then set to work on modernizing an army for the new method of warfare.

Colonel Burns wasted little time. He was convinced that parachute troops were "no longer just a 'stunt'," but rather, because of their mobility, an important element of any modern army.[29] And so, on 13 August 1940, he submitted his first proposal for the establishment of a Canadian airborne capability to Colonel J.C. Murchie, the Director of Military Operations in NDHQ. However, Murchie flatly dismissed the idea. He expressed the concern that "although the value of the parachute troops in certain situations was very great, the provision of such troops by Canada would be a project of doubtful value to the combined Empire war effort in view of the expenditure of time, money and equipment which would be involved."[30] Murchie further explained that any Canadian parachute units would likely be part of a British Parachute Corps, and as a result would be difficult to administer and more importantly, would be largely out of Canadian control during operations. He counselled that "if any additional commitments are accepted these should be limited to the formation of units to which Canadians are particularly adapted by reason of the nature of this country."[31]

The issue of national command remained an important one for Canadians during the Second World War. General McNaughton fought fiercely throughout his tenure to retain strict Canadian control. "We had to keep the command in our own hands," he insisted, "otherwise we would have had a succession of people coming in and the order and counter-order would have been similar to what we'd been through on Salisbury Plain in 1914."[32] McNaughton recalled the struggle to claim national control over the CEF during the Great War. Those successful efforts transformed the CEF into a distinct national entity, and its many achievements fuelled national pride and a sense of collective accomplishment. McNaughton was intent on applying that hard earned lesson to the present conflict.[33]

Colonel Burns remained undaunted by the initial rejection of his paratroop ideas, as well as the tendency to couple them with the larger issue of national command. He submitted a second memorandum to the CGS two weeks later. This time, Burns wisely reverted to a venerable Canadian approach when introducing an apparently unpopular subject. He cloaked his proposal in the mantle of home defence. He argued:

> In the defence of Canada against raids or a serious attempt at invasion, they [paratroops] would be the quickest means of building up a front against an attacker, and also could harass his communications. We have often thought of the problem of preventing an enemy from establishing a base for supplying submarines in remote sections of the coast which could not easily be reached by land. If we had even a battalion of Paratroops who could be landed to counter-attack such bases, it would make their establishment very much more difficult for an enemy; it would probably be necessary for him to send about a brigade of troops for land defences.[34]

Burns attempted to sweeten the idea further by emphasizing the stimulating effect that parachute training would have on the morale of the public and the armed services.[35] The year 1940 was part of a very low period for the Allies. Defeats, retreats and withdrawals, seemed to be all there was. Perhaps, Burns thought, the training of a corps of aggressive and inherently offensive-minded paratroopers could be a potential tonic to morale and to the war effort.

Major-General Crerar, although in apparent philosophical agreement with the concept of creating an airborne force, replied, "It is not a project of importance to the winning of the war just now."[36] He directed that the matter be set aside and brought to his attention in three months' time. Burns faithfully staffed yet another paper to the CGS on 12 November 1940. He reiterated the points from his earlier submissions and also emphasized the concept of paratroops in the form of an enhanced military capability. He asserted, "airborne troops are merely the most mobile form of land forces, and the fact that some of them land by parachute is due to the characteristics of the aeroplane."[37]

Significantly, in an attempt to win support for his proposal, Burns also linked his scheme to a distinctly national theme. He explained that "Canada is often claimed to be a country essentially adapted to air transport—witness development of the Northland." Therefore, "training airborne troops," he argued, "would be a development in line with the emphasis on air training generally."[38] Burns also suggested that Canada might make a contribution with respect to the parachute training which was then being conducted in England.[39]

Regardless of Burns's innovative approaches to convince those at home, he repeatedly expressed one key idea. "We hope to turn to the offensive against Germany some day," explained Burns, "and it appears that full advantage must be taken of all forms of mobility in carrying out operations."[40] Unquestionably, to Burns, paratroopers represented mobility and offensive power. They also personified a modern army. He argued passionately that airborne forces "would be a step toward a 'quality' army, and would show that we were actually doing something to create a force with offensive capabilities."[41] And so, at least in Burns's mind, airborne forces became inextricably mixed with national maturity and the development of state of the art military capability.

Yet Colonel Burns's superiors were not completely convinced. In December 1940, the cautious Crerar directed that further exploration of the concept be pursued. Crerar ordered that the views of both the British War Office and the Overseas Commander (McNaughton) be solicited. The War Office promptly reported that parachute troops were in fact being organized and that one special service battalion was undergoing active training. The British concept of employment was explained as filling the role of Light Cavalry to "seize bridge crossings, defiles and aerodromes well in advance of the slower-moving main body of the army."[42] Lieutenant-General McNaughton felt that the use of airborne troops had distinct possibilities. Moreover, he favoured the idea that Canada "should commence the organization and training of both parachute and glider-borne troops."[43] However, he stated that he would acquiesce to Major-General Crerar's decision. Crerar, in turn, proclaimed that he was "agreeable to a proportion (say a platoon) in each infantry battalion being trained in this work, [parachuting] [but] he is not in favour of training special airborne units unless the War Office make specific requests for them, which is unlikely."[44] As a consequence no further action was undertaken.

In sum, Burns's aspirations for the establishment of a Canadian airborne capability were fraught with impediments. His attempts at marketing, and later repackaging, the need and utility of parachute troops met limited success. The greatest obstacle was the failure to convince the decision makers that a pervasive role existed that warranted the expenditure of scarce resources. Surprisingly, the concept of a Canadian parachute force started to slowly take on a life of its own.

In the early part of August 1941, the idea resurfaced in the faceless tomb of NDHQ. This was inevitably linked to an Allied change of heart about airborne troops. The startling success of the German *Fallschirmjäger* in their conquest of the Mediterranean island of Crete in May 1941, prompted the British to adopt a more ambitious program for airborne forces. An update from the War Office stated that a force of 2,500 parachutists was to be formed and it even implied that this number might be increased to a division-sized organization.[45]

As far as Canadian commanders in England were concerned the latest British initiative would not be matched by Canada. They believed that creating specialized troops, who were perceived at that time as lacking a credible role, was a waste of resources. Specifically McNaughton, who at the meeting in December 1940 had left the impression that he was actually inclined to support airborne forces, now surprised many. In response to the latest attempt to establish an airborne capability he declared, "I do not advocate the establishment of any separate parachute troops in the Canadian Forces."[46] Several months later, he again repeated this sentiment at a meeting with General Sir Bernard Paget, Commander-in-Chief Home Forces (UK). Paget, in turn, acknowledged that he agreed with McNaughton's policy in regard to not forming special paratroop units.[47] In McNaughton's view there were only two reasons that justified the creation of a special airborne force. The first was the probability of early and continued employment in a special role, and the second was the need for specialized training along lines greatly different from that of regular units.[48]

Despite the perfunctory rejection by the Canadian Overseas Commander, the renewed airborne effort lingered. Amazingly, the continued interest was not driven by the Army, but rather the Royal Canadian Air Force (RCAF). In October 1941, the RCAF began to query Ottawa in regard to the policy on parachute troops. Furthermore, RCAF staff officers received an offer from the Royal Air Force (RAF) to provide instructors and equipment to assist the Army in the event they wished to proceed with training airborne forces.[49]

As no definitive answer was forthcoming from the Army, the RCAF continued to forward a stream of messages requesting an update on the Army's policy on parachute troops. In January 1942, Major-General Maurice Pope, the Vice Chief of the General Staff (VCGS), directed that the effort be indefinitely deferred because Canada's home army had no requirement for the employment of parachute troops.[50] An Appreciation on Air Landing Troops conducted the same month reinforced Pope's assertion. It noted that "Parachute troops will not be considered except in passing. Our operations at home are largely static (coast defence), and, as a consequence, do not provide scope for the employment of parachute troops."[51] This belief became institutionally entrenched. The annual Army Programs for the period 1940 to 1944, included no mention of airborne troops. More importantly, in the discussion of forces for the defence of Canada, absolutely no reference was ever made to the employment of, or the requirement for, paratroopers.[52]

Remarkably, despite the repeated assertions that parachute troops were of limited relevance to the Canadian Army, a letter from Canadian Military Headquarters (CMHQ) in mid-February 1942 stated that "the policy to be adopted by the Canadian Army with regard to paratroop training is [still] under consideration by NDHQ at the moment. According to our latest information no decision was to be given until this matter had been thoroughly discussed with Lt.-General McNaughton."[53] Apparently, the continued efforts of the RCAF had kept the issue of airborne troops alive. It was not lost on the Air Force that paratroopers required aircraft. More aircraft meant an expanded RCAF organization and role. This suggests that airborne advocates, and equally its enemies, would promote or impede the idea according to their self-interest. It could be a dangerous game for the airborne itself.

Although the issue continued to simmer, little evident headway was made. The continuing resistance to establishing a distinct Canadian airborne capability was reinforced by none other than the Minister of National Defence (MND) in the spring of 1942. The Honourable J.L. Ralston explained in the House of Commons that "the formation of an actual paratroop unit is not being gone ahead with at the present moment, but rather the training of men so that they can be used as paratroops when the time comes, with additional training to be done with aircraft."[54] The policy seemed consistent. So too was the continuing lack of action in regard to the "training of men" for paratroop employment.

However, two months later things changed again. In early June, Lieutenant-Colonel R.H. Keefler, from the Directorate of Military Training (DMT), NDHQ, was sent to Fort Benning, Georgia, to report on the state of parachute training in the United States. Coincident with the submission of his final report, were discussions with Air Vice Marshal Steadman of the RCAF, who had just returned from a visit with the 6th British Airborne Division. As a result, Major-General Murchie reversed his earlier opposition and forwarded a proposal to the Minister of National Defence for nothing less than the organization of a parachute battalion.[55]

Approval was not long in coming. The Canadian Cabinet War Committee gave its blessing on Dominion Day 1942. Astoundingly, the stated purpose of the unit was for home defence, specifically, "to provide a means of recapture of aerodromes or re-enforcements of remote localities by air-borne troops."[56] The apparent inconsistency seemed to go unnoticed. For years the rationale given for the rejection of a distinct Canadian airborne capability had been based on its lack of relevance in regard to the Home Army. Now, at the same time as the general strategic situation was beginning to improve for the Allies, the Canadian Army professed that there was "a definite requirement to train one battalion of 600 paratroops by 1st January 1943."[57] A mere month later there was another contradictory change. An assessment of the Army's requirement for gliders stated that a demand did exist for paratroopers, but only one company in strength.[58] Still again, by early December 1942, it took on another form. The Directorate of Military Operations and Plans (DMO & P) now envisioned the need for approximately 1000 personnel for airborne operations in Canada, exclusive of the newly designated 1st Canadian Parachute Battalion.[59]

Clearly, even in these early years one can see the inconsistency and lack of coordination in Canadian military thought on airborne forces. During the dark days of the war, when Britain was at its weakest, when the Commonwealth stood alone against the Axis juggernaut, and when Canada had little in the way of defensive forces, the mobility and rapid reaction capability of airborne troops was dismissed as irrelevant for use in Canada. Later in the conflict, when the tide of the war shifted in favour of the Allies, a decision was taken to develop airborne forces, but only for a home defence role, when that risk was declining.

The key to understanding the paradoxical approach taken to the concept of a Canadian airborne capability is not found in the "officially" stated role. One must look beyond the rhetoric. There was little conviction, either militarily or politically, that Canada faced a serious threat to its security.[60] The home defence rationale for the parachute force was used merely to entice doubting military and political decision makers to support their case. Then-Major Fraser Eadie, who became the last Commanding Officer (CO) of the wartime 1st Canadian Parachute Battalion, was convinced that, in view of the consistent opposition to the idea of a Canadian airborne element in the Army the MND only agreed to the concept on the basis that the force was designated for home defence.[61]

Yet despite this public rationale of the defence of Canada, the recruitment terms of the airborne troops were in reality far different. There was never any question that the type of soldier required for parachute training was the "aggressive individual who was anxious to serve overseas."[62] In fact, the acceptance of National Resources Mobilization Act (NRMA) volunteers for the 1st Canadian Parachute Battalion meant that the respective individuals must first join the Canadian Active Service Force (CASF).[63] This cleared the "potential obstacle" of overseas service.

Further evidence of the muddy state of affairs was given in early December 1942, in a note to the CGS. In this correspondence his deputy insisted, "I do not consider that it is feasible at present to decide the ultimate role of the 1st Parachute Bn."[64] Instead, he suggested that the unit continue its training, which was not expected to be completed prior to the end of March 1943, at the earliest. Not surprisingly, even before the newly formed parachute unit was deemed fit for active service, overtures were made to the British War Office for its inclusion in a British airborne formation. Eadie, the eventual paratroop commander, later recalled a telephone conversation with Major Jeff Nicklin, the Battalion's Deputy Commanding Officer. Nicklin confided that neither the Canadian government nor the field commanders in England had any idea what to do with the paratroopers and as a result, they were being offered up to the British.[65] On 18 March 1943, General Paget welcomed the offer and stated that the battalion could be included in the establishment of a second British airborne division which was then forming.[66]

It became apparent that the issue of national control was a rather hit and miss notion in regard to a Canadian parachute unit even though senior commanders and politicians were applying this policy to the larger conventional units elsewhere. The latest turn in events also underscored another inconsistency; namely, in Canada, the ultimate aim was never to develop the airborne capability for use in the country's defence. That was merely a sop to sidetrack opponents and to gain supporters. The advocates wanted to use the paratroops in the active theatres of Europe. Indeed, airborne forces had become a symbol of modern warfare. More important, they represented the cutting-edge of offensive action. The British, as a result of their study of German *Fallschirmjäger*, viewed parachute troops as "a highly mobile force of shock troops which can be projected at short notice into an enemy area which might otherwise consider itself immune from attack." They saw the airborne weapon solely in terms of the offense.[67]

The emphasis on the offensive seemingly struck a chord with the Canadians. Colonel Burns's original argument was finally accepted. It is not coincidental that the decision to adopt a paratroop unit came at the same time that both the Americans and British were overwhelmingly committed to the large scale offensive use of airborne forces.[68] The British authorized the establishment of an airborne division in November 1941. The Americans converted the 82nd Motorized Infantry Division to the airborne role on 26 June 1942.[69] Furthermore the airborne arm, as an extremely aggressive combat-ready force, took on a public image of herculean proportion.[70] It was seen as a way for the Allies to crack "Fortress Europa" or attack the Japanese. The change in thinking was clearly reflected in the US War Department's 1942 strategy book which stated:

> The Use of Parachutists. ...Nowadays one cannot possibly hope to succeed in landing operations unless one can be assured of the cooperation of parachutists <u>on a scale hitherto undreamed of</u>. In fact, only the parachutist will be able to take enemy territory from the rear, thus preventing destruction of the attacking forces by artillery fire and enabling them to get a foothold on the coast....25,000 men set down in advance at every important point of attack should be able to do the work, especially if it proves possible to get them assembled. They must obviously be regarded as the pivot of success of the entire operation.[71]

The airborne's supporters in the Canadian military wanted to ensure that they were part of this neophyte club.[72] An eloquent entry in the battalion War Diary demonstrated the undercurrent of motive present. It read, "We members of the 1st Canadian Parachute Battalion, are well aware of our unique position as a newly born unit in a new phase of warfare. We are therefore, confident of our success and trust that we well be given the opportunity to prove our value."[73] Lieutenant-Colonel G.F.P. Bradbrooke, the first Commanding Officer of the unit, clearly explained his understanding of his unit's purpose as being "the tip of the spear." He elaborated that "they must expect to go in first, to penetrate behind enemy lines and to fight in isolated positions."[74] To the military community, being a modern offensive minded army meant, rightly or wrongly, the possession of paratroops. Canada was now in the game with the "big boys."

Possession of paratroopers who were worthy of taking their place in the vanguard of any future offensive action, however, required a solid commitment and special people. The Army, despite the initial resistance to the idea of airborne soldiers, now undertook an all-out effort. The parachute battalion became a select unit worthy of the title of "elite."[75] A very discerning screening process ensured that only the finest candidates were selected for further training. Army psychiatrist, Dr. A.E. Moll, developed a rating system which was used to grade volunteers during selection boards. His system ranked an individual within a range of "A" to "E", "A" representing the most preferred, and "E" the least. Only those who achieved an "A" score were kept for airborne training. Moll was certain that the "A" candidates were clearly the best material. He was equally sure that the "E" personnel should not be considered. He did confess to some uncertainty about the eighty percent who fell into the grey area in between. However, Moll and his staff decided that as long as the supply of volunteers remained strong they would continue to accept only the best.[76]

The requirements imposed on the volunteers demanded an exceptionally high standard of mental, physical, and psychological fitness. The aspiring paratrooper was required to be in good physical condition, preferably with a history of participation in rugged sports or a civilian occupation demanding sustained exertion. Aggressiveness, emotional stability, high motivation, and self-reliance were also necessary prerequisites to achieve an "A" rating. The volunteer was also expected to be Basic Training qualified and needed a minimum education of Grade VI, a higher standard than that required by conventional Canadian infantry.[77]

The screening procedure was so severe that an average of thirty percent of volunteers were rejected during the screening process alone.[78] One draft was as high as sixty percent.[79] This was just the beginning. A further thirty-five percent loss of personnel was anticipated due to the normal parachute training wastage rate.[80] Lieutenant Ken Arril, a veteran of that training, recalled that an individual had to be a "superb infantryman—top of the line" to make it. He stated that the army examiners were focussed on people who were more mature, motivated, and particularly experienced.[81] Former paratrooper Lance-Corporal H.R. Holloway remembered that the examiners "watched your reaction to everything." He stated that any sweating whatsoever was an automatic ticket back to an individual's original unit.[82]

The unit's training provided another indicator of its special status. A *Canadian Army Training Memorandum* (CATM) on the instruction of paratroops noted that "parachute warfare is tough—even in training." It explained that the new airborne arm needed alert, clever and daring young men, "who can exploit a chance and who have the guts necessary to fight against overwhelming odds and win."[83] The commentary concluded that the training process made "rugby look like child's play."[84] The training was gruelling. Lieutenant Bob Firlotte, a veteran of 1 Cdn Para Bn reflected that "commando training became normal training."[85] An official description of the regimen explained:

> The advanced training of parachutists is reported to be about 2% jumping and 98% rigorous commando training requiring great physical stamina and courage of a high order. Parachute troops have about 60 lbs. of equipment to carry, including a Tommy or Sten gun, hand grenades, high explosives, radio, ammunition, respirator, rations, etc. They frequently have to travel for long periods on foot with a full pack and almost at a run. As part of their training they take forced marches of 35 miles a day.[86]

Another veteran, Private T.A. Gavinski remembered that "they always tried to see how far you could go, to keep you on edge." He recalled that they were always culling out the slow and that on average, the unit was "losing a man a month because he didn't have that extra step."[87] The aim of the activities was clearly defined in the training syllabus. It declared that the objective was "to produce a formidable fighting man like an expert hunter—always alert and seeking an opportunity of striking his quarry or watching his movements with a view to future opportunities, confident and expert in the use of his weapons, skilled in the use of ground and able to stand fatigue without undue loss of efficiency. He must be determined, inquisitive and self-dependent, but must always remember that he is acting as one of a team."[88]

By March of 1943, after many confusing contortions, Canada possessed a battalion of highly motivated and trained paratroopers, officially described by the Army as a "corps elite."[89] The spectre of actually employing them now became the issue. However, their official raison d'être, home defence, as the critics had always maintained, was not a requirement. As a result, even before the battalion completed its collective training or was declared operationally ready, it was not only offered to the British, but was also alerted for overseas duty.[90] Despite the unit's imminent departure, it was still estimated that the paratroopers would need a further two months' training in the United Kingdom before the unit was fit for active service.[91] This sequence of events further underscored the feebleness of the "airborne for home defence" role. But there were not too many who were bothered by these inconsistencies in wartime.

If the rationale to justify the establishment of a parachute unit was questionable, the end product certainly was not. During the war the 1st Canadian Parachute Battalion fought valiantly in the Normandy Campaign, the Crossing of the Rhine, and during the pursuit of enemy forces in Northwest Europe. In all of this tough combat it suffered 128 killed, 294 wounded and 84 captured as prisoners. This represented a casualty list of more than 500 in a battalion which was officially established at only 618.[92] By war's end, the Battalion had earned a proud and remarkable reputation whose legacy would challenge Canada's future paratroopers and imbue them with a special pride. The Battalion never failed to complete an assigned mission, nor did it ever lose or surrender an objective once taken. The Canadian paratroopers were among the first Allied soldiers to land in occupied Europe and the only Canadians to have participated in the Battle of the Bulge in 1944-45, in the Ardennes. Additionally, by the end of the war they had advanced deeper into Germany than any other Canadian unit. Field-Marshal Sir Alan Brooke, Chief of the Imperial General Staff, wrote to his Canadian equivalent:

> The Battalion played a vital part in the heavy fighting which followed their descent on to French soil in 6 June 1944, during the subsequent critical days and in the pursuit to the Seine. Finally, it played a great part in the lightning pursuit of the German Army right up the shores of the Baltic. It can indeed be proud of its record.[93]

In spite of the war record, the unit's exemplary performance did little to guarantee its future. With the end of hostilities came the requirement for demobilization and the dilemma of deciding on a drastically scaled down peacetime force structure. The fate of the paratroopers was even worse and not difficult to predict. Once the paratroops had been transferred to the British, they were basically abandoned by Canada. Lieutenant Ken Arril recalled, "we called ourselves the forgotten battalion."[94] Sergeant Art Stammers noted that the "Canadian Army forgot we existed."[95] The paratroopers at large felt no link with their national army and received no visits from its commanders. Lieutenant-Colonel Fraser Eadie plaintively stated that "Canada had forsaken us for everything but pay and clothing."[96] The paratroopers were never fully integrated with the national army. For all intents and purposes, they were orphans.

Once peace broke out, the enigmatic debate over a Canadian airborne capability began anew. The first indication was not promising. Beginning in May 1945 no training was conducted at the parachute training centre since Army HQ anticipated no requirement for airborne forces in the postwar army.[97] In the following months it became apparent that the 1st Canadian Parachute Battalion was in fact designated for disbandment. Its existence was prolonged only long enough to serve as an administrative tool to process the orderly release of those unit members who did not sign on to serve in the Canadian Army Pacific Force.[98] The unit was officially disbanded on 30 September 1945.[99] Most of its members took their release and rejoined the civilian world. For the paratroopers who remained in the Active Force, the prospect of continuing airborne service was anything but bright.

ENDNOTES—CHAPTER ONE

1. National Archives of Canada (NAC), RG 24, Vol 12260, File: 1 Para Tps / 1, Message (G.S. 1647), Lieutenant-General McNaughton to Major-General Crerar, 19 August 1941.
2. Virtually every book on the history of Airborne Forces includes this quote. A sampling of examples includes: War Department (US) *Enemy Air-Borne Forces* (Washington D.C.: War Department, 2 December 1942), 3; Major-General James Gavin, *Airborne Warfare* (Washington D.C.: Infantry Journal Press, 1947), vii; Matthew B. Ridgway, *Soldier: The Memoirs of Matthew B. Ridgway* (New York: Harper & Brothers, 1956), 69; Charles MacDonald, *Airborne* (New York: Ballantine Books, Inc., 1970), 57; Brigadier M.A.J. Tugwell, "Day of the Paratroops," *Military Review*, Vol 57, No.3, March 1977, 40-41; William B. Breuer, *Geronimo* (New York: St. Martin's Press, 1992), preface; and Tom Clancy, *Airborne* (New York: Berkley Books, 1997), xvii.

3. Brigadier-General William Mitchell, *Memoirs of World War I* (New York: Random House, 1928), 268.
4. Major-General Archibald Wavell, the British military attaché to the Soviet Union witnessed the 1935 Airborne demonstration in Kiev, where approximately 1000 Soviet paratroopers were dropped on exercise. His report noted, "This Parachute descent, though its tactical value may be doubtful, was a most spectacular performance." David Glantz, *The Soviet Airborne Experience* (Fort Leavenworth: US Army Command and General Staff College, 1984), 2; and Steven J. Zaloga, *Inside the Blue Berets* (Novato: Presidio Press, 1995), 15. The Americans, similar to the British, failed to grasp the potential of airborne forces. They did not create an airborne "Test Platoon" until 26 June 1940. Gerard M. Devlin, *Paratrooper* (New York: St. Martin's Press, 1979), 34. They too relied on the reality of events, rather than the foresight of "visionaries," to guide their military preparedness and structure.
5. Glantz, *The Soviet Airborne Experience*, 2-11; and Zaloga, 4-16.
6. Charles Dick, "Soviet Operational Art," *International Defense Review*, 8/1988, 904.
7. General Kurt Student began his military career in 1911 in an elite *Jäger* (light infantry) unit. He later transferred to the new Army Air Force and in the mid-1930s became the preeminent champion of the German airborne cause. See Callum MacDonald, *The Lost Battle, Crete 1941* (New York: The Free Press, 1993), 6; and General Sir John Hackett, "Student," in *Hitler's Generals,* Corelli Barnet, ed., (London: Weidenfeld & Nicolson, 1987), 463-478.
8. MacDonald, *The Lost Battle*, 13.
9. Ibid., 13.
10. Ibid., 13.
11. Air Chief Marshal Sir John C. Slessor, "Some Reflections on Airborne Forces," DND Directorate of History (henceforth DHist; however, note that it has since been officially re-designated the Directorate of History and Heritage) file 112.3M2 (D232). The Americans too were impressed by the use of paratroopers. The official War Department publication *Enemy Air-Borne Forces* (dated 2 December 1942), attributed the speed at which the "German arms came triumphantly to the Channel" in a large part to the success of their airborne operations. *Enemy Air-Borne Forces*, 9.
12. Winston S. Churchill, *The Second World War.Vol II: Their Finest Hour* (Boston: Houghton Mifflin Company, 1949), 246-247 & 466. There is some discrepancy regarding the actual date. Most sources, based on the seminal work done on the British Parachute Regiment (*The Red Beret*), state that General Ismay, Chief of the Imperial General Staff, received instruction to establish a parachute corps on 22 June 1940. See Hilary St. George Saunders, *The Red Beret: The Story of the Parachute Regiment at War 1940-1945* (London: Michael Joseph, 1950), 27.
13. See Cohen, *Commandos and Politicians*, 37-40; Maxwell Schoenfeld, *The War Ministry of Winston Churchill* (Ames: Iowa State University Press, 1972), 124; and Patrick Cosgrove, *Churchill at War Alone 1939-1940* (London: William Collins Sons & Co. Ltd., 1974), 95.
14. David Jablonsky, *Churchill: The Making of a Grand Strategist* (Carlisle Barracks: Strategic Studies Institute, US Army War College, 1990), 125.
15. Ibid., 92.
16. F.A.M. Browning, "Airborne Forces," *RUSI*, Vol 89, No. 556, November 1944, 351. The need for support from the highest levels for new ideas was fully appreciated by David Stirling. By means of subterfuge, he submitted his proposal, for the establishment of the SAS, direct to the C-in-C Middle East. This was done to avoid the "layer on layer of fossilized shit [staff]" which he thought "ludicrously swollen, unnecessarily big and wholly obstructive to anything that looked like a new idea." Anthony Kemp, *The SAS at War* (London: John Murray, 1991), 6.
17. Robert W. Black, *Rangers in World War II* (New York: Ivy Books, 1992), 8.
18. Churchill, 247.
19. J.L. Granatstein, *The Generals: The Canadian Army's Senior Commanders in the Second World War* (Don Mills, Ontario: Stoddart, 1993), 116-117.
20. Burns published the "Mechanization of Cavalry" as early as 1923 in the *Canadian Defence Quarterly* (*CDQ*) Vol 1, No.3, 1923-1924, 37. During the years 1933-1938 he produced a further seven articles.

See also John A. English, *The Canadian Army and the Normandy Campaign: A Study of Failure in High Command* (New York: Praeger, 1991), 48-49. It is interesting to note that no writings on airborne warfare or the application of parachute delivered infantry was contained in the *CDQ* during the interwar years. The only reference to parachutes was an article entitled the "Thrills of Parachute Jumping," (Vol 12, No. 2, January 1935, 214-220), which gave the account of a pilot's familiarization training with the parachute as a method of emergency escape.

21. Major E.L.M. Burns, "Prize Essay—Protection of the Rearward Services and Headquarters in Modern War," *CDQ*, Vol 10, No. 3, April 1933, 295-313. Burns's notion of "motor-guerillas" raiding enemy rear areas was an extension of Fuller's concept born from his observations during the German offensive of 21 March 1918. The German penetration severed the command and control, and logistics between the Allied rear and the front line. This in turn created a state of paralysis in the Allied armies. From this experience Fuller developed the belief that the key was to employ mobility as a psychological weapon to paralyse not only an enemy's command but also his government. See J.F.C. Fuller, *Conduct of War* (London: Eyre & Spottis Woode, 1961), 256-257; A.J. Trythall, *Boney Fuller: The Intellectual General 1878-1966* (London: Cassell, 1977), 60; Brian Holden Reid, *J.F.C. Fuller Military Thinker* (Basingstoke: Macmillan, 1987), 49-51; and Field Marshal, F.M. Lord Carver, *The Apostles of Mobility: The Theory & Practise of Armoured Warfare* (London: Weidenfeld & Nicolson, 1979), 40.

22. DHist, File 112.1 (D32): Airborne Troops, Cdn 1940, Memo from Burns to CGS, 13 August 1940; and NAC, RG 24, Vol 12260, File: 1 Para Tps / 1, Memo from Burns to CGS, 12 November 1940, 1.

23. Captain F.O. Miksche, *Paratroops* (London: Faber and Faber Ltd, 1942), 38-39. See also MacDonald, *The Lost Battle,* 38. A GHQ memo reported, "There were constant rumours and alarms during operations with regard to parachute troops and fifth column activities. It is essential that means to deal with this menace be thought out...An efficient 'parashot' organisation is of high importance since it is essential to maintain mobile reserves to deal with the situation in case of enemy break throughs." GHQ Home Forces, "Notes on the Operations in Flanders and Belgium 10th to 31st May with Particular Reference to the Present Problem of Home Defence," 28 June 1940. DHist, File 146.141009 (D2)

24. E.L.M. Burns, *General Mud: Memoir of World War II* (Toronto: Clarke Irwin, 1970), 100-101.

25. Churchill, 285.

26. Ibid., 176; G.G. Norton, *The Red Devils* (Hampshire: Leo Cooper, 1971), 254; and Philip Warner, *The Special Forces of World War II* (London: Granada, 1985), 8.

27. John Swettenham, *McNaughton, Volume 2 (*Toronto: The Ryerson Press, 1969), 117-119. See also C.P. Stacey, *Six Years of War: The Army in Canada, Britain and the Pacific. Volume 1* (Ottawa: Queen's Printer, 1966), 287-295. Bob Firlotte, a junior NCO with the Carleton & York Regiment in England at the time, recalled the period as one of constant alarms and drills. He stated, "you were never sure if it was an exercise or the real thing." Firlotte concluded, "they never failed to scare the hell out of us!" Interview with R.B. Firlotte, 20 November 1998. Bob Firlotte later received a commission and served with the 1st Canadian Parachute Battalion.

28. Burns, *General Mud,* 102.

29. NAC, RG 24, Vol 12260, File: 1 Para Tps / 1, Memo from Burns to CGS, 12 November 1940, 1.

30. Major D.H. Cunningham, "Further Material Relating to the Organization and Training of the 1st Canadian Parachute Battalion," Appendix A, To Historical Section, C.M.H.Q. Report No. 138, 5 December 1949, 1. DHist C.M.H.Q. Report No. 138 (7 July 1945) and DHist, File: Hist 1B.

31. Ibid., 1.

32. Swettenham, *McNaughton, Vol 2,* 30.

33. Stacey, *Six Years of War,* 212-221.

34. DHist, File 112.1 (D32): Airborne Troops, Cdn 1940, Memo from Burns to CGS, 28 August 1940, 2. This memorandum was further evidence of Burns's maturation of thoughts on modern warfare. In his article, "The Defence of Canada," *CDQ,*, Vol 13, No. 4, July 1936, 379-394, he foresaw only a very limited role for infantry. It consisted merely of garrisoning bases to protect air and naval forces, which were seen as the defenders of Canada's vulnerable coastal areas.

35. DHist, File 112.1 (D32): Airborne Troops, Cdn 1940, Memo from Burns to CGS, 28 August 1940, 2.
36. C.M.H.Q. Report 138, 2.
37. NAC, RG 24, Vol 12260, File: 1 Para Tps / 1, Memo from Burns to CGS, 12 November 1940, 1; and Canadian Airborne Forces Museum, (hereafter CAFM), Research Papers on Canadian Airborne Organizations, Part 1, 1.B, Document 3—"Canada," 1. See also C.M.H.Q. Report 138, 1.
38. NAC, RG 24, Vol 12260, File: 1 Para Tps / 1, Memo from Burns to CGS, 12 November 1940, 1.
39. Ibid.; and C.M.H.Q. Report 138, 1.
40. NAC, RG 24, Vol 12260, File: 1 Para Tps / 1, Memo from Burns to CGS, 12 November 1940, 1.
41. Ibid., 2; and C.M.H.Q. Report 138, 2.
42. NAC, RG 24, Vol 12260, File: 1 Para Tps / 1, Message (G.S. 3140), Major-General Crerar, CGS, to H.Q. Cdn Corps., 16 December 1940; and C.M.H.Q. Report 138, 1.
43. NAC, RG 24, Vol 12260, File: 1 Para Tps / 1, Memo CMHQ, 6 December 1940, 2.
44. DHist, File 112.1 (D32): Airborne Troops, Cdn 1940, message Canmilitry [sic] (CGS) to Defensor (DCGS), undated: "Historical Notes 1942-1945, First Canadian Parachute Battalion," 1; DHist, File 145.4013 (D1); "Historical Reports 1 Cdn Para Bn, 1942-1945," CAFM, Document A 87.002.61, 1; and C.M.H.Q. Report 138, 1-2. During the December 1940 meeting in question, McNaughton stated that he would not press his views in regard to the establishment of paratroops in light of Crerar's comments and the scale of the War Office (UK) efforts.
45. NAC, RG 24, Vol 12260, File: 1 Para Tps / 1, Message (G.S. 0493), Major-General Crerar, CGS, to HQ Cdn Corps., 15 August 1941. See also Lieutenant-General R.N. Gale, "Aircraft for Army Uses," *RUSI*, Vol 65, No. 579, August 1950, 424; and Slessor, 2.
46. NAC, RG 24, Vol 12260, File: 1 Para Tps / 1, Message (G.S. 1647), Lieutenant-General McNaughton to Major-General Crerar, 19 August 1941. See also C.M.H.Q. Report 138, 1-2.
47. "Historical Notes 1942-1945," 2.
48. NAC, RG 24, Vol 12260, File: 1 Para Tps / 1, Letter, G. G. Simonds, Brigadier General Staff Cdn Corps to C.M.H.Q., "Paratroop Training," 30 October 1941; and C.M.H.Q. Report 138, 2. McNaughton obviously lacked an understanding of the concept of airborne forces. Apparently, he visualized nothing more than using the parachute to land conventional infantry from the heavens. In fact he advocated that if the prospects of operations indicated the need for troops to land by parachute, existing units would then be selected and given the appropriate specialized training. Letter from Director Operations and Intelligence to CGS, Re: "Parachute Troops," 5 January 1942. DHist, File 112.3M2 (D232). See Chapter Eleven for a detailed explanation of the "airborne battlefield."
49. NAC, RG 24, Vol 12260, File: 1 Para Tps / 1. The file contains no fewer than ten letters / messages from the period 24 October 1941 to 17 February 1942, which both offer RAF assistance for parachute training and / or request clarification on the latest policy in regard to the subject.
50. C.M.H.Q. Report 138, 2. Similar to McNaughton's views, or perhaps because of them, a belief existed at NDHQ that if, or when, parachute troops were needed they could be formed easily and rapidly by the conversion of existing infantry units.
51. General Staff, "Appreciation Re Air Landing Troops," 24 January 1942. DHist, File 112.3M2 (D232)
52. NAC, Ralston Papers, MG 27, III B11, Vol 38—Army Programmes 1940-1944.
53. C.M.H.Q. Report 138, 3. All historical reports noted to date highlight the lack of any existing documentation on the continuing discussion of an airborne capability.
54. Canada, *House of Commons Debates* (hereafter *Debates*), 22 April 1942, 1851.
55. "Minutes of a Meeting of the Inter-Service Committee on Air Borne Troops, Held at NDHQ, 1000 hours, 25 July 42," 28 July 1942. DHist, File 112.3M2 (D232), 1; C.M.H.Q. Report 138, 3; and John Willes, *Out of the Clouds* (Port Perry: Port Perry Printing Ltd., 1981), 10. The military historical reports attribute the ultimate decision to go forward with the proposal as a function of NDHQ action, regardless of McNaughton's position on special troops.

56. *Minutes of the War Committee of the Cabinet,* Vol 7-11 1942, Reel 3, 1 July 1942. The official authorization, in accordance with the caveat which was imposed by Cabinet on 1 July, was actually given on 8 July 1942, upon the concurrence of the Finance Minister. Ibid, 8 July 1942.

57. "Minutes of a Meeting of the Inter-Service Committee on Air Borne Troops, Held at NDHQ, 1000 hours, 25 July 42," 28 July 1942. DHist, File 112.3M2 (D232), Appendix A. A letter from Lieutenant-Colonel C.G.M. Grier, Canadian Army Staff in Washington D.C., to Major Proctor in NDHQ, on 25 July 1942, highlighted the abrupt change. He wrote, "The Canadian Army has suddenly expressed an interest in parachutes." DHist, File 314.009 (D321).

58. Directorate of Military Operations and Planning (DMO & P), "The Army Use of Gliders," 5 August 1942. DHist, File 112.3M2 (D232).

59. DMO & P, "Policy—Airborne Troops," 7 December 1942. DHist, File 112.3M2 (D232).

60. The next chapter deals with this issue in great depth.

61. Interview with author, 23 June 1998. Canada's military leaders have often used the argument of home defence, or benefit to the national interest, to cloak a desired military requirement. McNaughton used this tactic on a number of occasions during the thirties. Defence Scheme No. 3 ensnared both home defence and the dispatch of an overseas expeditionary force in the same plan. The military leadership convinced their political masters that national self-defence involved commitments beyond Canada's borders, despite the government's aversion to a potential repeat of the great losses of World War I. This allowed the military institution to equip, man and train to levels greater than required for a strictly territorial defence force. Similarly, McNaughton parlayed his depression era relief scheme into a network of military bases and airstrips spanning the country. Stephen Harris, *Canadian Brass: the Making of a Professional Army, 1860-1939* (Toronto: University of Toronto, 1988), 166 & 178-187; and Granatstein, *The Generals,* 59.

62. Many saw the Parachute Battalion as a way out of instructional duty and "a way to see action." Interviews with Lieutenant R.B. Firlotte, 20 November 1998 and Lance-Corporal W.B. Delory, 3 November 1998. Rifleman H.G. Ives asserted that, "They all thought it was a great chance to get action and quick." "Toughest in Canada's Army Back for Paratroop Course," *The Star,* 21 September 1942, (CAFM). Another common sentiment was that the unit "was the best way of getting at the enemy." Dave Campbell, "Parachuters' Reunion Raises Old Memories," *The Brandon Sun,* 7 June 1971, 3.

63. Appendix A (1949) to C.M.H.Q. Report 138, 5.

64. DCGS (A), "Role of 1st Parachute Bn.," 6 December 1942. DHist, File 112.21009 (D197). Every veteran of 1 Cdn Para Bn interviewed unequivocally stated that they were never told the role of their unit. Private T.A. Gavinski stated that "no explanation of what the unit was for was ever given. It was just hard to get in and keep up." Interview with author 1 November 1998.

65. Interview with author, 23 June 1998.

66. NAC, RG 24, Vol 12260, File: 1 Para Tps / 1, Message (G.S. 142), CGS, Major-General Stuart to Lieutenant-General McNaughton, 6 March 1943, and (G.S. 583) McNaughton to Stuart, 18 March 1943. See also C.M.H.Q. Report 138, 4; and Saunders, 152.

67. War Office (UK), *Army Training Instruction #5. Employment of Parachute Troops, 1941* (London: War Office, 20 August 1941), 3-5. The emphasis on the offensive was rooted in the analysis of the German victory in the spring of 1940. A memorandum sent to the minister, in September 1940, noted three major lessons learned. The first was the need to base the army on mechanized power, which included artillery, armoured fighting vehicles and close support aircraft. The second was the necessity to possess an industrial base capable of producing all essentials of war material. The final lesson was the conclusion that "reliance on an army of the defensive type is bound to end in defeat; the failures of the Allies have been due to the lack of attacking power." NAC, Ralston Papers, MG 27, III B11, Vol 37—"Memorandum for the Minister of National Defence—The Canadian Army—Synopsis," 3 September 1940, 5.

68. By October 1941 the British raised the possibility of forming an airborne division. This concept was implemented the following month and the Airborne Division was created. It was self-contained and

considered a strategic reserve. Its missions, based on experiments and training, were given as: (a.) The capture of a line or focal point in the communications in rear of the enemy to isolate them from reinforcements; (b.) The attack of the enemy in rear, in conjunction with the advance of the main force; (c.) The capture of an aerodrome or aerodromes; and (d.) Subsidiary operations in conjunction with seaborne expeditions. Major-General F.A.M. Browning, "Extracts from Memorandum on the Organization and Employment of the Airborne Division." DHist, File 112.3M3009 (D98).

69. Ridgway, 54; and Breuer, 9.

70. The newspaper headlines and reporting clearly reflected the image of the paratrooper as the ultimate, invincible fighting machine. A sampling of descriptive phrases included: "tough...hard as nails,"in James Anderson "Tough, Hard-As-Nails Paratroopers Arrive to Open Shilo School," 22 September 1942, (CAFM); "toughest in Canada," "Toughest in Canada's Army Back for Paratroop Course," *The Star,* 21 September 1942, (CAFM); "perfect physical specimens," in Larry Gough, "Parachutists Want it Tough," *Liberty,* 4 December 1943, (CAFM); "toughest ground infantrymen in the world," in Trent Frayne, "Parachute Course Aim is Tough Fighting Men," 17 July 1944, (CAFM); "utterly fearless...a package of high explosives," "sky-dynamite," in *Canadian Parachute Training Centre Newspaper, Souvenir Issue,* No.35, Volume 1, No. 1, November 1944, 1, (CAFM). The official British historian of the British Parachute Regiment also stated that the paratroopers "suffered from the misplaced enthusiasm of a section of the press." Saunders, 320.

71. US War Department Operations Division, General Staff, Strategy Book, November 1942, 212-213 & 219. National Archives, Washington D.C., RG 165, entry 422, Box 2, Item 10A, Exec 1, File OPD Strategy Book, November 1942. Sourced from the Joint Military Intelligence College, Washington, D.C.

72. The favourable manpower position in Canada in 1942 undoubtedly assisted with the decision. Stacey noted, "there was still a considerable pool of manpower in the country which could be tapped...in fact more men and women were enlisted into the Canadian Army than in any other year of the war." *Six Years of War, Volume 1,* 117. The manpower situation was so positive that a decision was reached that "there was no immediate urgency to despatch personnel from Canada surplus to the man-power ceiling especially if this would help Canada in providing the required tradesmen and specialists at a later date." It was projected that by the end of September 1943 the Canadian Army Overseas would be about ten thousand personnel over the manpower ceiling. "Record of a Meeting Held in the Office of Minister of National Defence At CMHQ on 4 August 1943." DHist, File 112.33S2009 (D164) Vol 2.

73. *1 Canadian Parachute Battalion War Diaries*, 15 January 1943. CAFM, A84.019.01, Envelope 2 of 22, January 1943.

74. Brian Nolan, *Airborne* (Toronto: Lester Publishing Ltd., 1995), 34. This concept was officially sanctioned as early as September 1942, at which time a series of National Film Board (NFB) pictures, depicting training in Fort Benning, carried the caption, "Canadian paratroopers are specially-picked, physically perfect, behind-the-lines fighters who drop from the skies." NA, Photo Collection, WRC (NFB), FA 19, Acc 1970-71, DND Indexes—Army Series, WRC Series, Box 5 of 6.

75. A discussion of the concept of elite is undertaken in Chapter Eleven. On 10 July 1942, the formation of 2 Canadian Parachute Battalion was authorized. However, this title was only given for security reasons. This unit was re-designated the First Special Service Force Battalion on 25 May 1943 and represented the Canadian element of the joint US / Canadian First Special Service Force.

76. Letter, 15 November 1985, from Dr. Bill McAndrew (DHist Historian) to Brigadier-General Beno. The data was based on McAndrew's research and personal interview with Dr. Moll. CAFM Files. Lieutenant-Colonel Fraser Eadie recalled the word association test. The first word was "mouse" which made him reflect immediately upon the type of individual he would be soldiering with. Interview with author, 23 June 1998.

77. DHist, File 163.009 (D16)—File—"Selection of Personnel—1st Parachute Battalion." See also "Selection of Paratroops—Specifications," 17 May 1944. DHist, File 171.009 (D223).

78. "D.G.M.S. Circular Letter No. 193 1942," 24 December 1942. DHist, File 163.009 (D16).

79. "Examination of Personnel—Para-Troops," 25 January 1943. DHist, File 163.009 (D16). The high wastage rates for both screening and training remained consistent throughout the war.

80. "A.35 Canadian Parachute T.C.," 19 November 1943. DHist, File 112.21009 (D197) Folder 6. Sergeant R.F. Anderson stated that, based on his discussions with others, a minimum of 60-70% of volunteers failed the selection / training process. Interview with author, 11 June 1998. This is consistent with the recollection of other veterans.

81. Interview with author, 25 August 1998. One official report noted, "Examination procedures became more refined and more sophisticated as more information became available on personal performance at Fort Benning...In particular examiners were looking for individuals capable of undertaking a highly specialized type of training which required them to possess a 'high degree of stability and perseverance, and at the same time an ability to think for themselves." Willes, 14.

82. Interview with author, 4 November 1998.

83. "Training Paratroops," *Canadian Army Training Memorandum* (C.A.T.M.), No. 20, November 1942, 10. Great emphasis was placed on the need to encourage and build self-confidence. Specific direction stipulated, "In view of the terrific mental strain which accompanies the physical strain it is of utmost importance that the man should be encouraged and given confidence. Under no circumstances will instructors do otherwise than build up the man's confidence." Canadian Army, *Canadian Parachute Training School—Parachute Training Syllabus* (Ottawa: King's Printer, 1943), 4.

84. CATM, No. 20, 8.

85. Interview with author, 20 November 1998.

86. "Selection of Personnel: 1st Parachute Battalion," 23 December 1942. DHist, File 163.009 (D16).

87. Interview with author, 1 November 1998.

88. *Canadian Parachute Training Centre—Standard Syllabus 1944*. DHist, File 145.4036 (D2)

89. "Training Paratroops," CATM No. 20, November 1942, 10.

90. The War Cabinet Committee authorized the battalion's inclusion in a second British airborne division which was being formed on 7 April 1943 and directed that the unit be ready to sail anytime after 15 May. *War Cabinet Committee Minutes*, Volume 11-14, 1942-1943, Reel 4, 7 April 1943. See also "1st Cdn Para Bn—Despatch Overseas," 15 April 1943. DHist, File 163.009 (D16). See also NAC, RG 24, Vol 12260, File: 1 / Para Tps / 1, Letter CMHQ to HQ First Cdn Army, 23 March 1943; and Messages (CGS 728), dated 5 April 1943, and (CGS 212), dated 7 April 1943. Upon confirmation of the availability of the Canadian paratroopers, the British quickly intended to utilize them as part of their plans for the upcoming invasion of North Africa. However, The Canadians insisted that 1 Cdn Para Battalion was only intended for inclusion in the British Expeditionary Force intended for the return to Europe.

91. C.M.H.Q. Report 138, 4.

92. DND Historical Section (G.S.) Army Headquarters, Historical Report No. 17, 27 October 1947, "The 1st Canadian Parachute Battalion in Low Countries and Germany Final Operations (2 January-18 February and 24 March-5 May 1945), 33-35; Historical Report No. 26, 23 August 1949, "The 1st Canadian Parachute Battalion in France, 6 June—6 September 1944, 19-20. The established strength often quoted as 616 is the original establishment. It was increased by two effective 19 May 1944. The change reflected an adjustment from 26 officers and 590 other ranks to 31 and 587 respectively. C.M.H.Q. Report No. 138, 3.

93. Letter from Field-Marshal Sir Alan Brooke to Lieutenant-General J.C. Murchie, 26 June 1945. On display at the CAFM. See also Willes and Nolan, for unit history and wartime exploits.

94. Interview with author, 25 August 1998. Even the post of liaison officer (rank of major) which was originally established in July 1943 as a link between 6 (UK) Airborne Division and the Canadian Military Headquarters was terminated after only four months because it was felt that the two entities were well enough established to maintain normal liaison without the need of a specially designated staff officer. NAC, RG 24, Vol 12260, File: 1 / Para—Tps / 1 / 22 -1.

95. Interview with author, 16 June 1998. It must be noted that there is no bitterness or recrimination in these observations. All paratroop veterans interviewed noted that they were proud of their origins but fit in with and were fiercely loyal to their British airborne formation.

96. Interview with author, 23 June 1998. The battalion suffered from a chronic reinforcement problem from its inception. Early in its formation it was directed to transfer 96 qualified personnel to the newly forming 2nd Para Battalion (FSSF) and two months later an additional 125 personnel. See *1 Cdn Para Bn War Diary,* 1 December 1942 and 27 February 1943. The unit was eventually sent overseas under strength in the order of 100 Other Ranks (OR). "1st Cdn Para Bn," 19 July 1943. DHist, File 112.21009 (D200). Reinforcement continued to be a problem. Between 4-20 July the Battalion, having suffered 300 casualties since D-Day, was reinforced by 7 officers and 100 other ranks, who were not para-trained, from the Canadian Reinforcement Unit. CAFM Research Document Part 1, 1.B, Document 2, "1st Canadian Parachute Battalion," 2. An arrangement for a flow of trained parachute reinforcements from Canada was effected with the establishment of 814 Canadian Parachute Training School at Shilo, in May 1943. The school was established to have 100 men in the Parachute Training Wing, 200 in the Advanced Training Wing, and 480 in the Trained Soldier Companies. After 14 November 1943, the quotas were reduced to 50, 100, and 240 respectively but the system was unable to provide a sufficient flow of replacements to keep the Battalion reinforced. C.M.H.Q. Report No. 138, 5 & 13. By 3 March 1944 the shortages of officers and ORs had increased to 16 and 340 (or 58% of unit strength). "Paratroop Reinforcements," 7 March 1944. DHist, File 112.21009 (D197) Folder 9.

97. Thomas Clark and Harry Pugh, *Canadian Airborne Insignia 1942—Present* (Arlington, VA: C & D Enterprises, 1994), 24. See also Darrel L. Harris, *Close Up & Stand In the Door! The Parachute School Airborne Command US Army / Canadian Parachute Training Centre A-35 Camp Shilo.* Private printing, Rivers, Manitoba, 1996, 74. The debate in regard to maintaining a parachute training centre in Canada commenced as early as September 1943. The Canadian overseas headquarters continually insisted that paratroop recruits be sent directly to Fort Benning, Georgia, or Ringway, England for training. They maintained that qualifying individuals in Canada was redundant and inefficient for the numbers required. NDHQ resisted this pressure initially. However, as the war began to wind down, training and facility development was dramatically pared. NAC, RG 24, Vol 9830, File 2/paratps/1, Training / Parachute Tp—Memorandum, "Advanced Training—Paratroop Reinforcements," 27 September 1943; Memorandum, "Reinforcements—1 Cdn Para Bn," 23 February 1944; Memorandum, "Training of Parachute Reinforcements," 15 June 1944; and Memorandum, "Development and Testing Facilities," 13 October 1944.

98. NAC, RG 24, Vol 2258, File HQ-54-27-128-16. There is a series of memorandums in this file, dated 18-19 June 1945, indicating the decision to postpone disbandment in order to facilitate the process of demobilization. Another indication of the future was held in a letter, dated 26 June 1945, from Field Marshal Sir Alan Brooke to Lieutenant-General J.C. Murchie. He wrote, "I understand that it may not be possible for you to keep the 1st Cdn Para Bn in being as a full battalion. Nevertheless, I hope that the close ties formed in battle between the Canadian parachute troops and the airborne troops of the British Army may be retained in the future." CAFM, on display.

99. *General Orders 1946, Part "A",* Nos. 12-19, 17 January 1946, G.O. 18—Disbandment, Active Units, 8. Lieutenant-Colonel Fraser Eadie recorded in the Unit's diary, "The disbursing of the Unit began this week...all unit affairs were straightened up and the Unit brought to nil strength." *1 Cdn Para Bn War Diary*, 23-30 September 1945, NA and CAFM.

CHAPTER TWO

A QUESTION OF THREAT

The Defence of Canada and the Need for Airborne Forces, 1935-1945

The threat to Canada [during the war] was less than minor, and insignificant as it was, it was created almost entirely by the over-wrought imagination of too many of our otherwise sane and sensible people.

Lieutenant-General M. A. Pope[1]

The concept of a distinct Canadian airborne capability during the Second World War faced much opposition from the political and senior military leaders. They believed that such special troops did not have a credible role to play in the defence of Canada and as such did not warrant the expenditure of scarce resources. The Canadian parachute battalion that was eventually established during the war was not intended for home defence. It served overseas as part of a British airborne division and was disbanded at the end of the conflict. To fully understand the veiled debate that engulfs the sometimes pernicious controversy over the relevance of parachute forces in Canada, it is essential to examine the relationship between threat perception in Canada and the airborne idea. Put simply, after the Second World War, defence of the nation against an external military menace, particularly in the North, has paradoxically been both the Achilles heel of Canadian airborne forces, as well as the pretence for their existence. This contradiction is the key to comprehending the inherent reason why Canadian airborne forces were destined to lead a roller-coaster existence for nearly a half century—one that would eventually lead to their ultimate demise.

Before the Second World War Canadian military and political leaders consistently dismissed the possibility of any real peril to Canada's physical security as a result of foreign attack. At the end of the war, the Canadian military attaché in Washington, DC publicly admitted:

> It is doubtful whether any country in the world possessed a greater sense of security in pre-war days than Canada. Her only immediate neighbour was her friend. Oceans on three sides appeared adequate barriers against trouble from Europe or Asia.[2]

This was no great revelation. As early as 1938, Prime Minister Mackenzie King asserted, "that undoubtably Canada is the most secure of all countries."[3] He dismissed "the launching of fantastic expeditions across half the world [by belligerents intending to attack Canada]" and stated, "At present, danger of attack upon Canada is minor in degree and secondhand in origin. It is against chance shots that we need immediately to defend ourselves."[4]

Ian Mackenzie, then Minister of National Defence, supported these sentiments. He proclaimed that "there is danger, but so far as Canada is concerned, it is, as I have already pointed out, an incidental contingency."[5] He expressed the notion that the direct defence of Canada entailed the protection of "our coastal areas, our ports, our shipping terminals, our territorial waters, the focal areas of our trade routes adjacent to our harbour mouths."[6] Specifically, he noted that the threat consisted largely of raids, by submarine, aircraft or other craft, for the purpose of creating diversion and panic.[7]

The military perception was little different in the late thirties. Lieutenant-General Maurice Pope wrote, "the idea of our having to fight a major war on our own soil was absurd. As the forms and scales of attack to which it was judged Canada might be exposed in the event of even a major war comprised only limited naval and air bombardment and minor raids against our defended ports."[8] This judgment changed little, even with the commencement of hostilities. An army appreciation in February 1941 stated that "Canada's front line lies in and around the British Isles."[9] Furthermore, the Chief of the General Staff professed that "large scale attack on these [Canadian] shores is not a contingency which I believe we need plan for. Even if the very worst happened and the UK [were] overwhelmed, I would continue to hold that view."[10]

The apparent lack of concern for Canada's security emanated from the nation's geographic endowment. A military appreciation on Canadian defence problems noted, "The direct defence of the national territory...owing to our fortunate geographical position...has not been given a high degree of priority."[11] General Charles Foulkes reinforced this theme. As he explained, "prior to 1939 Canada was able to derive a considerable amount of security from her geographical position. The then available weapons precluded a direct attack on Canada."[12]

Geography and history provided the nation with another important element in its defence, namely, a powerful neighbour to the south. The close proximity to the United States prompted Colonel Burns to write, "we believe, reasonably or unreasonably, that our Southern neighbour would go to war before she would allow a foreign nation to establish itself on our territory."[13] Canadian military historian C.P. Stacey reiterated this thesis in his examination of Canadian defence policy in 1940. "It has long been generally recognized in Canada," he asserted, "that the most elementary regard for the security of the United States itself would render it impossible for that country to permit any aggressive power to gain a foothold on Canadian soil."[14] Stacey believed that "all Canada's pre-war defence planning was implicitly conditioned by the knowledge that Canadian territory was protected by geography and the naval power of the United Kingdom and the United States."[15]

These conclusions were not visionary. In 1936, in Chautauqua, New York, President Franklin D. Roosevelt raised the image of a benevolent neighbour when he stated, "We can defend ourselves, and we can defend our neighbourhood."[16] Two years later he erased any doubt with his famous declaration at Queen's University in Kingston. He proclaimed:

> The Dominion of Canada is part of the sisterhood of the British Empire. I give to you assurance that the people of the United States will not stand idly by if domination of Canadian soil is threatened by any other empire. We as good neighbours are true friends.[17]

Two days later King responded, "We, too, have our obligations as a good friendly neighbour, and one of these is to see that, at our own instance our country is made as immune from attack or possible invasion as we can reasonably be expected to make it, and that should the occasion ever arise, enemy forces should not be able to pursue their way, either by land, sea or air, to the United States across Canadian territory."[18] These courageous words were uttered at a time when there were neither real nor perceived threats to Canada due to its geographical location and the naval might of both Britain and the United States. King's pledge to guard the flanks of his neighbour seemed effortless and easily enforced. However, his words would return to haunt him and take on the dimensions of a curse. Soon after the Second World War technological developments and world events changed Canada's outlook on security forever, particularly in regard to its North.

The Arctic, more than any other region in the nation, and specifically in the postwar era, became intimately associated with Canadian airborne forces. This was not due to an overwhelming concern for security. Rather, it was a question of sovereignty. Prior to discussing the postwar development of airborne forces it is critical to understand the nature of the perceived threat to Canada, particularly its northern territory.

The Arctic has a very special hold on the Canadian psyche despite the fact that very few Canadians have actually ever seen it. Strategist Kenneth Eyre observed that "North to Canadians is more of an idea than a place."[19] It was during the Second World War that Canadian apathy toward the Arctic was actually broken. The war led to the implementation of a continental alliance which dictated the close cooperation between Canada and the United States in the defence of North America. It was also the catalyst which fuelled a new surge of interest in the North.

In late 1941, especially after Pearl Harbor, the looming Japanese threat to Alaska and the fear of a Nazi-occupied Siberia only a short distance away across the Bering Strait, raised American fears higher than they had ever been before. It quickly became evident that this perceived threat to North America was intimately tied to the Canadian North. Under immense pressure from the United States, the Canadian Arctic was transformed, overnight, into a hive of activity and development. Significantly, it was mostly American activity and American development.

The growing American presence, coupled with their dominating attitude, worried Canadian politicians. After the Aleutians campaign of 1942, when US forces successfully drove the Japanese out of the islands, Canadian anxiety became heightened. The latent concern prompted Prime Minister King's government to take action to safeguard Canadian sovereignty. Canada had always been defensive of its claim to ownership of the Arctic archipelago, and the growing occupation of the North by the United States was seen as a direct threat to Canadian proprietorship. The American presence, it was argued, could be seen as de facto control.

The Canadian government soon discovered the danger inherent in the new defensive partnership. It became evident that any threat to the security of the United States, as perceived by the Americans, whether realistic or not, represented a genuine danger to Canada. The Canadian political and military leadership promptly realized that it was critical that Canada be seen by its southern neighbour to be taking adequate steps to secure Canadian borders against any intrusion that could subsequently threaten the United States. This geographical reality was exacerbated at the end of the Second World War. New technology, weapons of immense potency, and the emergence of two diametrically opposed superpowers, which sandwiched Canada between them, fuelled what would become a continuing challenge to Canada's efforts to maintain the security and sovereignty of its Arctic region.[20]

Canadian defence policy became focussed more on frustrating the erosion of its sovereignty and minimizing American expansion into the Canadian Arctic than it did on meeting any real danger to its territory from hostile invasion. Although a degree of potential threat was always recognized, more so by the military than the political leadership, decisions taken on the defence of the North were primarily geared to countering American encroachment. This theme, which was initiated by Mackenzie King in the Second World War, is still valid today—even if the issue appears only periodically. In order to see how this Canadian fear of the southern neighbour played such a large role in the re-establishment of an airborne force after the war, one must go back and retrace some of the salient events that led Canada to that conclusion.

The Canadian political and military leadership placed very little emphasis on the Arctic prior to 1939. During this period interest in the North was limited primarily to the establishment of a few radio communication stations, weather reporting installations, and rudimentary surveys to assist civilian aviation.[21] The limited development pursued in the Arctic was a result of commercial interest rather than defence concerns. Eventually, a series of civilian airfields and emergency landing strips, largely based on the pioneering efforts of the early bush pilots, was established across the entire country by the Departments of Transport and Defence. These fields were utilized mainly by Trans-Canada Airlines, but they also yielded a network which could be used to concentrate military air strength in time of crisis.[22]

This network of national airfields was expanded even further during the mid to late thirties because technological advancements and economic incentive rekindled an interest in a transpolar air route to Alaska and Europe. As a result, a survey of northern airfields was conducted to determine whether expansion of existing sites was required and what additional landing fields were necessary.[23] Construction on this network of airfields was undertaken in 1939 and continued well into the Second World War. It eventually became known as the infamous North-West Staging Route. It later proved instrumental in the defence of Alaska and in the supply of aircraft and equipment to the beleaguered Soviet Union.[24]

Apart from the growing realization of the significance of the transpolar air routes, by 1940 the North was still seen as inconsequential to the security of the Canadian "fireproof house." C.P. Stacey's military appreciation of the period captured the prevailing sentiment. He wrote:

> On the Dominion's northern territories those two famous servants of the Czar,
> Generals January and February, mount guard for the Canadian people all the year
> round. It is not impossible that the continuing development of aircraft will lend
> these Arctic and sub-Arctic regions an increased military significance in the future;
> but for the moment, though they cannot be entirely forgotten, they are clearly not
> particularly important, and this fact greatly narrows, for practical purposes,
> Canada's actual area of defence.[25]

Similarly, Kenneth Eyre insisted, "the most significant military characteristic of the Canadian North is not the climate; it is isolation!"[26]

Paradoxically, by 1943 the emphasis on northern security became focussed primarily on protecting national sovereignty from the perceived encroachment of an ally rather than guarding an unprotected flank from hostile invasion. The catalyst which fuelled the evolution of the Canadian concern for its North was tied inextricably with the American focus on Alaska. Throughout the 1930s American political leaders experienced a common apathy with their Canadian counterparts in regard to their northern territories. "In the halls of Congress, Alaska was described as a 'frozen waste,' much as strategic Guam was passed off by some Representatives as a 'grain of sand'."[27] The military leadership shared a similar view and placed

Alaska on low priority status for receiving scarce military resources. Contemporary accounts noted, "it is no criticism of American military and naval leaders to say that they have been reluctant to lavish the taxpayer's money on Alaskan defenses."[28] In 1937, an official of the Army's War Plans Division reported that "there appears at present to be no necessity, from the viewpoint of national defense, of increasing the military garrison of Alaska."[29] Few acknowledged General Billy Mitchell's observation that Alaska, as the most central place on the globe in regard to aircraft, was also the most important strategic location in the world. He argued that "whoever holds Alaska will hold the world."[30]

It took the Axis juggernaut to galvanize American action in the North. The German attack on the Soviet Union in June 1941, "muddied the already seething situation in the Far East and seemed to bring closer to Alaska the danger that Alaskans had been advertising for years."[31] The realization that "in the possession of the enemy Alaska, [would] furnish a jumping-off point for invasion by air of the United States," soon resulted in the restoration of money to expand Alaskan defence.[32] The Permanent Joint Board for Defence (PJBD) noted on 26 February 1942, "that the effective defence of Alaska is of paramount importance to the defence of the continent against attack from the West, since Alaska is the area most exposed to an attempt by the enemy to establish a foothold in North America."[33]

In the aftermath of the surprise Japanese attack on Pearl Harbor a rising sense of panic began to emerge in the American public and a shrill cry of impending doom prevailed. Herbert Hilscher, the editor of the leading Alaskan territorial magazine captured the predominating attitude when he stated:

> All Alaskans and the US Army and Navy know that if the flags of the Nazis and the Japanese fly over Siberia our position in the Northland will be extremely grave….Alaska must be made into an arsenal of democracy. It must be made as impregnable a fortification as Gibraltar. For if Russia falls, who can say at what unannounced hour bombers, parachutists, and air-borne troops may not descend on Alaska?[34]

The theme of a northern threat via Alaska was very quickly absorbed by Canadians as well. Canadian historian Desmond Morton observed, "It was easy to believe, as Japanese power spread irresistibly across Southeast Asia…that it could also reach out easily to seize a foothold in North America. If the threat was far-fetched militarily, it was politically all too real."[35] Politicians and their constituents in British Columbia became increasingly agitated.[36] Even the premier of Ontario predicted a Japanese assault on Alaska. He went so far as to postulate the inevitability of enemy infiltration down the western coast of Canada.[37] Prime Minister King was another who believed the Japanese represented a real danger. He warned his military officials that it would be foolhardy to underestimate the strength of the Japanese. Furthermore, King cautioned his generals not to rule out the possibility of operations of a larger or more serious nature.[38]

The military, however, was not overly alarmed. Even after the Japanese seizure of the islands of Attu, Agatu, and Kiska, in the Aleutians in July 1942, the official analysis reaffirmed that "the forms and scales of attack envisioned on the entry of Japan into the war remained unchanged."[39] The Armed Forces' position rested on the basis that there was no military objective of sufficient importance to justify other than small scale tip-and-run raids, the effect of which would have had little military significance. In addition, the generals emphasized the fact that the Japanese were already overcommitted. The Chiefs of Staff Committee clearly professed that an actual attempt at an invasion on this coast by Japanese forces was considered highly remote.[40]

Nonetheless, the military chain of command took into account the anxiety of the public. An Army appreciation noted, "the question of increasing protection in British Columbia is one of vocal and increasing concern on the part of the civilian population. In view of the immense length of the coastline, greater mobility of Army personnel would seem a matter of urgent consideration and might do much to allay the present feeling of apprehension."[41] Surprisingly, this admission had no effect on the senior military command in regard to the establishment of an airborne capability. It did, however, result in the reinforcement of the West Coast in terms of artillery and manpower.[42]

The public consternation in British Columbia was neither the government's nor the military's greatest challenge. Lieutenant-General Pope realized the nature of the real threat. He explained, "it was clear that if...Canada should attempt to remain neutral and aloof, our American neighbours would ride roughshod over us and make use of our territory and facilities as it pleased them."[43]

Pope's observation was accurate. The response of the United States to the new northern threat was representative of the energy and seemingly unlimited resources of a great power. The American reaction was swift and all encompassing and created an intricate web that eventually entangled Canada. The expeditious American mobilization resulted in a massive influx of personnel to reinforce the Alaskan garrison, as well as to establish the logistical infrastructure required to support the new defensive effort in the North. By June 1943, more than 33,000 American soldiers and civilian workers had poured into northwest Canada.[44]

The American invasion was precipitated by their perception of the defensive steps required to protect the North. These included the expansion and upgrading of the North-West Staging Route,[45] the construction of a land route to Alaska, and the assurance of petroleum for military forces in the North. These projects all encompassed development on Canadian territory and were, theoretically, subject to consultation and agreement between the two nations. In accordance with the Ogdensburg Agreement, the Permanent Joint Board of Defence (PJBD) was responsible for the "broad consideration of the defence of the north half of the Western Hemisphere."[46] King explained to parliament that due to the global scope of the conflict, "recommendations were made from time to time by the joint board [PJBD] for the development...of projects of vital importance to the two nations for common defence and for the effective prosecution of the war."[47]

Although these projects were grounded in the noble pursuit of mutual defence, they quickly highlighted the dangers of a relationship between two unequal partners. The Ogdensburg Agreement was signed in haste, almost as a contingency plan for the imminent collapse of Britain.[48] As the tide of war began to shift the consequences of the agreement soon became apparent.

The "projects of vital importance" to the security of North America very quickly captured Canadian attention. One such project, the construction of the Alaska Highway, was representative of the difficulties which faced Canada. It also fuelled the growing Canadian concern for the North. As early as 1928, both Americans and Canadians had considered a land route to Alaska; however, the exorbitant cost and "negligible military value" precluded any official support.[49] American military planners viewed a road link to Alaska as being of little strategic importance, and primarily of economic benefit to civilians.[50]

The Japanese attack on Pearl Harbor, in December 1941, abruptly changed the American perspective.[51] Overnight, the construction of an all-weather road was seen as "one of the most important steps toward making Alaska defensible."[52] Once the Americans decided what was necessary, they took prompt action with little regard for Canadian sensitivities.

On 12 February 1942, the Canadian under-secretary of state for external affairs informed the War Cabinet Committee that the Americans had concluded that construction of a land route to Alaska on Canadian soil was necessary for continental defence, but they had not yet submitted a formal request to do so.[53] It was not until 26 February 1942 that the PJBD, as its twenty-fourth recommendation, advised that the construction of the Alaska Highway should be undertaken.

The Canadian dilemma was evident. The government was reluctant to proceed with the project. Nevertheless, a secret external affairs memorandum conceded that, "the United States Government is now so insistent that the road is required that the Canadian Government cannot possibly allow itself to be put in the position of barring the United States from land access to Alaska."[54] Furthermore, it stated that in the unlikely event that Japan was able to deny the United States access by sea to Alaska, and "if Canada had prevented the construction of land communications the Canadian Government would be in a completely untenable position."[55] The alternative, however, was daunting. It required Canada "to expend some $80,000,000.00 on the construction, and about $1,000,000.00 per annum on the maintenance of a road that would be a monument to our friendship for the US but would otherwise be pretty much of a 'White Elephant'."[56] Cabinet concluded that Canada had little choice but to agree. War Cabinet Committee approval was subsequently given on 5 March 1942.[57]

But it did not matter. The actual decision to proceed had already been made in the United States. "President Roosevelt had in fact considered the matter as a fait accompli, and had allocated ten million dollars for the project from his emergency fund on 11 February."[58] As a result, American engineers arrived in Dawson Creek to begin construction on the road two days before cabinet approved the request.[59] The highway eventually proved insignificant. By the fall of 1943 only 54 tons of supplies had been delivered to the Alaska Defence Command by motor transport.[60]

The American presence quickly struck a disharmonious chord with Canadians, particularly Prime Minister King. Alarming reports, emanating from the North, painted a grim picture for a country that laboured to maintain a decorum of autonomy and independence. One report stated that the Americans in Edmonton were openly describing themselves as an "Army of Occupation."[61] To King the spectre of American encroachment was very real. "I said I was not altogether without feeling," confided King to his diary, "that the Alaska Highway was less intended for protection against Japan than as one of the dangers of the hand which America is placing more or less over the whole of the Western Hemisphere."[62]

The Alaska Highway was not the only source of concern. The CANOL (Canadian Oil) project provided similar hazards to the Canadian hosts. Its intention was to provide a guaranteed supply of fuel to Alaska and military traffic en route, by means of a pipeline from Norman Wells in the Northwest Territories, to a refinery in Whitehorse, Yukon, for subsequent distribution. By the time the project had been completed it had expanded to include a series of airfields, numerous construction camps, pumping stations, supplementary pipelines and additional roads.[63] Its utility, as well as efficiency, was questioned from the beginning. It has since been labelled a "junk-yard of military stupidity."[64] Lieutenant-General Pope commented, "The CANOL project as a defence measure has always seemed to me so far-fetched as to be absurd."[65]

Of greater concern was the fact that the decision to proceed with the project was once again taken without proper approval from the Canadian government. Donald Creighton ascertained that "the United States Army authorized the pipeline and signed a contract with Imperial Oil more than a fortnight before the Canadian government signified its approval."[66] Furthermore, additional airfields were constructed in support of the project without consulting the Canadian government.[67] The American insensitivity to Canadian control prompted Vincent Massey, the Canadian High Commissioner to the United Kingdom to comment, "They [Americans] have apparently walked in and taken possession in many cases as if Canada were unclaimed territory inhabited by a docile race of aboriginies."[68] His diary recorded further disquieting observations. Massey noted, "the Americans who unfortunately under cover of the needs of the war effort are acting in the North-West as if they owned the country....We have for too long been far too supine vis-à-vis Washington and the only threat to our independence comes from that quarter."[69]

The American encroachment in the North became extremely worrisome. As the war progressed, all perceived threats to the North American land mass, particularly in the Arctic, diminished dramatically.[70] Suspicions of American intentions did not. Malcolm MacDonald, the British High Commissioner in Canada visited the northern projects and reported to the Canadian Cabinet War Committee that "it was quite evident that these vast undertakings [American defense projects] were being planned and carried out with a view to the postwar situation." He further warned that "Canadian representatives in the area were few and quite unable to keep control or even in touch with day to day developments."[71]

Civilian entrepreneurs also questioned the long-term motives of the Americans. J.K. Cornwall, an Edmonton businessman remarked, "I visualize the USA. controlling to a large extent the development of Canada's north land, due to their financial power and experience."[72] But no one was more suspicious than the prime minister. J.W. Pickersgill recorded, "Despite his close friendship with Roosevelt, Mackenzie King was never without suspicions of the ultimate designs of the Americans....He referred to 'the efforts that would be made by the Americans to control developments in our country after the war.'"[73] King's own diaries are testimony to these misgivings. He wrote, "I viewed the Alaskan Highway and some other things growing out of the war, which was clear to my mind that America had had as her policy, a western hemisphere control which would mean hemispheric immunity, if possible, from future war but increasing political control by United States Forces greater than those of any one country working to this end."[74] He went so far as to confide in Vincent Massey that "he had grave doubts whether international agreements [on US withdrawal from bases and installations on Canadian soil] on this which Canada had secured from the United States [would] provide any practical guarantee against the United States' claims and pretensions."[75] King went on to say that "Canadians were looked upon by Americans as a lot of Eskimos."[76]

This fear of "possible domination of postwar Canada by the Americans" led King to decide that "we ought to get the Americans out of the further development there, [Canada's North] and keep control in our own hands."[77] As a result of the Canadian political perception of the American encroachment into Canada's North, action was taken to regain control and assert ownership. The Canadian government now embarked on a vigorous program intended to "re-Canadianize the Arctic."[78]

The new focus on the Arctic, although initiated by the spectre of Japanese invasion, later evolved into a fear of the Americans usurping the Canadian North. This new realization etched itself into the consciousness of Canada's military and political leadership. A military appreciation warned that "it is of great importance that Canada should carefully safeguard her sovereignty in the Arctic at all points and at all times, lest the acceptance of an initial infringement of her sovereignty invalidate her entire claim and open the way to the intrusion of foreign interests of a nature which might create an ultimate threat to national security."[79]

As the threat of a Japanese invasion waned, a shift in emphasis appeared. Alarm over the nation's physical security was replaced by concern over territorial jurisdiction. Action to regain control of Canadian sovereignty began as early as the spring of 1941 with the initiative to peel back the "command principle" that vested the responsibility for the strategic direction of American and Canadian forces in North America in the United States. The Canadians originally agreed to this principle in 1940 as part of the *Joint Basic War Plan, United States-British Commonwealth Plan 1* (ABC 1). Britain's precarious future at the time cast the United States as potentially Canada's only, and overwhelmingly stronger, ally.

This contingency further postulated that operations would probably be confined to the North American continent.[80] The favourable change in the direction of the war and the drafting of the *Joint Canadian-United States Basic Defence Plan 2* (ABC-22) provided Canada with the opportunity to change the former arrangement. The Canadian military and political leadership were opposed to the continuing American control of strategic direction. There was a distinct and powerful Canadian sentiment that "Canada should [now] retain strategic, as well as tactical control of her own forces and that a satisfactory solution of the problem of command could be found in cooperation."[81] Despite American reluctance the Canadian position was accepted.[82]

The government also took specific action to regain control of the Canadian North. The appointment of a special commissioner for defence projects in north west Canada was announced in parliament in the spring of 1943. His task was to supervise and coordinate the activities of the government and "to maintain close and continuous cooperation with all agencies of the United States government in the area."[83] In addition, the King government began an information campaign to reassure the political opposition parties, the public (and itself), as well as to give notice to its ally, that the American presence was strictly a temporary war measure. "To carry out joint plans for the defence of this continent, and to facilitate the transportation of war materials to fighting fronts," stated King, "the Canadian government has agreed to the stationing of United States military units at certain places on Canadian territory....It is not contemplated that the contributions which the United States is thus making to the common defence will give that country any continuing rights in Canada after the conclusion of war."[84]

Notwithstanding these initiatives, the most influential Canadian action in regaining control of its Arctic region was the policy of reimbursing the Americans for the cost of construction and development undertaken in the North. The tight-fisted King government realized that retention of clear ownership and title to Canada's North required payment for those bases and facilities of a permanent nature built by the Americans. What made this decision more painful was the fact that many of the projects were never supported as necessary by the government, and almost all were constructed to standards far in excess of Canadian requirements.

Despite these realities, the requirement to buy back control was seen as paramount and a new financial agreement was reached between the two nations in June 1944. It resulted in the acceptance of a further war debt of $123.5 million, in order to reimburse the Americans for work that had been done.[85] The principle in question was simple. King himself, prior to the outbreak of war, enunciated it:

> Domestic ownership, maintenance and control of all military stations and personnel is one of the really indispensable hall marks of national sovereign self government...Outside its homeland a state may have military stations and quarter military personnel in countries which it 'owns,' in its colonies or 'possessions,' or in its mandated territories according to the trust deed, or in countries which it has assumed or been yielded, by some arrangement, what amounts to a protectorate. But no country pretending to sovereign self control could permit such a state of affairs or its implications and consequences.[86]

This fundamental belief led the government, in the interest of sovereignty, to buy back the North and ensure clear title of Canadian ownership. The *Final Report of the Advisory Committee on Post-Hostilities* reported in January 1945, "As time went on, it became increasingly apparent that the existence of major military installations in Canada built, paid for and operated by the United States might impair Canada's freedom of action. This difficulty has been mitigated, if not eliminated, by the Canadian Government's decision, agreed to by all the United States, to reimburse the United States for construction costs of all airfields and certain other facilities of continuing value erected in Canada by the United States."[87]

The lessons learned through painful experience during the war were not lost. According to Desmond Morton, "the war had taught Canadians how swiftly the Americans could move when their minds were made up and how little weight Ottawa's appeals really carried in Washington."[88] At the time a government official conceded that "if Canada had refused or failed to undertake projects which formed part of United States plans or measures in Canadian territory for the special protection of the United States, the United States was willing and even anxious to proceed alone."[89] Seventeen years later, defence analyst R.J. Sutherland echoed those same observations when he opined, "Canada must not become through military weakness or otherwise a direct threat to American security. If this were to happen, Canada's right to existence as an independent nation would be placed in jeopardy."[90]

The realization that American security concerns represented a genuine threat to Canadian sovereignty was entrenched by the end of the Second World War. Nowhere was this more evident than in the Canadian North. McNaughton affirmed, "We had to discharge our obligations to make sure that nobody attacked the US over our territory. If we had not done so there was the danger that the US might have taken over the Canadian North in the interest of their own security."[91] This fear led to a new focus on the North and the acceptance of an enormous debt for unwanted infrastructure. The motive was primarily to preserve control and sovereignty of Canadian territory, it was not the result of any concern for security. The reality of the new world was that Canada and the United States formed a strategic unit and American security was of vital interest to Canada.[92] As King noted, "...because of the gateway which Canada opens to an enemy...the defence of this continent is bound to be increasingly that of the United States itself."[93]

This realization, combined with the dramatic improvements in technology and the growing antagonism between the newly emerged superpowers, cast King's prewar pledge in a new light. It now took on the likeness of a curse. Sandwiched geographically between the two rivals, Canadians quickly deduced the hazards and the potential penalty of attempting to remain aloof. The comment that "the United States military men refer, whether nervously or menacingly, to the 'undefended roof of North America' and claim the right to return en masse to the Canadian Northland which they left so recently," underscored the danger.[94] If the Second World War forced the nation's political and military leadership to take a direct interest in the North due to a fear of losing Canadian control and ownership, then the postwar era burned the issue of Arctic sovereignty into their very soul.

And so, for the future airborne force a marriage of convenience was in the making. The tight-fisted King government, which had never lost its disdain for the military, was intent on minimizing defence spending. However, it also grasped that its paranoid neighbour to the south would not tolerate an "open flank" to its north. As a result, a solution was required that could appease an apprehensive and potentially dominating ally and, more importantly, fulfill the Canadian government's agenda, namely minimum defence expenditures. It seems for the Canadian government of the day actual military capability was not the issue. The government was not convinced that a direct threat to the nation existed. The key was appearance. It was critical to demonstrate to the Americans that the Canadian government was conscious of its responsibility to secure the northern 'gateway to invasion.' More importantly, to prevent American interference, it was essential to furnish the illusion that actual forces were earmarked to undertake the mission if required. Paratroopers with their characteristic mobility and strategic reach seemed to be the government's politically expedient solution.

Notes for Chapter Two

1. Lieutenant-General M.A. Pope, *Soldiers and Politicians. The Memoirs of Lt.Gen. Maurice A. Pope* (Toronto: University of Toronto Press, 1962), 180.
2. Radio Broadcast by Colonel Guy V. Gurney on the Atlantic Coast Network. Transcript of speech, DHist, File 314.009 (D15).
3. W.L. Mackenzie King, "Canada's Defence Policy," *CDQ,,* Vol 15, October 1937-July 1938, 135.
4. *Debates,* 16 May 1938, 3179.
5. *Debates,* 24 March 1938, 1644.
6. Ibid., 1644. See also *Debates,* 19 May 1936, 2979; and "Royal Canadian Air Force," *The Royal Air Force Quarterly,* Vol 9, No. 1, January 1938, 10-13.
7. *Debates,* 24 March 1938, 1650, and 26 April 1938, 3236-3237.
8. Pope, 83 & 93. See also Stacey, *Six Years of War,* (Defence Scheme No. 3), 30-31.
9. "C.G.S. Appreciation of Military Situation, February 1941," DHist, File 112.3M2 (D496).
10. Ibid. See also Canada, *Documents on Canadian External Relations, Vol 7, 1939-1941* (Ottawa: External Affairs, 1980), 941; and NAC, Ralston Papers, MG 27, III B11, Vol 37—"An Appreciation of the Military World Situation with Particular Regard to its Effect on Canada," (as of 31 July 1942).
11. Joint Staff Committee, DND, 5 September 1936 (Army Records), as quoted in James Eayrs, *In Defence of Canada: Appeasement and Rearmament* (Toronto: University of Toronto Press, 1965), Document 1, 213.
12. General Charles Foulkes, "Canadian Defence Policy in a Nuclear Age," *Behind the Headlines,* Vol 21, No. 1, May 1961, 1.
13. E.L.M. Burns, "The Defence of Canada," *CDQ,* Vol 13, No. 4, July 1936, 379. Over thirty years later the same observation held true. Jon McLin in his study on contemporary Canadian defence policy wrote, "What protects Canadian security...is partly its isolation, and partly the fact that for geographical reasons, Canada's security interests are so closely identified with those of the US that it is assured of American protection." *Canada's Changing Defense Policy* (Toronto: The Copp Clark Publishing Co., 1967), 3.
14. C.P. Stacey, *The Military Problems of Canada* (Toronto: Ryerson Press, 1940), 29-30.
15. C.P. Stacey, *Arms Men & Governments: The War Policies of Canada 1939-1945* (Ottawa: Queen's Printer, 1970), 130.
16. Stacey, *The Military Problems of Canada*, 29.
17. Monica Curtis, ed., *Documents on International Affairs 1938, Vol 1* (London: Oxford University Press, 1942), 416. See also *Canadian Annual Review of Politics & Public Affairs,* 1937-1938, 141; and *Debates,* 12 February 1947, 346. FDR's speech was made in Kingston, Ontario on 18 August 1938. There was a degree of pragmatism involved. It has been well established that "the American Army has always taken the position that an attack on Canada is equivalent to an attack on the United States. For it is axiomatic that such an invasion...would merely be the prelude to an assault on the industrial heart of this country." Edgar P. Dean, "Canada's New Defence Program," *Foreign Affairs,* Vol 19, No. 1, October 1940, 236.
18. *Debates,* 12 February 1947, 346. The reliance on American protection led King to retort, as early as 1938, "The talk which one sometimes hears of aggressor countries planning to invade Canada...is, to say the least, premature. It ignores our neighbours..." *Debates,* 24 May 1938, 3179.

19. Kenneth Eyre, "Forty Years of Military Activity in the Canadian North, 1947-87," *Arctic,* Vol 40, No. 4, December 1987, 293.

20. *Documents on Canadian External Affairs, Vol 12, 1946,* 1617-1618; and Shelagh D. Grant, *Sovereignty or Security?* (Vancouver: UBC Press, 1988), 158-59; Foulkes, 1.

21. J.A. Wilson, the Controller of Civil Aviation maintained a great interest in developing flying in the North. He envisioned the establishment of a transpolar route to Europe. As a result, in 1922 he dispatched Squadron Leader R.A. Logan, of the fledgling Canadian Air Force, to conduct a survey of suitable landing fields in the Arctic archipelago. Trevor Lloyd, "Aviation in Arctic North America and Greenland," *The Polar Record,* Vol 5, No. 35, 36, January-July 1948, 164; and Swettenham, *McNaughton, Volume 1,* 210-214. General McNaughton, the CGS, was another who actively supported the initiative in the North. He orchestrated several programs on a shared cost basis with other government departments. For instance, the Royal Canadian Air Force, in cooperation with the Topographical Service and Geographical Survey, initiated a program of aerial photography. In addition, a series of radio stations was established which provided an invaluable system of communications. Swettenham, 214-216. The author noted that in 1941, this established network proved invaluable to provide communications for the many defence projects which were quickly undertaken. See also Grant, *Sovereignty or Security,* 15. The cost of the radio stations was shared between the Department of the Interior and Defence.

22. Stacey, *The Military Problems of Canada,* 112. Two commercial Airlines, Canadian Airways and Mackenzie Air Service, commenced operations in the Arctic in the late-twenties and did much to open the North. H.W. Hewetson, "Arctic Survey," *Canadian Journal of Economic & Political Science,* Vol 11, 1945, 462-463. See also Vilhjalmur Stefansson, "The American Far North," *Foreign Affairs,* Vol 17, April 1939, 517-521; and J.A. Wilson, "North-West Passage by Air," *Canadian Geographical Journal,* Vol 26, No. 3, March 1943, 107-115. Many of the fields were built as relief projects during the depression. C.D. Howe (Minister of Munitions and Supply) stated that, "Pioneering for this airway was carried out by Canadian bush pilots who first operated in that area, in seaplanes, in the early twenties." *Debates,* 28 February 1944. See also Vilhjalmur Stefansson, "Routes to Alaska," *Foreign Affairs,* Vol 19, No. 4, July 1941, 869.

23. The perceived viability and increased importance of a transpolar route was rekindled in 1937 when three Soviet airmen flew non-stop from Moscow to Vancouver in 63 hours and 17 minutes. W.M. Franklin, "Alaska, Outpost of American Defense," *Foreign Affairs*, Vol 19, No. 1, October 1940, 247. It was quickly noted that "On the maps of tomorrow's air age Canada holds a strategic position that can shape our future as a world power...In practise every plane from Europe or Asia reaching the United States by great circle courses will cross the Dominion." Trevor Lloyd, "Canada: Mainstreet of the Air," *Maclean's*, 3 April 1943, 34. See also Stacey, *Arms Men & Governments,* 379-380; F.H. Ellis, "New York to Nome and Back," *The Beaver,* September 1949, 28-32.

24. Stacey, *Arms Men & Governments*, 380. See also Stan Cohen, *The Forgotten War—Vol I* (Missoula, Montana: Pictorial Histories Publishing Company, 1988), 10-22; and Wilson, 116-127.

25. Stacey, *The Military Problems of Canada*, 5.

26. Eyre, 293.

27. Jean Potter, *Alaska Under Arms* (New York: The Macmillan Company, 1942), 35.

28. Franklin, 247.

29. Ibid, 247.

30. Potter, 74. Despite Alaska's strategic geographic location, it was the last of the overseas departments to receive combat planes. S. Conn, R. Engelman, R.C, and B. Fairchild, *The US Army in World War II. The Western Hemisphere. Guarding the United States and Its Outposts* (Washington D.C.: Department of the Army, 1964), 247.

31. Conn, 392. Alaska was described as, "Not exactly a soft under belly but rather the big toe an enemy can stand on while he slugs you." M. Young, "Defence Dilemma on North Frontier," *Saturday Night,* 13 Oct 1951, 28.

32. Potter, 35-36. It was noted that it took less than four hours to fly, in a bomber, from the Southern Alaskan bases to Seattle. Ibid., 13. An article in the *New York American*, titled "Unguarded Alaska," as

early as 21 January 1935, attempted to trigger public opinion against the state of military unpreparedness in Alaska. It stated, "Once an enemy base be established at any point in Alaska the foe could spread devastation by military planes against American cities. Dhist File 112.3M2.009 (D32). See also the Canadian General Staff commentary on the article, "Unguarded Alaska?" 5 February 1935, DHist, File 112.3M2.009 (D32).

33. *Documents on Canadian External Relations, Vol 9, 1942-1943*, 1180.

34. Potter, 23. The Vice-President of the United States warned the American people in May 1941, to be prepared for an attack on Alaska by Japan. E.R. Yarham,"The Alaska Highway," *RUSI,* Vol 87, No. 547, August 1942, 227.

35. Desmond Morton, *Canada and War. A Military and Political History* (Toronto: Butterworths, 1981), 110.

36. *Debates,* 11 June 1942, 3257. This was reflected by the concern shown by the member of Parliament for Cariboo in Question Period following the initial announcements of Japanese occupation of some islands in the Aleutians. He stated, "there will be much uneasiness in British Columbia, Alberta and other parts of Canada..."

37. Yarham, 227.

38. Galen R. Perras, "An Aleutian Interlude: Canadian Participation in the Recapture of the Island of Kiska," (Unpublished RMC War Studies MA Thesis, April 1986), 9.

39. NAC, Ralston Papers, MG 27, III B11, Vol 37 "An Appreciation of the Military World Situation with Particular Regard to its Effect on Canada," (as of 31 July 1942), completed by the General Staff (GS), 4 August 1942, 7.

40. NAC, Ralston Papers, MG 27, III B11, Vol 37 "Brief Appreciation of the Situation as of 24 Feb 1941," GS estimate 25 February 1941, 2; and "Japanese Occupation of the Aleutians Islands," GS estimate 15 July 1942, 3.

41. "Appreciation Re Air Landing Troops," 24 January 1942, 2. DHist, File 112.3M2 (D232).

42. Stacey, *Six Years of War*, 174-175. At its peak in June 1943, the Army attained a strength of 34,316 men on the West Coast. See also Perras, 3-4.

43. Pope, 91.

44. Col Stanley W. Dziuban, *The US Army in World War II. Special Studies. Military Relationships Between the United States and Canada 1939-1945* (Washington D.C.: Department of the Army, 1959), 199.

45. C.D. Howe described the North-West Staging Route as, "One of Canada's most important airways...composed of a chain of main aerodromes, with intermediary fields, extending from Edmonton to Alaska." *Debates,* 28 February 1944. A Northeastern staging route, code named Crimson, was also developed which was used to ferry aircraft and supplies to Europe via Northern Canada (The Pas, Churchill, Fort Chimo, Frobisher Bay, Northern Quebec), Labrador and Greenland. See Conn, 399-403; and Dziuban, 130-133.

46. The Ogdensburg agreement between President Roosevelt and Prime Minister King (18 August 1940) was a result of discussions relating to the mutual problems of defence. The agreement established the PJBD which was charged with coordinating the joint defence planning between the two countries. King stated, "The common approach of the governments of Canada and the United States to the problems of North American defence was formally recognized in the Ogdensburg agreement." *Debates,* 10 May 1943, 2504. The PJBD consisted of "four or five members from each country, most of them from the services." See J.W. Pickersgill and D.F. Forster, *The Mackenzie King Record, Vol 1* (Toronto: University of Toronto Press, 1960), 137-142; and Dziuban, 22-30. See also "Canada-US Permanent Joint Board on Defence—Twenty-Fifth Anniversary," *External Affairs,* Vol 17, No. 9, September 1965, 384-388; and H.L. Keenleyside, "The Canadian-US Permanent Joint Board of Defence, 1940-1945," *Behind the Scenes,* Vol 16, No. 1, Winter 1960-61, 51-75.

47. *Debates,* 10 May 1943, 2504.

48. Adrian Preston, "Canada and the Higher Direction of the Second World War 1939-1945" in *Canada's Defence. Perspectives on Policy in the Twentieth Century*, eds., B.D. Hunt and R.G. Haycock, (Toronto:

Copp Clark Pitman Ltd., 1993), 116. J.T. Jockel echoed this assessment. He noted, "Canada had been prepared to accept US direction of continental defences in early plans which assumed a defeated Britain and a retreat to Fortress North America." Jockel, "The Military Establishments and the Creation of NORAD," in *Canada's Defence,* 166. See also *Documents on Canadian External Relations, Vol 8, 1939-1943,* 192; and Grant, *Sovereignty or Security?* 131. The impression of a "sense of panic" at the imminence of Britain's collapse (as well as a perceived lack of faith and loyalty) caused Prime Minister Winston Churchill to initially look upon the Ogdensburg Agreement in an unfavourable light. This was reflected in an uncomplimentary telegram sent to King. See Pickersgill, *Record, Vol 1,* 139-143; and C.P. Stacey, *Canada and the Age of Conflict, Vol 2, 1921-1948* (Toronto: University of Toronto Press, 1984), 312.

49. Grant, *Sovereignty or Security?* 46. See also Stacey, *Arms, Men and Governments,* 382-384; Yarham, 228-230; and Stan Cohen, *The Trail of '42* (Missoula, Montana: Pictorial Histories Publishing Co., 1979).

50. K.S. Coates, and W.R. Morrison, *The Alaska Highway in World War II* (Toronto: University of Toronto Press, 1992), 25-26. This source provides an unrivalled account of the social impact of the "American invasion" on the Canadian North.

51. Dziuban, 53-54; Cohen, *The Forgotten War, Vol 1,* 16-17; Yarham, 227; G.L. Smith, "War Unlocks Our Last Frontier—Canada's Northern Opportunities," *Maclean's,* 3 April 1943, 11.

52. Stefansson, "Routes to Alaska," 868.

53. *Documents on Canadian External Relations, Vol 9, 1942-1943,* 1175.

54. *Documents on Canadian External Relations, Vol 9, 1942-43,* 1183. The author, H.L. Keenleyside noted, "I do not like the idea of Canada allowing the US to construct a highway on Canadian territory (thereby acquiring a moral if not a legal right to its continued use, at will, in peace or war).

55. *Documents on Canadian External Relations, Vol 9, 1942-43,* 1183. See also Keenleyside, 54-55.

56. Stacey, *Arms, Men and Governments,* 383.

57. "Summary of Cabinet War Committee Decisions on Canada—United States Joint Defence Construction Projects in the North-West." DHist, File 348.013 (D2). See also Stacey, *Arms, Men and Governments,* 348; and Dziuban, 220-221.

58. Stacey, *Arms, Men and Governments,* 348; Grant, *Sovereignty or Security?* 74-78; and Dziuban, 41.

59. Grant, *Sovereignty or Security?* 76.

60. Stacey, *Arms, Men and Governments,* 383.

61. Grant, *Sovereignty or Security?* 123.

62. *Mackenzie King Diaries,* Queen's University Archives (QA), File (Microfiche) T172 (21 March 1942).

63. Grant, *Sovereignty or Security?* 82-86; O.B. Hopkins, "The 'CANOL' Project," *Canadian Geographical Journal,* Vol 27, No. 5, November 1943, 241; Cohen, *The Forgotten War, Vol 1,* 34-38; and W.O. Kupech, "The Wells and CANOL: A Visit after 25 Years," *Canadian Geographical Journal,* 1968, 137-139. The eventual price tag for the project was $134,000,000.00.

64. Coates, 36. See also Dziuban, 229; and Cohen, *The Forgotten War, Vol 2,* 30.

65. Pope, 219.

66. Donald Creighton, *The Forked Road* (Toronto: McClelland & Stewart, 1976), 73. See also D. Grant, "CANOL—A Ghost From the Past," *Alternatives,* Vol 9, No.2, Spring 1980, 23.

67. Grant, "CANOL," 23; Dziuban, 214; and R.S. Finnie, "The Origin of CANOL's Mackenzie Air Fields," *Arctic,* Vol 33, No. 2, June 1980, 274-277.

68. Vincent Massey, *What's Past is Prologue* (Toronto: Macmillan Company of Canada Ltd., 1963), 371.

69. Ibid., 372. Creighton commented, "All too often they behaved as if they were on their own soil, or on a separate but tributary and submissive part of the Empire of the United States..." Creighton, 73. Stacey commented, "Canadian officials were often troubled by a tendency on the part of Americans to disregard Canadian sovereignty. American officers and officials...were sometimes as little disposed to worry

about respecting Canadian national rights...and acted as if they were on their own soil." Stacey, *Arms, Men and Governments,* 385.

70. Stacey, *Six Years of War,* 145-183. See also Nils Orvik, *Canada's Northern Security: The Eastern Dimension* (Kingston: Queen's University Press, 1982), 2.

71. Stacey, *Canada and the Age of Conflict, Vol 2,* 362. Trevor Lloyd, assigned to the Wartime Information Board, reported that it was apparent that the Americans were far advanced in their study of the Canadian Arctic. He observed that the American Army "was deeply entrenched in the north and that they have first class research facilities and an Arctic information centre." He added, "We have nothing." Grant, *Sovereignty or Security?* 122. Norman Robertson exclaimed, "The American presence had been allowed to grow in a fit of absence of mind" and he recommended that "a good, competent Canadian staff would have to be sent to the area, capable of collaborating with and controlling American development activities." J.L Granatstein, *Canada's War: The Politics of the Mackenzie King Government 1939-1945* (Toronto: Oxford University Press, 1975), 322.

72. Coates, 36.

73. Pickersgill, *Record, Vol 1*, 396.

74. *Mackenzie King Diaries,* QA, File T172 (18 March 1942).

75. Massey, 396. Minutes from the Cabinet War Committee meeting on 7 April 1943 noted, "It was feared that despite these agreements the United States, after the war, might seek to base an equitable claim to special concessions upon these large expenditures in Canada. *Documents on Canadian External Relations, Vol 9, 1942-43,* 1259. King also noted a similar conversation with Malcolm MacDonald in his diary. He wrote, "I said we're going to have a hard time after the war to prevent the US attempting control of some situations. He [MacDonald] said already they speak jokingly of their men as an army of occupation." *Mackenzie King Diaries*, QA, File T184 (29 March 1943).

76. Massey, 396.

77. Pickersgill, *Record Vol 1*, 644.

78. *Documents on Canadian External Relations, Vol 18, 1952,* 1201.

79. "Sovereignty In the Canadian Arctic in Relation to Joint Defence Undertakings," 29 May 1946. DHist, File 112.3M2 (D213).

80. *Documents on Canadian External Relations, Vol 8, 1939-41,* 197. ABC-1 was intended for use in the unlikely event of Great Britain being overrun by the enemy or if the British Navy ceased to control the North Atlantic. Ibid, 192. This arrangement was made during the period when Britain's survival was in grave doubt. See Endnote 39. Prime Minister King raised the issue in his War Cabinet. He noted that "consideration would require to be given, at once, to the possibility of having to provide bases in Canada for the British Fleet, if the military situation in Europe continued to deteriorate. The position with respect to the defence of the Atlantic Coast should be fully reviewed. *Memorandums Regarding the Meeting of the Cabinet War Committee*, Reel 1, Vols 3-5, 1939-1944, 14 June 1940. An excellent synopsis of Basic Plans 1 & 2 is given in *Documents on Canadian External Relations, Vol 8*, 192-196. Also see Dziuban, 113-114.

81. *Documents on Canadian External Relations, Vol 8, 1939-41,* 199. See also S. T. Ross, ed., *Coalition War Plans & Hemispheric Defence Plans, 1940-1941* (New York: Garland Publishers, Inc., 1992) for detailed text of defence plans.

82. The Americans felt that since "the defensive effort would fall nine-tenths to the United States, the strategic responsibility should be vested in that country." Dziuban, 114-115.

83. *Debates,* 10 May 1943, 2504. The commissioner, Brigadier W.W. Foster, reported directly to the War Cabinet Committee. See also Grant, "CANOL," 24.

84. *Debates,* 29 January 1943, 20-21.

85. "Summary of Cabinet War Committee Decisions on Canada—United States Joint Defence Construction Projects in the North-West." DHist, File 348.013 (D2). See also Grant, *Sovereignty or Security?* 132; Conn, 403-404; and Stacey, *Arms, Men and Governments,* 381.

86. *Debates,* 1 July 1938, 4527.

87. *Documents on Canadian External Relations, Vol 11, 1944-45,* 1570. See also L.B. Pearson, "Canada Looks 'Down North,'" *Foreign Affairs,* Vol 24, No.4, July 1946, 641-643. In 1969, SCEAND reiterated the importance of "paying your own way" and denounced the "free ride theory." It noted that it was convinced that Canada must be prepared to incur reasonable expenditures for its own defence in order to maintain its independence and freedom of action as a nation, and to ensure that Canadian interests are taken into account when continental defence measures are being taken. Cited in E.J. Dosman, ed., *The Arctic in Question* (Toronto: Oxford University Press, 1976), 90.

88. Morton, *Canada and War,* 156.

89. *Documents on Canadian External Relations, Vol 11, 1944-45,* 1570.

90. R.J. Sutherland, "Canada's Long Term Strategic Situation," *International Journal,* Vol 17, No. 3, Summer 1962, 202. A group of twenty influential Canadians (politicians, scholars, bureaucrats) reached this same conclusion in July 1940. They wrote *A Program of Immediate Canadian Action,* which stated in part, "A United States bent on large-scale preparations for its own defence and that of the hemisphere would be determined to take adequate measures wherever they might be needed. If concerned about the inadequacy of the meagre Canadian defences, it might and probably would insist on acting to augment them. Canada would have to co-operate voluntarily or involuntarily." Cited in Dziuban, 18. As if time stood still, over two decades later, Professor David Cox commented, "What is important to Canadians is not what we think the Russians will do; it is what we think the Americans think the Russians will do." Canada, *Canada's Territorial Air Defence* (Ottawa: DND, 1985), 35.

91. Swettenham, 176.

92. P. Buteux, "NATO and the Evolution of Canadian Defence and Foreign Policy," in *Canada's International Security Policy*, eds. D.B. Dewitt, and D. Leyton-Brown (Scarborough, ON: Prentice Hall, 1995), 160-161. R.J. Sutherland commented, "in the final analysis, the security of the United States is the security of Canada." Sutherland, 203.

93. Pickersgill, *Record, Vol 1,* 203.

94. Grant, *Sovereignty or Security?* 156.

Mass drop for Exercise Cooperation in England, 7 February 1944. (Photographer unknown, NA Negative PA206060.)

Above: LCol G.F. Eadie, CO 1 Cdn Para Bn, Grelingen, Germany, 8 April 1945.
(Lt C.H. Richer, NA, Negative PA169240.)

Opposite top: On 9 August 1948, in response to the VCGS's request for volunteers to serve in the new airborne battalion, the men of the PPCLI respond by saluting and saying "I volunteer to be a jumper, Sir."
(Maj Stirton, NA, Negative PA204973.)

Opposite bottom: R22eR paratroop officers of the Mobile Strike Force.
(Courtesy of the Canadian Airborne Forces Museum.)

Opposite top: Keeping a capability alive—members of the Defence of Canada Force conduct a drop.
(Courtesy of the Canadian Airborne Forces Museum.)

Opposite bottom: Colonel D.H. Rochester, first Regimental Commander, the Canadian Airborne Regiment.
(Courtesy of the Canadian Airborne Forces Museum.)

Above: Paratroopers practice helicopter rappelling during the first Regimental exercise conducted in Canadian Forces Base Chilliwack, 1968.
(Courtesy of M. Barr.)

Opposite top: Major Mike Barr, first CO of 2 Airborne Commando assists his CSM, Master-Warrant Officer B.C. Robinson, during an exercise in Wainwright, Alberta, 1968. Robinson was a veteran of 1 Cdn Para Bn, the SAS Company and the MSF/DCF parachute organizations. (Courtesy of the Canadian Airborne Forces Museum.)

Opposite bottom: General J.V. Allard, the father of the Canadian Airborne Regiment, congratulates Major Barr for the achievement of 200 parachute descents during the Change of Command parade between Colonels D.H. Rochester and R.G. Therriault in the summer of 1969. (Courtesy of M. Barr.)

Above: Paratroopers conducting jungle warfare in Jamaica, March 1972. (Courtesy of H. Pitts.)

Top: General Allard inspects the Regiment during the Trooping of the Colours at Clark Stadium, Edmonton, 9 June 1973.
(Courtesty of H. Pitts.)

Left: Regimental Change of Command, (left to right) Major-General J. Paradis, Colonel Herb Pitts, Colonel G. Lessard, August 1973.
(Courtesty of H. Pitts.)

Top: Trooping of the Colours, 3 Mechanized Commando, June 1975.
(Courtesy of M. Barr.)

Right: Colonel of the Regiment (retired Lieutenant-General) Stan Waters accompanied by the CO, Lieutenant-Colonel Mike Barr, inspects the unit, June 1975.
(Courtesy of M. Barr.)

Top: The officers of 2 Airborne Commando, Montreal Olympics, 1976. Standing (l to r): Rod Mckay, Murray Allen, Don McInnis, unknown, Peter Bradley, Brian Vernon (CO) Dave Varnot, Shawn Tymchuk, and Dennis Tabbernor. Kneeling (l to r) Bruce Wilson, Ed Ring, Don Krause, Jeff Labelle, Ray Elliston, and Peter Kenward.
(Courtesy of P. Bradley.)

Bottom: HRH Prince Charles chats with Regimental officers in Cyprus, 1986, as part of the ceremonies which formally affiliated the Canadian Airborne Regiment with the British Parachute Regiment.

CHAPTER THREE

POLITICAL EXPEDIENCY

Paratroopers as the Guardians of the Canadian North, 1946-1967

It is felt that the whole Mobile Strike Force to fulfill the role given it in the "Emergency Plan for the Defence of Canada" and the "Canada—US Emergency Defence Plan" should be airborne and trained for Arctic operations but as this would require tremendous airlift and, as the Brigade Group has the added commitment of retaining and developing the techniques of conventional warfare, a compromise is necessary.

Army Appreciation, 1949[1]

At the end of the Second World War, the 1st Canadian Parachute Battalion was swiftly disbanded. And so for the moment the argument in regard to the relevance of an airborne capability in Canada had returned to its original position. Namely, there was no threat to Canada so there was no need for specialized paratroops. By late 1945, the debt-conscious Liberal government was fully aware that the war-weary public held little sympathy for continued defence expenditures or large forces. As a result, an Interim Force was established for a two-year period which would allow the Department of Defence time to carefully craft the type of military the government considered sufficient to fulfill the nation's requirements.

Paratroopers were not part of that vision. The cessation of parachute training at Shilo and the spoliation of the only existing airborne battalion was a clear signal. In June 1945 one glimmer of hope lay in the proposed order of battle for the postwar Militia (reserve Army). For planning purposes it included the possibility of a parachute unit being perpetuated in the form of a reserve infantry battalion, although no unit was specifically designated.[2]

Lieutenant-Colonel Fraser Eadie, now in the capacity of a Reserve Force officer, actively pressed for such a commitment. He took his case to Major-General Church Mann, the VCGS, whom he had known during the war in 7 Brigade Headquarters. Eadie pressed Mann for the conversion to airborne status of his present unit, the Winnipeg Light Infantry. The VCGS' response was brutally frank. He stated that there was "no use for airborne" and went so far as to suggest that Eadie "was living in the past."[3]

Such a narrow view was not unique. The postwar army was to be anything but extravagant. First, it was to consist of a representative group of all arms of the service. Second, in the view of the government, its purpose was to provide a small but highly trained and skilled professional force which, in time of war, could expand and train the citizen soldiers who "would fight that war."[4] The Department of Defence explained the role of the postwar army in similar terms. It stated that the duty of the permanently employed Active Force was "to assist in the training and administration of the Reserve Force and to supply the necessary staffs, services and scientific research and development personnel, augmented by a small formation of essential field units. This field formation would be maintained as a trained field force, fully equipped and organized on war establishments, ready to meet whatever commitments might arise."[5] In either case, airborne forces were not in the cards.

The strength of the postwar army was to be its mobilization potential. Brooke Claxton, the newly appointed Minister of National Defence, announced to Parliament in 1946 that the proper role of the military, "at the present time, is as a training force for future staff officers and leaders, and for the reserve force of Canada."[6] This statement was consistent with Claxton's appointed mandate, namely to slash defence spending. Prime Minister King gave clear direction to his new MND. Claxton's task was to ensure "the utmost economy consistent with security should be effected in the Defence Department."[7] Claxton in turn had no illusions regarding his priority. He realized that "the most important question in defence planning after the war was: how much should be spent on defence?"[8] Any confusion was dispelled by King's rhetorical declaration that Canada had to decide whether to spend money for increased military expenditures or to implement the Liberal program for social legislation.[9] The military's lack of priority in the government's agenda soon became apparent. Claxton's official biographer recorded that the minister's "effort to define a realistic role for the military clashed with the prime minister's desire virtually to eliminate defence spending."[10] Claxton's success in reducing military expenditures prompted King to joyously remark in his diary, "Claxton has done wonderful work in compelling the defence forces to cut down different establishments, effecting a savings of something like $100,000,000."[11]

In this austere climate of "minimum peacetime obligations," the future of any airborne capability for Canada seemed dubious at best.[12] The training of new paratroopers at the Canadian Parachute Training Centre in Shilo ceased in May 1945.[13] Even the school's existence was only temporary until the blueprint of the postwar army could be solidified.[14] However, the efforts of individuals such as Major George Flint, the CO of the airborne training centre, were directed at maintaining a degree of airborne expertise. He selectively culled the ranks of the disbanding 1st Canadian Parachute Battalion. He chose the best from the pool of personnel who had decided to remain in the active force as instructors and staff for his training establishment. The parachute school, largely on its own initiative, worked to keep abreast of airborne developments and to perpetuate links with American and British airborne units.[15] Lieutenant Bob Firlotte, one of the hand-picked individuals to serve at the training centre recalled, "no one knew what we were supposed to do and we received absolutely no direction from Army Headquarters."[16]

The perpetuation of links with Canada's closest allies, as well as the importance of staying abreast of the latest tactical developments in modern warfare, specifically air-transportability, provided the breath of life that Flint and others were seeking. An early postwar NDHQ study indicated that British peacetime policy was based on training and equipping all infantry formations to be air-transportable.[17] Furthermore, closer discussions ascertained that both the Americans and the British would welcome an airborne establishment in Canada that would be capable of "filling in the gaps in their knowledge." These "gaps" included the problem of standardization of equipment between Britain and the United States, and the need for experimental research into cold weather conditions. To the Allies, Canada was seen as the ideal intermediary for both.[18]

It was not lost on the Canadian study team that cooperation with its closest defence partners would allow Canada to benefit from an exchange of information on the latest defence developments and doctrine. A test facility was not an airborne unit, but it would allow the Canadian military to stay in the game. During the interim period, NDHQ considered various configurations for an airborne research and development centre and/or parachute training school. In the end, for the sake of efficiency in the employment of manpower and resources, NDHQ decided that both entities should be incorporated into the single Canadian Joint Army/Air Training Centre. As a result, on 15 August 1947, military headquarters authorized the formation of the Joint Air School (JAS), in Rivers, Manitoba.[19]

For the airborne advocates the JAS became the "foot in the door." The military command now entrusted the Joint Air School with the retention of skills required for airborne operations, for both the Army and the RCAF. Its specific mandate included:

a. Research in Airportability of Army personnel and equipment.

b. User Trials of equipment, especially under cold weather conditions.

c. Limited Development and Assessment of Airborne equipment.

d. Training of Paratroop volunteers; training in Airportability of personnel and equipment; training in maintenance of air; advanced training of Glider pilots in exercises with troops; training in some of the uses of light aircraft.[20]

More importantly, the JAS, which was later officially renamed the Canadian Joint Air Training Centre (CJATC), provided the seed from which airborne organizations could grow.[21]

Once the permanent structure of the Army was established in 1947, the impetus for expanding the airborne capability began to stir within the Joint Air School. The growth manifested itself in the form of a proposed Canadian Special Air Service (SAS) Company. This organization was to be an integral sub-unit of the army component of the JAS. Its purpose was defined as filling a need to perform army, inter-service, and public duties such as army/air tactical research and development; demonstrations to assist with army/air training; airborne firefighting; search and rescue; and aid to the civil power.[22] Its development, however, proved to be another case of the surreptitious.

The initial proposal prescribed a clearly defined role. The Army, which sponsored the establishment of the fledgling organization, portrayed the SAS Company's inherent mobility as a definite asset to the public at large for domestic operations. A military appreciation eloquently expressed the benefit of the unique sub-unit in terms of its potential benefit to the public. It explained that the specially trained company would provide an "efficient life and property saving organization capable of moving from its base to any point in Canada in ten to fifteen hours."[23] The official *DND Report for 1948* reinforced this sentiment. Its rationale for the establishment of the SAS Company was the cooperation "with the R.C.A.F. in the air search-rescue duties required by the International Civil Aviation Organization agreement."[24]

The proposed training plan further supported this benevolent image. The training cycle consisted of four phases broken down as follows: tactical research and development (parachute related work and fieldcraft skills); airborne firefighting; air search and rescue; and mobile aid to the civil power (crowd control, first aid, military law).[25] Conspicuously absent was any evidence of the commando or specialist training the organization's name implied. After all, the Canadian SAS Company was actually titled after the British wartime Special Air Service that earned a reputation for daring commando raids behind enemy lines.[26] Yet, the name of the Canadian sub-unit was a total contradiction to its stated role. It was also not in consonance with the four phases of allocated training. Something was clearly amiss. Either the sub-unit was named incorrectly or its operational and training focus was misrepresented.

Several months later the Director of Weapons and Development forwarded the request for the new organization to the Deputy CGS. This submission affixed two additional roles to the SAS Company. One was "public service in the event of a national catastrophe." The other was the "provision of a nucleus for expansion into parachute battalions."[27] Once the CGS authorized the sub-unit, a dramatic change in focus became evident. Not only did its function as a base for expansion take precedence, but also a hitherto unmentioned war fighting role emerged. The new terms of reference for the employment of the SAS Company, in a revised priority, stated:

a. Provide a tactical parachute company for airborne training. This company is to form the nucleus for expansion for the training of the three infantry battalions and parachute battalions.

b. Provide a formed body of troops to participate in tactical exercises and demonstrations for courses at the CJATC and service units throughout the country.

c. Preserve and advance the techniques of SAS [commando] operations developed during WW II 1939-1945.

d. Provide when required parachutists to back-up the RCAF organizations as detailed in the Interim Plan for Air Search and Rescue.

e. Aid Civil Authorities in fighting forest fires and assisting in national catastrophes when authorized by Defence Headquarters.[28]

The change in focus in regard to the terms of reference for the SAS Company was in part pragmatic. It represented the Army's initial reaction to the government's announcement in 1946, that airborne training for the Active Force Brigade Group was contemplated and that an establishment to this end was being created.[29] This issue will be dealt with later. The dramatic mission shift also represented another case of "gamesmanship." It allowed the strong airborne lobby within the CJATC, the majority of whom had wartime airborne experience, an opportunity to perpetuate a capability that they believed was at risk.[30] This was clearly evident in the 1948-1949 historical report for the Joint Air School. The army component of the JAS wrote in regard to the establishment of the SAS Company, "The Special Air Service originated during World War II when after numerous operations military authorities were convinced that a few men working behind enemy lines, could, with sufficient bluff and daring wreak havoc with supplies and communications. Results obtained during the war assured its continued existence."[31] The report was not only incorrect in its assessment of the value placed on special operations units during the war, but more importantly, it clearly reflected a war fighting rather than public service orientation.[32] This was in complete contrast to the rationale used to justify the establishment of the sub-unit. It was, however, in line with the beliefs of those who were selected to serve in the organization.

If there was any confusion in regard to the purpose and role of the SAS Company it certainly did not exist in the mind of the CO. The new organization was established at company strength (125) and comprised one platoon from each of the three regular infantry regiments, the Royal Canadian Regiment (RCR), the Royal 22nd Regiment (R22eR) and Princess Patricia's Canadian Light Infantry (PPCLI). Captain Guy D'Artois, a wartime member of the First Special Service Force, and later the Special Operations Executive (SOE), modelled this new command in accordance with his wartime experience. He trained his sub-unit of carefully selected paratroopers as a specialized commando force.[33] D'Artois's intractable approach and trademark persistence quickly made him the "absolute despair of the Senior Officers at Rivers [CJATC]."[34] Veterans of the SAS Company explained that "Captain D'Artois didn't understand 'no.' He carried on with his training regardless of what others said."[35] Another veteran recalled that "Guy answered to no one, he was his own man, who ran his own show."[36]

Although organizationally the sub-unit was solid, its future was not. Its ultimate function and role were obscured by varied interpretations. Was the SAS Company in fact the nucleus of a larger airborne force? Was it designed to be an elite commando unit? Or was it simply a demonstration team for the Canadian Joint Air Training Centre? Evidence exists to support each perspective.[37] This confusion was merely a symptom of a larger problem, namely there was no clear understanding of or agreement on the role the paratroopers were to fulfill. It was characteristic of the blight that over the years permeated the entire Canadian airborne experience.

As noted the major problem was the lack of a coherent and pervasive role for Canadian airborne forces, which not only justified their existence, but also warranted the full support of the entire military and political leadership. The continued survival of the CJATC and its limited airborne capability, as represented by the SAS Company, was largely due to an American and British preoccupation with airborne and air-transportable forces in the postwar period. This was based on a concept of security established on smaller standing forces with greater tactical and strategic mobility. The cash-strapped Canadian political and military leadership also came to realize that such a force would provide a great political expedient. It provided the shell under which the government could claim it was meeting its obligations, yet minimize its actual defence expenditures.

The 1946 Canada/US Basic Security Plan imposed on Canada the requirement to provide one airborne/air-transportable brigade, and its necessary airlift, as its share of the overall continental defence scheme.[38] This obligation necessitated the retention of the Canadian Joint Air Training Centre. It also prompted the spark which fuelled the need for the Special Air Service Company which would act as a training tool and potential nucleus for an expanded airborne force.[39] As noted earlier, the government had briefed Parliament, as early as 1946, that airborne training for the Active Force Brigade Group was planned. Yet, no action was taken. For more than two years, the SAS Company represented the total sum of Canada's operational airborne capability. Incredibly, for most of that period contentious debate over its actual function and role still dominated.

The explanation for the continuing reluctance to do positive things for the airborne idea lies in the government's actions and not in its words. Defence analyst Colin Gray has stated that the concentration on historical decisions and subsequent policies should be based less on well meaning political speeches and more on actual realities. Gray maintains that if there is real commitment and motive, there must also be concrete actions, such as equipment purchases and military strength.[40] Here lies the answer. The issue faced by the government was how to overcome the problem of defending the vast north in the face of a perceived Soviet threat, at the lowest possible cost, while preserving Canadian sovereignty in light of the growing American concern over the potential northern enemy line of approach. The government's ultimate solution was as operationally effective as it was sincere. And it was not much of either.

The dilemma lay once again in the nation's Arctic region. Any respite from American encroachment in the north that the Canadian politicians had hoped to gain at the cessation of hostilities in 1945 quickly disappeared. Years later, Lester B. Pearson, then the Canadian Secretary of State for External Affairs, captured the essence of the Canadian dilemma:

> Canadians have abandoned the indifference which they once displayed towards their Arctic regions...The advance of the air age has taught them that across their northern frontier, only a few hours away, is a new neighbour, the USS.R. They realize, with something of a shock, that they stand between that neighbour, who has not been a friendly one, and their good neighbour to the south.[41]

The geographical reality which plagued the nation was clearly defined in 1946 in a classified American military appreciation on the problems of joint defence in the Canadian Arctic. It concluded that: "the physical facts of geographical juxtaposition and joint occupation of the North American continent have at all times carried the implication that the defence of Canada and the defence of the United States cannot be artificially divorced. Recent technological developments rendering Canada's Arctic vulnerable to attack and thereby exposing both Canada and the United States to the threat of invasion and aerial assault across the northern most reaches of the continent have greatly heightened the compulsion to regard the defence of the two countries as a single problem."[42]

The Canadian assessment, although similar, was more blunt. Norman Robertson, then the Under-Secretary of State for External Affairs, wrote, "To the Americans the defence of the United States is continental defence, which includes us, and nothing that I can think of will ever drive that idea out of their heads. Should then, the United States go to war with Russia they would look to us to make common cause with them, and, as I judge their public opinion, they would brook no delay."[43] Prime Minister Louis St. Laurent quipped, "Canada could not stay out of a third World War if 11,999,999 of her 12,000,000 citizens wanted to remain neutral."[44]

Once again, Canada was caught in the vortex of American security concerns. The United States perceived the North as an unprotected gateway to invasion that required immediate and costly measures to minimize its vulnerability.[45] Canadian politicians and senior military commanders quickly supported the new emphasis on the defence of the North, but they did so to minimize American encroachment in the Arctic. The motive behind Canadian defence policy largely remained one of countering perceived American penetration in the interest of sovereignty. Security, although a concern, was considered by the military and political leadership as the lesser threat. As a result, the military forces required to meet this need were tailored as such.

Although an element of Soviet menace was recognized, the Canadians consistently questioned their ally's assessments of risk. This difference between American and Canadian threat perception is an important indicator that reinforces the true motive behind the government's focus on the North and the subsequent force structure. By 1946, joint military planning committees warned of a serious threat, within a few years, to the security of Canada and the United States by means of attacks on North America by manned bombers equipped with atomic weapons.[46] The updated *Canada-US Basic Security Plan* (revised ABC-22) noted more accurately that "up to 1950, the Soviets could use subversion and sabotage by internal groups; covert biological and chemical attacks; air attacks against Alaska, Iceland and Greenland and the use of airborne irregular forces ranging throughout the continent."[47] By 1952, military planners projected "the use of the atomic bomb delivered by long range aircraft and the occupation of Newfoundland, Alaska and Greenland for the forward basing of Soviet bomber aircraft and airborne forces."[48] As a result, the Americans maintained a worrisome interest in the Canadian Arctic.

However, it was this American attention in the North, more than the threat posed by a possible Soviet invasion, which concerned Canadian politicians. Their perception of the risk of invasion was completely different. Scholars have shown that Canadian defence analysts were "less alarmist" than their American counterparts about Soviet intentions and the pace of technological advancements.[49] A Canadian intelligence report explained that "the USSR is not considered capable at the present time of endangering, by direct action, the security of Canada and the United States."[50] It tersely stated that the present American outlook depicted an impression of a greater threat to the security of Canada and the United States than actually existed. The Deputy CGS confessed, "I feel there is often a tendency for the Americans to place the worst picture before us in our discussions, with the result that our thinking is often along the lines of 100% protection and does not take into account a more realistic policy of calculated risks."[51] The British Foreign Office concurred. They affirmed that "Russia, so far as we can judge, is neither prepared for nor in the mood for war, and Stalin is a sober realist."[52]

The Canadian intelligence assessment also disagreed with the American assertion that the Soviets had the potential capability to seize objectives in Alaska, Canada, or Labrador, from which they could operate to strike vital strategic targets in North America. The report commented that the Americans "credit a potential enemy with greater capabilities than we consider reasonable.[53] Norman Robertson candidly stated, "I hold that the scales of attack, to which it could reasonably held we were exposed, were, are and will be almost insignificant."[54] Claxton, the Minister of National Defence, echoed those sentiments. He clearly believed that Canada faced no imminent threat. "On the information as is available to the Canadian government," he wrote in November 1946, "it appears most unlikely that the Soviet Union would be in a position to wage another war in the near future, and for this reason it is highly improbable that the Soviet Government would run the risk of deliberately provoking such a war."[55] Claxton postulated that the Soviet Union required a period of fifteen years before it would be physically capable of contemplating war.[56]

The skepticism over the actual threat was also fuelled by an inherent distrust of the military which was shared by many Canadian politicians. The Defence Minister himself felt that "the great danger of planning activities of this kind is that the planners, generally very bright officers of the rank of colonels, majors or captains, live and work without regard for the facts of national life. Unless they are very closely supervised, they are apt to draw up plans that are utterly unrealistic and impossible of fulfilment."[57] By 1947, he and General Foulkes, the CGS, were both concerned that the "planners were getting out of hand."[58]

The political concern for Arctic sovereignty, compounded by the requirement to address the American threat assessments, or more importantly the US concern for their northern flank, necessitated a Canadian response. However, Prime Minister King felt that "any attacks which might develop would be of a diversionary nature which would not warrant the establishment of an elaborate defence scheme employing our resources in a static role."[59] As a result, he directed that "in view of the immense financial outlays involved, it might be more appropriate to adopt measures of more modest proportions."[60]

The government required a politically expedient solution. Salvation was found in the form of airborne forces. Their existence proved conveniently advantageous to the present dilemma. In essence, possession of paratroopers represented the nation's ready sword. They afforded a conceivably viable means to combat any hostile intrusion into the North. Better still, they could be incredibly cheap, if they were maintained simply as a "paper tiger."

This less than sincere approach to the concept of parachute troops fuelled the continuing and invidious debate concerning the role of airborne forces in Canada. This stemmed from a deficiency of coherent vision, which in turn originated from a lack of strategic direction. Ultimately, the dilemma was rooted in the absence of either a commitment to or conviction of the relevance of an airborne capability. Furthermore, the Canadian nation and government wanted to spend its limited resources elsewhere, particularly on social development programs. This in turn was fuelled by government reluctance toward defence spending. The continuing internal debate within the Department of National Defence served only to exacerbate the problem.

The confusion within DND in regard to the concept of an airborne capability was clearly evident. In the autumn of 1947, the Chiefs of Staff submitted a memorandum to the Cabinet Defence Committee which described the Active Force Brigade as a "Mobile Reserve" that could provide an immediate and rapid counter to any enemy lodgement on Canadian territory. The military advisors insisted that this meant the Brigade Group was to be organized as a force "immediately available, fully equipped, and trained for airborne operations."[61] The Cabinet Defence Committee noted the submission but deferred consideration. After all, the proposal implied a substantial investment of resources, particularly costly equipment purchases such as transport aircraft.[62]

Roughly a year later, the Chiefs of Staffs made another pitch to their political masters. However, this time the proposal entailed a slower, more conservative approach. The Active Force Brigade Group was now designated the Mobile Striking Force (MSF). The military explained that the Brigade Group would concentrate initially only for formation training. Furthermore, the Army directed that merely one infantry battalion would be converted into an airborne/air-transported unit at a time. Only after the first infantry battalion had completed its training would the remaining units, in a consecutive manner, undergo conversion to airborne status, until the entire Brigade Group was air-transportable.[63]

The nebulous nature of the operational necessity for airborne forces quickly became apparent in the new plan. Internal DND commentary admitted that the broad uses of the words airborne and air-transported "caused considerable confusion as to our requirement."[64] Another document observed that imprecise terminology created the perception that the "present requirements in airborne and/or air-transported forces is most ambiguous."[65] Once again the relevance of an airborne capability was not rooted in a clear, pervasive role. It became a compromise, a stopgap to meet an immediate requirement. As with most expedient solutions, its life expectancy would be predictably short.

The renewed interest in a viable national airborne capability was not the result of a sudden shift in the government's, or military's, philosophical support for parachute troops. Rather it was inextricably tied to the American concern for Canada's northern regions and the avenue of invasion that they perceived it to represent. As a result, the lethargy in fulfilling the Canadian commitment to the 1946 Basic Security Plan came to an abrupt end. By the summer of 1948, some form of action was required. The creation of the airborne/air-transportable Brigade Group had not advanced beyond the conceptual agreement of the senior military commanders. The plan finally moved forward with the Joint Air Committee decision that:

> The CGS, Canadian Army desires to commence the training of one battalion of infantry for airborne/air-transported operations. This one battalion is the Canadian component to meet the immediate requirements of the BSP. The air training of this battalion (less collective battalion exercise) is required to be completed by 1 April 1949.[66]

The spark was prompted not by governmental or military diligence, but again by the spectre of the Americans. Two years before, the Basic Security Plan had obligated the Canadian Army to be prepared for Arctic airborne and/or air-transportable operations, to counter or reduce enemy lodgements in Canada—on a prescribed schedule of availability. This program compelled the Canadian government, by 1 May 1949, to have a battalion combat team prepared to respond immediately to any actual lodgement, with a second battalion available within two months, and an entire brigade group within four months.[67] Time was running out. Until now, with the possible exception of the Special Air Service Company, nothing had been done.

Two years had elapsed since the government's public declaration that the Active Force Brigade Group would become an airborne/air-transportable organization. Yet, it was not until July 1948 that NDHQ granted authority to commence airborne/air-transportable training. It was another month before these words were finally translated into action. At this time the VCGS, none other than Major-General Mann, visited the PPCLI battalion in Calgary and asked them to convert to airborne status. Training, he stated, was to commence in three months' time and was to be completed by May 1949. The effect was profound. The unit in its entirety volunteered for airborne service.[68] A western, or more precisely PPCLI ("Patricia"), airborne tradition was born. The first concrete step to establish the airborne/air-transportable brigade, as required by the 1946 Basic Security Plan, had finally been taken.

The effect on the existing small SAS Company was immediate and corrosive. Initially the sub-unit lost only its PPCLI platoon which formed the training cadre for the conversion of the Patricia battalion. However, once this task had been completed, Army headquarters directed that the SAS Company's Patricia platoon be permanently stripped from the sub-unit so that it could return to Calgary with its parent regiment, to provide a core of experienced paratroop instructors.[69] Although a replacement platoon, recruited from the service support trades, was raised, the fate of the SAS Company was sealed.[70] Its personnel were increasingly drafted as instructional staff for the Canadian Joint Air Training Centre training scheme to convert the remaining two infantry battalions into airborne/air-transportable units. By the time the program was terminated, the SAS Company had virtually ceased to exist. Its personnel melted away and rejoined their parent regiments.[71]

The SAS Company served as a bridge linking the 1st Canadian Parachute Battalion and the three infantry battalions which conceptually formed an airborne brigade.[72] It perpetuated the airborne spirit and kept the requisite parachute skills alive. However, its existence suffered from a lack of clarity and commitment. Its 'successor' would be similarly handicapped. The actual implementation of the airborne and air-transportable brigade group, as we have seen, was slow in coming and would never achieve the scale originally envisioned.[73]

And so airborne forces remained orphans. They were never fully accepted by the Army because their relevance was never convincingly established. In Ottawa, NDHQ and the military establishment at large believed that paratroopers were too resource-intensive, particularly since their exact role was unclear.

If the Mobile Striking Forces's gestation was at best tenuous, its existence was nothing short of ethereal. From its inception, the MSF was intended to be the "smallest self-contained force" capable of meeting peacetime requirements.[74] The original design concept supported the idea of airborne battalions, or at a minimum a single paratroop unit. The staff assessment argued that "the role of the force [counterattacking enemy lodgements in Canada] would indicate that there is justification for the organization of one airborne battalion."[75] It further stated that the airborne element should be in a homogeneous group which was best achieved by "the formation of one para-battalion—organized, equipped and trained in this role."[76]

The prevailing confusion and debate in regard to the airborne role and concept resulted in the scaling down of the entire airborne idea. By late 1948, Army Headquarters had decided that the respective airborne units would be established in accordance with an organization identical to a normal infantry battalion, with the exception that one rifle company be designated as a parachute company. Despite the observation that it was considered unsound in principle and practice for the airborne element of the force to be split among two or three battalions, the decision was taken to give each battalion its own component of paratroops.[77] Contrary to the accepted conventional wisdom, the MSF was never established, nor intended, to consist of entire parachute battalions.[78] The misconception, which originated with the designation of the PPCLI for conversion to airborne/air-transportable status, was addressed immediately with apparently little success. The Director of Infantry issued a clarifying memorandum in September 1948, which stated:

> The impression is prevalent in some quarters that the PPCLI has been converted into a Parachute Battalion. This is not correct...The organization of the battalion has been changed in that one rifle company has been designated for the airborne role, i.e. parachute troops, and the remainder of the battalion as air-transported troops.[79]

Despite the confusion over the concept of an airborne battalion, staff planners quickly established a training schedule to realize the goal of the airborne/air-transportable brigade. This meant that other regiments would be involved. Soon Army Headquarters designated the RCR to commence their conversion upon completion of the Patricia training cycle. In turn, the R22eR were to follow the RCR. The DCGS anticipated that the long term objective of forming the nucleus of the Active Force Brigade, around three infantry battalions, trained in airborne/air-transported operations, would be realized by April 1951.[80] Not surprisingly, this too failed to comply with the 1946 Basic Security Plan requirements. While the staff officers buried in the labyrinth of NDHQ may have sincerely believed in their task, their conviction, however, was not matched by that of their military or political masters. Once again it was a question of political priority. Political reality valued economic frugality, particularly in the sphere of defence. It also utterly dismissed the idea of a potential threat to the Canadian homeland.

The question of risk was also fundamental. Despite the impenetrable mistrust which overshadowed relations between the West and the Soviet-dominated sphere, the impression of a direct peril to Canada had not changed from the Second World War or the immediate postwar era. Canadian politicians refused to embrace the beliefs of their southern neighbour. They were not convinced that the Canadian North was "ground zero" for a possible invasion of North America. As a result, the government remained loathe to invest money in the defence of the northern flank from a danger which they thought was largely due to the active imagination and paranoia of their chief ally.

The lack of concern for a threat to the North was not a function of blind ignorance. The politicians maintained the belief that there was no danger to the physical security of Canada, even at a time when the bogey of communism reached its zenith in the early fifties. They recognized an international threat, but not one to Canada itself. Gordon Graydon, the

Parliamentary Advisor to the Canadian delegation to the UN, speaking on the subject of Soviet intentions warned of the "defiant and undisguised steps toward world domination."[81] In addition Prime Minister St. Laurent and Lester B. Pearson both went on record as stating "the international situation was never more serious."[82] Other parliamentarians were representative of the prevailing climate, viewing communism as "a diabolical dynamic thing...aiming at the destruction of all the freedoms and the inherent hard-won rights of man" and describing it as "the darkest and direst shadow that has ever fallen upon this earth."[83] But, to their minds the threat would come from somewhere outside Canada.

Indeed it all seemed so true when the North Koreans crossed the 38th Parallel into South Korea in the early summer of 1950. The government viewed the international environment as so volatile that it authorized the expansion of its armed forces and dramatically increased its defence expenditures. But this was done not only to facilitate the dispatch of an expeditionary force to fight the evils of communism in Korea, but also to raise a special brigade for service in Europe where some thought the real communist blow would fall.[84] Both these steps dramatically lowered the importance of the Mobile Striking Force.

Despite the abovementioned actions to combat the growing international menace, the perceived danger to the Canadian Arctic was still seen as minimal. Claxton declared, "the danger of direct attack upon Canadian territory was extremely remote...any attack on North America would be diversionary, designed to panic the people of this continent into putting a disproportionate amount of effort into passive local defence."[85]

This confidence was based on an assessment of practicality, probability and risk. Claxton explained the factors that were important in determining Canada's defensive posture. He insisted that consideration had to be given to: "the geographical position of Canada; the capacity of any possible aggressor to make an attack; the disposition of friendly nations; and what may be called the international climate."[86] Based on these criteria, the threat to the Canadian North was quickly discounted. The government asserted, "We have to discard from any realistic thinking any possibility of an attack by ground forces on the area of Canada either by air or by sea. Anyone who has any knowledge of the terrain of the outlying parts of this country will realize that such an attempt would be worthless and useless and is not likely to be part of any aggressive plans which may be launched against Canada."[87] Furthermore, the Liberal government emphasized that invading the North "would in no way destroy our war-making potential nor would it have any decisive effect on winning a war on this continent by invasion...you have only to look at this vast continent to see how formidable such a task is."[88] R.J. Sutherland, one of the country's pre-eminent defence analysts, soon reached the same conclusion:

> There is nothing of any particular strategic value in the Canadian Arctic. The two great bastions of polar defence are Alaska and Northern Greenland. The Canadian Arctic is a sort of strategic desert lying behind these two strong points.[89]

The military assessment was similar. Army appreciations recognized the chance of enemy airborne attacks as extremely slight because of the difficulties of re-supply and re-embarkation of the attacking force.[90] In 1951, the official NDHQ assessment regarding the direct defence of Canada contained in the military's strategic operations plan, *Defence Scheme No. 3: Major War*, concluded that as a result of the extremely limited base facilities in eastern Siberia, the Soviets were not capable of more than isolated airborne operations, none totalling more than a few hundred men. Furthermore, it explained that the lack of a fighter escort would make sustained operations impossible. Even the use of the North for transitory aircraft operations was discounted. The Defence Cabinet Committee rationalized that "if the Soviets attempted to use a

Canadian Arctic station as a bomber base, warning would be received and it was expected that such a base, which would have immense supply problems, could be immobilized rapidly."[91]

More importantly, the official defence plan identified only western Alaska and the Aleutian Islands as targets of potential enemy airborne forces.[92] Joint Intelligence Committee assessments from the early 1950s clearly remarked that the data available "implies that the Soviet Union cannot land any airborne forces on Canadian territory."[93] Nevertheless, prudence necessitated caution. Moreover, it was instrumental that the government demonstrate that a contingency plan to protect the Canadian North was in place. As a result, the MSF threat scenario it was required to respond to was defined as limited to the landing of small parties of approximately thirty to a maximum of one hundred personnel, "by air or submarine, in the hinterland areas of Canada, with the intention of establishing a refuelling airstrip, a weather or electronic station or just to cause alarm and despondency."[94] Government statements, however, failed to harmonize with how important Canadian decision makers saw the issue.

To understand the apparent dissociation between word and intention one must take a brief step back in time. By the late forties Prime Minister King readily embraced, and actively encouraged, the view that the North in itself did not represent a grave security risk. He endorsed the then governor general's observation that stations in the Arctic "may become bases from which the enemy himself may operate were they not there."[95] He subsequently formulated the strategy that "our best defence in the Arctic is the Arctic itself."[96] Claxton reiterated this belief. He proclaimed, "In working out the doctrine of defence of our north, the fewer airfields we have the fewer airfields we have to defend against the possibility of the enemy using them as stepping stones from which to leapfrog toward our settled areas. Indeed, were it possible the greatest single defence throughout our northland would be the rough nature of the ground and the extent of the territory itself."[97] McNaughton agreed with the concept that "ice is something of a defence in itself," and Pearson from the Department of External Affairs quickly dubbed the government's position the "scorched ice policy."[98]

However, the American apprehension regarding its northern flank remained an issue that could not be downplayed convincingly. In 1947, the MND reiterated that Canada's role in joint defence should be focussed specifically on the defence of the nation and on doing the things the country could and should do "in preference to the United States, particularly in the North."[99] This sentiment was consistent with the government's active "re-Canadianization" program which, since the end of the war was aimed at "keeping the Canadian Arctic Canadian."[100] Government reports highlighted the necessity of ensuring effective protection of Canadian sovereignty against American penetration. One note from the Privy Council Office (PCO) remarked, "our experiences since 1943 have indicated the extreme care which we must exercise to preserve Canadian sovereignty in remote areas where Canadians are outnumbered and outranked....Of much greater concern is the sort of de facto US sovereignty which caused so much trouble in the last war and which might be exercised again."[101]

Canadian concern for the North was aptly described in an editorial in *The Canadian Forum*, "We must be certain that we defend it [Canada] as much from our 'friends' as from our 'enemies'."[102] Norman Robertson, the Under-Secretary of State for External Affairs, explained, "what we have to fear is more a lack of confidence in United States as to our security, rather than enemy action....If we do enough to assure the United States we shall have done a good deal more than a cold assessment of the risk would indicate to be necessary."[103]

Supposedly, the Mobile Striking Force was to provide the assurance for the Americans. The MSF paratroopers were the guardians of the northern gateway. The MSF's existence, however, was also wedded to Claxton's directive that "everything possible must be done to ensure that we obtain the utmost value for the defence dollar."[104] The Minister of Defence did not believe in the Soviet threat to Canada. As a result, he felt little devotion to the MSF. Claxton held a firmly entrenched conviction that a "direct attack upon Canadian territory was extremely remote and there was no need to maintain the MSF as a powerful fighting unit."[105]

The lack of commitment to the MSF became readily apparent elsewhere. The Active Force Brigade Group suffered from neglect even before it was fully established. As early as 1948, the training of the three infantry battalions was fraught with shortages of instructors, equipment and aircraft. One report bluntly stated that "the training and preparation for war of the Mobile Striking Force is not proceeding as quickly and as efficiently as is desirable at this time."[106] Further turmoil was experienced from internal dissent at high levels within DND. Obviously frustrated and perturbed over his loss of control over the infantry battalions which were converting to the new MSF role, the Director of Infantry wrote, "I consider that air, whether for parachutists or air transported troops, is only a means of delivering the infantry where it is required. Therefore, once personnel have been trained in that 'new' kind of transportation, I feel that they should come down to earth and train as infantry." He further charged that the "PPCLI were NOT trained to conventional operational standards when they started air training and the same situation will apply to RCR and R22eR in varying degrees depending on how much interference these units will have with their training prior to becoming airborne."[107] Such dissent only made the situation for the airborne concept more confused and fragile.

The credibility of the embryonic airborne/air-transportable brigade group also suffered another severe blow even before it was fully established. In 1949, the final phase of training for the newly converted PPCLI battalion was an exercise to test the unit in its new role as an airborne/air-transported infantry battalion. The scenario for Exercise Eagle painted a picture of a lightly armed force of Russians landing and capturing the airfield at Fort St. John and the Peace River Bridge, in British Columbia. The task to conduct a rapid counterattack and destroy the enemy penetration was assigned to the PPCLI. The plan required D Company, the airborne company group, to seize the airstrip by parachute assault. With the bridgehead secured, the remainder of the battalion was to air land and conduct follow-on operations.[108]

But the exercise misfired badly and destroyed any credibility the fledgling Mobile Striking Force had hoped to attain. The Patricias were short of transport aircraft and were so wanting in equipment that they were forced to borrow jump jackets and parachutes from the Canadian Joint Air Training Centre, at Rivers.[109] Further difficulties were encountered when the lead aircraft missed the Drop Zone (DZ) during the parachute assault. The final nail in the coffin was the fact that the "enemy" dominated the airspace throughout the entirety of the exercise. Senior newspaper reporter Ross Munro of the *Calgary Herald* was present, and what he saw did not impress him. He let his readers know that "the Joint Army—R.C.A.F. Exercise Eagle has shown that these defence arms, in their present stage could not deal rapidly and effectively with even comparatively small landings by enemy airborne troops and fighter aircraft along the Alaska Highway and on these Northland aerodromes."[110] Even the PPCLI itself agreed with Munro's brutal assessment. Regimental reports pointed out that their troops had insufficient training or experience in airborne operations. They admitted that the unit in a real situation "would have had much difficulty had there been the slightest opposition."[111]

Immediately upon the completion of the exercise, the media and parliamentary opposition savaged the government, particularly the Minister of Defence, for the lack of military preparedness. Brooke Claxton, a man who was described as extremely sensitive to criticism of any kind, was subsequently given a "roasting that he never forgot."[112]

As a direct result of the furor which the exercise raised, the CGS appointed Brigadier George Kitching as the Commander Designate of the MSF. The CGS gave Kitching the responsibility for planning operations for the parachute battalions and for mapping out in detail the defence of the Arctic. The importance assigned to the new position was such that the CGS told Kitching he would be given special priority and all the resources he required.[113] Now optimists felt that, with the reputation of the MND at stake, support for the MSF seemed assured.

The test came six months later. In February 1950, another exercise was conducted to redeem Claxton's reputation and that of the progeny Mobile Striking Force. Military communiqués described Exercise Sweetbriar as a joint Canadian-American training operation along the Alaska Highway. It involved 5,000 military personnel from Canada alone. Its officially stated aim was to develop "procedures, doctrine, and techniques for the employment of combined Canadian and US Armies and Air Forces operating in the Arctic."[114] Unofficially, the MND planned to use it to compensate for the "debacle of Eagle."[115] He personally briefed Kitching that he wanted good press and he did not care how the brigadier got it.[116]

The exercise scenario was similar to that of Eagle less than a year earlier. It was based on the premise that an enemy force had captured the airfield at Northway, Alaska and was conducting an advance down the Alaska Highway to Whitehorse. The allied forces, including the elements of the Mobile Striking Force, were tasked with destroying the enemy penetration and recapturing the aerodrome. The outcome of the endeavour was officially touted as an outstanding success. It was also the last major exercise conducted by the Active Force in the MSF role.[117]

As for the defence minister, the success of Sweetbriar restored his reputation. But he did not seem too anxious to do anything more with the airborne force. Claxton had demonstrated the government's ability to respond to a hostile incursion on Canadian soil through a successful operation. But having achieved the intended aim, he and others in government quickly lost their enthusiasm for the MSF airborne/air-transported brigade group. Ministerial, even Cabinet, belief in its necessity was simply nonexistent; nor in their minds was there the will to finance an organization of questionable utility. Continuing internal debate within DND exacerbated the problem. By the early fifties the outbreak of the Korean hostilities as well as the looming communist threat in Europe gave the Army a new focus. The peacetime Canadian Armed Forces were no longer obliged to find a legitimate excuse for their existence. International tensions and growing public fear provided support for large standing peacetime forces, even in Canada.[118] The MSF now became a burden. Consequently, it was downplayed even before it was fully established.

Undeniably, overseas commitments provided impetus for growth in the military but these augmentations ultimately changed its focus, and it was not for the better for airborne advocates. During the 1950-1951 period, the three Active Force infantry regiments expanded to provide forces not only for duty in Korea but also to man the brigade group being established for NATO in Europe.[119] Although a parachute force was maintained in Canada for territorial defence, it was a far cry from that originally envisioned in the MSF concept.

The initial plan had called for the force to be centrally located with operational command retained by Army Headquarters.[120] Instead, after 1950, the individually assigned units remained scattered across the country. Command of the widespread elements was placed under control of their respective geographic Army Commands. Furthermore the new focus, compounded by the dismissal of any substantial threat to Canadian territory, resulted in another reorganization of the airborne component of the Mobile Striking Force all of which reflected doubt and decreasing support. An army appreciation explained:

> "It is felt that the whole MSF to fulfill the role given it in the 'Emergency Plan for the Defence of Canada' and the 'Canada–US Emergency Defence Plan' should be airborne and trained for Arctic operations but as this would require tremendous airlift and, as the Brigade Group has the added commitment of retaining and developing the techniques of conventional warfare, a compromise is necessary. The prime need is for a force to carry out air-ground reconnaissance and small scale offensive operations."[121]

Accordingly Army Headquarters determined that one airborne company in each battalion together with the necessary support troops would be sufficient.

In the same vein, another staff assessment at NDHQ made it clear that there was at best more confusion and waning support for the MSF. This time the justification for minimizing the airborne component was not credited to resource constraints. Rather, it was now determined that the requirement for offensive action would not likely exceed one infantry battalion group and "in practise it will more probably be a company group or platoon group."[122] Major-General C. Vokes, General Officer Commanding (GOC) Western Command, went so far as to suggest that "a platoon or squad of fifteen men well-trained for northern operations would be a compact, hard-hitting group with greater mobility than one of normal strength."[123] The RCAF added their own ideas and challenged the basic MSF concept by declaring that in many cases "air action alone might be sufficient to reduce an enemy lodgement."[124] The widespread reassessment of the relevance of the MSF had its effect. Hence, the MSF would operate as three independent airborne/air-transported infantry battalion groups, each responsible for ground action against enemy lodgements in a specific sector of Canada's northern approaches.[125]

The MSF was on a slippery slope. Its marginalization as a viable force continued with ever accelerating speed. In 1950, an Army policy statement reported that the training role of the Active Force infantry battalions "now" took on a dual function. Significantly, the two functions turned out to be mutually competitive. The policy claimed that the "primary role of the parachute battalion will be to prepare to operate in an airborne/air-transportable role in Arctic and sub-Arctic; and its secondary training role will be that of keeping alive the techniques of operating in the normal infantry ground role in temperate climates."[126] In reality, the priorities were reversed. General Foulkes asserted, "by 1950 Canadian defence policy was wholly concerned with NATO and with the U.N."[127] The reversal of actual priorities to those at NDHQ was evident. The Director of Military Operations and Plans wryly commented:

> At present the MSF trains in conventional operations, superimposed upon which is airborne and Northern training. This leads to a lack of economy in both numbers and training and adds to the length of time required. It further imposes on the man a variety of roles which may tend to reduce his effectiveness.[128]

It became apparent that the supposedly primary function of the MSF was being shoved into a declining secondary role or worse. The Acting VCGS announced that the MSF plan for the reduction of enemy lodgements in Northern Canada did not mean that "the aircraft or troops should be kept at the ready, but that these forces would be concentrated and made available if and when occasion required."[129] He evidently was not familiar with the obligations under the joint Canadian/US Basic Security Plan which required Canada to have the aircraft and troops available to respond immediately to any hostile incursion on Canadian territory.[130]

As noted strategic analyst Colin Gray has observed, the real confirmation of commitment is only evident in concrete action, not words. The acid test of reality indicated that the Mobile Striking Force was not taken seriously by NDHQ or the government. The airborne/air-transported infantry battalions were consistently hamstrung with resource limitations. Equipment deficiencies, particularly aircraft, and manpower shortages crippled the MSF units. In April 1950, the severity of the problem prompted the PPCLI to protest to the GOC Western Command. The unit's concerns were clearly identified. The regiment's commanding officer wrote:

> The Regiment is entirely dependent upon a few personnel who were trained at the CJATC as Parachute Instructors and Parachute and Safety Equipment workers. These numbers are gradually diminishing. At present trained personnel have to be borrowed from all companies for such duties and all other training and activities are affected.[131]

But little changed. The PPCLI complaint was not a profound revelation. By 1952, an assessment by the Directorate of Military Operations and Plans reiterated that the "Mobile Strike Force battalions have the dual role of training overseas replacements and preparing for their MSF role. Units are generally short of instructors and overburdened with recruits; they are thus under considerable strain and their operational capabilities leave much to be desired."[132] Another official report candidly observed that the Army, for all intents and purposes, had disregarded the special arctic/airborne nature of the MSF and consistently denuded it of resources. It conceded that the heavy drain on the force to supply trained officers and NCOs to 25 Canadian Infantry Brigade Group in Korea had stripped the units of key personnel and reduced their operational efficiency an estimated fifty percent.[133]

The erosion of the MSF's airborne/air-transported capability became so severe that in April 1953, the Director Military Operations and Plans outlined the problem yet again in an official letter to the brigadier responsible for the planning cell of the General Staff (GS). He explained that the operational efficiency of the MSF battalions had decreased since 1950 because of the "posting of a considerable number of Arctic and parachute trained personnel to units of 25 Brigade; the use of the first battalions (MSF battalions) to train personnel of the second battalions to the detriment of their own training; and the channelling of infantry recruits to units of 25 Brigade rather than to MSF battalions."[134] He further warned that "it is noted with alarm that the operational efficiency of the MSF has been so reduced and continues to be threatened by the present expansion of the Army."[135]

The Director of Infantry concurred. He confessed that because of the existing rotation plan battalions spent a comparatively short time in the MSF role. He further elaborated that "during this period of service units are required to become proficient in parachute and airborne operations and operations in the Arctic both summer and winter."[136] In addition, he explained, MSF battalions are responsible for the training of two to four hundred reinforcements for Korea. The Director of Infantry concluded that these conflicting priorities placed an extremely heavy load on the MSF.[137] The multiplicity and duality of tasks, without a proper priority would become a chronic problem for Canada's airborne forces, if not for the Army as a whole in later years. This issue will be dealt with in later chapters.

The director's concerns, however, were irrelevant. The existence of a strong and viable Mobile Striking Force was never a priority for the military or political leadership. Their actions, or more precisely inaction, sent a clear message in regard to the MSF's precedence. Critics of the government's defence policy quickly seized the opportunity to attack. In April 1953 for instance, the Conservative opposition in Parliament declared that the "airborne brigade serves only to lull the people of Canada into a false sense of security."[138] They noted that "the airborne striking force has already been broken up and its personnel distributed not only among the forces raised for Korea but also the forces sent with the 27th brigade, with the result that today we have no striking force of units which have been accustomed to work together and which have carried out any extensive training under arctic conditions."[139] Finally, they accurately charged that the MSF "has not trained; it has not carried out many exercises, if any, at unit level or any operations which it would be called upon to do in the future."[140]

The opposition protests did little to sway the political or military leadership. The Liberal government juggernaut was very hard to overcome for the well-outnumbered opposition. Not surprisingly, public and external criticism was not very effective. In short, an increase in support was implausible. There was no belief in the MSF's actual relevance to a NATO-centred military establishment.

To add fuel to the fire, a 1954 sub-unit level exercise highlighted the MSF's continuing shortcomings, providing further ammunition for its detractors. Exercise Bulldog II, conducted in Baker Lake, Northwest Territories, was designed to practice the RCR parachute component in a defence of Canada role. Area Headquarters tasked the RCR paratroopers with recapturing the local radio station and destroying the hypothetical enemy lodgement. Unfortunately, equipment problems and poor weather held the rescue force at bay. The exercise was called off before the RCR soldiers were able to conduct their assault.[141] Again the effectiveness of the airborne idea was questioned.

The experience was another severe blow for the MSF. In Ottawa, as well as in the Army at large, knives were quickly drawn. Other military interests, themselves short of resources or perceived support, wanted to carve up the corpse. Their autopsy of Bulldog II revealed a major problem with the MSF concept. One report commented that the exercise "indicated that paratroops cannot be relied on as an effective striking force in arctic regions and that many problems of mechanical maintenance have yet to be solved."[142] Another was more blunt. It asserted that "many officers feel that the day of the paratrooper and the glider-borne soldier are finished...and it is felt that some new means of carrying this soldier to the attack area must be evolved."[143] Similar to Munro's reporting on Exercise Eagle years earlier, the media attacked the prevailing fiction of northern defence. One reporter commented, "For years now, Canadians have been lulled into a false sense of security and have been completely misled on the capabilities of Canada's defence forces to defend this country against aggression from the north."[144] The issue of resource constraints and multiple taskings, however, were not addressed. The intent was not to find a cure for the MSF's problems, but rather to justify its destruction.

The myriad of negative reports and press presented a false dilemma. The Mobile Striking Force fulfilled exactly the role politicians and many soldiers had intended it to fill. A 1955 DND publication entitled *The Defence of Canada (Notes on CF for NATO Troop Information Lecturers)* clearly documented that the most probable threat to North America was by air, specifically by manned bombers with atomic weapons. This tract cursorily dismissed the role of airborne troops with a single vague line: "the army maintains a mobile striking force for defence against airborne attack." In total the role of the army in the defence of Canada merited but a single paragraph of the thirty-two page document.[145] In the end, by the mid 1950s the hapless MSF provided a financially inexpensive means of mollifying the Americans and calming the public in regard to the "vulnerable" North. The political and military leadership never postulated a serious threat to Canadian territory. Similarly, they never accepted the need for a strong or viable airborne capability. It simply provided an expedient with which other goals could be achieved.

As a result, resources were never fully committed to such a force. Internal debate and dissent were never reconciled. Most telling, the Mobile Striking Force was never allowed to exist as a viable organization. Instead, it was used to nourish and nurture the Army's true concern, its conventional forces in NATO and the UN.

Notes for Chapter Three

1. "Appreciation on the Employment of the Active Force Brigade Group in Defence of Canada," 7 November 1949. DHist, File 112.3M2 (D400).
2. Memoranda entitled "Alliance—Canadian Parachute Battalion," 18 & 19 June 1945. NAC, RG 24, Vol 2258, File HQ-54-27-128-16.
3. Interview with Fraser Eadie, 23 June 1998. The Reserve concept, with the assistance of Eadie's protestations, showed some resilience. In April of 1946 the issue was still alive. It was noted in NDHQ that "The Winnipeg Light Infantry, one of two infantry battalions surplus to our six Divisional requirements, is earmarked as Para, but it is not being so designated, and whether or not it will in fact be able to train as such, is a matter of some conjecture. This, of course will not be known for some time." "Alliance—Canadian Parachute Battalion," 26 April 1946. NAC, RG 24, Vol 2258, File HQ-54-27-128-16.
4. *Debates*, 19 August 1946, 5059.
5. Canada, *DND Report 1946* (Ottawa: DND, 1946), 27.
6. *Debates,* 9 July 1947, 5327. Claxton became MND on 12 December 1946. Canada, *Canada's Defence* (Ottawa: DND, 1947), 17. See also R.J. Sutherland, *Report of the Ad Hoc Committee on Defence Policy,* 30 September 1963, 21.
7. Pickersgill, *Record* Vol 3, 394.
8. David Bercuson, *True Patriot: The Life of Brooke Claxton* (Toronto: University of Toronto Press, 1993), 164. See also *Debates,* 13 February 1947, 394 and 9 July 1947, 5327. The financial reality was noted by Burns as early as 1936, when he wrote, "We cannot do much defence planning, in Canada or elsewhere, before we are faced with the question 'Where is the money coming from?" Burns, "The Defence of Canada," 382. This reality remained with the military. A DCGS memorandum on "Postwar Army Planning," dated 27 January 1944, stated, "Plans for the postwar Army in Canada are now under consideration at NDHQ. There are many factors to be taken into account, a number of which will be dependent on the attitude of the government at the time." NAC, Ralston Papers, MG 27, III B11, Vol 81.
9. Bercuson, *True Patriot,* 164. King, known for his hostility towards the military felt strongly that the Liberal caucus was the place to test feeling on issues of military importance. He stated, "That was the place to get the views. Not as sent in by persons interested in army to the Minister of War." Pickersgill, *Record, Vol 4,* 10. C.P Stacey stated, "King himself was one of the most unmilitary products of an unmilitary society. Hating war, he also hated the military services." C.P. Stacey, *Mackenzie King and the Atlantic Triangle* (Toronto: Macmillan, 1976), 29. See also J.L. Granatstein, *Canada's War: The Politics of the Mackenzie King Government 1939-1945,* 26; C.P. Stacey, *Arms Men & Governments: The War Politicians of Canada 1939-1945,* 71; C.P. Stacey, *Canada and the Age of Conflict Vol 2: 1921-1948,* 17 & 396; Stephen Harris, *Canadian Brass: The Making of a Professional Army, 1860-1939,* 161 & 165-167; James Eayrs, *In Defence of Canada: From the Great War to the Depression* (Toronto: University of Toronto Press, 1966), 168; and Pickersgill, *Record,* Vol 1, 259-60.
10. Bercuson, *True Patriot,* 166. The author also noted that "despite Claxton's hope that budget cuts would flow from policy, policy was going to flow from the budget cuts." He clearly asserted that the Department of Finance helped shape Canadian defence policy during this period. Ibid., 167 & 170. C.P. Stacey recorded that King told his Cabinet on 3 January 1947, "What we needed now was to get back to the old Liberal principles of economy, reduction of taxation, anti-militarism, etc." Stacey, *Canada and the Age of Conflict Vol 2,* 397.
11. Pickersgill, *Record,* Vol 4, 9.
12. See *Debates,* 13 February 1947, 394.

13. Clarke, 24. See also Chapter 1, endnote 97.
14. As a member of the training centre staff, Bob Firlotte recalled that they were told that the parachute capability would remain during the Interim Army for two years until a decision was made on the requirement for the Regular Army. Interview with author 20 November 1998.
15. Interviews with Ken Arril and Bob Firlotte, 25 August and 20 November 1998 respectively; and Harris, 74.
16. Interview with author, 20 November 1998.
17. To avoid confusion, the designations of the period are as follows: *Airborne* is used "for those troops, units and their equipment which form part of airborne formations and for which specific airborne war establishments exist. They are composed, equipped, and trained primarily for the purpose of operating by air and of making assault landings. They include parachute and air landing troops. *Air-transportable* designates units other than those of airborne formations which can be transported by air and employed in a tactical role. They may be part of a light division already specially equipped for movement by air in transport aircraft or they may be part of any other formation whose equipment has been exchanged or modified as necessary for a particular operation and for an approach by air instead of by land or sea." Canada, Army, Directorate of Military Training, *Military Science Part I and II,* 1948/49, 97.
18. See DHist, File 168.009 (D45), specifically "The Organization of an Army Air Centre In Canada," 29 November 1945 & 27 December 1945; A-35 (No.1 ARDC), 7 December 1945; and "Notes of a Conference—NDHQ," 8 February 1946, HQC 88-5(DSD (w)). Arril, the Officer Commanding the Technical Tactical Investigation Section (TTIS) in 1945-1946, stated that he was primarily focussed on making contacts and keeping abreast of the latest airborne developments. Interview with author, 25 August 1998.
19. See DHist, File 168.009 (D45) for a series of memoranda and proposals on the "A-35 Canadian Parachute Training Centre and the No. 1 Airborne Research and Development Centre." See also "Reactivation A-35 Canadian Parachute Training Centre," 28 December 1945. DHist, File 163.009 (D16).
20. "The Organization of an Army Air Centre In Canada," 29 November & 27 December 1945. DHist, File 168.009 (D45). It was also noted that an organization would be required at NDHQ whose responsibility included the "complete direction of Airborne activity such as coordination of policy, liaison, air intelligence, personnel, equipment, training, war organization and particularly long-term planning to ensure rapid expansion in case of necessity." See also *DND Report 1949,* 13; and CAFM Research Papers on Canadian Airborne Organizations, Part 1, 1.C, Document 2—"Canadian Air Service," by Berkley Franklin.
21. The organization, as well as its name, was actually in perpetual evolution. Although the title Joint Air School was officially in effect until 1 April 1949, many in NDHQ and the JAS itself utilized the term CJATC prior to this date. See endnote 28 this chapter. Nevertheless, in accordance with Joint Organizational Order No. 6, dated 5 March 1949, the title Canadian Joint Air Training Centre was to take effect 1 April 1949, upon reorganization and relocation to Shilo, Manitoba. *War Diary— JAS/CJATC,* 5 March and 1 April 1949 respectively.
22. "SAS Company—JAS (Army)," 13 June 1947. NAC, RG 24, Reel C-8255, File HQS 88-60-2; and CAFM research information sheet entitled "The Canadian Special Air Service Company."
23. "SAS Company," 30 October 1947, 4. The proposed SAS Coy was specifically included in the Interim Plan for SAR. "Requested Amendment to Interim Plan—SAR," 11 September 1947. NAC, RG 24, Reel C-8255, File HQS 88-60-2. In the SAS Coy's short existence, its only two operational tasks were in fact aid to the civil power. The first was Operation Canon in October 1947. A four-man team from the embryonic Canadian SAS Company dropped into Moffet Inlet, Baffin Island, to assist an Anglican missionary who had been seriously injured by a firearms accident. The second was in May 1948, when the entire sub-unit participated in Operation Overflow, the DND relief effort in response to massive flooding in British Columbia. "OP CANON," CAFM, File AB- Research SAS History; J.M. Hitsman, "Parachuting in the Canadian Army," 5 March 1956, 4. DHist, File 145.4 (D2) and 112.3H1.003 (D5). See also B.A.J. Franklins, *The Airborne Bridge. The Canadian Special Air Service Company* (Private Commemorative Publication, 1988), 50.

24. *DND Report, 1948*, 25.
25. "SAS Company—JAS (Army)," 13 June 1947, Appendix A. NAC, RG 24, Reel C-8255, File HQS 88-60-2.
26. See Tony Geraghty, *Inside the SAS* (Toronto: Methuen, 1980); Anthony Kemp, *The SAS at War*; and Philip Warner, *The Special Air Service*. Contemporary accounts of the Canadian SAS often state erroneously that the organization was originally established to provide Canada with such a capability.
27. "Special Air Service Company—Implementation Policy," 12 September 1947. NAC, RG 24, Reel C-8255, File HQS 88-60-2.
28. "SAS Terms of Reference," 16 April 1948; "Duties of the SAS Coy," 29 January 1948; "SAS Coy—Air Training Directive," December 1948. NAC, RG 24, Reel C-8255, File HQS 88-60-2. The establishment of the SAS Company was effective 9 January 1948. See also "Aviation Teamwork in Canada," *Military Review*, Vol 28, No. 5, August 1948, 96-97.
29. *Debates*, 19 August 1946, 5056. The government's sincerity is questionable. When grilled by the opposition on how this airborne force would be transported, the reply stated, "But I only said the group would be trained."
30. This was a tactic along the lines discussed in Chapter 1(see text and endnote 61). In this case the SAS company (the choice of name alone explains its true purpose), the Army element of the CJATC, all strong airborne advocates, used the benign tasks as a means to secure authorization for the required unit. Once established, training philosophy and practise could easily be co-opted.
31. Canadian Airborne Centre Edmonton, UIC 1326-2695, Vol 1, Annual Historical Report, 1 April 1948—31 March 1949, Sect XVIII—SAS Coy. DHist.
32. There has always been a recognized institutional hostility towards special forces units. The conservative military mind shuns the unique, special or unconventional. During the Second World War there was much resistance to the establishment of such units and as hostilities neared completion those that did exist were quickly disbanded or at best, severely curtailed. Among the casualties were such well-known organizations as the First Special Service Force (FSSF), Long Range Desert Group (LRDG), Layforce, the Office of Strategic Services (OSS), Phantom (GHQ Reconnaissance Organization), the Rangers and Raider Battalions, and the Special Air Service (SAS).
33. Franklin, 2 & 7; Interviews with Firlotte and B.C. Robinson (member of SAS Company), 21 September 1998. Selection standards included the requirements to be: a bachelor; in superb physical condition; able to demonstrate initiative, self-reliance, and control; immensely quick in thought and action; and have a strong sense of discipline and an original approach. CAFM, Research Papers on Canadian Airborne Organizations, Part 1, 1.C, Document 1—"Canadian Special Air Service Company," 1.
34. Interview with Ken Arril, 25 August 1998.
35. Interview with Ken Arril, 25 August 1998. Contrary to popular mythology Captain Guy D'Artois was not selected as OC of the SAS Company based on his wartime experience or exploits. In fact, he was not originally considered at all. His posting to the unit was as the Second-in-Command. However, because the "future of the SAS Coy was in doubt" little effort was made to find a qualified Major to fill the billet as OC. As a result, Captain D'Artois became the Acting OC. By late October 1948, the sub-unit's existence was considered secure and efforts were made to find a suitable candidate. In what could be considered testimony to military bureaucracy the demise of the sub-unit occurred prior to the appointment of a new OC. Consequently, D'Artois was the first and only OC, albeit in an acting capacity. His performance, however, was outstanding by all accounts. "SAS Company," 27 October 1948. NAC, RG 24, Reel C-8255, File HQS 88-60-2.
36. Interview with Bob Firlotte, 21 September 1998.
37. Numerous memoranda exist clearly stating the role of the SAS Company as that of a nucleus for a larger force. See NAC, RG 24, Reel C-8255, File HQS 88-60-2. The perceived "commando" role was held by virtually all who served in the sub-unit. Interviews and CAFM, Research Paper, Part 1, 1.C, Document 1—"Canadian Special Air Service Company." The commando function was later added to the SAS terms of reference (see endnote 26) which prompted debate. A NDHQ memo to the DCGS noted disagreement with "what appears to be the present concept of the role of the SAS Company." It stated that "first and foremost that its name should be changed." It further explained that the possession of

such a commando force was a luxury that could not be afforded in the peacetime armed forces. "Training the Active Force—Airborne and Air-transported Aspects," 7 September 1948. NAC, RG 24, Reel C-8255, File HQS 88-60-2. The final role as a demonstration and test group was clear. This took up a large portion of their time. In fact, it was directed that approximately one platoon of basically trained airborne personnel should be available at most times for demonstration duties, allowing the remaining two to carry on with normal training. "Demonstration Commitments 48/49—JAS," 5 March 48. NAC, RG 24, Reel C-8255, File HQS 88-60-2.

38. George Kitching, *Mud and Green Fields. The Memoirs of Major-General George Kitching* (St.Catharines, ON: Vanwell Publishing Ltd., 1986), 248; "Command, Mobile Striking Force," 21 October 1948. DHist, File 112.3M2 (D369); Lieutenant-Colonel D.J. Goodspeed, *The Armed Forces of Canada 1867-1967* (Ottawa: DHist, 1967), 213; and Sean Maloney, "The Mobile Striking Force and Continental Defence 1948-1955," *Canadian Military History*, Vol 2, No. 2, August 1993, 78.

39. "Special Air Service Company—Implementation Policy," 12 September 1947. NAC, RG 24, Reel C-8255, File HQS 88-60-2. The memo clearly stated, "As it is intended that all three infantry battalions will in future be trained as parachute battalions it is recommended that the Company should comprise one platoon from each of the three battalions."

40. Colin S. Gray, *Canadian Defence Priority: A Question of Relevance* (Toronto: Clarke, Irwin & Company, 1972), 22-23. He also concluded that Canada never invested adequately in its defence, but rather continually depended on strength through affiliation.

41. Pearson, "Canada's Northern Horizon," 581-582. Prime Minister John Diefenbaker later dubbed the postwar period as the era of the "Arctic peril." *Debates*, 10 June 1958, 993.

42. *USAAF Study on Problems of Joint Defence in the Arctic*, 29 October 1946, quoted in Grant, *Sovereignty or Security?* Appendix G, 302-311. General Foulkes wrote, "Canada is physically joined to the United States just like Siamese twins. If one of the twins gets hurt the other one suffers." Foulkes, 10.

43. *Documents on Canadian External Relations*, Vol 11, *1944-45*, 1535.

44. M.A. Conant, *The Long Polar Watch. Canada and the Defence of North America* (New York: Harper and Brothers, 1962), 73. Even Nikita Khrushchev later stated, "This time Canada would not be geographically secure." Norman Hillmer, and J.L. Granatstein, *Empire to Umpire. Canada and the World to the 1990s* (Toronto: Copp Clark Longman, 1994), 221. Pearson observed, "In 1946 there is no isolation—even in the Arctic ice." Pearson, "Canada Looks Down North," 647. Reg Whitaker and Gary Marcuse concluded after their in-depth study that "Neutrality in the Cold War was never an option for Canada." *Cold War Canada* (Toronto: University of Toronto Press, 1994), 126.

45. The new perceived vulnerability was the result of "the principal advancements in the science of war," namely, "The increased range of application of destructive power and armed force resulting from the development of modern aircraft, amphibious technique, guided missiles, and advancement in technique of submarine warfare, as well as the increased destructive capacity of weapons such as the atomic bomb, rockets, and instruments of biological warfare." *Documents on Canadian External Relations*, Vol 12, *1946*, 1617-1618.

46. J.T. Jockel, "The Canada-United States Military Co-operation Committee and Continental Air Defence, 1946," *Canadian Historical Review*, Vol 64, 1983, 352. During the 1947 May Day flyover of Red Square, the Russians revealed that they now had bombers (copied from an American B-29 which made an emergency landing in the USS.R. during the war) capable of striking the United States. Ibid, 355. See also *House of Commons Debates Official Report—The Defence Programme*, 5 February 1951, 1.

47. "Command, Mobile Striking Force," 21 October 1948 and "Operational Requirement of Airborne Forces for the Defence of Canada," 29 November 1948. DHist, File 112.3M2 (D369). *Documents on Canadian External Relations*, Vol 12, *1946*, 1618-1623 and Vol 15, *1949*, 1560-1561 & 1566-1567.

48. Maloney, 76. See also "If the Russians Attack Canada," *Maclean's*, 15 June 1951, 8-9 & 68.

49. "Extract from the 355th Meeting of the Chiefs of Staff Committee," 20 June 1946. DHist, File 112.3M2 (D325) and 112.3M2 (D213). See also Ron Purver, "The Arctic in Canadian Security Policy," in *Canada's International Security Policy*, ed., D.B. Dewitt, 82. Colin Gray stated, "There is no doubt that

in the late 1940s Canadian-United States differences over the scale of 'the threat' were quite considerable." Gray, *Canadian Defence Priority*, 71. Stacey noted, "Canadian ministers, officials and officers were probably somewhat less disposed than their American opposite numbers to believe that the USSR intended to attack the West..." Stacey, *Canada and the Age of Conflict*, Vol 2, 406.

50. *Documents on Canadian External Relations*, Vol 14, *1948*, 1581 & 1585.
51. "Intelligence Aspects—PJBD Canada—USA.," 15 October 1946. DHist, File 112.3M2 (D213).
52. James Eayrs, *In Defence of Canada. Vol IV: Growing Up Allied* (Toronto: University of Toronto Press, 1985), 6.
53. *Documents on Canadian External Relations*, Vol 14, *1948*, 1581-1582. A memorandum from the MND to PM, in 1947, reiterated this belief. He wrote, "...war is improbable in the next five or even ten years..." Ibid., Vol 13, *1947*, 1482. Furthermore, Ernest Ropes of the US Department of Commerce stated that Russia's industrial production would be "insufficient to support a war against the USA. for at least 25 years." J.W. Warnock, *Partner to Behemoth* (Toronto: New Press, 1970), 50. A Strategic Appreciation completed by the Joint Intelligence Committee stated that "[Soviet] Economic self-sufficiency for a major war, involving large-scale movements and supply problems, may not be attained before 1960." *Documents on Canadian External Relations*, Vol 13, *1947*, 347. A Canadian military appreciation also noted that "The Soviet road and rail system is also at present an overall weakness in the national economy and defence." "Extracts from an Appreciation of the Possible Military Threat to the Security of Canada and the United States," Appendix A to *Defence Scheme No. 3*, 16 September 1948. DHist, File 112.3M2 (D10).
54. *Documents on Canadian External Relations, Vol 11, 1944-1945*, 1534. In this respect Escott Reid, the Assistant Under-Secretary of State for External Affairs, stated clearly, "It is a mistake to believe that those who conceived the North Atlantic Alliance [NATO] were obsessed with the possibility of an open armed attack by Russia. Indeed there was no assessment in the summer of 1948 that the Russian Government was planning a military aggression as an act of policy." Escott Reid, "The Birth of the North Atlantic Alliance," *International Journal*, Vol 22, No. 3, Summer 1967, 433.
55. "Political Appreciation of the Objectives of the Soviet Foreign Policy," 30 November 1946. NAC, Claxton Papers, MG 32, Vol 95, Box 5, File "Canada -US Defence Collaboration."
56. NAC, Claxton Papers, MG 32, Vol 95, Box 5, File "Canada -US Defence Collaboration."
57. Eayrs, *Growing Up Allied,* 132. Eayrs compared this assessment to an American bureaucrat working in the US State Department's Policy Planning Staff who wrote, "The military planning process...turns out tidy and complete results...It is easy for the unwary to jump to a fallacious conclusion...." Ibid, 132. An External Affairs memorandum noted, "Whereas it is the duty of the military advisers of the Government to assess the military capacities of the Soviet Union to attack the North American continent, it is the responsibility of the Department of External Affairs to estimate the possibilities of the outbreak of such a war. We can dismiss the idea that Canada alone might be involved in war with the USS.R.; even in the very likely event of an unprovoked Russian attack on Canada we could rely on the immediate and full support of the United States." *Documents on Canadian External Relations*, Vol 12, *1946*, 1632.
58. Eayrs, *Growing Up Allied,* 132. See also James Eayrs, "Now That Canada's Armed Forces are Nicely Sorted Out, What Are We Going To Do With Them?"in *International Involvement*, ed. Hugh Innis, (New York: McGraw-Hill Ryerson Ltd., 1972), 57-59.
59. "Minutes of the Cabinet Defence Committee," 13 November 1946. DHist, File 112.3M2 (D125) Cabinet Defence Committee Papers, 8 December 1945—March 1947.
60. Ibid.
61. "Operational Requirement of Airborne Forces for the Defence of Canada," 29 November 1948. DHist, File 112.3M2 (D369).
62. Ibid.
63. Ibid; and "Operational Requirement of Airborne Forces for the Defence of Canada," 3 December 1948. DHist, File 112.3M2 (D369).

64. "Operational Requirement of Airborne Forces for the Defence of Canada," 3 December 1948. DHist, File 112.3M2 (D369).
65. "Operational Requirement of Airborne Forces for the Defence of Canada," 29 November 1948. DHist, File 112.3M2 (D369). The definitions for airborne/air-transported were promulgated as follows: *Airborne Forces are those forces equipped and trained to land by parachute or glider in the assault role. Air-transported or Air-transportable forces are those forces other than Airborne Forces who can be transported by air and employed in a tactical role.*
66. "Training of the PPCLI for the Airborne/Air-transported Operations," 28 July 1948. NAC, RG 24, Vol 2371, File HQ-88-33, Army/Air Training of Airborne Infantry, Vol 1.
67. "Brigade Headquarters—Army Component—Mobile Striking Force," 29 April 1949; and "Operational Requirement of Airborne Forces for the Defence of Canada," 29 November 1948. DHist, File 112.3M2 (D369). The commitment prior to 1 May 1949 was for the availability of a one-battalion combat team capable of responding within two months of a lodgement, two battalion-size combat teams within four months and a brigade with six months. Throughout this period the military was incapable of meeting these demands.
68. Major-General C.C. Mann, " The New Role of the Princess Patricia's Canadian Light Infantry," *Canadian Army Journal,* Vol 2, No. 4, July 1948, 1; and G.R. Stevens, *Princess Patricia's Canadian Light Infantry 1919-1957* (Edmonton: Historical Committee of the Regiment, 1959), 262-263.
69. "PPCLI Airborne/Air-transported Training—Employment of SAS Company," 2 October 1948; "SAS Company—PPCLI Platoon," 14 October 1948; "SAS Company," 12 November 1948. NAC, RG 24, Reel C-8255, File HQS 88-60-2.
70. Continuing conceptional turmoil prevailed even at this late period in the development of both the SAS Company and the embryonic airborne brigade group. In October 1948 it was directed that "On completion of the PPCLI airborne/air-transportable training the SAS Company will resume normal training in accordance with the block training program." NAC, RG 24, Vol 2371, File HQ-88-33, Army/Air Training of Airborne Infantry, Vol 1. However, this never happened. The SAS personnel became training cadre. Their position was furthered hampered by the loss of a platoon. It was noted that the "departure of the PPCLI platoon of the SAS Company to rejoin its parent unit further aggravated the shortage of competent instructors." NAC, RG 24, Vol 2371, File HQ-88-33, Army/Air Training of Airborne Infantry, Vol 2. Despite the SAS Company's employment as instructors, a proposal, in May 1949, to expand the SAS Company to regimental strength to fulfill a reconnaissance and pathfinder role was staffed to the DCGS. The next month it was decided that the SAS Company would remain indefinitely. As a result action was directed to bring it up to full strength. However, during this period its function remained that of instructional staff and it was allowed to quietly die in late 1949. "Special Air Service Company," 6 May 1949 and 4 June 1949. NAC, RG 24, Reel C-8255, File HQS 88-60-2.
71. The disbandment was so low key that no official date has been discovered. See endnote 70 this chapter. Sergeant B.C. Robinson recalled that Captain D'Artois informed the Company that they had been disbanded because the Mobile Striking Force (MSF) was starting up. Interview with author, 21 September 1998.
72. The "bridge" analogy was coined by Lieutenant-Colonel Moncrief, a platoon commander in the SAS Company and later a PPCLI Battalion Commander. See Franklin's, "Airborne Bridge," 4.
73. As previously noted the requirement was identified and embraced in the spring/summer of 1946, yet no action to commence training was taken until October 1948. It was not until 1949 that DND mentioned, "of primary importance was the conversion of one infantry battalion into a parachute-airtransported battalion." *DND Report 1949*, 14. It was not until 1953 that DND officially noted the brigade's existence by title of the MSF. *DND Report 1953,* 46.
74. "Operational Requirement of Airborne Forces for the Defence of Canada," 3 December 1948. DHist, File 112.3M2 (D369).
75. Ibid. Another document stated, "the whole force must be airborne." It further noted that "the nature of the task of the MSF and the swiftness at which it is required to strike will not allow the preparation of airstrips immediately after the initial drop, therefore the whole force must be either dropped by parachute or landed in gliders." "Operational Requirement of Airborne Forces for the Defence of Canada,"

29 November 1948. DHist, File 112.3M2 (D369). The Adjutant-General's Appreciation also recommended the formation of a separate parachute unit. It explained that the existence in one unit of volunteers and non-volunteers, further heightened by a difference in pay scales would prove to be highly divisive and ultimately bad for morale. "AG Appreciation Conversion PPCLI to Airborne/Airtransported Role," 1 July 1948. NAC, RG 24, Vol 2371, File HQ-88-33, Army/Air Training of Airborne Infantry, Vol 1.

76. "Operational Requirement of Airborne Forces for the Defence of Canada," 3 December 1948. DHist, File 112.3M2 (D369).

77. "Parachute/Airtransported Training PPCLI," 13 January 1949 and "Army/Air Training Directive No. 1 Parachute/Air Transported Training the RCR," May 1949. NAC, RG 24, Vol 2371, File HQ-88-33, Army/Air Training of Airborne Infantry, Vol 1. See also "Operational Requirement of Airborne Forces for the Defence of Canada," 3 December 1948. DHist, File 112.3M2 (D369). The actual requirement for paratroopers within a battalion totalled 186 all ranks. This represented: an Airborne Company Combat Team (5 Officers/125 ORs); a Battalion Support Team (2/27); and supernumeries to allow for normal wastage (2/25—this group trained as paratroopers solely to compensate any loss within previously listed groups). The decision to base the structure on decentralized parachute capability was based on the perception that increased operational flexibility could be attained by having an airborne capability within each unit, which in turn allowed the skill to be provided across a larger geographical area in the country. "Training of the PPCLI for the AB/Air Transported Operations," 28 July 1948. NAC, RG 24, Vol 2371, File HQ-88-33, Army/Air Training of Airborne Infantry, Vol 1.

78. This misconception originated from the fact that all members of the subject battalions who volunteered were trained to the level of basic parachutist. This was the result of an Adjutant-General's appreciation which noted that for ease of future training, and to lessen the need for compulsory transfers of personnel at a later date, all those who volunteered during the battalion conversion training should be so qualified. This was accepted and the training was broken into two distinct phases: Phase I—airborne training for the airborne company and air-transported training for the whole battalion; and Phase II—airborne training for the complete battalion (volunteers only). "AG Appreciation Conversion PPCLI to Airborne/Airtransported Role," 1 July 1948; and NDHQ Directive, 23 Aug 1948. NAC, RG 24, Vol 2371, File HQ-88-33, Army/Air Training of Airborne Infantry, Vol 1. The fact that the Maroon Beret was authorized for wear by the entire battalion, based on its dual role, also led to misunderstanding.

79. "Airborne/Airtransported Training," 27 September 1948. NAC, RG 24, Vol 2371, File HQ-88-33, Vol 1.

80. DCGS Letter, 1 January 1949. NAC, RG 24, Vol 2371, File HQ-88-33, Army/Air Training of Airborne Infantry, Vol 1. Interestingly, Claxton redefined the role of the Active Force Brigade in June 1948. He stated, "The Active Army in the first place, is to include a brigade group or later such additional force as may be considered necessary, trained and equipped to deal with any diversionary attack. Secondly, the Active Army is to provide administrative and training staff—the cadre of officers, N.C.O.s and tradesmen—to train the reserve army and with it form the nucleus for as large a force as Canada may need." *Debates,* 24 June 1948, 5785. Three short years later this was refined once again in adjustment to the volatile international environment. Claxton now defined the objectives of the National Defence Policy as, "(a) The immediate defence of Canada and North America from direct attack; (b) the implementation of any undertakings made by Canada under the charter of the UN, or under the North Atlantic treaty or other agreement for collective security; and (c) the organization to build up our strength in a total war." *Debates,* 5 February 1951, 91.

81. *Debates,* 5 February 1951, 77.

82. *Debates,* 12 February 1951, 267.

83. *Debates,* 8 May 1951, 2833. The shrill screams of fear included such manifestations as claims that "We also have no reason to believe that the Russians have not at this time, somewhere in the north, set up camouflaged rocket installations. It is not entirely beyond the realm of possibility;" and "We have no reason to believe they could not send suicide bombing missions, and if they did central Canada would make a beautiful target." Ibid., 2834.

84. *Debates,* 12 February 1951, 260. The government program called for an armed force of 115,000 men and an expenditure of $5 billion. See also *House of Commons Debates Official Report—The Defence*

Programme, 5 February 1951, 1-7; *Canada's Defence Programme 1951-52,* 5-10; Desmond Morton, *A Military History of Canada, 3rd ed.,* (Toronto: McClelland and Stewart, 1994), 233-237.

85. Eayrs, *Peacemaking and Deterrence,* 100, 107 & 401. See also D.J. Bercuson, *True Patriot,* 195; and *Documents on Canadian External Relations,* Vol 11, *1944-45,* 1583. The case for a diversionary attack to tie up resources merits consideration. In WW II, the violation of American territory, namely the Aleutian Islands of Attu and Kiska, resulted in the investment of an Alaskan garrison of a quarter of a million troops. James Stokesbury, "The US Army and Coalition Warfare, 1941-1945," in *Against all Enemies*, eds., K. J. Hagan and W.R. Roberts (New York: Greenwood, 1986), 290.

86. *Debates,* 9 July 1947, 5270; and Canada, *Canada's Defence* (Ottawa: DND, 1947), 7.

87. *Debates,* 17 June 1955, 4925. One military officer stated, "In Canada's northern regions there was no place to go from a military point of view and nothing to do when you got there." Dosman, 23.

88. *Debates,* 8 May 1951, 2834-2835.

89. Sutherland, 209.

90. "Composition of Mobile Striking Force for Defence of Canada," 3 December 1948; and "Appreciation on the Mobile Striking Force," 13 May 1949. DHist, File 112.3M2 (D369). See also "Appreciation on the Employment of the Active Force Brigade Group in Defence of Canada Operations," 1 November 1949. DHist, File 112.3M2 (D400). Major-General Mann's address to the Patricias also betrayed the lack of belief in the threat. He stated, "Our geographical position no longer is as valuable a defensive asset as it once was. Today it is possible—I do not say probable—for our only potential enemy to deliver formed bodies of troops in moderate quantities almost anywhere in our territory." Mann, 3.

91. *Documents on Canadian External Relations,* Vol 17, *1951,* 1249.

92. *Defence Scheme No. 3—Major War,* Chapter V, "The Direct Defence of Canada," 16 September 1948, Appendix A, 2 & 4. DHist, File 112.3M2 (D10). See also *Documents on Canadian External Relations,* Vol 15, *1949,* 1560-61. The Joint Intelligence Committee noted that "the radius of aircraft restrict area of operations to points in Alaska west of Fairbanks and Anchorage and to the extreme west of the Aleutian chain." "The MSF," 29 March 1950. DHist, File 112.3M2 (D400).

93. "The Employment of the MSF for Reduction of Enemy Lodgements in Canada," 2 May 1950. DHist, File 112.3M2 (D400). Claxton's position on the possibility of an enemy landing is puzzling. He consistently professed the belief that there was no direct threat to Canada, yet, he stated on 26 June 1950 that "We do not estimate that there is any possibility of any attack on Canada except by an airborne force." This was contradictory to all military appreciations completed, as well as counter to his earlier, and later, statements on risks to Canadian security. *Debates,* 26 June 1950, 4135.

94. "The Employment of the Mobile Striking Force in the Reduction of Enemy Lodgements," April 1950. DHist, File 112.3M2 (D400); "MSF Plan for Reduction of Enemy Lodgements in Northern Canada," 23 August 1950. DHist, File 112.3M2 (D401); "MSF Directive," 14 August 1951. DHist, File 112.3M2 (D371); and DHist, File 112.3M2 (D388). It was also decided that any enemy lodgement beyond the limits of Northern Continental Canada (the mainland) would be dealt with only by air strike. This was based on the premise that distances involved would make the mounting and enlargement of forward staging bases for parachute operations too slow for a timely response. A further pragmatic advantage was also considered. The smaller geographic area of responsibility made the employment of parachute forces more manageable. "Mobile Striking Force Concept," 23 July 1951. DHist, File 112.3M2 (371).

95. Pickersgill, *Record,* Vol 3, 370; and *Documents on Canadian External Relations* Vol 17, *1951,* 1249. It was also realized that any forward base would be extremely vulnerable to air action. Dosman, 126.

96. Eayrs, *Peacekeeping and Deterrence,* 344.

97. *Debates,* 15 April 1953, 3920. An American perspective observed that "winter warfare in the Arctic is such a serious problem that it is believed no nation would risk it unless it felt that it had sufficient force available to achieve a quick, easy victory and push through into the vital areas farther south." Colonel P.V. Kane, "If War Comes to the Arctic," *Military Review,* Vol 27, No. 10, January 1948, 25.

98. Alan Harvey, "Scorched Ice Policy," *Globe & Mail,* 27 November 1948, 17.

99. *Documents on Canadian External Relations*, Vol 13, *1947*, 1482. Years later, the CGS continued to stress that the "USA was still sensitive to an attack over the Alaska route." "Extract from Minutes of CGS Conference No. 110 Held 9 April 1951," 30 April 1951. DHist, File 112.3M2 (D369).

100. *Documents on Canadian External Relations*, Vol 15, *1949*, 1471.

101. Ibid., Vol 18, *1952*, 1197-1198. It was noted that "US activities now far surpass those of Canada, and there have been numerous incidents of US military personnel throwing their weight about." Ibid., 1117 & 1195-1196. G.W. Smith noted, "a massive and quasi-permanent American presence in the Canadian North such as we have seen during and since World War II could in due course lead, gradually and almost imperceptibly, to such an erosion or disintegration of Canadian sovereignty that the real authority in the region, in fact if not in law would be American." R. St. J. Macdonald, ed., *The Arctic Frontier* (Toronto: University of Toronto Press, 1966), 213. The Secretary of State for External Affairs, during a briefing to Cabinet reiterated the danger of de facto American control as a result of increased American activities in the Arctic which would "present greater risks of misunderstandings, incidents and infringements of Canadian sovereignty." *Documents on Canadian External Relations*, Vol 19, *1953*, 1048.

102. *The Canadian Forum*, Vol 27, No.3, 18 July 1947, 75. Colin Gray claimed that "the only plausible challenger to the writ of Canadian law in the Arctic is Canada's principal ally, the United States." Gray, 128.

103. *Documents on Canadian External Relations*, Vol 11, *1944-1945*, 1535.

104. *Documents on Canadian External Relations*, Vol 13, *1947*, 1483.

105. Eayrs, *Peacemaking and Deterrence*, 107. See also *Debates*, 8 May 1951, 2835.

106. "Command, Mobile Striking Force," 21 October 1948. DHist, File 112.3M2 (D369).

107. "Training of the Active Force Brigade Group—Active Force Battalions, 11 January 1949. NAC, RG 24, Vol 2371, File HQS 88-33, Vol 1.

108. "Minutes of a Meeting Held at the PPCLI, Currie Barracks, Calgary Alberta, 4 January 1949 to Discuss the Army/Air Training Problems of the PPCLI." NAC, RG 24, Vol 2371, File HQS 88-33, Vol 2; HQ Western Command, *Joint Operation Order No. 1—Exercise Eagle*, Army File—WC 4-9-24 (GS), 1. DHist, File 489.009 (D29); and "Ex Eagle—PPCLI Unit Exercise Diary," 20 December 1949, 1. DHist, File 145.2P7.033 (D1).

109. Stevens, 265.

110. Ross Munro, "Canada Needs Better Defences," *Calgary Herald*, 8 August 1949, 1. Cited in Canadian Airborne Regiment, "Canadian Airborne Forces 1945-1968," *Maroon Beret*, (20th Anniversary Issue, 1988), 30; and Floyd Low, *Canadian Airborne Forces 1942-1978* (Unpublished thesis, University of Victoria, 1978), 38.

111. "Ex Eagle—PPCLI Unit Exercise Diary," 20 December 1949, Appendix A. DHist, File 145.2P7.033 (D1).

112. Kitching, 249.

113. Low, 38. Low interviewed Brigadier Kitching.

114. "Ex Sweetbriar—Vol III, Report of Canadian Army, " February 1950, v; Headquarters Western Command, *Joint Operation Order No.1—Exercise Eagle*, Army file WC 4-9-24(GS), 3; and Stevens, 266. The focus of the exercise was described as northern training and survival operations. No mention is made in the final report of airborne operations.

115. Kitching, 252.

116. Ibid, 252.

117. *DND Report 1951*, 14. Not surprisingly no mention was ever made of Exercise Eagle in the annual reports. Air Vice Marshal C.R. Dunlap stated, "It can be said without contradiction that the exercise [Sweet Briar] was a success." *Report on Allied Air Force Participation in Joint & Combined US—Canada Arctic Ex "Sweet Briar,"* 1950. DHist, File 181.003 (D1462). The questionable priority put on northern exercises was discernable from the aim assigned to Ex Sun Dog II. The concept statement read, "Enemy forces have landed in Canada and are in possession of a frozen lake in the Churchill area." "Joint Exercise Directive No. 4—Ex Sun Dog II," 15 June 1950. DHist, File 112.3M2 (D240).

118. Defence spending, as a percentage of the Gross National Product, rose from 1.7% in 1947 to 7.6% in 1953. J.L Granatstein and D. Bercuson, *War and Peacekeeping* (Toronto: Key Porter Books, 1991), 2. The CGS planned for authorized Army strength to increase approximately 31% from 22,000 to 30,800 officers and men. *Documents on Canadian External Relations,* Vol 16, *1950,* 112. That same year the MND was able to report that military establishments had already increased by 40%. "Memorandum to Cabinet," 7 August 1950. NAC, MG 32, Vol 94, Box 5, Claxton Papers.

119. Canada, *House of Commons Debates Official Report—The Defence Programme,* "Speech by the Hon. Brooke Claxton, MND," 5 February 1951, 3-7.

120. "The Direct Defence of Canada," Chapter V, *Defence Scheme No. 3 Major War,* 16 September 1948, 10. DHist, File 112.3M2 (D10).

121. "Appreciation on the Employment of the Active Force Brigade Group in Defence of Canada," 7 November 1949.

122. "MSF Directive," 14 August 1951, and "Mobile Strike Force Plan For the Reduction of Enemy Lodgements in Northern Canada," 1 October 1951. DHist, File 112.3M2 (D371).

123. Letter, Vokes to the Acting VCDS, 22 August 1951. DHist, File 327.009 (D388). Vokes opined that "long range armed reconnaissance by the RCAF, should be adequate to eliminate lodgements immediately such are spotted, in the Barrenlands of Northern Canada and the Arctic Archipelago." Ibid. Similarly, the brigadier responsible for General Staff plans questioned the need for a large airborne force. He reminded the DMO & P staff that the resources of the Americans, namely two airborne brigades should not be forgotten in planning for northern defence. He also remarked, "It would surely be more economical to use small parties of infantry carried in light craft to deal with enemy sea landings *than the expensive parachutist.* [italics are mine]. DHist, File 112.3M2 (D369). The ultimate reliance on the US to come to Canada's aid was bluntly admitted by a former CDS of the period. He wrote in his memoirs, "We were at this time, and probably are today, dependent on our neighbour to the south to come to our aid in the event of a hostile encroachment or attack upon Canadian territory." H. Graham, *Citizen and Soldier. The Memoirs of Lieutenant-General Howard Graham* (Toronto: McClelland & Stewart Ltd., 1987), 230.

124. Letter, Acting VCGS to GOC Western Command, 14 August 1951. DHist, File 327.009 (D388). The nebulous nature of the threat prompted Western Command and the Tactical Air Group to demand: (a) further amplification on the three main reasons for an enemy lodgement with direction as to the degree of probability of each; (b) more detail as to how the enemy would make such a lodgement, its size, duration, and possible action after primary mission was completed; (c) The number of lodgements which might be expected simultaneously; and (d) most likely targets. "Estimate of Enemy Lodgements in Northern Canada," 2 September 1952, DHist, File 112.3M2 (D264).

125. Minute of VCGS to CGS, 21 April 1950, DHist, File 112.3M2 (D400); "MSF Planning," 5 July 1951. DHist, File 327.009 (D388); and "Reorganization MSF," 4 October 1951. DHist, File 112.3M2 (D371). The geographic areas were broken down as follows: Area I—The Great Slave, Mackenzie, Coppermine area; Area II—The Central Barrens and Arctic Islands, exclusive Baffin Island; Area III—Northern Quebec, Labrador, Baffin Island. Areas I and II were the responsibility of GOC Western Area. Area III was under control of GOC Eastern Area. Unit responsibilities broke down as follows: the PPCLI, operating out of a forward staging base in Calgary, were accountable for Area I; the RCR out of Dundurn (later changed to Winnipeg) for Area II; and the R22eR out of Valcartier for Area III. "Mobile Strike Force Plan For the Reduction of Enemy Lodgements in Northern Canada," 1 October 1951. DHist, File 112.3M2 (D371).

126. "Draft Canadian Army Policy Statement—The Organization & Training of Parachute Battalions, RCIC (Active Force)," no specific day/month designation 1950. DHist, File 112.3M2 (D418). The use of the term "Parachute Battalions" is incorrect. The "Parachute Battalions," as noted in this document itself, were based on establishment E/RCIC/2/3/ dated 1 June 1950, which is a normal infantry battalion establishment in which only certain personnel (those required to parachute in the assault role) are qualified as parachutists.

127. Foulkes, 4.

128. DMO & P document, 2 October 1950. DHist, File 112.3M2 (D369).

129. "MSF—Plan for Reduction of Enemy Lodgements in Northern Canada. Extracts from Minutes of the 4th Meeting of Vice Chiefs of Staff Committee Held 30 October 1950." DHist, File 112.3M2 (D369). Contrary to the VCGS's comments, Chapter V, The Direct Defence of Canada, *Defence Scheme No. 3,* dated 16 September 1948, clearly stated that the "MSF constitutes the striking element of Canadian defence" and "will be available at a moments notice." DHist, File 112.3M2 (D10).

130. "Active Force Brigade Group HQ—Summary of Activities," 2 June 1950. DHist, File 112.3M2 (D400). The obligations under the BSP were not totally forgotten. The MND made great press in Parliament of keeping the paratroopers at home to meet the subject commitment and the necessity of home defence. (*Debates*, 5 February 1951, 91-91). Yet, there was little sincerity in these proclamations. The MSF forces were eroded to a state of inefficiency and the aircraft required to lift them were never available. The issue of aircraft shortages was continually raised in Parliament. See *Debates,* 14 March 1950, 729 & 760; 10 May 1951, 2880; 12 February 1951, 288; 14 April 1953, 3816 & 3829; and 16 June 1955, 4870; and Kitching, 249.

131. Letter, PPCLI to HQ West Command, 15 April 1950. DHist, File 169.009 (D207). In regards to equipment shortages see also DHist, File 112.3M2 (D369).

132. "Memorandum for File—Summary of MSF Activities in 1952," 7 January 1953. DHist, File 112.3M2.009 (D264).

133. "Mobile Striking Force Operations," 5 March 1951, 2. DHist, File 112.3M2 (D402); and "Information on MSF," 5 October 1951. The identical sentiment, word for word, was also submitted in the "Summary of MSF Activities in 1952." "Memorandum for File—Summary of MSF Activities in 1952," 7 January 1953. Both memos from DHist, File 112.3M2 (D371).

134. "Operational Efficiency—MSF Battalions," 9 April 1951. DHist, File 112.3M2 (D369).

135. Ibid.

136. "Training—MSF Units," 12 January 1953. DHist, File 112.3M2.009 (D264).

137. Ibid. Chief Warrant Officer (retd) Henry Sampson served in CFB Petawawa from 1949-1956 with an MSF unit. He recalled that he spent most of that time instructing troops going overseas. He also stated that most of the brigade training was combined arms, infantry—armour cooperation and that very little emphasis was placed on Arctic training. He himself undertook Arctic training in Fort Churchill, for a week or two, only once in seven years. He noted that the unit as whole never sent more than a troop (platoon) and this only occasionally. Interview with author, 21 October 1998.

138. *Debates,* 14 April 1953, 3829.

139. Ibid., 3816.

140. Ibid., 3816-3817. The actual lift requirement for a parachute company and airborne battalion was twelve and thrity-five C-47 type aircraft respectively. "Airlift MSF BDF," 13 August 1951; "Aircraft Requirements for Airborne/Airtransported Operations," 26 April 1946; and "Capabilities and Limitations of Aircraft in Trans-Polar Airborne and Airtransported Operations, 15 May 1946." DHist, File 112.3M2 (D232).

141. Kitching, 260-261. See also "Army No Longer Smug in Arctic," *Winnipeg Free Press,* 8 December 1954. DHist, File 112.3M2.009 (D264).

142. "Canadian Combined Forces Exercise Bulldog II, 1954," *The Polar Record,* Vol 7, No. 51, September 1955, 492. The problems with aircraft were legion. It was noted that the serviceability figures for temperatures below 30 degrees Celsius on runways is very low, which is not surprising considering the serviceability rate in Montreal is only 50%. During the exercise, on the second attempt at a drop only two of seven aircraft were capable of take-off even after a 1.5 hour warm-up. This was of little consequence since the winds during the day were an average of 19 miles per hour (mph), a full four mph more than the permissible velocity. A night drop was out of the question since, as noted by the Director General of Army Plans and Operations, "we cannot drop at night because the night drop is no longer a part of the para course." He admitted, "If we can't drop in darkness we might never get into certain places in the North at all." Not surprisingly, the press was asked not to publicize this point. Amazingly, they complied. Letter by Brigadier R.P Rothschild, 31 December 1954. DHist, File 112.3M2.009 (D264). See also Colonel W.N. Russel, "Airborne or Heliborne?" *CDQ*, Vol 7, No. 3, 1978, 41.

143. "Change Due in Arctic Warfare: The Lesson of Bulldog II," *Ottawa Citizen,* 10 December 1954. The final report of Exercise Bull Dog II recommended that "airlandings be practised on MSF exercises to determine whether this method might prove a more reliable means of delivering troops." "Airlandings—MSF Operations," 30 August 1956. DHist, File 112.3M2.009 (D264)—both documents. Once again it was a question of threat. The unnamed officers stated the targets such as weather stations would not be worthwhile targets to an enemy.

144. Jim Senter, "Observer Says New Concept Needed to Ensure Canadians Can Deal Effectively With Invaders," *Hamilton Spectator,* 8 December 1954. DHist, File 112.3M2.009 (D264).

145. *The Defence of Canada* (Notes on CF for NATO Troop Information Lecturers), dated June 1955, 4.

CHAPTER FOUR

THE WINDS OF CHANGE
Embracing the Concepts of Rapid Reaction Forces and Strategic Mobility, 1964-1968

The special service force concept, announced in the White Paper to apply to one brigade, has now been expanded and current plans call for two brigades to be converted, on a planned basis, to this concept of air transportability, with an additional airborne battalion group for added flexibility and quick response to domestic needs and overseas commitments as they arise.

Paul Hellyer, Minister of National Defence, February 1966[1]

Clearly, given the capricious circumstances surrounding the Mobile Striking Force in the late 1940s and early 1950s, one can see that its future was tenuous at best. Professor David Bercuson claimed that the "MSF remained largely a concept rather than an operational reality."[2] As we have seen, the problem lay in the fact that very few believed the MSF was relevant. Its role was never fully accepted as credible.[3] Quite simply, many saw the Mobile Striking Force, and the airborne capability it represented, as a potential diversion of resources required for the more important NATO or UN roles.

Although support for the MSF was already minimal, its fortunes languished even further as the 1950s progressed. By mid-decade a shift in the strategic nature of war, with its new emphasis on thermonuclear weapons delivered by manned bombers, and later the inter-continental ballistic missile (ICBM), prompted a reassessment of the threat to the North America continent. This in turn, sealed the fate of the MSF. In the process, the military and political leadership clearly demonstrated the magnitude of their commitment, or lack thereof, to the idea of Canadian airborne forces.

In those same years the assaults against the belief that the North represented Canada's Achilles heel—a veritable gateway for invasion of the North American land mass—picked up momentum. This was so because bombers and missiles would fly over the North and technological advances were rapidly increasing the range of possible detection and early warning capabilities. By mid decade it was universally accepted, by the government, military and public, that the only probable method of attack, as highlighted in the 1954 *Defence Program*, was by air, specifically by the manned bomber. The Minister of National Defence bluntly affirmed "that in the final analysis the task of Canadian defence is defence against aerial attack over the north pole. We have to discard from any realistic thinking any possibility of an attack by ground forces on the area of Canada either by air or by sea."[4]

The change in the threat perception provided Canadian politicians with a welcomed respite both financially and in having to carefully define all aspects of defence policy. The emphasis of military activity in the North shifted from a focus on active defence to one of simply surveillance. This subtle shift was reflected in DND annual reports. In the years between 1946 and 1957, the stated aim of Canada's defence program underwent a distinct evolution. Initially, the narratives contained in the publications, *Report on the Department of National Defence* and *Canada's Defence Program*, for these years defined the military's efforts in terms of "defence of Canada from direct attack." With the change of the threat assessment, the wording was amended to a more ambiguous "to provide for the security of Canada."[5]

The reports also demonstrated a transformation of the officially pronounced definition of risk. Originally, the annual summaries documented the primary peril facing the Dominion as a potential surprise land attack in coordination with a campaign of aerial bombardment of North America. This was soon modified. By the mid-1950s, the defence department expressed the risk to the nation in terms based almost exclusively on the manned bomber. Not surprisingly, this significantly affected the need for land forces capable of responding to the perceived menace. From 1949 to 1955, DND's annual summary, *Canada's Defence Program*, spoke of the need to repel "surprise attacks." In 1956, the wording was changed to reflect a scaled down level of direct danger to Canadian territory. The reports now noted that troops were required to deal only with "possible enemy lodgements."[6] This was a subtle change in emphasis. Unfortunately, it meant different things to different parties in the airborne debate. One defence analyst observed, "As the Cold War developed, soldiers looked at the North as an approach. There were a few extremists who posited the notion of 'Slavic hordes' invading North America via the Yukon-Mackenzie Valley route; their voices soon vanished once the geographic realities of the concept were examined. What came to be known as the 'lodgement scenario,' however, refused to go away."[7]

By mid-decade the enigmatic "lodgement scenario" quickly became tied to Canada's airborne forces. Paradoxically, it provided the justification for both the retention of paratroopers, as well as the rationalization for their marginalization.[8] In the summer of 1958, the GOC Western Command lamented, "it is difficult to plan anything in the face of a threat which is defined so vaguely."[9] He went on to question, "If the threat of lodgement is so nebulous, why do we bother about it at all? Could it not be taken on by air bombardment?"[10] Similarly, the Director of Military Operations and Plans confessed that "many commanders and staff officers are under the impression that the threat of enemy lodgements is a rather nebulous one."[11] In the RCAF, the Chief of the Air Staff agreed. "The concept for reduction of enemy lodgements," he stated, "does not appear to be in consonance with the threat and should be scaled down accordingly. It follows that the Canadian forces allocated to this task are either not warranted or should be scaled down considerably."[12]

The question became largely redundant. The final death knell for the Mobile Striking Force was sounded on 26 August 1957, when the Soviet Union announced it had successfully launched its first inter-continental ballistic missile.[13] The air threat to North America was now further amplified. The vacillating commitment to the airborne/air-transported infantry battalion capability, as represented by the MSF, collapsed. In January 1958, the MSF was officially downsized to a reinforced company group for each of the respective parachute battalions, and the force was renamed the Defence of Canada Force (DCF).[14]

The new shrunken organization represented a significant resource saving for the Army. The resultant Canadian airborne establishment, although largely conceptual, was dramatically decreased in terms of requisite equipment and aircraft. The level of actual commitment to the concept of airborne forces still remained minimal and never reached the required level. The old cliché, "the more things change, the more things stay the same" clearly applied. What few paratroopers there were, were still seen publicly—and conveniently politically—as an insurance policy for the North. As before, the politicians and senior military commanders viewed the risk as negligible and as a result, the lowest possible premium was paid.[15] The importance of mere appearance substantially outstripped the reality or the desire for operational capability for the Defence of Canada Force.

If the public cared to look, the evidence of the sad state of airborne capability was readily conspicuous. In 1958, Western Command Headquarters concluded that "the present resources of defence [the airborne force] against enemy lodgements have a very limited capability and, for all practical purposes, are non effective."[16] Additionally, the summary explained that "the authorized establishment of parachutists will NOT guarantee the provision of a para company group in contact with the enemy because there is an insufficient reserve of trained parachutists with the battalion."[17] The warning was wasted. Frankly, no one cared.

As the perceived threat further evolved over the next few years, the relevance of paratroopers subsequently declined. This was especially true for the Diefenbaker Conservative government of 1957-1963. Despite the prime minister's "Northern Vision," Conservative defence policy concentrated on the politically, militarily and publicly well accepted belief that the only significant threat to North America was by air. The ill-fated CF-105 Avro Arrow, intended to "fly high and fast over the Canadian tundra to intercept Soviet bombers as far north of populated North America as possible" and its eventual replacement, the nuclear tipped Bomarc surface-to-air missile were representative of their focus. To the Tory government, defence of the North implied air defence not paratroopers.[18]

A new Liberal government in 1963 maintained a similar outlook in regard to the North. Paul Hellyer, the Minister of National Defence, stated, "the air threat to North America consists of long range ICBMs, submarine or ship launched intermediate range ballistic missiles and manned bombers."[19] Hellyer further added that there was no protection against ballistic missiles at the moment.[20] Dr. Harold Brown, Director General of Research of the United States Department of Defence, supported this assertion. His analysis claimed that "the problem of developing a defence against a missile is beyond us, and beyond the Soviets technically, and I think many who work on it feel that perhaps it can never be successfully accomplished."[21]

The growing ICBM threat relegated the Arctic's importance simply to one of strategic depth. This interpretation minimized the need for an airborne capability which was perceived as inexorably expensive. General Charles Foulkes explained that the new reality meant that "we will have to rely on the deterrent and retaliatory effect of the US strategic [nuclear] force. So that with the passing of the bomber, the Canadian contribution to the defence of North America will be greatly diminished and the importance of Canadian air space and territory in the defence of North America will be seriously reduced."[22] In 1963, the Chief of Operational Research at the government's Defence Research Establishment, R.J. Sutherland, one of Canada's most important defence scientists and then the chairman of the Ad Hoc Committee on Defence Policy, stated that "with the decline in the importance of the bomber threat to North America, a question will arise with regard to the future of the NORAD agreement. From a military point of view NORAD could be dispensed with now."[23] He further warned that, "with the declining importance of continental air defence, the special relationship with the USA will tend to diminish in importance."[24]

Sutherland's dire warning was overly pessimistic. The special relationship with the United States did not diminish. American strategic interest in the Canadian North, however, declined dramatically during this period, owing to the change in the threat and a fatalistic reliance on the policy of massive retaliation. In addition, international attention became focussed on counter-insurgency and regionalized brush-fire wars that were seen as potential catalysts of larger global conflicts.[25] Predictably, as the menace of American encroachment in the Arctic disappeared, so too did Canadian interest.[26]

The shift in attitude was not long in manifesting itself. The Liberal's 1964 *White Paper* highlighted the prevailing lack of concern. The document did not include a single reference to the Arctic. This omission is not surprising and it appears in consonance with Colin Gray's observation that "since the mid-1960s there has been no military incentive to urge the Canadian Forces to be active in the North. Reference to 'foreign incursions,' let alone 'lodgements,' should be treated with the contempt they merit."[27] But Gray missed the point. "Military incentive" was never the motive. The rationale behind Canada's defence policy in the Arctic was primarily to protect its sovereignty against perceived American penetration. Only when American attention died in the late fifties did Canadian interest wane. The primacy of Arctic sovereignty was always the driving force behind Canadian military action in the North. As a result, with the absence of American concern, the charade of an airborne capability to defend the northern frontier was not required. Accordingly, it was left to wither.

Nonetheless, over the next few years the DCF was allowed to survive, but just barely. The resilient and lingering scenario, which held that a diversionary attack could be launched against Canada's North, necessitated some sort of a response because it was dangerous for the political and military leadership to ignore it completely. This provided the impetus to maintain a parachute capability, albeit completely decentralized. During this period, the DCF conducted no joint exercises that included all the scattered jump companies. Nor was there a designated headquarters to control the different parachute sub-units should there be a need to bring them together.[28]

The jump companies, which were the core of the Defence of Canada Force, continued in the same vein as they had in the Mobile Striking Force; namely, appearance over capability. Lieutenant-General Stan Waters, a wartime veteran of the First Special Service Force and the 1st Canadian Parachute Battalion, who continued to serve in airborne staff and line positions in the peacetime Army lamented that all postwar airborne forces of Canada "suffered from a lack of clear, coherent and consistent policy on the role, the equipment and the training to meet that role."[29] The paratroopers serving with the DCF complained that there were no special standard operating procedures, no special training and no special equipment. Furthermore, the parachute soldiers perceived that the application of airborne doctrine was very disorganized, if existent at all. The shortage of aircraft and adequate mounting facilities for exercises led another paratrooper with much peacetime airborne service to assert that the DCF had "more of a PR [public relations] value than any real tactical training value."[30]

The Defence of Canada Force's lack of substance was apparent to many, especially those in the units. Parachute companies' establishment and organization were identical to the other standard rifle companies within the respective battalions. Parachuting was seen strictly as another means to deploy to the battlefield and no effort was made to keep those on jump status current. Paratroopers on average jumped only two to three times a year. One DCF paratrooper remembered that in eighteen months he participated in only one parachute company exercise. He added that normally they operated as a normal rifle company and although the jump company did in fact have a unique additional role, namely the defence of the North, it was never exercised.[31]

Individuals who served in the DCF harboured no illusions of its proficiency. One former member recalled that "it was not an operationally sound structure" and that "it would have been criminal to have deployed it in a real situation."[32] Another described the DCF as "essentially a Jump [parachuting] Club,"[33] while another insisted that as a viable airborne force the DCF was ridiculous.[34] Virtually all former serving MSF/DCF paratroopers agree that the jump companies had "no operational rationale nor capability, but existed only to keep alive the parachuting capability."[35]

Further testimony to the peripheral importance placed on airborne capability is also clear in the half-hearted effort placed on training replacement parachutists. Between 1952 and 1956, newly qualified parachutists graduating from the airborne training centre in Rivers, fell by twenty percent. In 1958, 24 candidates graduated. Only two years previously 1094 individuals were qualified in a single year. By 1959/1960 the numbers climbed back to 272 and 255 respectively; nevertheless, the trend had been set.[36] The senior leadership, both military and civilian, placed little emphasis on an airborne capability. It was in a hiatus that no one wished to disturb. For those who strongly believed in the utility of airborne forces the DCF provided a skeleton from which a more robust frame could one day be shaped. However, until the opportunity arrived, the fragile existence of paratroopers was strapped to the "Guardians of the North" concept. The idea of enemy lodgements on Canadian territory, as theoretical as it was, represented the only accepted rationale for maintaining airborne forces.

The truth was not difficult to discern. Military parachuting served a very limited purpose, namely, as assurance to the Canadian public and to the nation's domineering ally to the south. The airborne capability was not intended, nor was it ever allowed, to become an operational reality. The focus of the Army was mechanized forces for NATO and the European battlefield. Increasingly, the government, specifically the Department of External Affairs, became interested in UN deployments.[37] At that time, airborne forces were not perceived as relevant to either of these roles. As a result, the paratroopers were on the verge of veritable extinction.

However, in the mid sixties fortunes began to change. A fresh wind was blowing that would carry the seeds of new growth farther than the staunchest airborne protagonists could have hoped. The roller coaster that represented the very existence of Canadian airborne forces was on the ascent once again. This time it would have a powerful champion. Indeed the catalyst had occurred a few years before the "winds of change" were felt by the airborne advocates.

The intervention of the United Nations in the Suez crisis of 1956, through the use of an emergency force, furnished the events for a growing Canadian interest in UN operations. The fact that the idea had been a Canadian one further propelled the nation's interest. The following year, Lester B. Pearson, the Canadian Secretary of State for External Affairs and originator of the Suez Emergency Force concept, wrote of the need for countries to earmark small forces for UN duty to perform such functions as securing ceasefires that had been agreed upon by belligerents.[38] In January 1958, Canada officially designated a "stand-by battalion" for UN duties.[39] Here was the genesis of the "rapid reaction" concept that eventually came to the aid of the airborne force idea.

Nothing moves swiftly in a bureaucracy, but motion is perpetual. By 1963 the idea of an Army rapid reaction capability had gathered steam. The former CGS, General Foulkes, testified before the Special Committee on Defence that the Canadian defence effort should concentrate on the "operation of a mobile ready reserve available immediately for NATO or to meet an UN task anywhere in the world or maintain our sovereignty in the Arctic."[40] In a similar vein, the outspoken General Simonds recommended the organization of the military along the lines of a "conventionally armed tri-service, highly mobile force adapted to deal with brush fire wars in support of the United Nations or our allies."[41] This outlook was already rooted in the minds of many at NDHQ. Insiders there released information which indicated that "a new defence policy based on a small, mobile and airborne army with tactical air support is beginning to take shape."[42] The ultimate goal of this conventional multipurpose force was to serve NATO and/or the UN.[43]

The rumours were soon substantiated. The 1964 *White Paper* embodied a new philosophy for the Canadian Armed Forces (CAF). It represented the then current and popular idea which stressed strategic mobility. Lieutenant-General Jean Victor Allard, a key player in bringing about the change planned for the CAF, explained that "the [1964] White Paper subsequently set out a new concept for the utilization of our forces, based on their mobility, so that they could serve with the UN, with NATO, or within our own territory."[44] In short, the soldiers at NDHQ were trying to adapt to a changing world in which Canada was having a harder and harder time competing for an international role with the "big boys."

The "mobile force" approach was quintessentially Canadian. It appealed to many people for many different reasons. It appeased those who saw a need to address alliance commitments. But it also soothed others who maintained that Canadian sovereignty was the primary concern. Most importantly, as in the past, it was seen as cost effective.[45] Mobile forces could be earmarked against a number of different tasks. Much like a shell game, it would be difficult to confirm which shell held the pea. Nevertheless, the fresh outlook sparked what was soon to be a new and expanded role for airborne forces in Canada. This in turn generated development in the airborne realm.

The change in fortunes was not a chance of nature. The government of the day was Liberal under Prime Minister Pearson, who had a long history of advocating a national capability of this nature. Furthermore, his dogmatic and intractable MND, Paul Hellyer, ensured a climate of acquiescence within the military. Hellyer swept through DND like an ocean squall. He admitted his dismay at the "lack of coordination at the top, and the seemingly haphazard determination of priorities" within the defence department.[46] Hellyer quickly decided that each service was preparing to fight a completely different type of war. As a result, he personally wrote the first draft of the *White Paper* in longhand.[47] Hellyer was unyielding in his pursuit to ensure that not only the new *White Paper*, but the Department of National Defence as well, would be irretrievably imprinted with his vision.

Moreover, Hellyer intended the new defence document to provide a fresh blueprint for the entire Canadian Armed Forces for the next decade. "The purpose of our forces in being," asserted Hellyer, was "to preserve peace by deterring war."[48] He planned to achieve this by restructuring the military into a global and very mobile force that could meet the widest range of potential requirements in the fastest possible time.[49] The theory was that these forces could then contain conflict and prevent it from escalating into a more dangerous and less manageable crisis. The Defence Minister's mobile and flexible force was designed specifically to "answer the call of the UN or the Western alliance anywhere in the world."[50]

Fundamental to the then current ideology was the formation of a mobile command. And so in 1965 Force Mobile Command (FMC) became the new organization which consisted of the entire Army, as well as elements of the Air Force which were responsible for supporting and transporting the ground troops. The MND proclaimed:

> Mobile Command is basic to the philosophy of Canada's new defence policy. The largest of the new functional commands, its task is to operationally train and maintain the land elements of the Canadian force and its tactical air support, and to keep this force in a state of combat readiness which will enable it to be deployed in units of the required size to meet Canadian commitments and undertakings anywhere in the world. The prime ingredients in the force are quick reaction-time, the ability to go where required with dispatch, and to perform its tasks with maximum effectiveness.[51]

The new philosophical shift in thinking, however, could not be implemented by the MND himself. Therefore, Hellyer looked to those who shared and supported his prescience to take the reigns of control. Lieutenant-General Allard was one such individual.[52] He believed strongly in the underlying principles of a flexible and strategically mobile army. Not surprisingly, he became the first commander of Force Mobile Command.

Allard's support of the new strategy was unmistakable. He informed the Standing Committee on National Defence that FMC was the result of a defence analysis that had examined the Canadian commitments and potential conditions of conflict which faced the nation's soldiers. Allard visualized a scale of conflict ranging from peace and peacekeeping operations to limited and total war. He explained that different elements of the Army were seen as better suited to respond to different circumstances along the scale. Hence, he believed that FMC must be structured to provide an effective and capable response for the entire spectrum of conflict. Allard pointed out that at present, the Canadian Army was designed primarily for only the upper end of the scale, namely a total global war. As a result, Allard felt that the Army demonstrated great deficiencies in the lower range of activities such as peacekeeping, counter-insurgency, guerilla and limited warfare.[53]

Based on the anticipated range of potential confrontations, an Army appreciation deduced that a "significant portion of the Canadian Army Field Force must be capable of operating in limited war in any part of the world. They must be strategically mobile and possess tactical mobility suitable to the scale of conflict and appropriate to the areas of operations."[54] The analysis concluded that the Army's organization should be based on two basic types of formations and units. Firstly, "light airborne/air-transportable forces for the Defence of Canada—US Region, peacekeeping, the ACE Mobile Force, and small limited wars; and secondly, heavier armoured and mechanized forces to fulfil the Canadian Army's role in NATO Europe."[55] But this force mix was not compatible. One force could not sustain the other. Nor could units be rotated between Canada and overseas.

Nonetheless, this assessment was in accord with Allard's proposal for the establishment of paratroops and light forces to deal with the type of conflict that could be expected at the lower end of the spectrum. As a result, FMC Headquarters proposed a Special Service Force (infantry brigade), which would be organized as a ready force of battalion group size with strong airborne capability.[56] This concept was later expanded to two brigades structured as air-portable and designed for rapid deployment. Allard wanted strategic mobility, and aimed for a completely airportable unit, with all its equipment, deployed and in the designated operational theatre within forty-eight hours.[57] Lieutenant-General W.A.B. Anderson, who was Allard's personal choice to eventually succeed him as the next FMC Commander, proclaimed, "the new structure [Mobile Command], would give the force increased mobility, greater fire power and a greatly reduced administrative personnel." He added that he expected "Mobile Command to be able to move fast, faster, fastest."[58]

The initial formulation of FMC's organization included proposals for the continuation of decentralized parachute capability as currently represented by the Defence of Canada Force structure, albeit with an increase in authorized strength of 250 paratroopers in one battalion of each of the three infantry regiments. The VCDS specifically directed that the RCR, PPCLI, and R22eR be responsible for maintaining the Army parachutist capability.[59] Importantly, however, at this time the alternative of grouping all paratroopers into a single parachute battalion began to emerge.[60] Moreover, this latter option was more in line with Lieutenant-General Allard's thinking.

Thus, by the late sixties, a revitalized airborne concept was definitely gaining credence as a direct result of a few visionaries who held key positions in the corridors of power. Central to the new doctrine of flexibility and mobility was the re-emergence of a true airborne capability. The MND announced that "the command [FMC] is also forming the Canadian airborne regiment whose personnel and equipment can be rapidly sent to danger zones."[61] Any doubt of his intention was dispelled by the Commander of FMC. Allard himself divulged that his new organization would have an airborne regiment that would provide the flexibility the Army required. Later he explained:

> We knew that the deployment of an infantry brigade overseas could take several weeks and even then only if it were already completely equipped and had received at least one month's thorough training. The light and rapid airborne regiment was meant to 'fill the bill' between the time the government acceded to a request for intervention from outside and the arrival of the main body of troops...This regiment was therefore designed to fill a gap in our strategy for modern warfare. In the minds of its planners, it was never intended to remain in the fighting line for more than a few weeks.[62]

In Allard's mind the airborne capability was more than just a sop to mollify the concerns of the US regarding their northern flank, or to allay the consternation of the public which had grown to fear the evil Soviet Empire. Importantly, the FMC's commander envisioned more than a token force. He realized that the current decentralized parachute capability, namely the Defence of Canada Force, was ineffective and had been for many years. In 1966, he testified before the Parliamentary Standing Committee on National Defence that the idea was now to change the philosophy and group the paratroopers permanently together. Allard further explained that at the time all "our troops are assigned to a multitude of tasks so we have to train them for all of them. One of the things we want to do is to stabilize them in one task."[63]

Allard also stressed the ineptitude of the DCF concept. An assessment done by his army headquarters staff in 1966 concluded that the "dispersal of parachutists in small operational and training packets leads to a loss of overall airborne effectiveness and efficiency. Furthermore, it violates the principle of economy by duplication of training facilities and other functions and it causes unnecessary disruption and resultant inefficiency to three battalions, at any one time, and, in the long term forces unwanted organizational changes on half the infantry corps."[64]

It clearly recommended that "every effort must be made to concentrate all airborne operational and training resources in the one unit."[65] Here was the key idea that would produce the revitalized airborne capability of later years.

The report went beyond merely the economic and organizational problems. It also highlighted the operational deficiencies of the current DCF scheme. The evaluation explained:

> Although three airborne company groups are under training at any one time, the operational effectiveness is frequently two or even one company group. This is caused by the rotation of infantry battalions between Canada and overseas. Furthermore, DCF units have been required to undertake other roles during summer months. The re-organization needed for these summer tasks greatly reduced their capability of mounting a DCF operation. It would be truthful to conclude that the effectiveness of the DCF parachutist element has been less than three company groups except possibly for a limited period during the winter months.[66]

The FMC commander's vision for a single viable airborne unit went beyond its operational capability. He also believed in its value as a training tool. Allard always felt that the Canadian Army needed parachute units if only for the training value of the parachute.[67] He clearly conveyed this notion to the Parliamentary Committee on Defence. Allard elucidated, "that this light unit is going to be very attractive to a fellow who likes to live dangerously, so all volunteers can go into it."[68] His creation was to be an all-services one, manned only by volunteers. "We intend to look at the individual a little more rather than considering the unit as a large body of troops, some of whom might not be suited for the task," he told the parliamentary group.[69] Indeed, it seemed that Allard had heralded the end of the marginalization of Canada's airborne forces. In his mind, they were to become a very special and vibrant element, and for this they had Lieutenant-General Jean Victor Allard to thank.

By the late 1960s, the improved position of airborne forces in the projected Army organization was rooted in the perceived contribution of the paratroopers to the general proficiency of the Army. Of great importance was the fact that the new vision encompassed a role for the proposed airborne regiment that exceeded a single, narrow focus on the defence of Canada. It was given a pervasive rationale for existence which had the support of a powerful segment of the military and political leadership of the day. The new organization was designed for commitment anywhere, as part of a UN mission to contain a brush-fire conflict, or to Europe as part of a NATO operation to counter a Soviet threat. As an afterthought, this new unit was also recognized as capable of covering the open flank to the North. A 1965 DND report, exclusively for "Canadian Eyes Only," stated that Canada had a responsibility, as a sovereign nation, to have forces capable of responding to a possible lodgement on its territory. It pointedly admitted, however, that "this is not to say, of course, that Canada must maintain military units exclusively for this purpose, but rather that this minor but indispensable responsibility must at all times be included among the tasks of Canadian military units stationed on Canadian territory."[70]

The task of protecting the Arctic was downplayed because DND believed the assessment of low risk of a direct threat to Canada through the north remained current. The air threat was still seen as the only real menace. In December 1966, Hellyer once more reinforced what is probably the most consistent theme of Canadian defence policy. The Minister reasserted, "forces for the direct protection of Canada remain necessary. While direct attack on Canadian territory is very low in the scale of probability, it is essential to provide appropriate surveillance of our territory and its sea approaches as well as to have the capability of dealing with lodgements of enemy forces in the unlikely event they should occur."[71]

Hellyer's public utterances were driven more by political than military necessity. But the root concern was clearly identified by Army Headquarters in 1968: "...it is of vital importance to Canada's continued existence as a viable and fully independent and sovereign nation that our military posture be considered a contribution and not a risk to the security of the United States."[72] This had been a consistent theme since the end of the Second World War. Whether in agreement with the American threat assessment or not, Canada had to ensure that Canadian policy addressed the concerns of the Americans in regard to the possibility of its territory being used as an approach of attack against the United States. Outside Ottawa's necessary military posturing to appease Washington however, a different reality was also present. From the standpoint of an actual threat within Canada itself, NDHQ insisted that "generally speaking, lightly-armed forces equipped with the means of riot control would be all that is required."[73] Once again, military analysis dismissed the threat of the North as a gateway to invasion. Internal security, they suggested, was the most likely task for soldiers stationed in Canada.

In spite of whatever public spin may have been put on it, the central driving force for the reborn airborne idea was not the potential threat to Canada. The new proposed airborne capability was more than able to meet the evaluated contingencies in the defence of Canada. The contemplated difference in the make-up of the new airborne force, specifically a single parachute organization instead of the decentralized MSF/DCF model, was due to two important factors. First, the new concept had a powerful sponsor, none other than the Commander of the Army, Lieutenant-General Allard who was heir apparent to the supreme position of Chief of the Defence Staff. Second, the paratroopers' existence was no longer rationalized on the basis of a threat that was equally dismissed by both the military and political leadership. Axiomatic to the evolution of Canada's airborne forces was a conviction that they had a much more pervasive role to fill. Based on a spectrum of conflict of variable intensity, and the need for strategic and tactical mobility, the new defence ideas seemed tailor-made for parachute troops.

Unfortunately, the development of the airborne was not to be that simple. Indeed, such a radical approach was not embraced by all among the soldiers. Military conservatism is not easily broached and new ideas are seldom accepted without deep internal resistance. The sudden enhancement of a perceived larger peripheral capability for airborne forces as espoused by Allard or Hellyer was resisted by others in the military establishment. This reaction is not hard to explain. Behavioural scientists have frequently recorded that significant resistance to change comes from the fact that "leaders have to indict their own past decisions and behaviours to bring about change."[74] Significantly, the academics also recognized that "cultures that require a great deal of conformity often lack much receptivity to change."[75] As far as the airborne was concerned, the Royal Canadian Infantry Corps (RCIC) was no exception.

The RCIC was not only slow to embrace Allard's vision, they also actively tried to ignore it. The Infantry Board established to review doctrine noted in December 1965 that "currently, it would appear that the shifting fortunes of political or service decisions demand the production of new organizations and establishments."[76] The Board recognized that the infantry battalion establishments would inevitably be influenced by non-operational factors such as financial considerations in concert with restrictions on manpower and equipment. Nevertheless, the Board considered it prudent to design a fixed infantry battalion establishment which would be "capable by tailoring, to suit the operational and training roles assigned to infantry, regular or militia, at home or abroad, in peace or war, mechanized, wheeled, air or foot mobile."[77] This "all singing, all dancing" organization also served the Board's other motives. The true intentions were soon obvious. The Board's single objective was to create the "ultimate in the infantry contribution to the mechanized battle in Northwest Europe."[78] Such a geocentric and force-specific limitation did not speak well for the airborne. In addition the Board 's vision also failed to reflect any political guidance or for that matter, the Army Commander's publicly declared direction.

The Board's presentation at the Infantry Conference in Camp Borden that same month underlined their true focus. The meeting quickly demonstrated the Infantry Board's ingrained resistance to the proposed unique airborne organization. The presentation was based solely on the postulated northwest European battle. Furthermore, it visualized a role almost exclusively for the mechanized all-arms battle team. The proposal put forward for approval was based on the principle of a one establishment multi-capable infantry battalion. The Infantry Board argued that the "battalion must be capable of standing on its own feet, unreinforced and make a worthwhile contribution to the destruction of the enemy through a range of combat intensity, from highly sophisticated USSR mechanized force in being, to the unobtrusive unsophisticated, yet deadly peasant band armed with homemade weapons."[79]

The intent, however, was unmistakably centred on the high-intensity battle in Europe. Despite the political direction and Lieutenant-General Allard's focus on the full spectrum of conflict, the RCIC clung to the establishment which had been their bread and butter since the early fifties, namely the mechanized army tailored for NATO. In fact, the throw-away mention of "unobtrusive unsophisticated, yet deadly peasant band armed with homemade weapons" contained in their fixed battalion capability statement was the only reference made to brush-fire conflicts. The remainder of the more than100 pages of text was devoted exclusively to high-intensity warfare.[80]

The Infantry Board tried to further deflect the momentum gathering for the politically necessary establishment of a specially designed force for rapid deployment to brush-fire conflicts. To provide for the flexibility and mobility demanded by the *1964 White Paper*, the Board proposed that the infantry battalions of the RCR, PPCLI, and R22eR, which were authorized a parachute element, would add one sergeant and one corporal parachute rigger to the administration platoon of the respective support companies. Evidently, the Board still clung to the Defence of Canada Force model of airborne capability. The incumbent Director of Infantry, Colonel E.M.K. MacGregor, admitted that the employment of airborne troops in Canada had had a hard time maintaining credibility because they could barely justify the use of 250 parachutists in the battalion parachute companies much less the proposed 900 of a new airborne unit.[81] Significantly, the Infantry Board was adamant that the designated battalion for the government's intended Special Service Force Brigade, which would be tasked as the UN stand-by battalion, would not be a special airborne organization.[82]

The myopic approach of the Infantry Board sparked rancorous internal debate. The commandant of the Royal Canadian School of Infantry wrote, "the aim of producing a so-called 'ultimate battalion' should be consistent with current and proposed defence policy."[83] He challenged whether the proposed establishment met the concepts as outlined by the MND, specifically the existence of two highly mobile brigades to fight brush-fire wars and one parachute battalion of one thousand personnel for immediate use anywhere in the world. The Infantry School Commandant reproached the Infantry Board and commented that any establishment which tries to be as many things as were outlined in the capability statement of the fixed infantry battalion, is "unfortunately doomed to failure." He further chided the Board to "avoid the narrowing of our perspective to the three battalions in Europe, or only 25% of our 'party'."[84]

With such disharmonious and divergent concepts concerning the organization of the new Force Mobile Command rampant throughout the senior military chain of command there was a high potential for emasculating the newly conceived airborne organization. After all, the ultimate administrators of such an organization, the Infantry Corps itself, held an unfavourable view of the utility of such a force. However, a viable airborne capability was in line with the aim of the MND, the very recalcitrant and mulish Paul Hellyer. Furthermore, an airborne unit was also close to the heart of Lieutenant-General Allard, the Commander of the Army, whose dedicated and loyal hand-picked staff enforced Army compliance. Douglas Bland, a respected Canadian defence policy analyst and scholar, remarked that Allard's selected staff officers "were aware of the latest systems of decision making and management and used their skills and his [Allard] command personality to bulldoze the headquarters into accepting the new unified structure and strategy."[85] Allard's subsequent appointment as Chief of the Defence Staff, from 1966 to 1969, ensured his aspirations were fully carried forth.

Colonel D.B. McGibbon a senior staff officer at NDHQ at the time dubbed this era the beginning of the "New Army." He maintained that prior to Hellyer and his genre of commanders, there was an ethic of listening to the staff and creating an environment conducive to critical thought. In McGibbon's view, supported by many others, healthy debate had given way to a mind-set of inflexible top down direction. McGibbon explained, "those who argued were out and those who quickly fell in line prospered."[86]

In spite of the rancour associated with the new strategic direction, it is important to note that the creative vision was not quite as innovative and freshly Canadian as the Defence Minister and Commander of the Army implied. Allard's assertion, before the Parliamentary Committee on Defence in 1966 that "in our thinking, we are ahead of the United States,"[87] was not entirely accurate. The concepts of flexibility of response, as well as the requirement for strategic and tactical mobility, had long been percolating to the south.

As early as 1950, American General Omar Bradley, in his capacity as Chairman of the Joint Chiefs of Staff, had warned the US Senate Appropriations Committee that "it is now evident that we must have an even greater flexibility of military power in the United States itself not only for our own protection, but also to give us a ready, highly mobile standing force which we can bring to bear at any threatened point in the minimum time."[88] Although directed largely at the need to rebuild the American Army after its rapid demobilization after the Second World War, the foundation of strategic thought was present. Six years later, General Maxwell Taylor, in the same capacity, cautioned that "our program must provide for mobile ready forces prepared for rapid movement...for use to resist local aggression in an unexpected quarter."[89] He insisted that a strategy of "flexible response" was needed to provide a capability to react across the entire spectrum of possible challenge, for coping with anything from general atomic war to infiltrations.[90]

The evolution of American thinking in the late fifties and early sixties was also recorded by Robert McNamara, the Secretary of State for Defence. He explained that by 1961, conclusions were reached "that improvements to organization, manning, equipment, training, mobility, and most especially, the balance among all elements of the forces" were required.[91] As a result, emphasis was placed on the amelioration of American Special Forces, the Marine Corps, as well as a quantum increase in airlift capability. The emphasis on innovation was such that McNamara pressed his army planners to take a "bold new look at land warfare mobility" which eventually ushered in the era of airmobility (widespread use of helicopters).[92] By 1962, McNamara had created "Strike Command," a joint Army-Air Force organization which combined the Army's two airborne divisions with Tactical Air Command and Military Airlift Command.[93] As a result, while the Canadian military establishment contemplated their new design, the Americans were already living it, needless to say, on a much larger scale.

The transition of American thought did not go unnoticed in Canada especially among airborne advocates. Much like the drive to form the 1st Canadian Parachute Battalion during the Second World War, and the desire to use the Canadian Joint Air Training Centre in the postwar years as a centre of excellence for airborne/air-transported research and development, the fresh push in the late sixties for mobile forces with strategic reach, based on a Special Force Brigade concept with a strong airborne element, was heavily influenced by the perpetual Canadian desire to be a member of the club and to associate with and gain access to doctrine and equipment which the major "club members" could provide. In short, the move to flexible, mobile, rapid reaction forces was by no stretch of the imagination a Canadian invention. It was not lost on the military and political leadership that to stay in the game, one must remain a player.

Once again, this desire to remain in the club provided a lifeline for the country's often hard-pressed paratroopers and they grasped at it eagerly. For the first quarter century of existence, Canadian airborne forces were peripheral to the main effort. To most in the military institution they represented nothing more than an extravagant diversion of resources from the Army's main focus. For most of the period their survival was directly related to their ability to provide a conduit to allied doctrine and influence. But for politicians, airborne forces remained an inexpensive political expedient.

It was in the latter role that the survival of Canada's paratroopers largely rested. They were the guardians of the North. This neatly placated an anxious and often overbearing ally to the south, and masked the irresolute Canadian response to formal commitments under the joint defence agreements. The overwhelming conviction that no direct risk to Canadian territory existed further increased the political utility of parachute troops. But with no threat, there was little reason for politicians or senior military commanders to keep Canadian airborne forces as a strong, viable organization.

Paradoxically, arguments about the defence of the North not only ensured the airborne's survival, as ethereal as it was, but also perpetuated their continued marginalization. The lack of a credible and pervasive role consistently supported by the military and political chain of command assured a tenuous existence for Canada's parachute troops. They became dependent on personalities in positions of influence and political expedients of the day. Paratroopers were seen as an anomaly in an army obsessed with mechanized forces and rooted to a scenario centred on a high-intensity battlefield in Europe. They were the "bastard sons," conceived in passion and with the best of intentions during the heady days of World War II; however, they were never fully accepted by the entire family. As a result, fair weather support was the best they could hope for. Condemnation and contempt were always nearby. During periods of calm, the extended family could be friendly and tolerant. But in a storm friends would be few, and the airborne soldiers were cast adrift to find assistance wherever they could.

Yet there seemed a chance to put it all on a firm footing. By 1965, the continual ebb and flow of fortunes showed a significant change. The affluence of the nation's airborne forces was on the rise. The new strategic concepts espoused by Hellyer and Allard gave the country's paratroopers real and renewed hope. Propelled by the commander of the Army, and soon to be CDS, a new, viable airborne unit was conceived. To some it seemed to fit comfortably with the Liberal government's strategic thinking. Such a new force could transform how the Canadian military establishment and public would view parachute troops. It was the beginning of a great new adventure. It remained to be seen if true viability could be sustained for the airborne.

Notes for Chapter Four

1. *Debates,* 17 February 1966, 1418.

2. David Bercuson, *Significant Incident. Canada's Army, the Airborne, and the Murder in Somalia* (Toronto: McClelland & Stewart, 1997), 50.

3. Major-General (retired) R.I. Stewart candidly wrote, "I do not believe the government nor the military leadership took the threat seriously and the loose structure of the MSF reflects this fact." Letter to author, 1 July 1998.

4. *Debates,* 17 June 1955, 4925. The MND also stated that "Anyone who has any knowledge of the terrain of the outlying parts of this country will realize that such an attempt would be worthless and useless and is not likely to be part of any aggressive plans which may be launched against Canada." The continuing belief was that "any attack on Canada will be in essence part of an attack on the United States." Ibid., 4925. See also *Canada's Defence Programme* 1949-50; Sutherland, 271; and A. Brewin, *Stand on Guard. The Search for a Canadian Defence Policy* (Toronto: McClelland & Stewart, 1965), 53-54.

5. *DND Reports* 1946-1953 and *Canada's Defence Program,* 1949-1957. Protection was never an issue. In later years the Parliamentary Special Committee on Defence noted the nation's irrefutable safety net. The Committee's report admitted, "the inviolability of Canadian territory is a sine qua non condition of the defence of the United States." *Special Committee on Defence. Proceedings*, 17 December 1963, 808.

6. Ibid.

7. Eyre, 295.

8. An excellent example of the period was a DMO & P assessment paper entitled, "Defence Against Enemy Lodgements," 8 July 1954. DHist, File 112.3M2.009 (D264). This report encapsulated the raging debate and dissent which engulfed the issue of enemy lodgements. The document noted that there was no agreement on the likelihood of airborne operations against Canadian territory. It admitted that the majority (Joint Intelligence Committee) view was that the enemy's purpose for attacking the continent could be "better served by air attack than by lodgement operations." It noted that Canadian military intelligence viewed lodgements as "possible but not probable." The conclusion reached in the paper was that "common sense demands that planning, so far as is practicable should cater for the worst case." It also asserted that "considering the extent of the territory to be defended, the inaccessibility of much of it, and the speed with which counter-attacks to be effective must be launched, the regular forces assigned to home defence must be airborne." The report went so far as to determine that the "three existing battalion-groups are the minimum number required." The problem with these unsigned reports is the fact that one is unable to determine any partisan link with the final conclusions. For instance Major Stan Waters, a former FSSF and 1st Cdn Para Bn veteran, and later Honorary Colonel of the Canadian Airborne Regiment, was a prolific writer during his tenure as a staff officer in the Active Brigade Headquarters. Not surprisingly, he championed the cause of airborne training, even at the cost of the conventional program. His suggestions, much like those of the above report, were simply ignored. See DHist, File 112.3M2 (D400).

9. Letter, Major-General Chris Vokes to the Director General of Plans and Operations, 6 June 1958. DHist, File 112.3M2.009 (D264).

10. Ibid. The DMI threat assessment noted, "Airborne or parachute attacks on Canadian targets are likely to be limited to company or platoon size if they are carried out at all." "Defence Against Enemy Lodgements. Summary of Discussions held at HQ Western Command, 15-17 Oct 1958," 27 October 1958. DHist, File 112.3M2.009 (D264), 1.

11. "Threat of Enemy Lodgements," 27 October 1958. DHist, File 112.3M2.009 (D264).

12. "Canada—United States Emergency Defence Plan" (MCC 300/11), 4 September 1959. DHist, File 112.012 (D1).

13. Right Honourable John G. Diefenbaker, Prime Minister of Canada, Text of Speech for Delivery on "The Nation's Business" Series of the CBC Television Network, 9 March 1959. The PM stated, "A revolution in technology has taken place in the last two years beginning with the launching of the sputnik, the Ballistic Missile with a range of some 5,000 miles, the moon satellites, and the expanding threat of

missiles with nuclear heads— frightening in their awfulness. Canadians as a whole realize that, for the first time in history, this country will be one of the first to be attacked if war begins."

14. CAFM—Research Paper, Part 1, 1.D, Document 1—"The Mobile Striking Force and the Defence of Canada Force," 2. This period is commonly referred to as the era of "Jump Companies;" and *Special Committee on Defence, Minutes of Proceedings and Evidence*, 11 July 1963, 142.

15. *Debates,* 21 May 1954, 4961; and L.B. Pearson, "Canada's Northern Horizon," *Foreign Affairs,* Vol 31, No. 4, July 1953, 584. Pearson explained, "The problem for Canada is to maintain a balance in committing her limited manpower and defense resources; to weigh carefully the alternative risks of the overrunning of Western Europe by a potential enemy, and the risks of attack by the polar route; and to formulate plans and priorities accordingly."

16. "Defence Against Enemy Lodgements. Summary of Discussions held at HQ Western Command, 15-17 Oct 1958," 27 October 1958, 8. DHist, File 112.3M2.009 (D264). The absence of mention is often more telling than an actual remark in passing. It is interesting to note that in the DND report "Defence Achievements 1957-1960," there is not a single reference in the twelve-page document to airborne capability or forces, the MSF or DCF, or parachutists. Conversely, NATO forces and the organization of a UN 'Stand-By' force were prominent. DHist, File 112.012 (D1).

17. Ibid., 2. The lack of concern was explained by the MND two years later. He noted, "there has not been quite the same emphasis placed on parachute training as there previously was, owing to the great difficulty in carrying out parachute operations in force in the arctic, and also owing to the fact that the arctic is gradually being opened up with respect to aircraft, and where there are more air fields than there were." *Special Committee on Defence Expenditures, Minutes of Proceedings and Evidence,* 7 July 1960, 450-451.

18. Hillmer and Granatstein, *Empire to Umpire,* 244-245.

19. *Statement by the Honourable Paul T. Hellyer, MND, to the Special Committee on Defence,* June 27, 1963, 1. See also Canada, *Territorial Defence,* 5-7; Macdonald, 271-272.

20. *Statement by the Honourable Paul T. Hellyer,* June 27, 1963, 1.

21. Canada, *Special Committee on Defence—Minutes of Proceedings and Evidence,* 22 October 1963 (Ottawa: Queen's Printer, 1963), 503. Field Marshal Montgomery told the California Institute of Technology that "trying to get a secure defence against air attack is rather like trying to keep the tide back on the seashore with a picket fence." *Debates,* 17 June 1955, 4926.

22. *Special Committee on Defence—Minutes of Proceedings and Evidence,* 22 October 1963, 503 & 507. Foulkes also wrote, "I submit that there is no direct defence for Canada no matter how much we are prepared to spend." Foulkes, 9.

23. R.J. Sutherland, Chairman, *Report of the Ad Hoc Committee on Defence Policy,* 30 September 1963, 67 (held at DHist). Sutherland was Chief of Operational Research at the Defence Research Establishment.

24. Ibid., 83.

25. L.P. Bloomfield, "The Arctic: Last Unmanaged Frontier," *Foreign Affairs,* Vol 60, Fall 1981, 92; Brewin, 76; and *Special Committee on Defence—Minutes of Proceedings and Evidence,* 17 October 1963, 439 and 22 October 1963, 504.

26. Kenneth Eyre noted, "The Navy gradually stopped its northern summer cruises. Army exercises ceased. The radio system and the Alaska Highway were turned over to civil departments of government. The Canadian Rangers were left to wither on the vine. Aerial surveillance flights were curtailed." Eyre, 296.

27. Gray, *Canadian Defence Priority,* 185.

28. CAFM—Research Paper, Part 1, 1.D, Document 1—"The Mobile Striking Force and the Defence of Canada Force," 2.

29. Waters was also the Colonel of the Regiment, the Canadian Airborne Regiment, 1971-1976. S.C. Waters, "Former Colonel of the Regiment," *Fragments of 1 Airborne Battery (RCA),* private regimental souvenir publication, 27.

30. J.M.R. Gaudreau, letter to author, 18 September 1998. The shortage of aircraft was mentioned by all those interviewed who had MSF/DCF experience.

31. Interview with Brigadier-General Walter Holmes, 17 July 1997.

32. Major-General R.I Stewart, letter to author, 1 July 1998. Stewart was a Platoon Commander in a DCF "Jump Company." Lieutenant-General Kent Foster is the only individual interviewed who actually contends that the parachute companies represented a "good capability." He agreed with the others that aircraft shortages were a problem and that the greatest benefit of the MSF/DCF was the fact the organizations allowed the skill and spirit of military parachuting to be kept alive. Interview with author 6 June 1998.

33. Interview with Holmes.

34. Interviews with Colonel Mike Barr and Lieutenant-Colonel Swan. Major-General Dan Loomis and Lieutenant-Colonel Swan both asserted that very little status was attached to belonging to the "Jump Companies" because their existence was not much differentiated from the other companies within a battalion. The only distinction was the maroon beret and the jump allowance of $30.00 per month which represented a substantial pay boost. (Interviews with author, 11 December 1997 and 16 August 1996 respectively). The monetary benefit was also seen as a factor contributing to the continuing marginalization of a sound operational airborne capability. Chief Warrant Officer B.C. Robinson recalled that the parachute company was often used as a "compassionate posting" for those with financial difficulties. (Interview with author 21 September 1998). Additionally, Lieutenant-Colonel Swan observed that the monetary bonus also resulted in a disproportionate number of officers and Senior NCOs filling the officially allocated jump billets. The net result was that motives other than optimal operational effectiveness were used to man the organization.

35. See endnotes 30-35, this chapter.

36. CJATC *Annual Historical Report*, Appendix D, AB School, 1955-1961, DHist; *Special Committee on Defence. Minutes of Proceedings and Evidence*, 7 July 1960, 450; David Charters, "Five Lost Years: The Mobile Striking Force 1946-1951," *CDQ,* Vol 7, No. 4, Spring 1978, 46; Low, 47; and Pugh, 31.

37. The MND stated that the Army had four primary roles. In priority, he stated: (1) commitment of a brigade group in Europe and the maintenance of sufficiently trained groups in Canada in order to rotate that brigade; (2) the maintenance of a stand-by force on call to meet any further United Nations request; (3) the maintenance of a force capable of taking action against any possible commando-type raid in the Arctic or elsewhere in Canada; and (4) survival operations [nuclear war scenario]. *Debates,* 3 August 1960, 7525-26. The emphasis on NATO was such that the MND and the CDS would later testify to the Special Committee on Defence that "to bring the balance of the division up to effective strength and to provide the initial reinforcements for the brigade in Germany, today's [1963] emergency plan calls for the withdrawal of a number of troops from the defence of Canada brigade." As a result, the militia was seen as fulfilling the role, as a minimum, of shadowing any raiding force which may be launched against national territory. *Special Committee on Defence. Minutes of Proceedings and Evidence,* 11 July 1963, 144. Even under the new plan for the Army, it was clearly written that "4 CIBG remains as a priority claim on our resources." "Force Structure—Mobile Command Guidelines." DHist, File 112.11.003 (D3)—Box 1.

38. Lester B. Pearson, "Force for U.N.," *Foreign Affairs,* Vol 35, No. 3, April 1957, 401.

39. *Debates,* 18 July 1958, 2363; *Special Committee on Defence. Minutes of Proceedings and Evidence,* 7 July 1960, 453, 11 July 1963, 147 and 22 October 1963, 505. A DND report noted that "during 1958 the government decided to maintain a stand-by battalion fully trained and prepared to be sent abroad in an emergency. The battalion designated is placed on constant stand-by alert and is prepared, if necessary, to leave this country at a moment's notice." "Defence Achievements 1957-1960." DHist, File 112.012 (D1). See also Lieutenant-Colonel R.B. Tacaberry, "Keeping the Peace," *behind the headlines,* Vol 26, No. 1, September 1966, 7.

40. *Special Committee on Defence. Minutes of Proceedings and Evidence*, 22 October 1963, 507; and *Debates,* 8 May 1964, 3076. He recommended the defence effort be focussed on two major activities. The first, as already stated, and the second "antisubmarine operations in the Atlantic-Pacific and perhaps in the Arctic."

41. *Special Committee on Defence. Minutes of Proceedings and Evidence*, 17 October 1963, 439; and *Debates,* 29 October 1963, 4141 and 8 May 1964, 3076. Simonds argued that in terms of the coun-

try's size and financial burdens, this type of role would be "our most useful role within the alliance." The concern for brush-fire wars was rooted in the fear of nuclear Armageddon. A special report noted, "The nuclear stalemate as well as the awesome potential of nuclear war have directed attention to the increasing need to deal effectively with local disturbances which hold the danger of escalating into major conflicts. The effectiveness of UN quasi-military operations to contain local brush-fire wars has won substantial support to the idea of an international force, a fact demonstrated to the extent of voluntary contributions to the UN forces in the Middle East and the Congo." *Special Studies prepared for the Special Committee of the House of Commons on Matters Relating to Defence,* Supplement 1964/65, 84.

42. *Debates,* 3 October 1963, 3169.

43. Ibid., 3169. Not surprisingly no mention was made of either the Arctic or enemy lodgements. By this time the idea of a land threat had been almost totally dismissed. Nuclear holocaust as a result of an ICBM attack was now the primary concern. This was evident in the complaint of the GOC Eastern Command, Major-General George Kitching. He protested that "national survival [assistance to the public in the wake of a nuclear strike] has completely obscured other tasks." DHist, File 112.012 (D1). See also *Special Committee on Defence. Minutes of Proceedings and Evidence,* 7 July 1960, 446 and 449.

44. Jean V. Allard, *The Memoirs of General Jean V. Allard* (Vancouver: The University of British Columbia Press, 1988), 234. The *1964 White Paper* reaffirmed, "It is, for the foreseeable future, impossible to conceive of any significant external threat to Canada which is not also a threat to North America as a whole....The major threat to North America at this time is from the air..." Canada, *White Paper on Defence* (Ottawa: DND, March 1964), 13-14. Andrew Brewin, a member of the Special Committee on Defence, later questioned in his book whether Canada really opted for a new role or continued an uneasy compromise between the new and the old. A. Brewin, *Stand On Guard. The Search for a Canadian Defence Policy,* 109.

45. Paul Hellyer, the MND, was quoted as stating "We must greatly increase defence spending or reorganize. The decision was to reorganize." Cited in Douglas Bland, *The Administration of Defence Policy in Canada, 1947 to 1985* (Kingston: Ronald P. Frye & Company, 1987), 33. The proposal for the Army reorganization also stated that, "it is appreciated that any re-organization must be designed to reduce the present high running costs (pers, ops, and maintenance) of the Armed Forces. It is noted that these costs have increased from 45% of the defence budget in 1953 to 77.6% in 1963." "Proposed Reorganization of the Army Field Force," 18 March 1965. NAC, RG 24, Acc 83-84/165, Box 34, File 2001-1/1. One witness before the Parliamentary Defence Committee was sceptical of the new plan. Air Vice-Marshal M.M. Hendrick confirmed that his interpretation of the *White Paper* indicated "we were going to do all the things we had been doing before, and create a mobile force, which is a brand new one, in addition to which we were going to save $100 million and fire 10,000 people, and I thought it was a pretty wonderful trick." He also admitted, "That is why I was baffled." *Special Committee on Defence. Minutes of Proceedings and Evidence,* 21 February 1967, 1474. The *1964 White Paper* notes that the employment of Canadian mobile forces on NATO flanks vice the present commitment to maintain a Brigade Group on the central European front would be a preferred course of action. It states that increased air transport will make it possible to move units to the European flanks, if and when required, from bases in Canada and the United States. It further explains that this would be "more economical than stationing mobile reserves in Europe." This was a precursor of things to come. *White Paper,* 21-22.

46. Paul Hellyer, *Damn the Torpedoes. My Fight to Unify Canada's Armed Forces* (Toronto: McClelland & Stewart Ltd., 1990), 34. Hellyer ordered a halt to all procurement plans as soon as he took office. Bland, *Administration of Defence Policy,* 35.

47. Ibid., 33-34. Hellyer's *White Paper* was heralded as "the most forward-thinking defence document produced by any government for the past decade, and probably since world war II" in some circles, but attacked in others. Former MND, Douglas Harkness, observed that the first fifteen pages of the *White Paper* were a simple restatement of basic defence facts. He further added that the document drew no new conclusion and provided no new strategic objectives. Editorial, *Canadian Aviation,* Vol 37, No. 5, May 1964, 15; and *Debates,* 11 May 1964, 3148. Hellyer's greatest goal was the unification of the Forces under a single chain of command. By 1968 the position of a single Chief of the Defence Staff

was in place and unification had been achieved. However, this was only accomplished after great internal struggle and turmoil.

48. *Special Committee on Defence. Minutes of Proceedings and Evidence*, 19 May 1964, 12.
49. Hellyer, 42-43.
50. "Defence," *Time,* Vol 83, No. 14, 3 April 1964, 11-12. R.B. Sutherland's special committee noted that "with comparatively minor exceptions, the purpose of Canadian defence programs and activities is to support an alliance policy. In terms of Canadian national interests, the rationale of Canadian defence is to maintain influence with our allies." *Report of the Ad Hoc Committee on Defence Policy,* 30 September 1963, 3.
51. *Debates,* 17 February 1966, 1417. The six functional commands were Mobile Command, Maritime Command, Air Defence Command, Air Transport Command, Material Command and Training Command. See also *Special Committee on Defence. Minutes of Proceedings and Evidence*, 9 June 1966, 149.
52. "Multi-Purpose Force Doctrine Paper," 12 February 1966. NAC, RG 24, Vol 23491, File 1901-2, Part 1. See also Allard, 220, 247 & 254.
53. *Special Committee on Defence. Minutes of Proceedings and Evidence*, 21 June 1966, 274-277. See also Dan Loomis, *Not Much Glory* (Toronto: Deneau Publishers, 1984), 48-56.
54. "Appreciation and Proposed Options for the Structure of the Canadian Army Field Force 1965-1970 Period," no date. DHist, File 112.11.003 (D3)—Box 3.
55. "Appreciation and Proposed Options for the Structure of the Canadian Army Field Force 1965-1970 Period," 5 April 1965, 2. DHist, File 112.11.003 (D3)—Box 3.
56. "FMC—Force Structure Guidelines." DHist, File 112.11.003 (D3)—Box 1; and "The Shape of Canadian Forces 1964-1974," *External Affairs,* Vol 16, No. 4, April 1964, 198. The breakdown of FMC was given as follows: (1) 4 CIBG—remains as a priority claim on our resources; (2) Training & Rotation Back-Up for 4 CIBG—retain one mechanized brigade group in Eastern Canada similar to 4 CIBG but modified in support elements; (3) headquarters—produce light field HQ from HQ Mobile Command Resources as when required; (4) support troops—develop and organize on a divisional basis balanced to support both light and heavy forces; (5) SSF—organize as a 'ready force' of battalion group size with strong airborne capability; (6) light forces—Canada (the remainder)—Organize remainder of forces in Canada as lightly equipped forces for employment in: the Defence of Canada, UN Operations and ACE Mobile Force.
57. *Special Committee on Defence. Minutes of Proceedings and Evidence*, 21 June 1966, 282 & 294. See also *Debates,* 17 February 1966, 1418. Sutherland's committee also noted that lightly equipped forces were a potentially valuable means of demonstrating political commitment. Furthermore, they observed that there were considerable areas of NATO Europe in which, owing to the nature of terrain, relatively lightly equipped forces were appropriate. *Report of the Ad Hoc Committee on Defence Policy,* 30 September 1963, 140. An DGT & O appreciation noted that "the force must be designed so it can be moved quickly from Canada to any likely spot in the world. It is desirable that 50 percent of the force should be able to reach the objective area within 48 hours, the remainder within seven days." "Mobile Force," 16 December 1965. CAFM, File AB. CAR History (1966) Definition: Requirement SSB/AB Unit (Canadian Airborne Regiment Working Papers).
58. "Special Parachute Force is Planned," *The Gazette,* 7 December 1966, 1. Anderson was appointed Commander FMC upon Allard's promotion to CDS in 1966.
59. "Proposed Reorganization of the Army Field Force," 18 March 1965. NAC, RG 24, Acc 83-84/165, Box 34, File 2001-1/1, 3. The entrenched view at this time was that the "only operational requirement for the parachutist capability is that reflected in MSC 100/16 relating to the Defence of Canada—US Region." Ibid., 3. See also "Special Service Force (SSF)—Organization and Employment," 30 November 1964, 3. DHist, File 171.009 (D299). This document, also signed off by the VCDS, noted that despite the establishment of the SSF, "it is not intended to change the responsibility of parachute training or the maintenance of the parachute force from those battalions which presently have the responsibility. Ibid., 3.

60. "Infantry Parachutist Battalions in the SSF," 2 February 1965; "Organization Canadian Army (Regular)—Infantry Battalions—Parachutists," 16 February 1965. DHist, File 327.009 (D432); and "Appreciation and Proposed Options for the Structure of the Canadian Army Field Force 1965-70 Period," 5 April 1965, 7.

61. *Debates,* 12 May 1966, 19, 7 December 1966, 10823 and 30 January 1967, 12417. See also Paul Hellyer, MND, *Address on the Canadian Forces Reorganization Act,* 7 December 1966, 19. At this point the name and actual composition of the airborne organization had not been determined.

62. Allard, 237-238. Lieutenant-General Allard also explained how the parachute regiment would be used to secure an airfield to allow heavier follow-on forces to airland. He asserted that "There was never any question between 1965-1969 that this regiment could only go into action by being parachuted. The most likely situation would be an intervention in hostile territory where, if landing was impossible, the regiment could be parachuted in. The men would then make use of the shelter of mountains, reefs and lakes to obstruct the enemy while awaiting the arrival of the forces who would undertake the major tasks." Ibid., 237; and *Special Committee on Defence. Minutes of Proceedings and Evidence,* 21 June 1966, 295.

63. *Special Committee on Defence. Minutes of Proceedings and Evidence,* 21 June 1966, 298.

64. "The Requirement for Parachutists in the Canadian Army," 14 February 1966, 2. CAFM, File AB. CAR History (1966) Definition: Requirement SSB/AB Unit (Canadian Airborne Regiment Working Papers). It was also considered unwise from a morale, teamwork and esprit point of view to create two levels of pay in such a small organization. This conclusion was identical to that of the Adjutant-General's postwar appreciation in 1946. See Chapter Three, endnote 74.

65. Ibid., 2.

66. Ibid., 2. Allard testified in front of the Parliamentary Committee of Defence that the rotation of units, for an overseas NATO tour of duty, shattered the already impotent airborne capability. He noted that during these rotations, for a period of over a year and a half at a time, there was only one effective unit that could muster an operational parachute company, if in fact it was up to strength. *Special Committee on Defence. Minutes of Proceedings and Evidence,* 21 June 1966, 298. By Allard's own admission he had "lots of experience in training parachutists" and was obviously a staunch proponent of airborne forces.

67. Major-General J.M.R. Gaudreau, letter to author, 18 September 1998. Gaudreau also wrote that Allard "considered himself to be the founding father of the Canadian Airborne Regiment." Allard was parachute qualified, having taken his training in the postwar period at the rank of brigadier. The theme that Allard wanted an organization that provided a test for the men was reinforced by Colonel Michael Houghton. He recounted a meeting between his father and Allard, at which time the FMC Commander spoke of developing an airborne unit which provided adventure and a challenge for the men, as well as a vehicle to develop a highly spirited unit. Interview with author 5 November 1998.

68. *Special Committee on Defence. Minutes of Proceedings and Evidence,* 21 June 1966, 298-299.

69. Ibid., 298.

70. Canada, *Rationale For Canadian Defence Forces* (Ottawa: DND, 14 May 1968), 29. DHist, File 90/452.

71. Hellyer, *Address on the Canadian Forces Reorganization Act,* 7 December 1966, 6.

72. "Appreciation and Proposed Options for the Structure of the Canadian Army Field Force 1965-1970 Period," no date. DHist, File 112.11.003 (D3)—Box 3. A defence policy review several years later reiterated the reality of the American shadow. The VCDS, Lieutenant-General F.R. Sharp observed that "no feat of Canadian policy or diplomacy can withdraw Canada from the North American continent or disentangle Canada's security interests from those of the United States." "Defence Policy Review," 6 December 1968. DHist, File 112.11.003 (D3)—Box 2. R.B. Sutherland's special committee recognized this verity years earlier. They recommended that for political reasons the defence of Canada be separated from the defence of North America, specifically that the preservation of Canadian sovereignty in "the great unoccupied expanses of the Arctic must be an important concern of Canadian policy." As a result, they recommended the specific capabilities for all three services. For the Army they concluded a

minimum of an airtransportable brigade group including a parachute element. *Report of the Ad Hoc Committee on Defence Policy,* 30 September 1963, 80.

73. "Defence Policy Review," 28 June 1968. DHist, File 112.11.003 (D3)—Box 1. This statement was strongly influenced by the recent US experience in controlling disturbances in some of their big cities.

74. N.M. Tichy, and M.A. Devanna, *The Transformational Leader* (New York: John Wiley and Sons, 1986), 77.

75. Ibid., 81.

76. "The Infantry Battalion Establishment," 10 December 1965, 1. NAC, RG 24, Vol 23604, File /REC/1920-1, Part 1.

77. Ibid., 2.

78. Ibid., 2.

79. "The Infantry Board Infantry Battalion Establishment Design Philosophy—Presentation to the Infantry Conference 1965 Camp Borden" 13-17 December 1965. NAC, RG 24, Vol 23604, File /REC/1920-1, Part 1.

80. Ibid.

81. CAFM, audio cassette tape, Floyd Low interview with Brigadier-General MacGregor, January 1978.

82. "An Infantry Battalion, RCIC, Special Service Force—Provisional Establishment (war & peace)," April 1965. NAC, RG 24, Vol 23604, File 1920-1, Part 1.

83. "The Infantry Battalion Relation to Current Thinking," 11 March 1966. NAC, RG 24, Vol 23604, File 1920-1, Part 1.

84. Ibid.

85. Douglas Bland, *Chiefs of Defence. Government and the Unified Command of the Canadian Armed Forces* (Toronto: Canadian Institute of Strategic Studies, 1995), 230. The resistance to Allard's new idea was also noted in David Bercuson's *Significant Incident,* 171. Bercuson wrote that Allard's idea was not well thought out and that the Airborne Regiment was operationally obsolete from the day it was formed. Allard, 247-254.

86. Interview with author 24 November 1998. Bland labelled this period as the start of the "Management Era." He dubbed the earlier period the "Command Era." See Bland, *The Administration of Defence Policy,* 11.

87. *Special Committee on Defence. Minutes of Proceedings and Evidence,* 21 June 1966, 296.

88. William W. Kaufman, *Planning Conventional Forces 1950-80* (Washington D.C.: The Brookings Institution, 1984), 3.

89. Maxwell D. Taylor, *The Uncertain Trumpet* (New York: Harper & Brothers, 1959), 191.

90. Ibid., 6. The concept of a Spectrum of War [the later Canadian version was titled Spectrum of Conflict] was actually entrenched in American doctrine by 1962. See Department of the Army Field Manual *FM 100-5, Field Regulations Operations,* February 1962, 4-5. The American focus on strategic mobility and airborne forces is not hard to understand. Historians and political scientists have observed that an astonishing number of young majors and colonels who served in the Airborne divisions of the Second World War had by the 1950s and 1960s risen to general officer rank and collectively ran the US Army. These leaders were attributed with setting both the tone and style. The presence of former commanders of the 82nd and 101st Airborne Divisions, specifically Matthew Ridgeway, Maxwell Taylor (both chairmen of the Joint Chiefs of Staff during this period) and James Gavin, in the senior echelons of command, further boosted American airborne interests. Ward Just, *Military Men* (New York: Knopf, 1970), 132-134; and Walter Millis, *Arms and Men: a Study of American Military History* (New York: New American Library, 1956), 317-319. The American acceptance of airborne forces, although slow in coming, was complete. Airborne forces since the Second World War have formed the nucleus of the American global rapid reaction capability. It has long been realized that "the deployment of the 82nd Airborne Division during an international crisis transcends the simple act of deploying a combat unit. It takes on a global significance that symbolizes the final US political solution being applied, once

efforts have failed...and has come to embody national will and commitment." See Tom Clancy, *Airborne*, 230-231; and V.M. Rosello, "The Airborne is not Obsolete," *Army,* Vol 42, No. 9, September 1992, 42.

91. Robert S. McNamara, *The Essence of Security* (New York: Harper & Row Publishers, Inc., 1968), 78-79 & 84.

92. Maurice A. Mallin, *Tanks, Fighters & Ships: US Conventional Force Planning Since World War II* (New York: Brassey's, 1990), 138.

93. A.R. Millet, and Peter Maslowski, *For the Common Defence* (New York: Free Press, 1984), 537-538; and Russel Weigley, *The History of the US Army* (Bloomington: Indiana University Press, 1984), 529.

CHAPTER FIVE

THE GREAT ADVENTURE
The Establishment of the Canadian Airborne Regiment, 1968-1970

Canada's military is planning the formation of a 1,200 man parachute special force which will be kept in a permanent state of combat readiness and available on a moment's notice for duty anywhere in the world.

Lieutenant-General W.A.B. Anderson, Commander FMC, 1966.[1]

In April 1968, despite the undercurrent of resistance within the Army, the "special parachute force" was created in the form of the Canadian Airborne Regiment. It was a protracted process that lasted more than two years and was only possible because of the sponsorship of powerful men such as Paul Hellyer the MND, and General Allard, the CDS. They had ensured that little public opposition materialized. The diligent work and loyalty of their hand-picked staffs also facilitated compliance. After all, as Lieutenant-General Anderson, the new Commander of Force Mobile Command explained, "such a force had been advocated by Canada for many years at the United Nations."[2] Nevertheless, the creation was not easy or smooth.

Although the internal military resistance to the new force was slowly stifled, it was never fully eradicated. Nonetheless, in synchronization with the current command philosophy, Army appreciations began to reflect a studied preference for the vision expressed by General Allard. It all started in early 1966, when the Mobile Striking Force/Defence of Canada Force model of decentralized parachute capability which had been touted for years began to be condemned by Allard's planning staff; who then quickly put a new option forward. What would the new force look like was the question. The answer came from FMC Headquarters which claimed that "quick reaction and the ability to undertake operations virtually anywhere in the world over a wide range of climatic, terrain and operational conditions are essential ingredients of the airborne force."[3] As a result, it concluded that for maximum effectiveness, efficiency and economy in a field force with a strictly limited manpower budget, the most suitable method of meeting the parachutist requirement was to form a permanent airborne regiment consisting of two small battalions with appropriate support arms.[4]

In the spring of 1966, Allard discussed the formation of the new Airborne Commando Regiment with Colonel D.H. Rochester who was well known for his interest in parachuting and skydiving.[5] A year later the CDS invited Rochester to Ottawa and gave him command of the new force. Surprisingly, and perhaps prophetically the foundation of the proposed unit was not solidly worked out despite the years of formulation and the numerous speeches professing the need and relevance of such a special airborne force. As a result, Rochester received a further year to refine the theory and bring Allard's "baby" to life.

For the enthused the prospects seemed unlimited. Colonel Rochester recalled that the "exciting thing about General Allard's concept was that this unit was to be radically different. Except for aircraft, it was to be self-contained with infantry, armour, artillery, engineers, signals and supporting administration."[6] Moreover, "all were to be volunteers and so well trained in their own arm or service that they could devote their time to specialist training."[7]

Rochester and his embryonic planning staff began to work out the details concerning organization, strength, training requirements and unit location. In spite of this enthusiasm outside interference was not long in re-emerging. NDHQ quickly directed that the name of the organization must be altered. The senior military leadership decided that the term "Commando," in the title, was too "aggressive."[8] It was then amended to simply the Canadian Airborne Regiment (Cdn AB Regt).

As well, during 1966 and 1967 further mutations occurred during the planning process. An imposed manpower reduction scaled the regiment down from the original 1,285 positions to 898.[9] As a result, the proposed armoured squadron was dropped. This turn of events was particularly welcomed by many in the Army. Colonel Mike Barr, then a Major and one of the first company commanders within the Canadian Airborne Regiment, recalled visiting the Director of Armour during the planning phase to consult on the type of tank that should be adopted for the proposed airborne armoured squadron. But Barr was unceremoniously "thrown out" of the office, along with his suggested "Sheridan" tank. The Director of Armour had little patience for new ideas such as Barr's. For him they represented competition for scarce resources. At the time he was preoccupied with his own struggles, trying to save the main battle tank of the Canadian Army. Besides, he told Barr, he was unequivocally against Black Berets dropping out of aircraft.[10]

Other latent hostilities against the new Canadian paratroopers boiled under the surface. Colonel Rochester found that in spite of Allard's support the process of trying to establish the new formation was really "hard slugging." The commander-designate felt that the principal problem in planning arose from the fact that very few people in or out of the military took the establishment of the Regiment seriously. It appeared that the general consensus was that this plan would never come to fruition particularly if one put enough obstacles in front of it while not rejecting the idea outright. Therefore, little assistance was forthcoming from various headquarters staffs since most felt it was a wasted effort.[11]

But Rochester believed otherwise. "General Allard," he recalled later, "was determined it would happen." He further added that Lieutenant-General Anderson, the FMC Commander, "was convinced." Rochester readily admitted, however, that "no one else seemed to be."[12] He also remembered being told as late as February 1968, "by a very senior officer, who was a friend of mine, that I might as well forget it because the Airborne Regiment would never be formed."[13] Such was the resistance.

Colonel Barr echoed those sentiments. He recalled that the World War II veterans still in the Canadian Armed Forces held onerous and overwhelmingly negative attitudes toward airborne forces. He observed that "they saw them [paratroopers] as elite and bathed in too much glory, with much too much pay." This "anti-airborne attitude" according to Barr followed the Regiment throughout its history.[14]

Brigadier-General E.M.K. MacGregor, then the Director of Infantry, also experienced this opposition. The leadership within the Infantry Corps, he later claimed, simply felt that the Regiment would never come about. Many of them believed that they could not justify diverting a great deal of resources to a parachute regiment because as it was, "there was no real mission for the existing MSF [DCF] except for a small role in the Arctic." In the end, however, as MacGregor noted, "this was Allard's baby and he simply directed that resources be made available and there was no arguing the point."[15]

Notwithstanding the undercurrent of opposition, once in the formation stage the new Regiment appeared to get off to a good start, at least in Allard's mind. But, the invidious opposition to the airborne concept was not the only crack in the buttress of Canada's latest airborne entity. The Airborne Regiment contained the same weaknesses as those airborne organizations that preceded it. A large element in the military questioned the relevance of the new unit. Supporters, who pushed their idea through, did so at great cost. They not only alienated a large segment of DND, but they also established an organization which was not clearly thought out. As a result, it became difficult later on to substantiate its relevance or role. This problem became even more difficult as circumstances, personalities, and time went on. These factors would make the Regiment a continuing and attractive target for its antagonists.

The failure to cement the Airborne Regiment on a firm footing within the Army structure, from the outset became a critical defect that haunted the paratroopers for their entire existence. The lack of precision and the outright confusion as to the guiding rationale for the Canadian Airborne Regiment was clearly evident from the start. Army Commander, Lieutenant-General Anderson's direction to Colonel Rochester about the new unit was both expansive and far too general. To date no in-depth analysis had been done. In fact, Rochester and his staff were instructed to assist the Army Chief of Staff in developing a concept of operations for the Regiment.[16] As a result, their particular views were able to take on a greater importance. Much like the evolution of the Canadian Special Air Service Company years before, once the organization had been approved, a shift in focus became discernable. Anderson's guidance directed that the Canadian Airborne Regiment was to be organized and equipped to perform a variety of tasks including:

a. Defence of Canada;

b. The Standby role in response to the UN;

c. Peacekeeping operations;

d. Missions in connection with national disaster;

e. 'Special Air Service' (SAS) type missions;

f. *Coup de main* tasks in a general war setting; and

g. Responsibility for parachute training in the Canadian Forces.[17]

Unlike Allard's original intention that the parachute troops were to fill a limited segment along the spectrum of conflict, the roles were now far too many and diverse. It was also evident that, once again, a new emphasis had been placed on Special Forces-type missions. This became increasingly apparent in the genesis of the Regiment's operational concept. The FMC commander specifically counselled Rochester and his staff to visit both the US Special Forces Centre, as well as the US Army Airborne Centre, at Fort Bragg. He deemed this essential to gather the "necessary stimulus and factual data upon which to develop your concept."[18] He also stressed the need to visit the British SAS Regiment. This had the danger of further complicating influences on the new Canadian formation.

Anderson continued to dabble in the details, especially training. For instance, he insisted that an element of the Regiment must be proficient at High Altitude Low Opening (HALO) team parachute descents, deep penetration patrols, underwater diving, obstacle clearance and laying of underwater demolitions, mountain climbing, and "Special Service Forces" team missions.[19] Although in consonance with the current American focus, the new theme was not exactly in alignment with the original intent of an UN stand-by/ready force.[20]

Not surprisingly, the operational concept that was finally conceived reflected the FMC commander's broad strictures. The scale of conflicts to which the Canadian Airborne Regiment would be able to contribute included "situations short of war, such as peacekeeping/restoring, and from limited to general war."[21] Likewise, its scope of operational environments was worldwide and encompassed any foe ranging from semi-civilized bands of insurgents to highly sophisticated armies.[22]

The Special Forces aberration was also enshrined in the operational concept, as well as in the later doctrinal manual, *CFP 310 (1) Airborne—The Canadian Airborne Regiment*. Under the heading 'Special Operations' a long list of tasks were included that were clearly Special Forces in nature. Specifically, the document stated that the "Canadian Airborne Regiment is to be prepared to carry out the following operations for which it is specially trained: disruption of lines of communications, destruction of critical installations; psychological warfare operations; special intelligence tasks; recovery tasks; deception operations; internal security operations; counter-guerilla operations; and support of indigenous paramilitary forces."[23] With such "mission creep" taking place in the formative stage it created future problems. For example, with so many added tasks how does one adequately train? What is the focus? What is the priority? What in fact is the pervasive role of the Regiment? The failure to establish answers to these fundamental questions at the start would haunt the Regiment throughout its entire existence.

Nevertheless, this very diverse operational concept was accepted. Only one dilemma was left; namely, where to locate the new formation. Possibilities included the military bases at Valcartier, Petawawa, Picton, Rivers, Wainwright, Penhold, Edmonton and Comox. After exhaustive analysis and study, Rochester's planning team chose Edmonton because of the excellent air facilities and abundant drop zones, its important strategic location from a global point of view, proximity to training areas at Wainwright, nearness to mountains and ski areas, and particularly because the PPCLI was moving to Calgary and the accommodation they were vacating was made to order.[24]

And so, amid all of these diverse ideas and impulses the Canadian Airborne Regiment was formally established on 8 April 1968.[25] The new organization certainly had capability. The Regiment "had all the elements required for true airborne operations in one unit, wearing one badge. The artillery had airborne howitzers, the engineers had airborne heavy equipment and we dropped everything we owned in the way of vehicles and equipment."[26] The all-arms organization consisted of an airborne headquarters and signal squadron, two infantry commandos, an airborne artillery field battery, an airborne engineer field squadron and an airborne service company. The Regiment now began to assemble in Edmonton, at Griesbach Barracks, with the exception of 1 Commando which remained in Valcartier for the interim.[27]

The new CO was certainly enthusiastic as were all the recruited members. When Rochester addressed his new command, he told the assembled troops prophetically, "ahead lies the great adventure of this new Regiment."[28] In 1968, he had reason to be optimistic. The Regiment, as intended by General Allard, took only volunteers and was designed specifically for exceptional individuals and seasoned soldiers. The type of soldier expected to flock to the Regiment prompted Rochester to postulate that the new members "would be so dedicated to their cause that normal disciplinary measures would not be needed."[29]

At the time the high quality of individuals who volunteered from the various combat arms units was incontestable. The FMC Force Structure study specifically stated that the Regiment was to be manned by volunteers from all components of the Field Force. In addition, it noted that the willing individuals for the Canadian Airborne Regiment would normally be above average and serve for a tour of approximately two years.[30] Official recruiting themes stressed the superior qualities of the new genre of airborne warrior. They emphasised the fact that the paratrooper had to be an excellent athlete, an expert at small arms and a survival specialist. Furthermore, they underscored the necessity to be robust, courageous and capable of a high level of endurance.[31]

Chief Warrant Officer B.C. Robinson, himself a veteran of 1 Canadian Parachute Battalion, the Canadian SAS Company, and the subsequent MSF and DCF Jump Companies recalled the exceptional quality of the first Canadian Airborne Regiment personnel. He remembered that when he arrived in Edmonton he was terribly impressed by "all the keen looking fellows" from the Canadian Army Field Force who answered the call to serve in the new formation. The calibre of manpower impressed him and as he later remembered, "by Jesus, this Regiment has the potential."[32]

Another early participant, Brigadier-General Therriault also recalled the "tremendous group of highly motivated people the Regiment received." He admitted that compared to other organizations, "we had a larger percentage of the more ambitious, determined and energized individuals."[33] His assessment was corroborated by Brigadier-General Ian Douglas who was a staff officer at FMC Headquarters at the time. He confirmed that the Airborne Regiment "got the cream of the crop" in the first rush of volunteers. Douglas added that the Regiment attracted those individuals from other regiments who "were dying to do something different."[34]

The other advantage for the new formation was the dictated prerequisites for volunteers. Only experienced officers and soldiers were accepted. All riflemen within the commandos had to be trained to the "5A" level, or in laymen's terms, they had to be qualified for the rank of corporal. This meant that the respective individual had previously served within a normal rifle battalion. As a result, they were already competent and experienced in the basic drills of soldiering. Equally important, they were generally older and normally more mature. The benefits were quickly realized. Major-General Stewart explained that "there was no need to conduct basic specialty courses and therefore we were able to direct the training effort to special skills training, a mountain school, ski school, patrol courses, pathfinder courses, and unarmed combat."[35]

The Canadian Airborne Regiment quickly forged a reputation for tough, dynamic and demanding activity. It set new standards for physical fitness and training realism. Specifically, it revolutionized the manner in which the infantry conducted live fire exercises and shooting ranges.[36] In the first years that followed, the new Regiment travelled throughout Canada, the United States, and Jamaica to practise its deadly craft. In the process, the airborne soldiers began to carve out a reputation for advanced and exacting fast-paced training. Although not recognized as such at the time, the exotic and unrestricted spectrum of training was actually due to a structural flaw that would have later implications. Rochester suggested what it could mean when he remembered those early days. "Few outsiders knew what we were and what we were supposed to do," he recalled, "so we did what we liked."[37]

At the start this uninhibited attitude benefited the soldiers of the Regiment immensely. It was also in concert with Allard's vision of an organization which provided adventure and challenge for the soldiers. However, it was a luxury that many antagonists would not tolerate. The at times abstract and subjective training mandate underscored the continuing confusion over the Regiment's purpose. The initial years of the Regiment provide a graphic example. The young Major Barr admitted that Colonel Rochester gave him free rein to run and train his unit (2 Commando) as he saw fit. Barr further noted that the conflict in Vietnam was a huge influence at the time, and prompted an emphasis on counter-insurgency and jungle training within his Commando.[38] This reflected the fact that some aspects of training, if not its total emphasis, could easily be influenced, if not misdirected, by every new unit commander. Such discretionary power was not good for consistency. Moreover, units became far too accustomed to doing what they wanted and difficult to control. Later events in the 1990s would prove this with a vengeance.

The inconsistency and confusion in training emphasis were underscored after Rochester's departure as CO. Brigadier-General Therriault took over command of the Regiment in 1969 with a completely different interpretation of their role than his predecessor. The new regimental commander candidly acknowledged that he was not given a briefing on what was expected of him by his superiors. Therriault admitted that he could have easily "played around with scenarios," but he interpreted his primary task as training. He explained that the Regiment "was a great big training school, the most magnificent training vehicle the Canadian Forces had." He thought that the Regiment's capability could be used anywhere in the world, but its role was to improve the people in it, so they could return to their parent regiments. In essence, Therriault viewed the Airborne Regiment as a "leadership nursery."[39] Major-General Stewart later reinforced this notion. He wrote, "it is my opinion that the Airborne Regiment was created less for a perceived operational requirement and more to provide an organization that would undertake adventurous, exciting special training for those soldiers of our peacetime army that needed something to break up the monotony of garrison life."[40] Although this point of view has value, it hardly represents a principal *raison d'être*.

The third Regimental Commander (1971-1973), Colonel Herb Pitts, construed his primary role differently yet again. He viewed the Regiment as a rapid reaction force for employment in any number of environmental conditions such as desert and jungle, but with a special focus on the Arctic. In his mind, the Regiment trained specifically for the airborne capability and not necessarily for any specific role.[41] As we can see in these first short years, none of the three regimental commanders had the same idea of what the Regiment was to do or be.

Not surprisingly, a later commander highlighted the continuing problem of operational focus, even within the Regiment itself. He cautioned his successor that it was important "to limit the units to training for their role [so they] don't try to constantly redo the raid at Entebbe." He noted that the commandos in the Airborne Regiment "were quick to get into unit raiding type ops and as a result they never really are prepared for the role they have been given, if indeed one was ever given."[42] It became evident there was a wide variance in perceptions of role and training requirements for each regimental commander, as well as each of their subordinate commanders. Needless to say, some had more acumen than others.

The hazard of doing "whatever one likes," no matter how one rationalizes it, is the loss of focus on the institution's legislated and primary function. Furthermore, organizational training, and its operational locus are liable to become hostage to the interpretations and whims of the incumbent commander, and his subordinate officers, instead of being embedded in a requirement to serve national policy. This danger is compounded by the lack of a precise role or mission statement. A systemic flaw of this nature is very dangerous to any organization. It is one that grows with every other adverse event that comes along.

Right from the late 1960s the Canadian Airborne Regiment rested on just such an insecure base. The rationale for its existence was never clearly reconciled. Its role had become wide and ever-expansive. Subsequently, the Regiment's purpose was interpreted in many ways. It represented many different things to many different people. Unfortunately, even as the Regiment matured in the seventies and beyond no effort was made to apply one consistent mandate. As a result it became a mirror image of the perceptions of those who held the reigns of power at the moment.

The confusion can be easily traced to the Regiment's original operational concept and the all-inclusive mission statement of 1968. That year the Canadian Forces Organizational Order 3.11 (CFOO) dictated that, "the role of the Canadian Airborne Regiment is to provide a force capable of moving quickly to meet any unexpected enemy threat or other commitment of the Canadian Armed Forces."[43] This message was echoed in the June 1968 edition of *Sentinel*, the official magazine of the Canadian Armed Forces. The article describing the debut of this fresh new formation asserted, "The Regiment is being formed to provide a versatile force capable of moving quickly to meet any enemy threat to Canada, and to participate as part of any force that Canada might deploy to meet national or international commitments. Its capability for quick reaction and its strategic mobility will make it a truly 'ready force,' capable for use on a world wide basis."[44] The Airborne Regiment's own keystone document also stressed the issue of global deployment. The publication explained, "The quick-reaction capabilities of the Regiment coupled with its strategic mobility make it suitable for deployment on a worldwide basis thus allowing maximum exploitation as a 'Ready Force'."[45]

The emphasis on strategic reach and swift deployment was fundamental to the original planners and design teams. They believed that the Airborne Regiment would be responsible for dispatching, within two days of a request being received, the first elements of a Canadian UN peacekeeping force. As a result, they organized the formation into two balanced infantry elements, each alternately maintaining 100 percent readiness and a lesser state of operational readiness.[46] Thus, it was clearly evident that a segment of DND also saw the Canadian Airborne Regiment as a strategic force for global employment.

The cause of the apparent role confusion is easy to discern. The Regiment rested on a precarious substructure. The all-inclusive role failed to provide the requisite priority guidance. For example, the regimental commanders and their immediate supervisors determined their training priorities based on their version of the operational concept, which gravitated more and more toward the exciting special operations sphere of activities. Canadian Forces planners and decision makers viewed the Regiment in accordance with the official CFOO, with a particular bent toward UN missions. The planning cell of Army Headquarters, on the other hand, saw the Regiment in a more North American persona.

As for the Army itself, a Force Mobile Command assessment in the late sixties stated the "role of the [Airborne] Regiment as specified in Mobile Command Headquarters *Operational Plan 100* is to provide an airborne rapid-development force for operational support of national security, North American defence and international peacekeeping."[47] The document further elaborated that the role broke down into the following tasks: national security, defined as defence of Canada and sovereignty operations; North American defence, defined as the joint defence of

Alaska and the West; and UN peacekeeping/ready force.

This Army interpretation was heavily weighted toward a traditional defence of the North perspective. The same brief noted that "the word <u>anywhere</u> is stressed because it is in this word that the Canadian Airborne Regiment's raison d'être lies. Implicit in the word sovereignty is the ability to impose the government's will, if necessary in any <u>part</u> of the country to which the government lays claim."[48]

Political reality of the late sixties and early seventies, however, soon reinforced the FMC translation of the Regiment's principal purpose. Moreover, that old ghost of American encroachment in the North once again sparked panic at a national level. In 1969, the Americans announced that the supertanker *Manhattan,* belonging to the Humble Oil Company, intended to conduct a voyage through the Northwest Passage as part of an experiment to study the feasibility of transporting Alaskan crude oil through the northern waters year 'round. The Americans did not seek Canadian permission. Contrary to the Canadian claim, Washington considered the Northwest Passage international waters. As a result, the *Manhattan* incident sparked another frenzy of politically directed military activity in the North. Maxwell Cohen captured the essence of the challenge when he wrote, *"Manhattan's* two voyages made Canadians feel that they were on the edge of another American 'steal' of Canadian resources and 'rights' which had to be dealt with at once by firm governmental action."[49]

Canada responded by increasing military activity in the North. Once again DND was given the principal role of protecting Canadian authority in the Arctic. Prime Minister Pierre Trudeau clearly stated, "Our first priority in our defence policy is the protection of Canadian sovereignty."[50] This affirmation was later followed by the admission of Mitchell Sharp, the External Affairs Minister, that the future role of Canadian Forces would be "in the surveillance of our own territory and coastlines in the interests of protecting our sovereignty."[51] Sharp bluntly acknowledged, "we have problems defending our sovereignty, not our security, but our sovereignty."[52]

Such a welter of conflicting ideas caused rapid changes in the Airborne. In mid-1969, Lieutenant-General Gilles Turcot, the FMC Commander, explained that the return to the North "was not so much a new departure as a return to priorities that were accepted in the Nineteen Fifties and early Sixties."[53] The writing was on the wall. The Airborne Regiment's versatility and rapid reaction capability quickly relegated the parachute force to its traditional role as protector of the North. Ominously, the Canadian airborne capability was once again being linked to a role and threat which carried no operational credibility. This in turn represented yet another fundamental danger to the Regiment.

The tabling of the new defence White Paper, *Defence in the 70s*, in 1971 solidified this perception. Not surprisingly, the White Paper emphasized sovereignty protection as the prime commitment of the Canadian Armed Forces.[54] The defence policy reflected the perennial concern over American encroachment. Clearly, security against a military menace was never an issue. Leo Cadieux, the Minister of National Defence admitted, "although we do not consider there is a military threat to the Arctic at the present time, we feel it is essential to develop the capability of keeping on top of the situation."[55] The historic necessity of reassuring the Americans that Canada did not represent a security concern was still present.

The politicians were not the only ones to be conscious of this. The military assessment was even more blunt. The NDHQ Directorate of Strategic Planning explained that "apart from the threat of aerospace attack on North America, which can be discounted as an act of rational policy, Canada's geographic isolation effectively defends her against attack with conventional land or maritime forces."[56] The report did, however, deem it necessary "to ensure that the minimum contributions we can make to our own defence must be adequate to assure the US of its safety without keeping our territory under surveillance herself."[57] It was further concluded that an important consideration was the American belief in the threat of direct attack, an idea that was still conditioned by memories of Pearl Harbor. The assessment bluntly stated that the "significant point is US perception, which is sometimes based less on reason than on emotion."[58]

Some of the government's critics were quick to point out the inconsistencies of the White Paper. They also wanted to score some political points against the incumbent Liberal government. One editorial writer noted "while Pierre Trudeau didn't invent the Arctic, he certainly seems determined to rediscover and exploit it for political purposes."[59] Others declared the "whole emphasis on the North as a sham." Predictably, once the storm over the *Manhattan* incident had died away, and the desired cuts to the Canadian forces in Europe had been implemented, the emphasis on Arctic sovereignty was allowed to dissipate. Kenneth Eyre felt that "in the government's view, while protection of sovereignty was the first military priority, the threat to that sovereignty was minimal and, under existing conditions, did not warrant a major commitment of men, resources and money."[60] A symbolic presence was all that was required.

Therein lay the danger to the Airborne Regiment. The primary assignment of the Regiment to a symbolic and largely superficial role undermined the argument for keeping it as a strong and viable force. Years later Colonel Ian Fraser, the Regimental Commander counselled his successor to remember that the Regiment's future lay in the North. "The defence of Canada is why we exist," he declared, "and your parish is north of 60 degrees, for God's sake, don't ever forget that!"[61] Fraser's sentiment was noble but the real question was how secure was the Regiment's future if it was based on a role or a threat that many said did not exist.

All through the 1970s internal discord further exacerbated the turn of events. Prime Minister Trudeau's shake-up of defence policy, in 1970-1971, seared the Army to its veritable soul. The new policy dramatically cut the heavy mechanized forces in NATO/Europe, which had represented the Army's primary focus since the early fifties.[62] The animosity aroused was such that Donald Macdonald, the Minister of National Defence, was faced by a very antagonistic and unhelpful military. As a result, he directed that the preparation of the White Paper that year be done without military advice.[63] The Liberal government was quite prepared to make defence policy alone if the soldiers were not prepared to cooperate.

The poisoned environment created real impediments. The Airborne Regiment's inescapable linkage with the North inevitably attracted further daggers. The government's stratagem of reallocating scarce resources for the Canadian Arctic, at the expense of Canada's mechanized NATO formations, piqued the fury of the Euro-centric Army Headquarters. A stirling example of the undercurrent of resentment was found in the case of a comprehensive appreciation on Canadian training activities in the North which was completed by Major Mike Barr in late 1970, while he was on temporary duty away from the Regiment with the Directorate of Force Development, at NDHQ.

Barr's assessment was stifled the moment it left his desk. The paper was returned for "private filing." The accompanying minutes on Barr's effort were surprisingly candid. His superior commended him for his excellent and thorough analysis, as well as for his stellar recommendations. However, the director also chided him for his naiveté. Barr's supervisor explained that "Withers [Brigadier-General Ramsey Withers] organized the nonsense of NRHQ [Northern Region Headquarters] to get himself promoted. It was done over considerable opposition from FMC!"[64] Therefore, "any thought of giving W [Withers] any part of the action," the director admonished, "is repugnant to FMC." An ominous margin note at the end of the attached minute sheet warned, "Your paper could get you into great trouble with FMC. Take it from an old friend—leave it alone."[65] And here is the basic contradiction: the Regiment's role was in the defence of the North but nobody else seemed to believe it.

With such latent hostility, the closer the Airborne Regiment was identified exclusively with the North, the dimmer seemed its future. In addition, the resentment of the Regiment's very creation still lurked under the surface. The Regiment was increasingly associated by many, some of whom were clear opponents, to be the private preserve of the formation's creators. The manner in which the Regiment was created was not easily forgotten.

Nevertheless, by the early seventies, internally the Airborne Regiment was at its zenith of power. It had the status of a mini-formation, with a peacetime establishment of 1044 soldiers. In tandem with its unique and privileged stature was the advantage of addressing its concerns directly to the commander of the Army.[66] Colonel Fraser reflected that despite the small size of the Regiment, "I was a formation commander and I was treated the same as the other Brigade Commanders that answered to Commander FMC."[67] Another Regimental veteran, Major-General Bob Stewart admitted, "we lived a charmed life." We were "a truly mini airborne brigade," he added, "separated from the rest of the Army."[68] But this, Stewart conceded, nurtured the resentment of some important officers who felt that the Regiment was being given both undue status, and too many scarce resources which were being taken away from other units.

Another commander of the time, Brigadier-General Therriault, agreed. He acknowledged that the Regiment was indeed favoured. We "had greater training opportunities; no summer taskings or commitments to the Reserves," he explained, "and a free reign to do our own thing."[69] Therriault candidly stated that in the early years, the Airborne Regiment "was given more, and other people didn't like it." He was convinced that this created a certain group of enemies who were determined to get rid of the organization. He lamented, "it goes back that far."[70]

The preferred position of the new formation was recognized by virtually all those within its ranks. Philip Bury, an officer in 1 Commando at the time, is representative of the feelings of those who served in the formative years. He remembered, "we really felt favoured." They were, he claimed, "protected from taskings and knew it."[71] Their environment was considered very favourable to the airborne soldiers. Furthermore, the paratroopers felt well regarded, at least to those who counted, that is, those who held power.

To the intrepid individuals serving in the Canadian Airborne Regiment, its existence truly represented a "Great Adventure." Some, such as Therriault however, knew it could not last. By the mid seventies the Trudeau government was propelling the Canadian Armed Forces toward another painful downsizing. This meant a smaller Army, which inherently implied bitter internal debate over roles and increasingly fewer resources. The first test of the Regiment's shaky foundation was in the offing.

Notes for Chapter Five

1. "Special Parachute is Planned," *The Gazette,* 7 December 1966, 1.
2. Ibid. The statement is misleading. Although Lester B. Pearson advocated the concept of a "stand-by" battalion for UN service as early as 1956, with implementation following two years later; it was never postulated or even suggested that the force had to be a self-contained airborne battle group as was now being established.
3. "The Requirement for Parachutists in the Canadian Army," 14 February 1966, 4, CAFM, File AB. CAR History (1966)—"Canadian Airborne Regiment Working Papers."

4. Ibid., 4; and "Proposed Re-organization of the Army Field Force," March 1965. NAC, RG 24, Acc 83-84/165, Box 34, File 2001—1/1, 5. For the sake of clarification, the terms "formation" and "Regiment" refer to the entire entity, namely the complete Canadian Airborne Regiment. The terms "battalion," "unit" or "commando" refer to sub-components of the Regiment. For variety, terms such as "organization" and "establishment" are used. The context of the text will indicate what level is being discussed, although it will normally pertain to the higher category. This clarification may not be valid when I am quoting others, specifically non-military individuals who may not be conversant with the nuances of the different words.

5. Colonel Mike Barr, the first CO of 2 Commando recalled that Don Rochester loved parachuting. He stated that Rochester was a true parachutist vice a hard core paratrooper. Barr also noted that the first Regimental Commander was loved by his soldiers. He remembered that "you never heard the troops say a bad thing about Don Rochester." Interview with author 6 January 1998.

6. "CANMOBGEN 098 Comd 2549, dated 022030Z December 1966, "Approval of MOBCOM Forces Structure Concept." NAC, RG 24, Vol 23491, File 1901-2, Part 1. See also Rochester, "Birth of a Regiment," 34. Rochester, a veteran of both WW II and Korea, was a Combat Engineer by classification. Colonel Rochester passed away on 18 August 1997. See Thomas Walton, "Biographie du Colonel D.H. Rochester, OBE, CD," *The Maroon Beret,* Vol 2, No. 3, December 1997, 6-7.

7. Rochester, "Birth of a Regiment," 34.

8. Ibid., 35. This provided a cure for another problem. The infantry components were called battalions but their "small size made it hard to stomach the term." As a result, the name commando was applied against the infantry units of the Regiment. Ibid., and Barr interview. Once again, much like the Canadian SAS, the name more closely reflected the perception of the formation's *raison d'etre* in the eyes of its officers and men, than its official mission statement.

9. Ibid., 34. Barr commented that the original "Royals Royce" version of the Regiment was quickly scaled down as a result of imposed manpower limitations. Consequently the battalions and their respective companies (two instead of three platoons in each) were kept small to ensure enough manpower credits for support troops such as engineers and artillery. It was also necessary to give up the infantry mortars and assault pioneers to ensure vacancies for the airborne battery with its mountain gun and mortars and Combat Engineers. The Combat Engineers were seen as critical since they alone, with their equipment, had the capability of improving and building runways in the North. Interview with author. Colonel Dick Cowling reminisced that in the early days the Regiment and engineers actually practised building ice airstrips. Interview with author, 8 December 1997.

10. Interview with author, 6 January 1998. Major-General Stewart affirmed that "the Armoured Corps resisted inclusion in the Regiment." From 1969-1972, Stewart was Regimental Major (RM) and CO of 2 Commando respectively. Letter to author 1 July 1998.

11. Audio cassette tape containing a 60 minute recollection by Colonel D.H. Rochester of his contribution to the establishment of the Canadian Airborne Regiment. The cassette was made in response to a request by Fred Low in 1978 who was writing an undergraduate paper on the Regiment. The tape, hereafter referred to as the Rochester Tape, is now held in the CAFM. The perception held by FMC and NDHQ staffs had a real effect on the Regiment. During the initial period of the Regiment's establishment it suffered from a dearth of equipment. This was due to the fact that no serious effort had been made to locate or obtain equipment by the various staffs because no one thought the Regiment would actually be formed. It was not until the actual stand-up that a concerted effort was undertaken.

12. Rochester, "Birth of a Regiment," 34. The negative World War II stereotype is accurate. A Canadian Military Headquarters memorandum captured the essence of the sentiment. It stated, "paratroops, as a whole, appear to be somewhat over-pampered and temperamental prima donnas..." NAC, RG 24, Vol 12721—File "Discipline—No. 1 Para Bn."

13. Rochester Tape, CAFM. Colonel Rochester also recorded that the only people who insisted the Regiment would be formed were the CDS, the FMC Commander and the FMC Deputy Commander.

14. Interview with author.

15. CAFM, Audio Tape, Fred Low interview with Brigadier-General E.M.K. MacGregor, 12 January 1978.

16. "Formation of the Canadian Airborne Regiment—Activation and Terms of Reference," 15 May 1967, 3. The document was accessed from Colonel Michael Barr's personal files, hereafter referred to as the Barr Papers. The Regiment was directed to be operationally ready by mid-1969.
17. Ibid., 1.
18. Ibid., 3. Colonel Barr, a graduate of both the British Royal Marine Commando Course and the US Special Forces (SF) Course, recalled that it was a direct result of these staff visits that he was selected as the first CO of 2 Commando. While on the SF Course, Barr's abilities came to the attention of Lieutenant-Colonel Herb F. Roy, a veteran of the original 1942 American Airborne Test Platoon. During Colonel Rochester's visit to Fort Bragg, Roy upon hearing what was afoot, strongly recommended Barr as a necessity for the new organization.Barr confirmed that Rochester and staff did in fact visit the UK Parachute Regiment, Royal Marine Commandos, and SAS, as well as the US Airborne Centre, Rangers and SF for ideas to create their operational concept. Barr Interview. Once again this underlines the prevailing focus. Needless to say it was not the monitoring of a cease-fire line.
19. "Formation of the Canadian Airborne Regiment—Activation and Terms of Reference," 15 May 1967, 2. Barr Papers.
20. The American influence is undeniable. See Chapter Four, endnotes 88-92. A steady increase in SF numbers transpired in the early sixties and virtually exploded by 1965. In that year alone the SF expanded by 6,500 personnel. President Kennedy's interest and vigorous support also catapulted SF fortunes. His sponsorship caused such rancour in the American Army that the Special Forces were dubbed "Jacqueline Kennedy's Own Rifles." See Charles M. Simpson III, *Inside the Green Berets. The First Thirty Years* (Novato, CA: Presidio, 1983), 68; and Eliot A. Cohen, *Commandos and Politicians* (Cambridge: Center for International Affairs, Harvard University, 1978), 40-41. During this period the French also established a rapid reaction/Special Forces role for elements of its Foreign Legion, specifically 2 REP. H.R. Simpson, *The Paratroopers of the French Foreign Legion* (London: Brassey's, 1997), 38-39.
21. "Canadian Airborne Regiment—Operational Concept," 1. Barr Papers.
22. Ibid., 1. The earlier advice of the Commandant of the Infantry School, who warned of creating an "all singing, all dancing" organization was obviously forgotten. His sage observation that an establishment that is intended to do so many things is "doomed to fail" was not heeded. See Chapter Four, text and accompanying endnote 83-84.
23. Ibid., Annex C; and *CFP 310 (1)—Airborne, Volume 1, The Canadian Airborne Regiment,* 1968, Chapter 1, Sect 2, "Role, Capabilities and Employment."
24. Letter, FMC Commander, W.A.B. Anderson, to CDS, 27 June 1967, "Location of Canadian Airborne Regiment." CAFM Files; and Rochester, "Birth of a Regiment," 35. Colonel Michael Houghton recalled that the estimate used to evaluate students at the Canadian Forces Command and Staff College in Toronto for many years was the assessment of where to locate the Canadian Airborne Regiment. He noted that this appreciation was conducted hundreds of times, by members of all three services, and almost without fail, the overwhelming recommendation was always to base the organization in Edmonton. Interview with author, 5 November 1998.
25. Message, CANCOMGEN 022, dated 111600Z April 1968, *Organization Mobile Command.* Colonel Rochester, the first commander-designate of the new airborne unit, mused, "the gestation period for a hamster is only sixteen days, for a horse eleven months but for a pegasus—two years!" Rochester, "Birth of a Regiment," 34.
26. Major-General Stewart, letter to author, 1 July 1998. He noted the only shortfall was the lack of a direct fire armoured vehicle. For organizational data see *CFP 310 (1)—Airborne, Volume 1, The Canadian Airborne Regiment,* 1968, Chapter 2, "Organization."
27. The delay was designed to allow for sufficient time to organize the required infrastructure for the influx of a large Francophone body. Specifically, adequate schooling in French for dependents was a concern. 1 Commando eventually joined the Regiment in Edmonton, in May 1970. In the interim it joined the Regiment for major exercises. CAFM Files, Message, CANFORGEN 03, dated, 142100Z January 1970, "Relocation 1 Cdo from CFB Valcartier to CFB Edmonton." The time delay was also required to improve the required francophone numbers. By the fall of 1969, a great improvement in 1 Commando strength was commended, however, alarming shortfalls were still noticeable. The command

inspection of the unit on 29 September, noted that the total strength was now such that 145 of the established 158 positions were filled. Shortfalls in leadership were stated as follows: only 11 senior NCOs of 16 required; only 2 warrant officers present out of a needed 12; and officers were adequate at 17 of the established 19 positions. NAC, RG 24, Vol 23506, File CAR 1370-1, Part I.

28. "Airborne in Edmonton," *Sentinel*, April/May 1994, Final Edition, 11.

29. Rochester, "Birth of a Regiment," 34. Nick Lees, then a reporter for the *Edmonton Journal*, quickly played on this theme and titled his article on the elite new paratroopers, "Their Choice: Danger." CAFM, article on file, Nick Lees, "Their Choice: Danger," *The Edmonton Journal*, 1968, no specific date. Brigadier-General R.G. Therriault, the second Regimental Commander, from 1969-1971, acknowledged that many people considered the Regiment elite, although he personally did not. He noted that in Canadian society it is not a good thing to produce a group who is favoured above others. Interview with author 28 April 1998. The term "elite" became a very sensitive issue that created a running and very acrimonious debate. It would also become a factor in later problems.

30. *FMC Forces Structure Study,* Chapter 7, "The Canadian Airborne Regiment," 3 April 1967, Barr Papers.

31. *Sentinelle,* November/December 1966, rear cover.

32. Interview with author, 21 September 1998. Robinson was hand-picked. He was summoned from Germany to take the position of RSM of 2 Commando. His assessment carries substantial weight. Robinson served as a private in the 1 Cdn Para Bn and participated in the Normandy drop, the parachute assault across the Rhine, and the pursuit in NW Europe. He was also a Sr NCO in the Canadian SAS Company and he participated in the Korean conflict as a member of the RCR. As well, he was later a member of the various MSF / DCF airborne organizations.

33. Interview with author, 28 April 1968. Therriault divided people in the military into three categories. The Top Group he defined as the more energized—the faster skaters; the Middle Group he typified as good solid people; and the Bottom Group he labelled as those the institution could do without. He used this scale to explain that the Airborne Regiment drew more than its fair share of the Top Group.

34. Interview with author, 18 March 1998.

35. Major-General Stewart's letter to author, 1 July 1998. The excellent calibre, particularly the experience and skill level of individuals was echoed by virtually all those interviewed from the specific era. Chapter Seven will further explore the effect of this generation of airborne soldiers.

36. Major-General Stewart commented the "live fire battle schools that the Regiment conducted became common place throughout the Army as a result of officers returning to their [parent] regiments with the knowledge, skill and courage to conduct sometimes dangerous, exciting and realistic field firing." Letter to author, 1 July 1998. Lieutenant-General Kent Foster, a former Regimental Commander and FMC Commander echoed this fact. Interview with author 6 June 1998.

37. Colonel D. H. Rochester, "Idle Musings While Standing in the Door," *Fragments of 1 Airborne Battery (RCA), The Canadian Airborne Regiment,* 3. In another account Rochester was equally as candid. He wrote, "We were given quite a free rein. Probably because our creation defied the odds, coupled with the fact that no one really knew what we were supposed to do, we were able to be imaginative and do just about anything we wanted." Rochester, "Birth of a Regiment," 36.

38. Interview with author 6 January 1998.

39. Interview with author 28 April 1998. Therriault's interpretation is closely aligned with the vision of his R22eR brother, General Allard. Therriault was not cut from the same bolt of cloth as Rochester. He never established the same close rapport with the men as did his predecessor, however, he was well respected for his calm, supportive leadership style which was well in evidence during the FLQ crisis, in Montreal. Therriault's strength as an administrator and organizer was also seen as critical to the Regiment's evolution. He was credited with putting the Regiment on paper, specifically formalizing SOPs and ensuring that the infamous "Quick Rig" procedure (call back of personnel and the rapid dispatch of the Regiment, or elements thereof to an operational theatre) was institutionalized.

40. Letter to author, 1 July 1998.

41. Interview with Major-General (retd) H.C. Pitts, 30 June 1998. Herb Pitts is easily one of the most respected figures in Canadian airborne history. This sentiment is held by both the officers and men

who served for and with the general, and those who simply became acquainted with the gentleman through his efforts on behalf of the Canadian airborne family.

42. Colonel I.S. Fraser, "Handover Notes Col J.J.B. Painchaud / Col I.S. Fraser, July 1977," 29. Documents accessed from Colonel Fraser's personal file, henceforth referred to as the Fraser Papers.

43. CF Organization Orders 3.11, Canadian Airborne Regiment, dated 25 April 1968. Commission of Inquiry into the Deployment of Canadian Forces to Somalia. *Information Legacy. A Compendium of Source Material from the Commission of Inquiry.* [CD-ROM], 1998, hereafter referred to as *Information Legacy*; and *CFP 310(1) Airborne*, 1-2 / para 105.

44. Major K. G. Roberts, "Canadian Airborne Regiment," *Sentinel,* June 1968, 2.

45. *CFP 310(1) Airborne*, 1-2 / para 106.

46. "Operational Concept," Annex B; and *Forces Structure Study*, Chapter 7, "The Canadian Airborne Regiment," 1. It was also recommended that the remainder of the Regiment be broken down into half units capable of alternately maintaining 100% readiness.

47. "Briefing Airborne Regiment and Components of the Regiment." CAFM, File AB-Research: CAR. Components and Structure. Part One, 1.E, Doc 4 & Part Two, 2.E, Doc 1.

48. Ibid.

49. Maxwell Cohen, "The Arctic and National Interest," *International Journal,* Vol 26, No.1, Winter 1970-1971, 72. The government tried to place a favourable spin on the event. Both Trudeau and Mitchell Sharp stated publicly that they "concurred with the project." Nevertheless, their approval was never sought and the research information was never shared. See *Debates,* 15 May 1969, 8721; and *Globe & Mail*, 18 September 1969, A7. Sharp explained that a large part of the problem lay in Canada's fear that its claims to the Arctic archipelago and adjacent waters, specifically the Northwest Passage which was disputed by the Americans, might be defeated in an international tribunal. Sharp stated, "the government continued to feel that a blunt declaration of sovereignty would invite a challenge from the United States, a challenge for which Canada, equipped only with legal and historical arguments of less than conclusive force, might be ill-prepared." *Canadian Annual Review For 1970,* 350. External Affairs had always candidly noted, "Due to the desolate nature of the areas in question, these claims have little support on the grounds of effective occupation, settlement or development. Thus while Canada's claims to sovereignty to these regions have not heretofore been seriously challenged, they are at best somewhat tenuous and weak." *Documents on Canadian External Relations, Vol 12, 1946,* 1556. See also Grant, 178 & 307; L.C. Green, "Canada and Arctic Sovereignty," *The Canadian Bar Review,* Vol 68, No. 4, December 1970, 740-775; and Dosman, 34-57.

50. *External Affairs,* Vol 21, No. 6, June 1969, 253. In a statement to the press in May 1969, the prime minister asserted the new defence priorities which would later appear in his government's Defence White Paper, *Defence in the 70s.* He stated that "the surveillance of our own territory and coast-lines, i.e., the protection of our sovereignty," was the first priority followed by "the defence of North America in co-operation with United States forces." Ibid., Vol 21, No. 5, May 1969, 215. See also *Debates,* 18 April 1969, 7724.

51. *The Globe and Mail*, 18 September 1969, A7.

52. Terrance Wills, "Developing Canada Priority over NATO critics told by Sharp," *The Globe and Mail,* 11 April 1969, 1.

53. Clyde Sanger, "Why Canada's Army is back in the Arctic," *The Globe and Mail,* 12 March 1970, 7. Year 'round training of soldiers in the North was re-introduced in March 1970. The following month a new permanent northern headquarters, to coordinate military activities in the north, was established in Yellowknife. *Canadian Annual Review For 1970,* 362; *Debates,* 21 May 1971, 6054; and Canada, *Defence 1971* (Ottawa: DND, 1972), 59-60. General Allard confirmed that the establishment of the new headquarters was a direct result of the *Manhattan* incident. Allard, 291.

54. Canada, *Defence in the 70s;* and Canada, *Canada's Territorial Air Defence,* 31. The White Paper confirmed reductions to the Canadian commitment to NATO. The government cleverly couched the withdrawal of half of its forces from Europe in the necessity of re-orienting Canadian resources to meet the needs of sovereignty and defence of its North. See also Nils Orvik, *Canadian Defence Policy: Choices and Directions* (Kingston: Queen's University Press, 1980), 1-2. Orvik noted the "so-called 'northern

orientation' in Canadian defence policy was never well defined in terms of defence objective and deployments." Joel Sokolsky commented, "the general thrust of the Trudeau policies was to de-emphasize collective defence in favour of national sovereignty protection." J.J. Sokolsky, *Defending Canada* (New York: Priority Press Publications, 1989), 5.

55. Sangar, 7. See also FMCHQ, "Study Group and Exercise," 13 February 1969. NAC RG 24, Vol 23499, File 3120-3, Part 1; and "Message from CDS—General Allard," 24 June 1969. NAC, RG 24, Vol 23491, File 1901-2, Part 1. General Allard asserted that "FMC will undergo some changes but will continue to maintain in Canada forces for a variety of roles related to the defence of Canada, aid to the civil power, cooperation with US Forces for the defence of North America and collective security and peacekeeping abroad. This will mean more emphasis on light, quick-reaction, airportable land-force units designed to meet these roles." In light of the budget cuts and force reductions he emphasized that FMC would continue to be organized in combat groups and that the Canadian Airborne Regiment would be retained.

56. "A Draft Study of the Future International Scene," 5 April 1968, 4 & 8. DHist, File 112.11.003 (D3)—Box 3. Another military assessment deemed the risk of any kind of hostile land operations against North America as "slight." *Rationale For Canadian Defence Forces,* 14 May 1968, 28. DHist, File 90/452.

57. Ibid. Brigadier-General Therriault noted the geographic trump card. He stated, "when you've been there and realize the difficulty of operating there, especially the distances, it boggles the mind." Interview with author, 28 April 1968.

58. "A Draft Study of the Future International Scene," 5 April 1968, 4.

59. *Canadian Annual Review for 1970,* 363.

60. Eyre, 297. He stated "While Canadian force levels in Europe were being halved, the withdrawn troops were not to be committed to the protection of sovereignty; the forces were to be reduced. Similarly, the new role, it was implied, would have to be fulfilled with equipment and facilities then in the Forces' inventory. No new 'northern-sovereignty' equipment was to be obtained..."

61. Fraser, "Handover Notes," 4. Fraser Papers. The actual concept for Defence of Canada operations stipulated that the country be divided into two geographic areas of responsibility. Within these areas the respective Combat Group Headquarters (Brigades) were responsible for conducting any DCOs within their allocated area. The West was the responsibility of HQ 1 Cbt Gp, and the East was the purview of HQ 5eGdeC. 1 Cbt Gp was also the designated HQ to conduct ALCANUS operations. The Airborne Regiment was to be capable of conducting operations independently or in support of these entities as required. An argument for redundancy can be, and was made. *The Canadian Airborne Regiment Operational Plan 300 / CAR, Defence of Canada / ALCANUS Operations,* March 1971, 1-4. DHist, File 81 / 80.

62. *Canada, Defence in the 70s* (Ottawa: DND, 1971), 4-8 & 16; J.L Granatstein and Robert Bothwell, *Pirouette. Pierre Trudeau and Canadian Foreign Policy* (Toronto: University of Toronto Press, 1990), 234-240.

63. Bland, *The Administration of Defence Policy*, 213.

64. Major Michael D. Barr, "Forces Development Objective Canadian Forces In The North Training Activities," July 1970. Barr Papers.

65. Ibid.

66. CFOO 3.11, Canadian Airborne Regiment, dated 25 April 1968; *CFP 310(1) Airborne*, 3-2 / para 303 & 304; and "Briefing Airborne Regiment and Components of the Regiment." CAFM, File AB-Research: CAR. Components and Structure. Part One, 1.E, Doc 4 & Part Two, 2.E, Doc 1.

67. Letter to author, 8 April 1998. See also SSF (Airborne Regiment) generated position paper, "The Canadian Airborne Regiment—A Proscribed Elite," November 1982, *Information Legacy,* Document Control No. 905211, 3.

68. Letter to author, 1 July 1998.

69. Interview with author, 28 April 1968.

70. Ibid.

71. Interview with author, 14 December 1998.

Top: Paratroopers participate in an Arctic Sovereignty Exercise, Igloolik, Baffin Island, March 1987.
(Courtesy of T.C. Elliot.)

Bottom: When in Rome....Two paratroopers don native garb during an Arctic deployment, March 1987.
(Courtesy of T.C. Elliot.)

Top: Brigadier-General Kent Foster inspects the Regiment accompanied by the Regimental Commander, Colonel J.M.R. Gaudreau, summer 1987. (Courtesy of the Canadian Airborne Forces Museum.)

Bottom: Regimental march from DZ Anzio back to the garrison, summer 1987. 2 Commando flies the Rebel Flag. (Courtesy of Don Halcrow.)

Opposite top: Regimental jump bivouac, Ex Coelis, summer 1988. (L to r): Brigadier-General Ian Douglas, Lieutenant-General John de Chastelain, Colonel Mike Houghton, (over his left shoulder) former CDS, General Maurice Baril, remainder unknown.
(Courtesy of M. Houghton.)

Opposite bottom: Loading a C-130 Hercules aircraft to conduct at Brown's Field, Petawawa.
(Courtesy of C. Nobrega.)

Above: Ramp jump onto DZ Anzio, Canadian Forces Base Petawawa.
(Courtesy of the Canadian Airborne Forces Museum.)

Top: Winter drop onto DZ Anzio, Canadian Forces Base Petawawa. (Courtesy of T.C. Elliot.)

Bottom: Vice-Admiral John Anderson, the VCDS, and Brigadier-General Ernie Beno, Commander of the SSF, discuss matters during the VCDS's visit to the Canadian Airborne Regiment during Ex Stalwart Providence, 16 October 1992. (Courtesy of E. Beno.)

Top: Belet Huen airfield, Somalia, December 1992. (Courtesy of E. Barry.)

Bottom: Defensive position and living quarters on the perimeter of the Belet Huen airfield. (Courtesy of R. Prouse.)

Opposite top and middle: 2 Commando acting as guides through Belet Huen during the Regiment's move from the airfield to their new camps, 3 January 1993. (Courtesy of D. Delaney.)

Opposite bottom: OC 1 Commando, Major Charles Pommet and members from the French Foreign Legion meet with elders from a Somali clan to discuss humanitarian and security issues, 1993.
(Courtesy of the Canadian Airborne Forces Museum.)

Above top: The strength of the Regiment—the determination and skill of the individual paratroopers. Members of 3 Commando, Somalia, 1993. (Courtesy of R. Prouse.)

Above bottom: 3 Commando on patrol in Yasoman, Somalia, April 1993. (Courtesy of R. Prouse.)

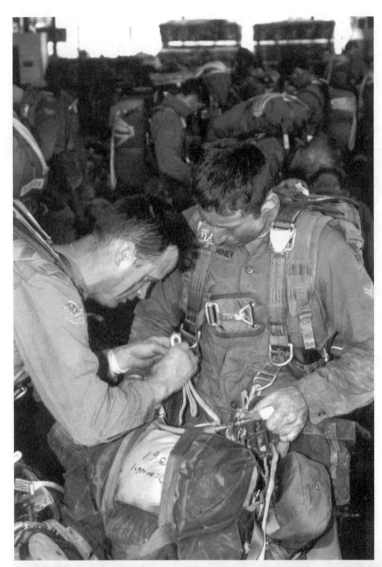

Teamwork and mutual trust. A paratrooper must not only trust his mates to ensure his safety in regard to parachuting, but must also count on them to pull their own weight. Once on the ground, the airborne soldiers are largely dependent on what they themselves can carry.
Top: (Courtesy of Canadian Airborne Forces Museum.)

Bottom: (Courtesy of R. Prouse.)

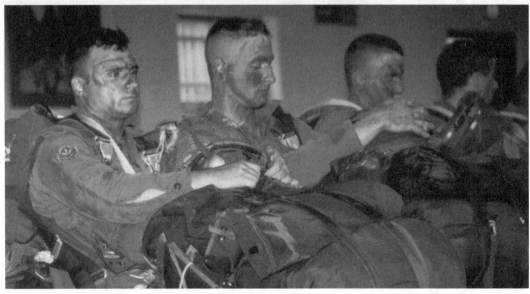

CHAPTER SIX

THE LONG KISS GOODNIGHT
The Canadian Airborne Regiment in the Seventies

An Airborne Regiment is extremely costly to maintain if dedicated solely to quick reaction situations that require light forces. I cannot / not in my judgement, afford to have any one formation of the Canadian Forces become unduly specialized.

General Jacques Dextraze, CDS, 1976[1]

In spite of all the internal debate in government and the military that was swirling around the Regiment and CF in general, the Airborne ushered in the 1970s with an auspicious start. The FLQ crisis in Montreal in October 1970 afforded the opportunity to exhibit the Regiment's value. The Quebec government officially solicited the assistance of the Armed Forces in aid of the civil power, citing the need to "help the police protect the public and public buildings."[2] The CDS received the request in Ottawa at 12:50 hours and, forty minutes later, two aircraft carrying the lead elements of the Airborne Regiment departed Namao airfield in Edmonton to begin the Regiment's participation in Operation Essay thousands of kilometres away.[3]

Once in Quebec, the Airborne was stationed at St. Hubert airfield, with smaller detachments scattered around Camp Farnham, Camp Bouchard, St. Sauver and Sorel. It was organized into four rapid reaction teams tasked with assisting the police to conduct sweeps, raids and other internal security missions. The Airborne Regiment's excellent and disciplined performance was such that Army Commander Lieutenant-General Turcot, wrote a letter to express his "deep pride and appreciation for the excellent manner in which the Canadian Airborne Regiment participated during their deployment in Montreal from 15 October to 17 November [1970]."[4]

Yet another operational test of the Regiment came a short four years later. In April 1974, 1 Commando assumed a peacekeeping rotation to Cyprus, as part of the Canadian commitment to the United Nations Force in Cyprus (UNFICYP). A coup staged by the Greek Cypriot National Guard in mid July triggered a Turkish invasion of the island. The resultant conflict necessitated the deployment of the remainder of the Regiment as reinforcements for the Canadian contingent there.

In Cyprus, the paratroopers quickly distinguished themselves. The airborne soldiers continually displayed a steely courage and again exhibited a firm, disciplined and resolute stand. By late August a demarcation line was finally established and the Canadian Airborne Regiment aggressively enforced it.[5] For their efforts, the paratroopers earned two Stars of Courage and six Medals of Bravery. However, a great price was paid for these honours. In the brief period the Regiment was engaged in the conflict, it suffered thirty casualties, including two dead.[6]

The accolades were short-lived. Despite the meritorious service, the Regiment's structural defects and its growing number of opponents could not be held at bay. By 1975, the winds had shifted. The Regiment no longer had the protection of the gods. The failure to define a specific role was no longer seen by many senior military commanders as an example of unlimited flexibility or versatility, but as needless elitism and wasted resources. The Regiment's special status, reviled by the conventionally minded, was perceived by many to be offensive and unwarranted. Whether the Airborne realized it or not, it was about to commence its "long kiss goodnight."

The Airborne Regiment was in no way a solitary target. The entire Canadian military establishment felt the immutable threat of the budgetary knife, but the continuing erosion of the Canadian Armed Forces irrefutably worsened the Regiment's problems. Resource constraints, particularly budgetary shortfalls and manpower deficiencies, inevitably inspired a reassessment of the relevance of a strong and costly airborne capability. One contemporary CO, Major-General Herb Pitts, recalled the comments of General Jacques Dextraze, the CDS, his Vice Chief, Rear-Admiral Robert Falls, and Colonel Andrew Christie, their COS, following their visit to the Regiment. At the completion of the tour, Dextraze queried his entourage. He simply asked them, "what did you think?" The VCDS's immediate response, which earned the approving nods of his two companions was, "lots of expensive equipment."[7] Pitts conceded that this exchange turned his stomach. The "paratroopers," he lamented, "couldn't help but impress those who saw them."[8] But evidently not the CDS and his deputies.

The reality, however, was not about impressive, specially trained, soldiers. It was quite the opposite. The military bureaucracy, struggling with perennial funding problems, loathed the special or unique. These types of organizations normally implied added costs. What was preferred among those who decried the Airborne was generic, general purpose organizations that fit a standard template.

In hindsight the erosion of the Airborne Regiment's special status is clearly discernable. But it was not quite so clear then. Nevertheless, in June 1970, the first sign of the erosion was the addition to the Regiment's organizational structure of a mechanized infantry battalion, designated 3 Mechanized Commando. This unit was stationed in Baden-Soellingen, Germany.[9] Although 3 Mechanized Commando wore the maroon beret, the vast majority of its members were not jump-qualified; the unit had no parachute role, and it never exercised in conjunction with the rest of the Airborne Regiment. To the paratroopers serving in Canada, 3 Mechanized Commando was an anomaly that should never have been directly associated with the Canadian Airborne Regiment.[10] It symbolized a retreat from the concept of a unique formation that provided adventurous and challenging training not found elsewhere. Furthermore, it represented a corrosion of the concept of a pure airborne entity that was capable of swift global deployment.

Another dangerous sign was the willingness to include the Regiment, or elements thereof, in the normal six-month rotation tours of conventional Canadian units in UN assignments such as Cyprus. If the formation was tasked with such a mission how could it fulfill its officially mandated role? How could it be a global quick reaction "fire-brigade," or an UN stand-by force, or the government's trump card in the defence of the Canadian Arctic? If it was tied up performing normal duties, how could it continue to be a strategic reserve?

The apparent retreat from the Airborne's original operational concept was disturbing to the paratroopers. Equally as ominous was a tasking chart published in the DND publication, *Defence 1972*, depicting programmed military activities and the current system of multiple assignments. The three Combat Groups (brigades), as well as the Airborne Regiment, shared identical missions. Namely, all four formations were shown to have a capability and responsibility to conduct: protection of Canada, North American defence, NATO collective defence, international security, and national support and development operations. As such, the Airborne Regiment, in accordance with this all encompassing list of duties, no longer represented a unique capability characteristic of special operations forces. In fact, one could argue it was actually depicted as inefficient. Notations to the afore-mentioned tasking chart specifically indicated that the Airborne Regiment was the only formation which was incapable of providing trained personnel for the mechanized battle group in NATO Europe.[11] Again the Euro-centric military posture seemed the dominant one.

Collectively these events, compounded by sullen resentment of some of those in NDHQ and the conventional regiments, strengthened the growing movement to establish the Airborne Regiment as nothing more than just another infantry unit. Some even argued it should simply not exist.

Whether those in the Regiment realized it or not ominous larger events were taking place. In December 1974, the cabinet authorized the initiation of a Defence Structure Review (DSR). The review was conducted by a committee which consisted of the Deputy MND, the Under-Secretary of State for External Affairs, the Secretary of the Treasury Board, and Dextraze, the Chief of the Defence Staff. Dextraze clearly announced that "hard operational needs would determine the basic structuring of the forces."[12] The underlying message was obvious. Only those organizations that had a pervasive and undisputable role to fill could breathe easily.

The Defence Review meant that the Airborne Regiment's fortunes had turned—probably for the worse. To date, the paratroopers had reaped the benefits of powerful and sympathetic mandarins. However, Dextraze changed that. Although Dextraze demonstrated the same ability as General Allard, especially in overcoming opposition and bulldozing his decisions through reticent headquarters, unlike Allard, he was not a fan of the Airborne Regiment.[13] The paratroopers would soon find that he was indeed a dangerous adversary.

General Dextraze, as well as his perceived protégé, Andrew Christie, were described by some as bullies. Colonel D.B. McGibbon, a senior long-standing staff officer at NDHQ at the time, felt that the two placed a heavy emphasis on the virtue of rank to ensure the implementation of decisions because "they lacked the intellectual horsepower" to do otherwise.[14] Major-General Pitts recalled that "it didn't matter what you thought was right; if he [Dextraze] believed otherwise, anything counter to what he wanted was a waste of time."[15] This observation was later supported by Professor Douglas Bland's comprehensive study of Canadian Chiefs of Defence Staff. Bland recorded that Dextraze's manner was not likely to "tolerate a long strategic discussion," and that he "bullied projects through" because he believed he had an "inherent right and responsibility to dominate the defence policy process in ways that other officers or bureaucrats cannot."[16] Not surprisingly, this new Chief of the Defence Staff was not respected or necessarily trusted by many of his subordinates. Nevertheless, he was at the top of the pyramid, and he would stay there for close to an unprecedented five years.[17]

If the enmity of the CDS was not enough to cause consternation, then the reversal of the government's emphasis on a northern defence policy was. The first indicator came in November 1975 when James Richardson, himself a new Minister of National Defence, addressed a gathering of Militia Honorary Colonels. At this forum, he stressed the government's re-commitment to NATO and Europe. Richardson, in a clear reversal of the 1971 White Paper, asked the rhetorical question, "Where is the threat?" He went on to answer, "The threat is largely in Europe, on the Central Front. The threat is not as we see it, in North America."[18] Once again the one role Canada's airborne forces had always been associated with, the defence of the North, was dismissed. By this statement even the government acknowledged the primacy of heavy mechanized forces for NATO.[19]

The CDS provided no respite for the Airborne. He shared the defence minister's assessment that there was no risk in Canada, let alone its North. Although concerned with exercising sovereignty in the Arctic, General Dextraze did not consider an airborne regiment the most effective means of performing that duty. He stressed a more tangible presence. In 1975 the CDS had proposed an organization centred on an older idea of a force of native peoples, such as the Canadian Rangers, who resided in the region and who would perform patrolling and surveillance duties. He postulated that this force would be supported by the Northern Region Headquarters, Canadian Forces airbases, and a new training facility on Devon Island.[20] His vision did not contain a role for the Airborne. Shortly thereafter the General initiated a series of events very disquieting for the Regiment's future.

In late December of that year, Dextraze told a gathering in Montreal that the structure of the Armed Forces was being reviewed and that "one of the units considered for disbandment or removal is the First Canadian Airborne Regiment in Edmonton."[21] During this time, Colonel Ian Fraser, the Regimental Commander of the Airborne Regiment also received a telephone call from (then) Lieutenant-Colonel Ian Douglas who was the CO of 3 Mechanized Commando in Europe. Douglas informed Fraser that he had just returned from a briefing given by the CDS, at which Dextraze clearly stated that the Airborne Regiment would be disbanded.[22]

A frantic Fraser immediately sent signals to the Army Commander and Brigadier-General Pitts, the senior serving paratrooper in the Canadian Armed Forces. It quickly became evident that neither of these individuals knew of such a plan. However, on 18 December 1975, Fraser received an exclusive telex from Army Headquarters confirming the CDS's comments. The telex stated that the Airborne Regiment would be disbanded and the responsibility given to an airborne company in central Canada.[23] Dextraze's belief that the Regiment was costly and redundant was obvious. After all, his perception was that the "Airborne Regiment's role is to assist every other formation and the Government of Canada in any missions we may be given."[24] For him, given no credible threat to the nation, and a formation with no pervasive role, a return to the Mobile Striking Force/Defence of Canada Force concept of airborne capability (and cost) was deemed only sensible.

The roller coaster ride was about to begin in which civilian and military personalities would be instrumental. In light of the threat that had emerged, Pitts, a former Regimental Commander and now Chief of Land Operations at NDHQ, began to work frenetically on an alternate plan. He had one goal—save a viable airborne capability for the Canadian military. This, however, was no easy task because Dextraze's ideas had no concrete formulation, so it was difficult for the Airborne advocates to devise a saving counterproposal.

The subsequent events became nothing short of chaotic. Colonel Fraser recalled, with respect to the future of the Regiment, the process of events from "December of 1975 until July of 1977, can at best be described as bizarre and funny, or at worst, tragic."[25] The tragedy, he explained, was that there was no adequate staff analysis, no effective operational plan, nor was there any real strategic concept.[26]

The announcements of disbandment fomented a storm of resistance. If the initial declarations had been floated to test the wind it became apparent a gale had erupted. Faced with the storm, the ever-resourceful General Dextraze now deftly took a new approach. In January 1976, the CDS addressed the Conference of Defence Associates at the Château Laurier in Ottawa. For years this group of mostly reserve force representatives and retired regulars had been used by ministers and their generals as a platform to announce new programs and test reactions. They usually supported conventional ideas for the good of the Canadian Forces as a whole. If Dextraze was mindful of this he was not disappointed, for they listened to him intently and there was not much reaction against what he said. He told them:

> My two major problems with the current army posture are that it could be better balanced geographically, and that I do not have enough people to fill the sharp end vacancies which exist. I could correct these problems in a number of ways. Something along the following lines could work well: The Airborne Regiment could be relocated and form part of the order of battle of another formation; we would then have three, rather than four, major army formations in Canada, each with integral supporting arms and services.[27]

Dextraze also painted a "hypothetical scenario" for the assembled audience. He informed them that he visualized the formation of a highly mobile, rapid reaction formation in the centre of Canada, with its headquarters in Petawawa. He outlined that the organization would consist of an air-landed battalion and a major airborne unit formed from the current Canadian Airborne Regiment in which there would be RCR, PPCLI, and R22eR commandos.[28]

The CDS's theoretical musings to the CDA members reflected his long held desire to establish a new Special Service Force (SSF) which would be a direct challenge to the Airborne Regiment. Some years later, Major-General Pitts would recall that no amount of his or any other's persuasion could change the CDS's direction once he set his mind on something. In light of the existing airborne force serious arguments and discussions should have surrounded the CDS's concept. But none was apparently forthcoming. Dextraze was likely promoting the relocation of the Canadian Airborne Regiment in order to transform it or amalgamate it with his envisioned SSF. In any event there was no doubt in anyone's mind that the CDS was the prime mover for the decision to relocate the Airborne Regiment. Pitts explained that Dextraze had commanded 2 Canadian Infantry Brigade Group in the mid sixties and had tried to convert it to an SSF organization. However, the Army had then scuppered his plan. As Pitts revealed, "he now [re-]created his pet project."[29]

The CDS directed Formation Mobile Command Headquarters to study and prepare a plan for the reorganization and relocation of the Army in Canada. Increasingly, resistance to the General's scheme mounted. Internal studies conflicted with Dextraze's assertion that the Airborne Regiment would be more operationally effective in Ontario.[30] So Dextraze tried to isolate the opposition. Colonel Fraser, the Regimental Commander, stated that "by August [1976], the plans with respect to the Airborne Regiment were being managed personally by Colonel Andy Christie who was the CDS's Executive Assistant. HQ Mobile Command was virtually cut out of the equation."[31] Fraser suggested this was due to the fact that the CDS was concerned that the weakness of the basic concept would be seriously challenged by the staff of FMC on the strength of military logic alone.

In October 1976, Colonel Fraser was summoned from Edmonton to see General Dextraze in his office in Ottawa. The CDS simply asked Colonel Fraser if he agreed with the move of the Airborne Regiment. Fraser conceded that he did not agree with the plan, but that he would support it to the best of his ability. Once again the CDS asked the determined Fraser the same question, to which he again gave a negative reply. Then Dextraze cooly told the astounded Colonel that "I [Fraser] would be well advised to leave the military because my career had come to a halt."[32] Ironically, years later, during an interview with David Bercuson, General Jacques Dextraze, then retired, lamented that "too often in peacetime it takes courage 'to rock the boat,' and I must admit that our peacetime system sometimes seems to have a built-in bias against those who have the courage to speak out against what they honestly believe to be wrong."[33] Analysis indicates that if this was a problem, Dextraze himself shared a great deal of responsibility for its perpetuation.

Dextraze also had opposition outside the military. Alberta politicians, concerned with the economic impact of the move, created much discomfort for the CDS.[34] To exacerbate the situation a protest movement calling itself the Save the Regiment Committee, composed of former serving members and concerned citizens and widely supported by the Royal Canadian Legion membership, began an active campaign to lobby the government. The committee went so far as to write a letter to Queen Elizabeth asking her to intercede on behalf of the Regiment.[35]

More effective, however, were the efforts of individuals such as the recently retired Lieutenant-General Stanley Waters. Waters was a staunch airborne supporter who personified credibility and respect. He was a former member of the First Special Service Force, 1st Canadian Parachute Battalion, and an operational and staff officer in the postwar period who crusaded for a credible airborne capability. At that time he was also the Colonel of the Regiment (Canadian Airborne Regiment). Waters attacked Dextraze's proposal relentlessly in private and public forums. In support of the actions being taken by the Save the Regiment Committee he wrote:

> Numerous Defence Studies and Reviews since the end of World War II have constantly confirmed the operational requirement to retain balanced, all-arms, combat capable parachute (airborne) forces as part of the Canadian Regular Active Force. This all-volunteer force is the Corps d'elite of the Canadian Armed Forces and can do the assigned operational missions superbly well—as demonstrated most recently during the Turkish invasion of Cyprus. Suffice it to say that it was a painful route to get to the present—virtually ideal—situation in which all the components of the Canadian Airborne Regiment are located together under a single commander which has all the obvious advantages of unified training, operational effectiveness, responsiveness and esprit de corps. In addition, the Airborne training centre and the parachute packing and maintenance centre are co-located with the CAR [Canadian Airborne Regiment] for the first time in Canadian military history, with clear advantages in effectiveness and economy. Finally, the airborne force is located on a superb, all-weather air base, soundly situated from a strategic viewpoint for access to the Canadian North. The air base is the home of one of the two air transport squadrons which provide the airborne forces with their tactical mobility and essential training support. It is worth stressing that for the first time, all the essential land/air components that make up an airborne capability, are located together on one base. To propose to change this ideal situation is, by any military yardstick, simply poor military judgement, as well as being very expensive if current facilities are to be duplicated elsewhere.[36]

In spite of this public resistance the CDS dismissed such criticisms and forged ahead. In an almost casual way, in spite of the pressure, he repudiated the comments of Lieutenant-General Waters almost with the condescension of an adult disciplining an errant child. Dextraze bluntly pointed out, "Waters has been out of the forces for over a year. He's out-of-date."[37] According to some, he vindictively punished Waters by refusing to extend him as the Colonel of the Regiment and denied him permission to go to Europe to say farewell to 3 Mechanized Commando.[38] Whether this was true or not there was little doubt that Dextraze would not tolerate opposition to his ideas. On 26 November 1976, the decision to move the Regiment to Petawawa was formally authorized by cabinet. Dextraze clearly announced that the decision was strictly a military one. He stated, "the plan comes from me, I made it."[39]

Despite this determination by the CDS he did have to defend his actions with some sort of justification. In doing so, he asserted that the redeployment plan was the result of a military appreciation and a military necessity.[40] He did not believe that the posture of the Army field formations in Canada was in balance with the military requirements. Almost a year to the day after his initial musing to the Conference of Defence Associations, Dextraze briefed the gathering once again on his final design. He had concluded, he said, that a "military appreciation" had led him to believe that "on mobilization day the minimum Field Force requirement is for four brigades and an Airborne Regiment manned to War Establishment."[41] Once again, he laid out a detailed rationale for the CDA delegates:

> I decided to go in peacetime with a standard brigade group in the West, a standard brigade group in the East and a force of Regimental size in the centre, which I have tentatively called "The Special Service Force."...The Special Service Force in the Centre is slightly different. It must be capable of executing the peacetime missions assigned to it with its "Peace Establishment" but be capable, using reservists, of expanding to a full Airborne Regiment plus a brigade in time of emergency/mobilization. This will allow us to maintain a relatively light—"Airborne—Airportable" Quick Reaction Force in the demographic centre of the country in peacetime which can be moved quickly to augment either of the flanking brigades for internal security tasks, to the Arctic, or to UN-type operations.[42]

By late summer 1976, General Dextraze had achieved his Special Service Force. The CDS clearly specified that the SSF would pick up the Airborne Regiment, which obviously entailed a move of the airborne organization from Edmonton, not only to Petawawa but also some elements thereof to the nation's capital.[43] He announced that the Airborne Regiment was now also responsible for doing the Allied Command Europe (ACE) Mobile Force (Land) task. Having achieved his goal, at times against very determined opposition, General Dextraze now delivered the coup de grâce. With complete confidence he boldly proclaimed that "rather than destroying the Airborne Regiment, in fact I have expanded it."[44] Not everyone agreed.

Several months later the inconsistency of the entire affair began to come out in various public forums. In Parliament, when questioned by the Standing Committee of External Affairs and National Defence (SCEAND) on his new plan, Dextraze amazingly declared "never have I said that moving the Airborne Regiment, from Edmonton to Petawawa, would make it far more operationally efficient or effective, no. Obviously, it is going to be less effective, operationally, but not that much."[45] Dextraze now admitted that the reason he amalgamated the Regiment with another formation was so that they would have "duties other than just airborne duties."[46] The CDS's new tack was not surprising. Dextraze was already on record as stating:

It would have been too easy to disband the Airborne Regiment and disperse the persons to other formations. However, we have a requirement for an Airborne component as one element in our general purpose force package...but an Airborne Regiment is extremely costly to maintain if dedicated solely to quick reaction situations that require Light Forces, let me here make a point very clear, parachuting is only one of the methods we use to insert troops into operations, and I cannot /not, in my judgement, afford to have any one formation of the Canadian Forces become unduly specialized."[47]

And so one can interpret the CDS's directed move of the paratroopers as a conscious step toward harnessing and subordinating Canada's airborne forces. Implicit in Dextraze's reasoning was a valid argument that had perpetually clung to the idea of a distinct Canadian airborne capability; namely, the relevance of paratroopers in the national context. Significantly for the Airborne, the senior leadership associated with the formative halcyon days of Edmonton failed to grasp this fact, nor did they appreciate the stark reality of the political and financial world in which Dextraze had to operate. Their inability to understand and correct this fundamental flaw would have severe repercussions later on. Clearly, the CDS's message foreshadowed the evolution of the Regiment to just another infantry battalion.

General Dextraze was not without opposition. The General's staunch defence of his Land Force Restructuring Plan before the Parliamentary Standing Committee of External Affairs and National Defence (SCEAND) was not the end of his troubles. He constantly had to reassert that his decision was a good one for the sake of the entire Land Force and the greater good of Canada's defence. Furthermore, Dextraze acknowledged that his real motive was to economize and establish better command and control in the Army Field Force. Nonetheless, problems continued to plague the General's personal plan of moving the Airborne to the east and transforming it. CFB Petawawa was unable to absorb such a large new lodger to its base in such a short period of time. By the end of March, Colonel Fraser recalled, "there was no decent accommodation in Petawawa, no Air Head selected, equipment scales were not established, confusion over drop zones, no stores accommodation, no Operations Plan for the move, no future training policy, no PMQs [military housing] in Ottawa [for the proposed move of 1 Commando to that location] and God knows what else."[48] The fact that Dextraze wanted to billet Francophone paratroopers of the Airborne Regiment in Ottawa was scoffed at by Prime Minister Trudeau and flatly rejected. Trudeau made it clear that there would be no combat troops in his capital. This now exacerbated the issue of overcrowding in Petawawa.[49]

The various forms of the controversy that now surrounded the relocation underlined the lack of analysis inherent in Dextraze's plan. As a sign of further trouble, the MND began to get cold feet, likely caused by the apparent confusion in costs and by ministerial questions about troops stationed in Ottawa. Consequently, he chaired a meeting on 16 June 1977, attended by the CDS, VCDS and a senior representative from FMC, to discuss a possible reversal of the decision to transfer the Regiment from Edmonton.[50] Not surprisingly, the strong-willed Chief of Defence Staff prevailed.[51] Dextraze once again declared that the move was a necessary military decision. A week later, Colonel Fraser was informed that the relocation for the Airborne to Petawawa was definitely on.

The move of the Airborne Regiment in the summer of 1977 proved to be a major watershed in its existence. Overwhelmingly, the consensus of those who supported the requirement for a strong airborne capability viewed the decision as a disaster. All of the senior regimental officers of the time agreed. Major-General Gaudreau assessed that "the move to Petawawa was the beginning of the end of Regiment."[52] Brigadier-General Therriault echoed those sentiments. He felt "the move brought about the demise of the Airborne."[53] Brigadier-General Walt Holmes thought that the Airborne Regiment "lost its fabric" as a result of the transfer and "was no longer the cohesive, effective organization it had been in Edmonton."[54] Finally, Brigadier-General Ian Douglas believed that "the entire structure and attitude of the Regiment changed" for the worse after the relocation.[55] Dextraze's scheme diluted it in focus, in task, and in ideal location. Morale in the Regiment plummeted.

But there was at least one voice which still loudly applauded the fateful move east. The CDS's former executive assistant, Brigadier-General Andy Christie, now the Special Service Force Commander, claimed that "it [Airborne Regiment] had limited capabilities in Edmonton and by drawing the Airborne from the West to the centre of Canada, we've put more punch in the sharp end of the fighting stick."[56] Obviously, Christie had not paid attention to his mentor's testimony in front of SCEAND the previous March in which Dextraze admitted that efficiency would be less.

The reasons for the hostility to Dextraze's scheme went well beyond the simple fact that the Regiment had put down roots in Edmonton and was accepted as a valued member of that community. The decision was not only extremely unpopular but operationally unsound. There were a large number of operational concerns which had not been adequately addressed. Petawawa did not have parachute training equipment or facilities, nor did it have a close accessible airfield to allow for rapid deployment. Another concern was the fact that the Parachute Maintenance Depot, where all parachutes were checked and packed, remained in Edmonton. Colonel Fraser was horrified at all of this:

> In Edmonton, we had one of the finest combined operation establishments located anywhere in the world. We were co-located on a major air base with a resident C130 Squadron, a resident Helicopter Squadron and a resident Air Reserve Squadron. The Canadian Forces Parachute Maintenance Depot and the Tactical Air Lift School were in the same barrack lines, as was the Canadian Airborne Centre. One of the largest supply depots in Canada was less than a mile away.[57]

It was not to be so in Petawawa.

But of prime importance, and instrumental to the Regiment's subsequent decline, was its loss of status as an independent formation. It was now simply an integral part of the newly created SSF. Furthermore, its subjugation to another brigade cast doubt on its claim to be a strategic reserve. In essence the move fulfilled its actual intent. It represented, in consonance with the CDS's plan, a wholesale depreciation of the importance of the Airborne Regiment.[58] A commission of inquiry would later conclude, "the reorganization [move to Petawawa] had the effect of diluting the CAR's former uniqueness in the army."[59]

The reality of Dextraze's plan quickly materialized. The Regiment was dramatically reduced. Its integral airborne engineer squadron and airborne artillery battery were removed from the order of battle. The Regiment was no longer a "stand alone mini-formation." Instead, it depended on other units within the SSF to augment it when required. On these occasions the Regiment took on a new designation, namely the Airborne Regiment Battle Group. For instance, the lost engineer and artillery capabilities, previously built into the Regiment's organization, now became the obligation of separate units: 2 Combat Engineer Regiment and "E" Battery, 2 Royal Canadian Horse Artillery respectively. They were responsible for providing airborne qualified personnel and equipment in support of the Airborne Regiment, on order from the SSF headquarters. But they were not an integral part of it.

The erosion of the Regiment's structure did not stop with the loss of integral combat capability. In addition, the Airborne Service Support Unit (ASSU) was also disbanded. First line service support was provided by the newly formed 1 Airborne Service Support Company, and second line support by 2 Service Battalion which was another unit within the SSF. Also stricken from the order of battle was 3 Mechanized Commando in Germany. Personnel serving in the unit were returned to Canada, and subsequently re-badged to form 3 RCR, which was also newly established in Petawawa. A new 3 Airborne Commando was authorized, but not yet organized.[60] In light of the final resolution of events, it was difficult to comprehend General Dextraze's public claim to have actually strengthened the Regiment.[61]

The designation of the Canadian Airborne Regiment as a "regiment" was largely in name only. It became nothing more than an airborne battalion and further evidence of a drastic reduction and role change continued to emerge. Direction given by the FMC Commander, in the *Land Force Restructuring—Detailed Implementation Plan,* specified that the Airborne Regiment was still to be exempted from normal taskings, in an attempt to keep it operationally ready as a quick-reaction unit. However, this direction was quickly forgotten. The Regiment, as just another member of the SSF, was tasked in the same manner as the other units to fulfill the SSF's voracious manpower bill.[62] The paratroopers' complaints fell on deaf ears. Neither the Army headquarters nor the SSF listened.

In all, the move of 1977 was the turning point for the optimism generated in the "Great Adventure" of the early decade. The chronic weakness of the unit's foundation, specifically the lack of a pervasive role, once again rattled the entire structure. Its lack of a recognized or unique mission, which was widely accepted by the military and political leadership, undermined its relevance. As a result, the Regiment was at the mercy of personalities in power. Unfortunately for Canada's paratroopers, many of the civilian and military mandarins of the day were not enamoured by airborne soldiers any more than Dextraze was.

The perception that the Airborne Regiment was a costly and redundant organization simply refused to go away. By the summer of 1978, while still reeling from its dramatic move, the Regiment's utility, as well as its existence, was once more questioned. This time it came from the MND himself. Barney Danson told newspaper reporters that he was thinking of disbanding the Airborne altogether. The ensuing public controversy prompted a clarification, at which time he declared: "Canada cannot afford the luxury of an unassigned unit to be inactive."[63] In another account he affirmed that "an elite unit, with no assigned tasks, seems out of place today."[64]

Once again, the minister's statements were testimony to the flaws in the Regiment's original operational concept. It was too all-inclusive in defining the Regiment's role. The Airborne was not recognized as filling a specific purpose, or providing a necessary task that no other organization could perform. Therefore, its existence as a strong, viable—and perceived costly—entity was open to serious scrutiny and inevitable attack. Its apparent high cost only made the viability arguments more poignant.

The none-too-subtle hints about disbandment prompted Colonel Painchaud, the well-respected and outspoken Regimental Commander to publicly criticize the MND. Audaciously, Painchaud actually called for Danson's replacement, if in fact the minister did not stop such "irresponsible" statements. Not surprisingly, Painchaud was swiftly "reassigned." He had crossed the acceptable boundary in civil-military relations. Even those officers who strongly supported the former regimental commander conceded that serving senior military commanders simply could not openly challenge and criticize their political masters. Indeed, Painchaud himself should have realized this.[65]

The most recent confrontation between the Airborne and its detractors was not an isolated event. Adding to the Regiment's misery in the late 1970s was the incessant undercurrent of hostility towards the paratroopers and the concept of "special" troops. Colonel Painchaud professed that the Airborne Regiment "has had enemies ever since it was formed."[66] This belief is widely held by most, regardless of rank, who have served in the Airborne. Lieutenant-Colonel, Dr. Peter Bradley, a former member of the Airborne and now the head of the Royal Military College's Military Leadership and Psychology Department, acknowledged that throughout his career he always noted a distinct anti-airborne attitude in the Army.[67] Brigadier-General Ian Douglas stated that he was "always aware that there was a group out there who were hostile to the Regiment." He explained that the paratroopers were "always being sniped at by people outside the organization."[68] Chief Warrant Officer Jim Vienneau, a senior NCO who spent the majority of his career in airborne related units and is viewed by many as the epitome of the airborne soldier, commented, "everyone who didn't serve in the Airborne Regiment had a negative opinion of the Airborne." He indicated this was due to the fact that "anywhere we went we stole the limelight and this created jealously."[69]

Similarly, Lieutenant-Colonel Richard Dick conceded he knew many officers who hated the Airborne. These individuals, he claimed, had nothing good to say about it. He remarked that the one thing the airborne critics all had in common was the fact that none of them ever served in the Regiment.[70] This observation is worth emphasizing. Brigadier-General Ernie Beno, a former airborne gunner, felt then as now that "there is no such thing as the 'Airborne' soldier. There are soldiers who parachute and those who *chose* not to."[71]

Another veteran of the Regiment, Lieutenant-Colonel Ron Bragdon, was less diplomatic. He flatly pointed to another recognized fact. "The only ones who haven't served in the Airborne Regiment," he stated, "are those who didn't want to."[72] Colonel Peter Kenward, who served three tours with the Airborne added that for numerous people, the Regiment was a reminder of their personal shortcomings. As a result, the Airborne created a level of dislike and discomfort for many. Kenward concluded that this created a distinct polarity. Individuals "either loved and had great loyalty to the Airborne or they thoroughly despised it." While all of this personal testimony smacks of special pleading by airborne soldiers, one truth is clear. There was no middle ground in this debate.[73]

Throughout his lengthy airborne service, Colonel Kenward felt that each time he left his parent unit he suffered an acute sense of separation. He adjudged that as paratroopers, the members of the Regiment were consistently "pit-lamped." Kenward explained that "there was always a feeling that you had to defend yourself, defend the capability you represented, and defend the unit."[74] There always seemed to be a challenge. Sometimes, he noted, it was overt, and often it was covert. But it was always there.

The antagonism between the Airborne and its detractors was noticeable even in the newspapers of the time. Several reported on the latent mistrust that faced the paratroopers. Journalist Peter Worthington recognized that the "Trudeau government is probably nervous of the Airborne Regiment." He quickly added, "so are the conventional military." The enmity, Worthington believed, stemmed from the fact that the "paras may be too good for their own good." In addition the "outspoken, irreverent, maverick" tendencies were repugnant to the military and political leadership.[75]

The issue was explored in other newspapers as well. National commentator and former war correspondent Charles Lynch also documented that "other units of the armed forces have long looked askance at the Airborne Regiment, partly out of envy but also out of unease about the hell-raising capacities of its members on and off the mock battlefield."[76] Lynch pointed out that "successive Canadian defence ministers have handled the airborne forces with tongs, never sure what to do with the unit, and never completely certain that civilian control over the force was absolute."[77] Worthington commented on the governmental angst as well. He wrote, "for those conditioned to watching how our federal government traditionally treats the military, the signs are unmistakable: they want to be rid of the Canadian Airborne Regiment which is usually referred to as 'crack' or 'elite' or similar adjectives that soldiers envy."[78]

The commentary of the press, and those in the Regiment, was not the result of casual or fleeting trouble. Rather, it was the inevitable outcome of the Airborne's systemic flaws. The Airborne Regiment was conceived with passion and with the best of intentions, but the "bastard sons" were never fully accepted by the civilian or military family. In 1968, a military patron had the power to ensure their creation but not the longevity to necessarily ensure their viability. Then in 1977, a military opponent began to erode its staus with a similar enthusiasm and the same power. The signal event of the shift from support to opposition was the fateful move of the Airborne out of Edmonton. The relocation to Petawawa signified all that had worked against the unit over the formative years—a flawed operational concept and a sea of resentment within other military circles. It was also the first clear sign that marked its eventual demise.

Notes for Chapter Six

1. "Text of CDS Speech to Press," Message CDS 424, 081800Z December 1976. DHist, File 77 / 31.
2. Major Guy Morchain, "Peacekeeping at Home," *Sentinel*, February / March 1971, 2-3.
3. Major-General Stewart recalled "we were ready to deploy to Montreal faster than they could assemble the airlift and once there we undertook helicopter and vehicle mounted search and cordon operations the next day!" Letter to author, 1 July 1998.
4. Letter, FMC Commander to Regimental Commander, Cdn AB Regt, "Aid to the Civil Power in the Province of Quebec Contribution by the Canadian Airborne Regiment," 4 January 1971. Barr Papers.
5. The Regiment undertook the task of establishing and enforcing the demarcation line, providing organization and security for prisoner of war (PoW) exchanges, and providing escorts for infrastructure repair. The Canadian troops assisted with 20,000 refugees and delivered tons of food and supplies, tents, blankets and cots prior to the arrival of the International Committee of the Red Cross (ICRC) and other agencies. In addition, they later delivered ICRC family messages to villages. The "can do attitude" and efforts of the paratroopers was noted by the Cypriots. A sign was erected outside one of the refugee camps in the Canadian sector with a hand drawn paratrooper under full canopy with the words, "All Canadians welcome." The Canadian Airborne Regiment, "The Regiment in Cyprus," *The Maroon Beret,* January 1975, 28-40.
6. Annex A to 1326-1(10), Canadian Airborne Regiment Historical Report, dated 8 February 1995. CAFM.
7. Major-General H.C. Pitts, interview with author 30 June 1998. Pitts who was the Chief of Land Operations at the time, declared that "senior people have no special love for special soldiers." He explained that many persons felt that the Regiment was an expensive organization. As a result, when money became tight the Regiment became a target. A prime example was the Air Force. During the C-130 Hercules transport aircraft rationalization, the Air Force argued for 26 aircraft so that it could deploy the Regiment in two lifts. However, when flying hours became short, the requirement to keep specially qualified aircrews (i.e., trained to drop parachutists) to man all these aircraft became an exorbitantly expensive proposition. The Air Force now changed its argument and priority. Major-General Stewart also asserted that the Regiment was always listed for disbandment by the budget bureaucrats in Ottawa in the annual fiscal economy studies. Letter to author, 1 July 1998.
8. Interview with author, 30 June 1998.

9. The new unit was a hybrid and represented an expedient solution to a potentially acrimonious dispute. In fact it was an easy out for NDHQ to name it as a unit of the Regiment and avoid the necessity of creating a new regiment to account for the composite nature of 3 [mechanized] Cdo." Letter to author, 1 July 1998. This was based on the FMC reorganization 1969 / 1970. The old structure had 11 infantry battalions (2nd Cdn Guards; 1, 2 RCR; 1, 2 PPCLI; 1, 2, 3, R22eR; 1, 2, RHC; and 1 QOR of C) and the Canadian Airborne Regiment consisting of 2 commandos. The re-organization cut several regiments but established three battalions for each of the RCR, PPCLI and R22eR. Therefore, the new structure now had 9 infantry battalions and the Canadian Airborne Regiment consisting of 2 commandos and a mechanized battalion (3 Mechanized Cdo). "Mobile Command Force Structure Conference 25-26 November 1969," Annex F, Appendix 1. NAC, RG 24, Vol 23571, File 1901-2, part 2. See also "3 Canadian Mechanized Commando," *The Maroon Beret,* Spring 1974, 14; Fall 1976, 6; and 1978, 81. The unit was relocated to CFB Petawawa where it was disbanded effective 15 July 1977 as part of the Land Force Restructuring. Although 3 Airborne Commando was created in its place, it was not authorized to be manned. Positions accruing as a result of the disbandment were reallocated within existing FMC units in accordance with priorities established by Commander FMC. 3 Airborne Commando was not manned until June 1979. Message CDS 220, 301905Z June 1977. DHist, File 77 / 502.

10. The 3 Mechanized Commando issue is one which still rankles many in the airborne family. Major-General Stewart recalled that the Airborne Regiment "objected strenuously to the naming of 3 Cdo." Those who served in the unit, particularly individuals who commanded, insist that it was an integral part of the Airborne Regiment. Brigadier-General Ian Douglas argued that the mechanized unit made a conscious decision to be airborne and entered a partnership with a German Jump Battalion and the British Parachute Regiment, which allowed members of the unit to conduct continuation parachuting in Europe. Colonel Mike Barr insisted that the unit gave Canadians, in the eyes of NATO, a contingent with a first class reputation. Interviews with author. However, the purists in Canada felt that this orphan was an embarrassment and a dilution of the airborne ideal. It is interesting to note that the *Maroon Beret, 20th Anniversary Issue,* makes no mention of 3 Mechanized Commando. Obviously, the purists forgot that under the original Forces structure study each company, within each of the battalions / commandos was to be mounted in "ten Commando Armoured Personnel Carriers." Cost quickly relegated this idea to the dustbin. *Forces Structure Study,* Chapter 7, "The Canadian Airborne Regiment," April 1967, 1-2. Barr Papers.

11. Canada, *Defence 1972* (Ottawa: DND, 1973), 6-7. The formations listed were: 1 Combat Group, Calgary; 2 Combat Group, Petawawa; 5e Groupe du Combat, Valcartier; and the Airborne Regiment, Edmonton.

12. D.W. Middlemiss and J.J. Sokolsky, *Canadian Defence: Decisions & Determinants* (Toronto: Harcourt, Brace, Jovanovich, 1989), 39.

13. Colonel Michael Houghton recalled that "there was a general feeling by all that Dex[traze] did not like the Airborne Regiment. Dex clearly had no use for the Airborne Regiment." Interview with author 5 November 1998. This sentiment was echoed by all those of senior rank during this period.

14. Interview with author, Colonel (retd) D.B. McGibbon, 24 November 1998. McGibbon was the principal staff officer in DLO, NDHQ, from the mid seventies to the early eighties. McGibbon observed that one of the greatest problems that emerged after integration (due to the personalities at the time and the effect they had on the choice of commanders, i.e. those who readily acquiesced and supported Hellyer initiatives) was the departure of those willing to argue in a collegial manner.

15. Interview with author, 30 June 1998.

16. Bland, *Chiefs of Defence,* 237 & 238.

17. Douglas Bland wrote "when Hellyer left the portfolio, the CDS, Allard, was the unchallenged centre of decision making in the CF and his staff, CFHQ, was the centre for military decisions in DND and the Armed Forces. After 1969, however, the authority of the office of the CDS began to erode and that trend continued to the present, interrupted only by the personal dynamism of General Jacques Dextraze." Bland, *Chiefs of Defence,* 92.

18. Gerald Porter, *In retreat. The Canadian Forces in the Trudeau Years* (Toronto: Deneau & Greenberg, 1980), 165.

19. The reversal is dramatic. A government report captured the essence of the government's original intent. It recorded, "In April 1969, Prime Minister Trudeau announced changes in defence policy which had a major effect on the land forces. It was decided to reduce the troops in Europe by roughly half. In 1971, a new Defence White Paper elaborated on these changes as well as giving greater emphasis to the protection of Canadian interests at home as a way of 'fostering economic growth and safeguarding sovereignty and independence.' It was also proposed that the Europe-based land force be reconfigured to give it a higher degree of mobility and greater compatibility with Canada-based forces—in short, 'a lighter, more mobile land force capable of a wide range of missions.' This involved, among other things, plans to abandon the main battle tank—a policy which, in fact, never materialized." Canada, *Report of the Special Committee of the Senate on National Defence, Canada's Land Forces*, October 1989, 3.

20. Bland, *Chiefs of Defence,* 236. His vision was largely based on a larger NRHQ and a revamped Canadian Ranger program.

21. Written brief by William Chmiliar, President Royal Canadian Legion Branch 178 contained in Documentary Book—*Save the Regiment Committee,* 31 May 1977. CAFM.

22. Colonel Ian Fraser Presentation Notes for his speech to the Halifax Royal United Service Institute (RUSI) in January 1993, hereafter referred to as RUSI Presentation, Fraser Papers.

23. Ibid., 2. The telex was given a very high security rating and was not to be communicated to the troops under any circumstances. Curiously, Fraser commented that despite the secrecy, he received a call from the Canadian Press asking for a comment. Apparently, Dextraze briefed the media. The next day, all of the details in the telex were in the press, including a few additional facts with respect to base closures. Colonel Fraser also stated that following an announcement on the television news program "W5" that the Regiment was to be disbanded, General Stan Waters called the CDS and had a forty minute conversation. During this discussion, Dextraze was reported to have said that the original announcements of disbandment had simply been a ploy to stir up interest in defence policy. Yet, a press article in February 1976 reported that "General Dextraze has mentioned that the RCR might fulfill that role [quick-response unit] bolstered by members of a disbanded CAR." "Legion Campaigning to Save Regiment," *Edmonton Journal,* 4 February 1976. Documentary Book—*Save the Regiment Committee,* 31 May 1977. CAFM. Five days later DND emphasized that "any reference to disbandment in the past has only been an example of what would be one option." DND (MND's office) Letter to Mr. W. Skoreyko, MP Edmonton-West, 19 Februay 1976. Ibid.

24. Canada, *Minutes & Proceedings & Evidence of the Standing Committee of External Affairs and National Defence,* hereafter *SCEAND*, Issue 7, 10 March 1977, 7:16. During this forum Dextraze undercut the Airborne Regiment's traditional mantle as defender of the North (and fail-safe rationale for existence). He enunciated that the Regiment's role is merely to assist the other regular formation to conduct DCO and ALCANUS on an as required basis. Ibid., 7:16.

25. RUSI Presentation, 1. Fraser Papers.

26. Ibid., 17.

27. Address by General J.A. Dextraze, CDS to the Conference of Defence Associations, 16 January 1976, 11. DHist, File 76/89.

28. Ibid., 12. Dextraze also postulated that 3 Mechanized Commando would be disbanded, thus freeing up almost 1,000 established positions which could be used to bring up other units to full peacetime strength.

29. Interview with author, 30 June 1998. Colonel Ian Fraser also related a conversation with Dextraze at which time the CDS conceded, "A special service force wearing that badge [pointing to a winged dagger similar to that of the British SAS hanging on the wall] is my dream and that is why the Airborne Regiment is going to Petawawa." RUSI Presentation, 8. Fraser Papers. Generals Beno, Douglas, Foster, Gaudreau, and Stewart all emphasised Dextraze's penchant for Special Forces and the creation of an SSF. Colonel Houghton reminisced that "when Dextraze came to NDHQ he brought Christie with him and the rumour going around at the time was that Dextraze was going to create an SSF and Christie would command it." Prophecy or rumour? Interview with author 5 November 1998.

30. Interviews with Major-General Pitts, Colonel D.G. McGibbon and Colonel Fraser.

31. RUSI Presentation, 6. Fraser Papers. Colonel Peter Kenward remembered the visit of General Dextraze during Operation Gamescan, the military security program for the 1976 Olympics. Kenward recalled that "Dextraze tore a strip off of us because there was resistance against the move." Interview with author 16 December 1998. In regards to the security mission to the Olympics, the bulk of the Regiment was stationed at the College Militaire Royal de St-Jean and was given the designation of "Task Force III." The Regiment was tasked as the CF immediate reaction force. See Annex A to 1326-1 (10), Canadian Airborne Regiment Historical Report, dated 8 February 1995, CAFM; and Captain A.J. Lavoie, "Airborne—Task Force III," *Sentinel,* January 1977, 24-25.

32. Interview with author, 31 July 1998 and RUSI Presentation, 8. Fraser Papers.

33. Bercuson, *Significant Incident*, 110-111.

34. All levels of governmental representatives lobbied Parliament and the prime minister. Premier Peter Loughheed, the various members of Parliament representing ridings in the area, and the mayor of Edmonton, all wrote letters of concern and protest to the prime minister and his responsible cabinet minister. Copies of this correspondence are contained in Documentary Book—*Save the Regiment Committee,* 31 May 1977. CAFM. See also *Debates*: 4 February 1976, 10626; 25 February 1976, 11242; 18 June 1976, 14658; 8 November 1976, 835; 18 November 1976, 1176; 3 December 1976, 1640; 6 December 1976, 1678; and 15 December 1976. Throughout, the government's position was that the proposed move was part of the military infrastructure review, and the Airborne Regiment, similar to other units and bases, was simply under consideration.

35. Documentary Book—*Save the Regiment Committee,* 31 May 1977. CAFM.

36. Letter from Waters to Chmiliar, 16 June 1976. Documentary Book—*Save the Regiment Committee,* 31 May 1977. CAFM.

37. Duart Farquharson, "Transfer of Airborne force 'all my idea' says General," *Southam News Service,* 8 December 1976. Documentary Book—*Save the Regiment Committee,* 31 May 1977. CAFM.

38. RUSI Presentation, 7. Fraser Papers.

39. CDS letter to the MND, "Land Force Restructuring," 11 January 1977, *Information Legacy,* Document Control No. 905,193, p 614,988. Fraser also noted that at that time Dextraze emphasized that the move was a military decision. RUSI Presentation, 7. Fraser Papers. Colonel Dennis Tabernor, as a platoon commander at the time, recalled that " Colonel Fraser aged dramatically during this time fighting for the Regiment." Letter to the author, 31 March 1997. Colonel Houghton recalled that on 12 September 1976, the CDS held a closed meeting in his office. Shortly after the meeting the decision to move was made. When Houghton asked a colleague, Major John Malarky, what had transpired, he was told, "I have been sworn to secrecy and cannot tell you what went on." Interview with author, 5 November 1998. Colonel Fraser provided another interesting anecdote. After General Dextraze's retirement, Fraser had an opportunity in December 1977, during the General's visit to the National Defence College, to query him on the move. The former Regimental Colonel simply asked "was the decision to move the Regiment political or military?" Without hesitation, Dextraze answered, "political." Fraser added that six months later he had the opportunity to pose the same question to Barney Danson. He replied, "it was strictly military." One must wonder if the former CDS had now realized his folly. Both James Richardson and Barney Danson, the respective MNDs involved, as well as Prime Minister Trudeau, always maintained the decision was purely a military one. Interview with Colonel Fraser, 31 July 1998; RUSI Presentation, Fraser Papers, 18; and *Debates,* 3 and 6 December 1976, 1640 and 1678 respectively.

40. "Text of CDS Speech to Press," Message CDS 424, 081800Z December 1976. DHist, File 77/31. This was echoed in the official DND publication *Defence 1976*. The document clearly stated that "Following a review of the land force structure, it was determined that better utilization of available resources would be achieved by moving the Canadian Airborne Regiment from Edmonton to a new location close to the demographic centre of Canada." Canada, *Defence 1976* (Ottawa: DND, 1977), 32.

41. Address by General J.A. Dextraze, CDS to the Conference of Defence Associations—40th Annual Meeting, 13 January 1977, 9. DHist, File 77/186; and "Text of CDS Speech to Press," Message CDS 424, 081800Z December 1976. DHist, File 77/31.

42. Address by General J.A. Dextraze, CDS to the Conference of Defence Associations—40th Annual Meeting, 13 January 1977, 10.

43. Dextraze CDA address, 13 January 1977, 11. His plan called for 1 Commando to go to Ottawa and the remainder of the Regiment to move to CFB Petawawa. See also "SSF Restructuring Brief" for Commander FMC and CDS, 25 January and 2 February 1977 respectively. CAFM.
44. Dextraze CDA address, 13 January 1977, 12.
45. *SCEAND,* 10 March 1977, 7:21. The CDS's myopic approach was witnessed when questioned how the Regiment would get to an airbase at the new location in Petawawa. He remarked, "Trucked or bussed. It is not any less reasonable than when we are trucking or bussing them from Griesbach barracks to the airfield." Dextraze was then chided by the querying member of Parliament (Steve Paproski), "there is a little difference there General, 3 or 4, or 5 miles compared to 80, a 100, maybe 200 miles." Ibid., 7:21. See also *Debates,* 14 March 1977, 3930.
46. *SCEAND,* 10 March 1977, 7:21.
47. "Text of CDS Speech to Press," Message CDS 424, 081800Z December 1976. DHist, File 77/31.
48. RUSI Presentation, 14. Fraser Papers.
49. On 20 June 1977, while the Regiment's advance party was in Ottawa to conduct a reconnaissance, it was announced by the MND that 1 Commando would not go to Ottawa. RUSI Presentation, 15. Fraser Papers. Lieutenant-General Kent Foster also testified to the Somalia Commission that the reason for the move of 1 Commando to Ottawa was simply because there was no room for the entirety of the Airborne Regiment in Petawawa. As a result of the cancellation, Foster asserted that the "decision was made to reduce the Regiment to make it fit into Petawawa." "Transcript of Evidentiary Hearing," *Somalia Commission,* Vol 3, 5 October 1995, 397-398.
50. RUSI Presentation, 16. Fraser Papers.
51. Bland's interview and study of Dextraze provides a possible answer to the CDS's power to override the MND's concerns. Bland wrote "Dextraze felt that he and Trudeau had a 'sound and honest relationship' and that 'he [Dextraze] was trusted implicitly.' Public acknowledgement of that confidence helped Dextraze in Cabinet and elsewhere because 'it was not only known to his staff and to the deputy minister of national defence and ministers in cabinet and one man who knew that, and knew it very well was Jim Richardson'." Bland added that Dextraze claimed "he never used his relationship with the prime minister to undermine his minister. Nevertheless, he realized that it gave him immense leverage over Richardson." Bland also noted that "Dextraze candidly admitted that if Richardson 'would not want to do the things that I [Dextraze] would recommend which were the right things, I knew damn well that if I would go and see the prime minister, the prime minister would tell Jim Richardson to do it this way.'" Bland, *Chiefs of Defence,* 136.
52. Letter to author, 18 September 1998.
53. Interview with author, 28 April 1998.
54. Interview with author, 17 July 1997. Virtually all those interviewed with experience during this period, whether in the Airborne Regiment or in a staff position in FMC or NDHQ, stressed the detrimental effect of the move.
55. Interview with author, 18 March 1998. Douglas conceded, "Lets call a spade a spade, you're nothing more than a Company Commander, and I'm a Battalion Commander. We'll play the 'Regimental' game, but the fact of the matter is that we no longer have the capability of a Regiment."
56. Jim McNutty, "The Canadian Airborne Farce," *The Hamilton Spectator,* 18 February 1978, 24. Colonel McGibbon reminisced that during the move controversy it was generally acknowledged that Christie was going to get his star and go to Petawawa to command the new SSF organization which was being pushed by Dextraze. Interview with author, 24 November 1998.
57. RUSI Presentation, Fraser Papers, 17. Major Pat Dillon stated, "We were taken away from our airplanes, out of our element where we could speak with the pilots and drink beer with them in the mess. After the move they were in Trenton, four hours away, in a totally Air Force environment and you would only see them half an hour before the drop for a quick briefing." Interview with author, 16 January 1997.
58. Letter, CDS to the MND, "Land Force Restructuring," 11 January 1977, *Information Legacy,* Document Control No. 905,193, p. 614,988; "SSF Restructuring Brief " for Commander FMC and CDS, 25 January

and 2 February 1977 respectively, CAFM; Message DOE 119, "Land Force Restructuring," 151915Z March 1977, DHist, File 77 / 257; and *Defence 1977*, 33.

59. Report of the Commission of Inquiry into the Deployment of Canadian Forces to Somalia (hereafter Somalia Commission), *Dishonoured Legacy. The Lessons of the Somalia Affair, Vol 1,* 1997, 175.
60. See endnotes 57 & 58 this chapter.
61. The authorized establishment strength of the Regiment actually was reduced from the original 1,044 ("Briefing Airborne Regiment and Components of the Regiment," CAFM, File AB—Research: CAR. Components & Structure. Part One 1.E, Doc 4) to 730 (Cnd AB Regt Annual Historical Report for 1979, dated 09 April 1980, 2. CAFM). This represented a loss of 340 positions, or 30 percent of its strength, not to mention the question of formation status.
62. Major-General J.P.R. LaRose, CLDO, memorandum, dated 20 January 1977, *Land Force Restructuring— Detailed Implementation Plan.* Major Pat Dillon noted, "The Regiment was 'nickled and dimed' to death by the SSF." Interview with author, 16 January 1997.
63. Neil Macdonald, "We have enemies. Airborne chief calls Danson 'irresponsible,'" *The Ottawa Citizen,* 11 July 1978, 1. Barney Danson was a member of the infantry Regiment The Queen's Own Rifles. Colonel Painchaud's rebuttal to the MND's comments was, "If we are anything, we are over-committed already." The enormous gulf between the two positions is testimony to the flaw in the Regiment's organizational concept. See also "The Airborne's Trauma," *The Citizen,* 14 July 1978.
64. Charles Lynch, " Airborne's Last Post?" *Ottawa Citizen,* 11 July 1978; Peter Worthington, "Value of 'elite' troops," *The Toronto Sun,* 13 July 1978, 11; and "The Unhappy Warrior," *Macleans,* 24 July 1978, 17. The MND later stated he was misunderstood. He insisted that he only wanted a more "specific role for them" so that the paratroopers "know what their role is in a period of tension." The "rumour" of disbandment was such that the FMC Commander sent a message to confirm that there was no intention of disbanding or eliminating the Airborne Regiment. "Future of the Airborne Regiment," Message FMCHQ Comd 142, 131245Z July 1978. CAFM; and Sarah Henry, "Defence Minister supports removal of Airborne chief," *Ottawa Citizen,* 13 July 1978, 1. Interestingly, at the beginning of the year the MND was quoted as speaking favourably about the creation of an elite unit for "anti-terrorist" duties. Reference was made to the recruitment of elements of the SSF and RCMP to form the subject unit. See Orland French, "From Dove to Hawk?" *Legion,* January 1978, 14-15.
65. Macdonald, "We have enemies," 1; and *Debates,* 5 December 1978, 1838. Colonel Painchaud was described as a popular CO who contributed greatly to the airborne cause. Notably, he overtly promoted an 'elitist' attitude for his Regiment. Press clips as given in endnotes 63 & 64 and personal interviews. Lieutenant-Colonel Lorne O'Brien remembered that Painchaud "gave you everything but took all the rockets." He conceded that Painchaud was rather confrontational with those outside the Airborne. Interview with author, 14 April 1997. Colonel R.A. Hatton recalled, "He did a lot of good for the Regiment, but the thinkers of the crowd realized that you can't have a Colonel speaking out against the MND." Interview with author, 16 December 1998.
66. Macdonald, "We have enemies," 1.
67. Interview with author, 26 June 1998.
68. Interview with author, 18 March 1998.
69. Interview with author, 13 April 1997. Colonel Michael Houghton echoed Vienneau's view. He maintained that the Airborne was always under scrutiny and those who continually criticised the paratroopers were largely those who had not served in the organization. He further declared their motives were largely envy and jealousy. Houghton added, "the Airborne Regiment was a threat to each of our conventional infantry regiments." Interview with author, 5 November 1998.
70. Interview with author 15 April 1998. Major Pat Dillon declared that the "Airborne was a group everyone loved to hate." Interview with author 16 January 1997. A report written for SSF HQ stated, "The anti-airborne feeling and criticism is strongest today among those who could not make the grade in the Airborne Battle Group and among those of in support functions who count the costs in static, technical and quasi-civilian terms, without thought of the military and personnel benefits." *Information Legacy,* "A Proscribed Elite," 8.

71. Brigadier-General Ernie Beno, "The attitudes and values of the Canadian Airborne Regiment and the 'Airborne' Solider." Accessed from his personal papers, hereafter referred to as the Beno Papers. Italics are my own.
72. Interview with author, 7 October 1998. Bragdon stated there were two distinct schools of thought on how the Airborne was treated by the Chain of Command. The first was those who had been in the Airborne or earlier jump companies. He stated they favoured the Airborne. The second school was those who never served. Conversely, they didn't favour the Airborne. Bragdon maintained that "everyone who wanted to serve, could have and should have." Furthermore, he elaborated that the most rabid anti-airborne individuals were those who never went on the jump course because of personal weakness. But far worse yet, he insisted, were those who "went on the parachute course and quit."
73. Interview with author, 16 December 1998.
74. Interview with author, 16 December 1998. Colonel Kenward served from 1975-77 as a platoon commander; 1986-88 as the CO of 2 Commando; and 1993-1995 as the last Regimental Commander.
75. Worthington, "Value of 'Elite' Troops," 11.
76. Lynch, "Airborne's Last Post."
77. Ibid. This perception was not aided by the commentary of the paratroopers or their leaders. Colonel Don Rochester set the tone when he wrote, "Of course after the first year, regulations and authority began to slip their noose over us and we became as restricted as an airborne soldier ever is, which he really ever isn't." Rochester, "Idle Musing," 3.
78. Worthington, "Value of 'Elite' Troops," 11. Master Warrant Officer Réal Gagné, a fifteen year veteran of the Regiment recalled that during this period he and his soldiers had the "definite impression that the government wanted to destroy the Regiment." Gagné also noted that everyone in the Airborne, including the vast majority of the francophones in 1 Commando had wanted to stay in Edmonton. Interview with author, 9 June 1998.

CHAPTER SEVEN

DESCENT INTO DARKNESS
The Continuing Degradation of the Airborne's
Unique Status in the 1980s

The greatest failing of the Regiment in its later life was its unwillingness to accept the reality of its situation and get on with life in the present. This negative attitude and desire to live in the past was particularly evident in the senior officers of the Regiment and was passed on as folk lore to the young officers who had no experience with the independent Regiment of the Edmonton years.

Major-General R.I. Stewart, Former SSF Commander, 1 July 1998[1]

The erosion of the Airborne Regiment's original concept continued to accelerate in the early 1980s. One component of the growing trouble was the continued schizophrenic approach taken to the Regiment's perceived role. The other chronic problem was the passionate dislike of "special" troops by many conventionally minded individuals within the military. Taken together, these factors and the country's defence milieu fostered unrelenting debate in regard to the relevance of airborne forces within the Canadian Army. The lack of consensus on the Regiment's primary purpose, compounded by the latent opposition to it, condemned it to an uncertain future.

The diminution of the Canadian Airborne Regiment's capability was also directly related to the emasculation of its status as an independent formation in 1977. In Petawawa it became just another infantry battalion, albeit with some special characteristics. However, it no longer received special treatment and as a result, was plagued by incessant taskings on the same basis as other units. One internal defence department report acknowledged, "as the Special Service Force's only infantry organization in Canadian Forces Base (CFB) Petawawa, the Regiment is the prime target for every field-oriented tasking which the SSF gives out."[2] This reality was directly linked to a decline in operational readiness. Additionally, the change in status meant that the Regiment ceased to have the inestimable privilege of direct access to the Commander of the Army.

By the mid eighties, this degeneration fuelled further instability. A litany of difficulties soon emerged and aggravated an already serious situation. First, because many in NDHQ, and the Army itself, considered the Airborne as just a normal unit, it only made sense to employ the paratroopers as such. Therefore, the Regiment or elements thereof were rotated through Cyprus on a regular basis. A fundamental question now emerged. If the Airborne Regiment could be spared for a six-month tour as well as the subsequent pre- and post-deployment training and leave without jeopardizing Canadian operational performance, then why was a special, and costly, airborne capability needed?[3]

To exacerbate the dilemma, amendments to the Regiment's Canadian Forces Organization Order (CFOO) did little to change the prevailing schizophrenic approach. The 1977 Army reorganisation resulted in an update of CFOO 3.21.5 (Canadian Airborne Regiment). Consequently, as part of this exercise the Regiment's role was redefined. The latest version directed that the "Canadian Airborne Regiment is to provide rapid deployment airborne forces for operations in support of national security and international peacekeeping."[4] Fatefully, the document also highlighted several new tasks. It specifically noted that the Regiment was now capable of acting as a "Canadian Cyprus commitment rotation unit." It also assigned the Regiment the nebulous mission to provide "a quick response airborne capability in mounting the national rescue plan in the event of a major air disaster."[5] In 1977, Colonel Fraser, just as he was handing over command, expressed his frustration in regard to the latest additional tasking. "I am not sure what the status of this one is," he wrote his successor, "we have a very obscure role which has not really been published in a particularly precise fashion, which indicates that we are supposed to be ready to leap into the frozen wastes of the arctic to pick up the pieces after a 747 [commercial airliner] thunders in."[6]

Fraser's concern over "nebulous tasks" was well founded. The new definition narrowed the original open-ended notion of providing a "force capable of moving quickly to meet *any* unexpected enemy threat or *other commitment* of the Canadian Armed Forces."[7] But a more narrow redefinition was only an illusion. The encompassing term "national security" cloaked continuing imprecision. The 1977 version of CFOO 3.21.5 went on to declare that "peacetime functions stemming from the role involve sovereignty, internal security, defence of North America, NATO and peacekeeping operations."[8] As a result, nothing changed for the Airborne to help clarify its role. The all-inclusive mission statement once again left the Regiment open to the wide interpretations of those in power.

The revised CFOO did little to correct the Airborne's structural flaw. Instead, it created even more turmoil. In April 1979, the Commander FMC issued a memorandum stating that the Airborne Regiment had two distinct roles, defence of Canada operations and domestic assistance operations.[9] Competing notions of what constituted the Regiment's principal responsibility became readily apparent. The Special Service Force, as well as the Director of Land Operations (DLO), envisioned a rapid reaction capability for the Airborne Regiment well beyond Canada's borders. These two entities argued that the Regiment's primary importance was in the context of an UN Ready Force, and as part of the NATO commitment. A DLO comment on the Regiment's assignment to both the Canadian Air-Sea Transportable (CAST) Brigade Group and to the ACE Mobile Force (Land), stated that the "exclusive tasks for the Airborne Regiment were DCO [defence of Canada operations] and membership to the CAST Brigade Group."[10] The report added, "More than any other NATO airborne force, the Canadian Airborne Regiment has the ability to operate within the arctic [North Norway] and is equipped to do so."[11] However, a 1980 review of the Airborne's CFOOs conspicuously made no mention of the NATO commitment. It simply declared that "functions stemming from the role involve sovereignty, internal security, defence of North America, and peacekeeping operations."[12] Nevertheless, the SSF was still heavily involved with NATO commitments, and the Airborne Regiment remained an integral element of the SSF.

Further confusion came in 1985. Yet another amendment to CFOO 3.21.5 foreshadowed a subliminal evolution of the Canadian Airborne Regiment. The published document directed that "the Canadian Airborne Regiment is to provide rapid deployment airborne/*air-transportable* forces for operations in accordance with assigned tasks, primarily in support of national security and international peacekeeping."[13] The goalposts still encompassed the entire field, but more importantly, there was now the inclusion of the term "air-transportable forces." This begs an obvious question. Why this sudden reversion to terminology reminiscent of the MSF's "airborne battalions?" Was this addition the result of attempts by the Regiment's opponents to further bury its last vestiges of uniqueness? A definitive answer is not possible. However, it is widely accepted by most of the senior leadership who served in the Regiment, FMC Headquarters or NDHQ, that a conscious attempt was made to remould the Airborne Regiment into just another infantry unit, albeit with a unique capability.[14] If so, such moves would destroy it as a separate, special and uniquely identifiable formation.

Despite the plethora of changes, such as the Army reorganisation, the amendments to the CFOOs, and the assignments of additional tasks, nothing had changed to shore up the Regiment's flawed foundation. The old flaws persisted. In 1993, Brigadier-General Beno captured the essence of the dilemma when he wrote in regard to the Regiment's historical experience. "Overall there are no commitments, roles or tasks," he acknowledged, "which are greatly different from other infantry units."[15] Colonel Houghton, a former regimental commander reinforced this perception. He recalled that during the eighties, in a "fight people would deny our special capability and say, no you're just a unit like us [regular infantry]."[16] The most glaring problem remained the failure to define and then carve out a defining niche. And so the lack of a credible role endured as the Regiment's Achilles heel.

With no well-defined purpose, the Regiment's operational and training focus in the 1980s once again became hostage to the interpretation of those who held the reigns of power. Lieutenant-Colonel Ken Watkin, then the legal advisor to the SSF recalled, "the biggest problem they [Airborne Regiment] had during my period there was the lack of a viable role. Nobody knew what their primary mission was."[17] "Everyone you asked," he added, "told you something different. There was no sense of a single unified entity." Watkin also highlighted the subliminal Special Forces persona which existed. He recollected that "3 Commando patterned themselves after the British SAS, 2 Commando the American SF [Special Forces], and 1 Commando, the French Foreign Legion."[18] Three tribes warring in the bosom of a single regiment.

Watkin's assessment is not hard to understand. The expansive role and contradictory direction nurtured a climate of confusion. Colonel Rick Hatton recalled that during his airborne related service in the late seventies and early eighties, the Regiment was perceived as a rapid reaction force, specifically as the UN Stand-By Force.[19] Colonel Dick Cowling, the Regimental Commander from 1980 to 1982, claimed that he interpreted his primary mission to be the defence of Canada. However, Cowling conceded that he failed to believe there was an actual threat. As a result, he rationalized that the Regiment was "required to be ready to do whatever we were told, therefore, we had to march, dig, and shoot."[20] He maintained that these were the building blocks and all else would fall into place.

The variance in interpretations is legion. Lieutenant-Colonels Ron Bragdon and Dave Pentney both served multiple tours during the eighties, and each was a commanding officer during that time. Bragdon recalled that the focus on the defence of Canada waned considerably from his earlier tour in the early seventies and a more standardized "regular" infantry approach became predominant. He maintained that "by 1986 and beyond, the Regiment was conducting conventional operations."[21] Not surprisingly, Pentney's perception was somewhat different. He stated that the Airborne "hung its hat on the UN stand-by role" during this time, but candidly acknowledged, "there was no clear mission."[22] This, he claimed, created a problem. Pentney confided that the absence of a clear role contributed to the perception of some that they in fact were a Canadian variation of the British Special Air Service and American Special Forces.[23]

The turmoil over mission, purpose and role bothered Colonel Houghton to the point that he felt "it was like the stock market, up and down, and basically dependent on who was in the chair at the time."[24] Major-General Gaudreau, another former regimental commander, concurred. He saw that the mutually competitive ideas of the defence of Canada versus UN stand-by were damaging. When it "suited the fancy" of the higher headquarters, Gaudreau claimed, the Regiment was simply told it could not go on a UN tour because of its DCO commitments. Yet, at other times the Regiment was sent overseas and the defence of Canada operations requirement was ignored. Similarly he said that compared to the conventional infantry battalions the Airborne's light equipment scales (particularly vehicles) were also used as an excuse not to use them on UN deployments. Gaudreau consequently thought that the process "was wishy-washy and lacked the substance of professional thinking."[25]

The inability to define the exact mission, compounded by the mutually exclusive nature of the multiple tasks, continued to weaken the Airborne's position. Astonishingly even Allard, the "Father of the Regiment," apparently could not come to grips with the raison d'etre for the Regiment. Although he had earlier spoken eloquently in front of SCEAND in 1966, convincing them of the need for an organization which could act as a rapid reaction force capable of deploying in advance of heavy forces to "seize and hold" an airhead, twenty years later in April 1986, he explained his motives for forming the Airborne Regiment in a completely different manner.[26] During a visit to 1 Commando that year, the aging general said, "qu'il avait forme le Regiment aeroporte dans le but d'avoir une force de reaction rapide a la porte du Nord: Edmonton."[27] Is it surprising that the edifice begins to wobble if the architect himself is unclear as to what supports the structure?

It was painfully obvious that commitments such as the defence of Canada, NATO, and UN stand-by were contradictory. If deployed on one task, they would automatically default on the remainder. More to the point, which mission was the focus of training? If the Regiment itself could not centre its energies on a consistent and pervasive operational role, how did it expect others to rationalize its existence during times of economic austerity or institutional reorganization.

One attempted solution was to concentrate on the airborne capability instead of any specific role. The Regiment's publicists soon proclaimed that "we are equipped to respond anywhere, at anytime, or any place."[28] Colonel Peter Kenward explained the evolution of thought. He pointed out that there was a strong linkage between training for the airborne capability and the various assigned tasks. For example, he accepted defence of Canada operations in the North as a primary mission, regardless of the weak threat probability. Although Kenward realized this contradiction, he went on to argue that "exercises in the North would build in my unit fundamental skills and qualities that would foster the characteristics of my organization which I wanted such as individual fieldcraft skills, preparedness and robustness."[29] The end product was a unit that could operate in any hostile, remote and rugged territory, whether in a DCO, NATO or UN scenario.

The approach is logical, although it does not necessarily provide a consistent internal focus. Once again it is highly dependent on the individual interpretation of the term "airborne capability." Furthermore, the outlook is effective only to those who believe in the relevance of airborne forces. Training for capability is dismissed as a costly and unwarranted luxury by those who consider the paratrooper an anachronism. The airborne detractors consistently put forward the question, Why expensive airborne troops if other generic, general purpose forces can equally handle the respective tasks?

The continuing absence of a credible threat to Canadian territory also fuelled the debate over the Regiment's relevance. The Airborne's trump card of being the only organization capable of dropping into desolate and remote Arctic regions is moot if this capability is not required. Supporting this conclusion was a 1979 joint Canadian/US intelligence estimate which reported the unlikelihood of the Soviet use of general purpose conventional forces to initiate hostilities against installations in the CANUS area. The document was clear that Soviet "airborne attacks, unlikely as they are, would consist of no more than small highly specialized teams."[30]

Subsequent appreciations began to identify, or more accurately transform, the potential land threat to North America. The risk evolved from the insertion of airborne forces to the more likely commitment of Soviet Special Purpose Forces (Spetsnaz) teams operating against the continental periphery, including the North. The intelligence reports assessed the most probable threat to CANUS, in the event of general war, as "a series of simultaneous small party raids in isolated communities, in conjunction with sabotage / terrorist operations in any of the major Canadian cities."[31] However, even this level of menace was hotly debated.

In early 1988, Admiral R.H. Falls, a former CDS and chairman of the NATO Military Committee, testified before a Special Senate Committee on Defence that "I just cannot imagine a scenario where Canada is under attack by land forces."[32] His doubt was shared by Dr. Cynthia Cannizzo of the University of Calgary. Her study of possible threats to the Canadian Arctic led her to believe that "the possibility of a land invasion over some five thousand kilometres of arctic terrain is minuscule."[33] Similarly, military historian John Marteinson, now the editor of the *Canadian Military Journal*, added, "I have never heard any really convincing argument that our most likely potential enemy has either the capability or the inclination to seize and hold even small bits of Canadian territory, be they in the Arctic or along our shores."[34]

Within the Army itself there was also serious scepticism. Former Regimental Commander Ian Douglas queried, "Who the hell will invade Canada?" "If the Russians attacked," he added, "the best defence would be to starve them out."[35] In a similar vein, another former airborne commander, Colonel Dick Cowling questioned, "What is the threat? Why would the Soviets want to take over an airfield in Canada?" He added that it was difficult to come up with a credible scenario. Cowling concluded that if they did seize a piece of the Canadian Arctic the most efficient response would be to "leave them there for a month and then mount a rescue operation to get them out."[36]

The new Spetsnaz threat emerging in the eighties was also met with similar reservation. Acknowledged targets for the Soviet Special Forces were given in priority as: nuclear delivery systems; command and control systems; key installations; key transportation or communications links; and key personnel.[37] Although the possibility was always acknowledged, the likelihood of attack was considered almost negligible. Most analysts concluded that Spetsnaz units would be concentrated on the target-rich and logistically supportable European theatre. As Admiral Falls remarked, "it would be suicidal on their part [to operate against North America]."[38]

Clearly, not much had changed from the post World War II era. Policy makers continued to believe with good reason "that geography and common interests with the United States would continue to afford the nation considerable security and relative immunity from distant conflicts."[39] In part, this was a more contemporary version of the old theme of Canadian military history since Confederation: lack of a clear threat. The major concern in the North was primarily one of surveillance and control over sovereign territory. The fact that sixty percent of Canada's land mass was accessible only by air often led the Airborne Regiment, and its supporters, to the misguided belief that paratroopers were irreplaceable.[40] However, in 1984, the Senate Defence Committee popped that bubble for those who were listening.

The Committee's announcement was a simple declaration of what many had, or should have, already known. Their report outlined the four roles of the Canadian Forces as: 1) the protection of Canada; 2) cooperation with the US in the defence of North America; 3) collective defence of the NATO area; and 4) peacekeeping. "Obviously," the report went on, "the protection of Canada, and the security of Canadians, is the ultimate priority of our defence policy and the underlying purpose of all four roles. However, this does not necessarily imply that the first role need have the highest priority in terms of force structure design, readiness, manning, or resource allocation."[41] This was the exact rationale which had marginalized airborne capability during the MSF/DCF era twenty years before. It would do so again.

Clearly, DCO was not the bedrock on which to solidify the Regiment's existence. Rather, reliance on this task could actually prove detrimental. The continuing lack of threat marginalized the importance of the DCO role and limited the resources allocated to it. Lieutenant-Colonel Dick, a former regimental administration officer commented, "if the role was to be meaningful, no effort was made to follow through on other aspects. There was no sustainability plan and we did not have the required equipment, specifically vehicles."[42] Douglas was even more blunt in his assessment. He recollected that opponents consistently argued, "What do we need the Airborne for? DCO? It's not realistic!"[43]

In 1985, the growing distance between the relevance of paratroopers and the perceived security of the Arctic became evident during a new crisis in Canada's North. Without any warning or request, the American government announced the impending voyage through the Northwest Passage of the US Coast Guard cutter *Polar Sea*. This unilateral act incited yet another shrill cry for protection of Canadian sovereignty.[44] And once again the military was mobilized to meet the non-military threat to its North. The *Canadian Strategic Review 1985-1986,* reported that the government's decision "to underscore Canadian sovereignty in the north with an increased air and naval presence was reminiscent of the steps taken by the Trudeau government during the late 1960s and early 1970s [after the Manhattan affair]."[45]

The increased emphasis on DND presence in the North was subsequently highlighted in the 1987 White Paper, *Challenge and Commitments.* Similar to its predecessor, the White Paper established as "its first priority the protection and furtherance of Canada's sovereignty as a nation."[46] It stated, "After the defence of the country itself, there is no issue more important to any nation than the protection of its sovereignty. The ability to exercise effective national sovereignty is the very essence of nationhood."[47]

The new government initiatives included the North American Air Defence Modernization Program (North Warning System),[48] a proposed new Northern (Army) Training Centre, the designation of five northern airfields as Forward Operating Locations (FOLs), the construction of the *Polar 8* icebreaker, and a new fleet of nuclear submarines.[49] The programs were designed to provide increased presence to monitor friend and foe alike. However, NDHQ focussed largely on an Air

Force and naval presence.[50] The need for paratroopers was minimal. Joseph Jockel, political scientist and authority on Canadian-American relations has recently noted that the true stimulus behind the Canadian government's programs was an "emphasis on sovereignty protection [which] places a premium on the presence of Canadians, rather than on the fulfilment of a defence mission."[51]

Fiscal realities and the end of the Cold War quickly dampened the latest surge of interest in the Arctic. Many of the programs proposed, such as the fleet of nuclear submarines, the northern training centre and the *Polar 8* icebreaker were never implemented. Nevertheless, six years later the *1994 Defence White Paper* still echoed the sentiments of its predecessors and emphasized that "sovereignty is a vital attribute of a nation-state."[52] It also expressed a consistent and historic theme, namely that Canada faced no direct threat. The underlying necessity was clearly the ability to protect its sovereignty.[53] But attitudes and events also indicated that the requirement for a strong airborne capability was not necessarily required to fulfill this aim.

Once again, into the 1990s, the Canadian Airborne Regiment's true viability was challenged because of its inability to demonstrate a pervasive role for itself. Its subordination to the SSF, its dramatic decrease in size and contradictory employment highlighted its weak foundation. Internal discrepancies in operational and training priorities further heightened the ever present scrutiny of the Regiment. In the end, one key question kept emerging. Why must a "special" and costly airborne unit be maintained if the other generic, general purpose forces could equally execute the respective tasks?

The second problem that propelled the Regiment on its fateful path into the 1990s was also rooted in the Airborne's loss of special status and resultant organizational changes. As it became defined and viewed as just another infantry unit, its claim on the very best experienced officers and soldiers was increasingly ignored. Fatefully, it lost its preferred manning. In short, it ceased to be a collection of the most talented people. It no longer received only experienced and mature leaders and men. This blow created a shock wave which would be felt by the entire Army, if not in all of Canada's military institutions.

As already noted, the Army reorganization and subsequent move of the Regiment from Edmonton in the late seventies eroded the status, as well as the very character of the Airborne Regiment. The greatest manifestation of this was the detrimental effect the changes had on the quality of leader and soldier the Regiment now received. Prior to the reorganization all riflemen within the commandos had to be qualified to the rank of corporal. As already explained, this meant soldiers were generally more mature and experienced. However, after the move to Petawawa, the former prerequisite of "5A" qualified soldiers was no longer followed. The resultant influx of more immature and junior soldiers subtly started to transform the very character of the Airborne Regiment during the 1980s.

Major Mike Blanchette in the unit at the time recalled that the Regiment changed dramatically within a year of its transfer from Edmonton. He explained that the influx of newer inexperienced soldiers created a dramatic decline in skill levels within the Airborne. Blanchette emphasized that the erosion of expertise continued to plummet on a yearly basis.[54] Similarly, another veteran, Colonel Dennis Tabbernor remarked:

> The Regiment in Edmonton was not the same as the Regiment in Petawawa. When I had gone to Edmonton, the only way a soldier could get into the Regiment was if he was highly qualified and if not a Corporal, soon to be one. Young officers were to have had a previous tour of Regimental duty. These requirements were slowly eroded and soon we were getting platoons of soldiers right out of the Battle Schools. They caused their fair share of problems.[55]

The critical manning problem was caused by a number of factors. It was symptomatic of a manpower crisis being experienced throughout the Canadian Forces as a result of financial constraints. Men who were there, like Lieutenant-Colonel Lorne O'Brien, explained the essence of the dilemma. Lowering the standards to get in the airborne, he said, was a function of the "realities of a downsized army." He added, "the gene pool just wasn't there and you can't give what you don't have."[56] Others stated that out of sheer necessity the Airborne began receiving basic qualified privates instead of corporals, or senior privates qualified to that level.[57]

The shortage of trained personnel was also due to a reluctance by many to volunteer for airborne service. Major-General Bob Stewart felt that it became clear that "there was not a large reservoir of soldiers in the remainder of the army that wanted to experience the challenge and hardship of airborne service, particularly [vital leaders and trainers like] Warrant Officers and Senior NCOs."[58] In May 1985, the manning issue became so sensitive that the Director of Infantry requested the FMC commander to consider modifying the voluntary aspect of service in the Canadian Airborne Regiment "because of the long-standing difficulties in obtaining sufficient numbers of volunteers, especially to fill Senior NCO positions."[59] Lieutenant-General Charles Belzile refused the request. He insisted that the regimental identification of the three infantry commandos for manning purposes was working well. Furthermore, Belzile believed that voluntarism was the core of the airborne spirit.[60]

Belzile's faith in the regimental affiliation of commandos with their parent infantry regiment (RCR, PPCLI, and R22eR), was perhaps naive. Regardless, it became a serious source of controversy. The original idea to connect the Airborne Regiment's commandos directly to their parent regiments was actually the brainchild of General Dextraze in the late seventies.[61] However, it was not until June 1979, when the last manifestations of the Airborne's reorganization—the establishment of 3 Airborne Commando—was complete that the concept was actually implemented.[62] In later years this final expression of the 1977-1978 reorganization became a bitter aftershock.

The Dextraze initiative to link the commandos to their parent regiments was intended supposedly to assist the Airborne Regiment. The Army's senior leadership believed it was possible to solve the Regiment's chronic manpower shortage by ensuring that each of the rifle commandos was independently manned by the three regular force infantry regiments. They felt that this system would ease the problem of replacements. Each parent infantry regiment had a quota to fill to meet the requirements of its respective commando. Any shortfalls could be easily attributed to the source. The senior Army commanders further postulated that affiliated commandos would create, within the parent infantry regiments, a distinct pride. Therefore, they argued, feeder regiments would send only their best officers and soldiers.[63]

However, those within the Airborne Regiment opposed this initiative. Warrant Officer Mark Miller captured the overall sentiment of the time. He thought that most of the serving paratroopers feared that the affiliation would introduce "regimental quiffs and practices." He emphasised that a prevalent worry was that the unit would become divided and that the uniformity and common standard of the Airborne Regiment would be lost.[64] As it turned out he was not far off the mark. Colonel Kent Foster, the Regimental Commander at the time, agreed. He argued for regimental integration instead of affiliated commandos. Foster explained, "I wanted the commandos to remain regimentally mixed...I thought it would provide a strength of them sharing each other's culture."[65]

The flaw in the new manning system soon became obvious. The relationship between commanding officers of the respective commandos and their parent regiments soon usurped the regimental commander's control on certain command appointments within his own regiment. He was no longer capable of ensuring that his strong leaders were spread throughout the entire Airborne Regiment.[66] Beno observed, "the Regimental method of manning 1, 2, and 3 Commando leads to a sense of independence [for each]. There is the potential for cliques to develop where otherwise undesirable individuals might be protected."[67] Alas, if any of the feeder infantry organizations failed in their responsibility to send only quality people, a major problem could, and did, arise.

The hypothetical dilemma was only too real. The three sponsoring regiments brought both their jealousies and politics into the Airborne. Originally the Regiment was commonly viewed by the other infantry regiments as a "Patricia" fiefdom. This was largely due to the Airborne's western roots, as well as the historic link which had been crafted when the PPCLI was designated as the first Canadian airborne unit in the post Second World War period.[68] Following the Airborne Regiment's move to the east, a definite shift of support away from the Patricias quickly emerged. Former paratroop officer Mike Blanchette remembered that there was "a definite mood that this is not the same Airborne Regiment as in Edmonton and we don't want to be here in the East." "From this time on," he added, "the depth of support was eroded and it appeared that no real effort was made to ensure that quality [PPCLI] personnel were sent. Often, trouble makers were sent to clear them out of the battalions."[69]

Similarly, Lieutenant-Colonel Dick saw that there was a distinct difference in the calibre of soldiers who started to arrive at the Regiment. The Patricia influx was not viewed as representative of the quality of soldiers available within the PPCLI.[70] Brigadier-General Douglas bluntly referred to the transformation in support as cancerous.[71] These observations are neither subjective, nor unique. A board of inquiry later acknowledged the intermittent decline of PPCLI personnel support to the Airborne Regiment.[72]

The Patricias, however, were not the only ones to dilute the quality of personnel to the Airborne. In the mid eighties, an FMC report on Army discipline noted that the Airborne Regiment was required to "live with the problems associated with a transient population." It further showed that this was a situation over which the Regiment had little control. The Army study explained that the Airborne had to "rely almost exclusively on the good will of the parent regiments for troop replacements."[73]

Unfortunately, the goodwill was not always there. The forced reliance on the parent regiments to provide suitable replacements was at times a legitimate concern. Commanding officers of the line battalions which comprised the parent feeder regiments were normally directed to transfer a quota of personnel to the Airborne Regiment on a yearly basis. They often found that a posting to the Airborne was an expeditious means of ridding themselves of undesirable individuals in their unit. The absence of controls, and a "take him or go short attitude" soon emerged. As a result, the Regiment no longer received the very best. In some cases, it actually had the dregs dumped on it![74]

Two former 2 Commando COs serving in the mid eighties reinforced this notion. Lieutenant-Colonel Bragdon acknowledged that there were definitely two schools of thought in the PPCLI. Those who had former airborne service sent their best. Those who did not, sent their garbage. Bragdon lamented that during his service years the controlling personalities, within the PPCLI in any case, were of the latter persuasion. As a result, 2 Commando received the individuals no one else wanted, the "cowboys" who were seen as ill-disciplined. Furthermore, as Bragdon also noted, "once they sent them, they just forgot about them."[75]

Major Pat Dillon was another who conceded, "the problems that caused the demise [of the Airborne Regiment] were there below the surface while I was there [1982-1984]." He claimed that the selection process was ineffectual and that he was burdened with numerous "weak officers and Senior NCOs." Dillon recalled, "I got rid of half my officers in the first year."[76]

The decline in support was felt nowhere more deeply than in the area of leadership. Major-General Pitts thought that leadership, or the lack of it, was at the root of the Airborne's demise.[77] Colonel Tabbernor recalled that a great deal of expertise was lost at the officer level when the Regiment moved to Petawawa. He explained that only two officers from 2 Commando, who had served in Edmonton, made the transfer to Petawawa. The new draft were "all new and the majority, if not all, had not served in the Regiment previously."[78] Brigadier-General Beno concurred. He believed that after the move east, the Airborne was seen as just another unit within a brigade, and consequently a lesser quality of leader was at times accepted at all levels of command. He also underscored the fact that even the infantry regiments had not consistently selected the most suitable individuals for command positions.[79]

Brigadier-General Greg Mitchell, who served two tours with the Airborne in the 1980s echoed these sentiments. During his second tour with the paratroopers in the latter part of the decade, it became evident to him that organizational strength relied heavily on the commander in the seat at the time. The depth of leadership was simply no longer there as it had been in his first tour earlier in the decade. Mitchell recalled that the Regiment had evolved into "little independent fiefdoms" formed around the commanding officers of the three commandos. He explained that the regimental commander required the strength of character and professional ability to come to grips with problems as they emerged. He admitted that not all those appointed were up to the task.[80]

A litany of additional problems grew out of the dilemma caused by questionable manning practises. A pool of soldiers labelled as "cowboys" and "ill-disciplined" began to collect within the Regiment. The chronic shortage of volunteers for airborne service, as well as the enmity of their parent regiments, meant that these soldiers began to serve enormously long tours, from four to eight years or more, within the Airborne. The perennial problem of attracting senior NCOs ensured that those so inclined could make a virtual career in the Airborne Regiment alone. Consequently there was no talent renewal as would be the case in rotations among the very best. Furthermore, the expedient solution of offering promotions, out of sequence on the merit list, to senior NCOs agreeable to an airborne tour further diluted the quality of leadership.[81]

These flaws caused other problems. First, the long serving senior NCOs were often looked to for guidance, particularly by junior officers. As a result, the ethos of the airborne was being passed on by the NCOs alone. Unfortunately, they were not always the best. As Lieutenant-Colonel Bradley explained, "no parent regiment would keep its streamers [best/upwardly mobile individual] in the Airborne for too long."[82]

Lieutenant-Colonel Watkin agreed. He remembered officers who tried too hard to be privates because they wanted to be accepted by the men. Furthermore, Watkin also felt that the ethos was being perpetuated by the NCOs. This was due to the reality that it was the junior and senior NCOs who consistently remained in the Airborne for extended periods of time. Watkin maintained that these circumstances created a climate where an unofficial chain of command emerged. It was controlled at the junior NCO level, particularly at the rank of Master-Corporal.[83]

The danger of the unofficial chain of command was obvious. The airborne ethos and culture, which was being promoted by some elements within the Regiment's NCO corps, centred on an elitist, macho, renegade attitude. Loyalty was defined in terms of the airborne itself, often to a particular clique therein. Moreover, airborne service became an end in itself. Service to Canada and the public, appreciation for national policy and the concept of the greater good was rejected. Outsiders were shunned and considered only worthy of contempt. Authority, especially the chain of command outside of the Regiment, was a target to be defied. The cancerous attitude that the unofficial chain of command perpetuated was nothing short of a renegade warrior cult.

Even during the eighties many of the paratroop commanders realized the danger of this growing problem. Bragdon also warned of the parallel command structure. He indicated this was an inherent problem which had become endemic with weak leadership at the top. To break this pathogenic cycle required strong officers and senior NCOs. Such deviant energies had to be transformed into constructive activity and direction. Bragdon agreed that the challenge was predominately with the master-corporal rank.[84]

Another critical shortcoming that became prevalent as a result of extended tours and weak leadership, and was intricately related to the parallel chain of command, was the advent of powerful, closely bonded cliques. Major-General Herb Pitts had predicted this latent pitfall in the seventies. During the rancorous debates over the establishment of the Special Service Force and the regimentally affiliated commandos, Pitts warned of the problem of sustainability and "inbreeding" within the Airborne. At that time he had foreseen that in the long term individuals would become so enamoured with the Special Forces persona that nothing else would matter.[85]

Kent Foster was another who believed it was important to prevent the emergence of cliques, as well as to eliminate the macho ethos within the ranks of the NCOs. He insisted the health of the organization rested on an invigorating exchange between the Airborne and the parent feeder regiments so that a leadership nursery effect occurred.[86] Unfortunately, as described by Brigadier-General Douglas, the necessary flow of rotation failed to happen. As a result, the Airborne Regiment evolved to the point where the backbone holding up the organization did not consist of the best leaders.[87] Rather they were individuals, who because of their longevity in the unit and their repertoire of airborne skills, were perceived by many, particularly the junior soldiers, as the embodiment of a paratrooper. Furthermore, these self-proclaimed airborne demigods, by virtue of their unrivalled airborne experience, now defined what was considered as acceptable behaviour for airborne soldiers. Consequently, a distinct impression of "how things are done" permeated throughout the ranks. Often this was based on bravado and a misguided "tough-guy—kill em all and let God sort them out" attitude instead of quiet professionalism based on superior performance.

In all, the manning issue caused serious problems for the Regiment. Many factors such as the shortage of volunteers, the decline in the quality of leaders and soldiers, the questionable level of support proffered by the feeder regiments, the acceptance of extremely long tours for individuals, and the insidious creep of a parallel sub-rosa chain of command all dragged the Regiment down. Like a hazardous silt build-up, the manning problem slowly accumulated. As this happened, discipline also declined.

The erosion of the Regiment's leadership and discipline increased substantially during the eighties. It made a mockery out of the optimistic hopes that the Airborne's first commander had had twenty years before. Then he had speculated that the paratroopers' dedication and pursuit of excellence would render "normal disciplinary measures unnecessary."[88] Over time, the reality became increasingly less palatable. The disciplinary problems within the Regiment during this time are incontestable. Many of its senior officers knew that there was something wrong. Lieutenant-Colonel Dick recalled that it "always felt as if you were sitting on a pressure cooker. In order for it not to blow you always had to make sure it was secure and provide for a control release mechanism."[89] Lorne O'Brien, a former 3 Commando commanding officer, felt the same pressure. "You had to run herd on them [the soldiers] all the time." He likened it to a professional athletic team. "You keep them pumped-up but that comes with certain problems," O'Brien explained, "you have to let steam off judiciously and you have to be ruthless with discipline."[90]

Another paratroop officer admitted, "discipline was far more precarious in the Airborne than anywhere else I served." He added that the unit had great potential because of the level of the soldiers and the training. He believed that the Regiment was untouchable when it had strong leadership and when a strong sense of discipline was enforced. However, when the "screws were loosened," he revealed, "it [Airborne Regiment] had enormous problems." The Regiment's last Commander, Colonel Kenward also thought it was so. He was convinced that "more rigid control, if not a tight rein is required because of the high level of energy in the ranks. Things can go adrift, and as a result leadership by example and being in people's face becomes very important."[91] But here is where the other flaw came into dangerous play: the Regiment's leadership was not always up to the task.[92]

By the mid to late eighties blatant manifestations of mediocre, even bad behaviour became conspicuous. Paratroopers in Petawawa refused to salute "LEG" (the pejorative term for non-airborne personnel) officers and amazingly were not held accountable.[93] Incredulously, a 1 Commando motorcycle club, called the Para Nomads, with known connections to the Hell's Angels existed within the Regiment and it seemed to be tolerated by senior leadership.[94] Furthermore, in addition to a large number of physical assaults committed by paratroopers, there was also a disturbing rash of weapon thefts from Regimental stores. These events created a sense of alarm. But little seemed to be done about stopping such acts other than the usual post-crime punishments. One serving member at the time recalled the sense of anarchy. He confided that "it is a bad sign when officers are threatened by the troops. You clearly have a problem."[95]

However, such events did not go unnoticed at the top even in the early days of the emerging problems. In the spring of 1984, Brigadier-General R.I. Stewart, then the Commander of the SSF stated:

> The problem in a nutshell is that we have far too many cases of ill disciplined behaviour, assault, disobedience, disrespectful behaviour; theft of private and public property by soldiers; impaired driving offenses; vehicle accidents; inadequate control of stores; ammunition/pyrotechnics, weapons and equipment that result in loss or theft; and a general laxness in properly controlling soldiers, all which contribute to an erosion of disciplined/soldierly behaviour. We have in many cases lost our regimented pattern of behaviour and our standards of performance are seriously in jeopardy. The danger of allowing standards to slip is self-evident. Once started on the decline, the process picks up momentum and reaches a point when we have no junior leaders who comprehend the standard and it is then impossible to reverse the process.[96]

Stewart outlined a program of remedial action to correct the malaise he saw within the entire formation, but particularly in the Airborne Regiment. However, he soon lamented that a number of serious disciplinary problems that were not properly addressed by the regimental commander continued to fester.[97]

Continuing weapon thefts and a highly publicized homicide, committed by a paratrooper from 1 Commando, brought the crisis to a head. In early August 1985, the machete murder of a civilian in Fort Coulonge, Quebec, mere weeks after a rash of weapon thefts, reportedly drove the CDS, General C.E. Theriault, to order the disbandment of the Regiment on the spot. Looking back, Bob Gaudreau, then the Deputy Commander of the SSF and soon to be Regimental Commander, thought that the beleaguered defence chief had reacted more out of fear of the continuing media flak in issuing such an extreme order than in concentrating on keeping the Regiment solvent and solving its problems.[98]

Fortunately for the Regiment, Major-General John de Chastelain, then acting Commander of FMC, managed to calm the CDS and a compromise was reached. By the end of August, the CDS agreed to the commission of an investigation titled the *FMC Study on Disciplinary Infractions and Antisocial Behaviour with FMC with Particular Reference to the Special Service Force and the Canadian Airborne Regiment.* This probe became known informally as the "Hewson Report." Its aim was to review disciplinary infractions within Force Mobile Command and investigate the factors which led to the excessive antisocial behaviour. General Theriault allowed the Army to write the guidelines, establish the terms of reference, and provide the committee members. However, NDHQ provided the chairman, Major-General C.W. Hewson, the Chief of Intelligence and Security.[99]

Nonetheless, a cynic could question whether the vehicle had been hijacked. The committee's all Army membership was no coincidence. Major-General Gaudreau admitted later that those assigned, Colonel Bob Alden, Lieutenant-Colonels Serge Labbé and I.N. Gervais, were all "pro-airborne guys." The chairman himself wrote "their loyalty to the Canadian Airborne Regiment and the Army was apparent." Not surprisingly, the report's findings were anything but critical of the Airborne Regiment or the Army.[100]

Sadly, in the end the report was of little concrete value. It concluded that there appeared to be a higher number of assault cases in the two infantry units in the SSF (1 RCR and the Airborne Regiment) compared to the remaining infantry units in the rest of the Army. Although statistically 1 RCR had a greater incidence of assault cases than the Airborne, the study team dismissed this difference as an unexplainable anomaly. The fact that 3 Commando, the RCR component of the Airborne Regiment, had the highest number of incidents of assault within the Airborne also seemed to go unnoticed. The FMC team then went on to rationalize the discrepancy in behaviour within the Canadian Airborne Regiment to a combination of factors such as: the absence of junior leaders, the immaturity and lack of experience of some of the replacements sent to the Regiment, and the semi-isolation of CFB Petawawa itself, which failed to provide an adequate number of drinking establishments and other social outlets off the base that could absorb the large single male population of the base.[101] These findings did not represent any fresh revelations. The study also failed to explain why other units, with similar problems, did not exhibit the same high number of incidents of anti-social behaviour.

Likewise, the report's recommendations neglected to provide any tangible direction to improve the Regiment's practices, procedures or its manning system. It noted that there was a need to base selection of junior leaders for service with the Canadian Airborne Regiment on the particular need for mature, capable leaders with good common sense. It added that previous experience in a regular infantry battalion should also be a prerequisite for all volunteers.[102] However, it failed to come to grips with creating real mechanisms to solve the identified problems. A perfect example of their lack of resolve was the committee's mild and innocuous comment that "this may necessitate the need to remind the three Regular Force infantry regiments of their continuing responsibilities to provide 'good' soldiers to the Canadian Airborne Regiment."[103] This was the grand sum of what the study team thought necessary.

Significantly, the Hewson committee members did spend a great amount of time in trying to show that the problems in the Regiment were "normal" or even better than normal. The final report declared, "there is no cause for alarm or requirement for precipitate action."[104] It went on to argue that "there appears to be a lower incidence of serious pathology and violent behaviour in the Canadian Forces than in the Canadian population at large."[105] Although the report promoted numerous initiatives, such as preferred manning and tasking exemptions—which would have returned the Regiment to its former privileged status—it failed to provide any tangible relief for the Regiment's structural defects.[106] The report had been a waste of time and resources. It had no impact and moreover, it had the distinct complexion of an "insider" exercise.

Amazingly, Ken Watkin, the SSF legal advisor during the period was never consulted for input. Not surprisingly, he believed that the end product was "very watered down."[107] One serving officer recalled that the study "didn't make a ripple."[108] The regimental commander at the time acknowledged that he received no special direction as a result of the report. Major-General Hewson himself, also later admitted, "I know of no specific action that resulted from our study."[109] This revelation suggests that there was also a leadership default at levels higher than the Canadian Airborne Regiment itself.

Nevertheless, the chaotic state of discipline appeared to wane. But this was primarily due to the appointment of a strong regimental commander. Bob Gaudreau was a very efficient and highly respected officer often described as a "superb field commander" and "forward thinker."[110] Furthermore, he had the confidence of Army Commander, Lieutenant-General Kent Foster who had great trust in his new commander's ability to run "a strong outfit."[111]

Gaudreau believed that the answer to the disciplinary problems lay in the tenets of good solid soldiering, namely firm discipline and hard challenging training. "These problems after all," he candidly explained, "although serious in nature, had been experienced in all other Combat Arms units in the past at one time or another."[112] Gaudreau's firm grip put a temporary lid on the problems, but they had not gone away. Perhaps even Gaudreau should have avoided the habit of all who looked at the Regiment's problems at this time—the comparison of the Airborne to others when indeed the only true measure was what one wanted from the Regiment itself.

In all, during the 1980s, the erosion of the Airborne Regiment's status, structure, and perceived importance was rooted in the absence of a credible, pervasive role. The Army reorganization and resultant move to Petawawa, and the corollary loss of formation status and strength, exacerbated the Regiment's decline. These combined factors, fuelled a further belief in the rest of the Army that the Regiment was simply another infantry unit and therefore not deserving of any special consideration. The subsequent degradation in manning and the absence of consistent support from the feeder regiments created further strain on an already overburdened structure. Weak leadership and a core of ill-disciplined rogues dragged the Airborne down even further. Incredibly, there was yet another problem that accelerated the Regiment's sorry descent. This one was purely self-inflicted—and it was at the highest command level within the Regiment.

The concepts on which the Regiment was founded, as well as its privileged status were no longer accepted or enforced by those in positions of power and those in the Regiment stubbornly hunkered down and refused to change. This sullen and reticent posture soon turned the unit into a pariah, even in the eyes of those who supported it. Major-General Bob Stewart, one of the Regiment's first "Regimental Majors," recalled his later frustration when he was the Special Service Force Commander. The Airborne Regiment which was an integral component of his SSF, he conceded, received some preferential treatment from his chain of command. The fact that the Regiment had a full colonel commanding and up to six other officers with the powers of a commanding officer, for a unit of approximately 700-800 personnel, made this special consideration almost a certainty. Stewart recalled that during his time as the SSF commander a great many of his staff were ex-members of the Regiment who loved the Airborne and "went out of their way to make life easy" for the paratroopers.[113] Despite this uncritical and "nurturing" environment, Stewart lamented that the Regiment could never accept the fact that it was no longer an independent formation, and as a result, was in constant conflict with other units of the SSF and SSF Headquarters. "It was interesting to me that the Regiment received from SSF HQ preferential treatment," he stated in bewilderment, "yet were always griping about every order or directive they received." Stewart explained that the senior officers within the Airborne resented the fact that they were not independent and felt it was below their dignity to take orders from a Brigadier-General. He added, "as a result they seldom did what they were ordered to do and sometimes, unfortunately, they got away with it!"[114]

Another former SSF commander was equally as candid. Ernie Beno commiserated that the "Airborne Regiment tried to be a mini-formation within a formation," which he explained, "caused no end of heart ache."[115] These observations are not subjective, nor inaccurate. Lieutenant-Colonel Richard Dick, the Regimental Administration Officer from 1984-1986, recalled, "we acted independently and did what we wanted to do." "Furthermore," he too added, "we got away with it."[116]

More telling were the impressions of the regimental commanders. For instance, at the time of his command hand-over, Colonel Fraser admitted to his replacement his inability to accept the subordination of the Regiment to the SSF. "I don't know how that's going to work," he advised the new commander, "a formation within a formation is doomed."[117] Colonel Cowling also conceded that he felt the SSF represented nothing more than an unnecessary headquarters between the Regiment and the Army Commander.[118] These sentiments were by no means unique. They represented a pervasive attitude, as well as a fundamental belief in regard to the Airborne's proper position in the Army chain of command. This debate endured until the Regiment's ultimate demise in the mid 1990s.[119]

But even as the Regiment entered its third decade of service, its acceptance as an integral element of the Army was by no means assured. Its raison d'être remained confused and hotly debated; its status and structure were dramatically pared down; it lost its preferential claim on experienced and mature manpower; and it was increasingly defined as just another infantry unit. Some of its commandos were riddled with serious and growing ill discipline. Furthermore, in an era of shrinking resources and personnel, the support of the parent feeder regiments was never consistent and often their personnel contributions were not good. The outside investigators knew there were problems but could find no real solutions. The leadership inside the Airborne sometimes acted as if they ruled their own fiefdom. Those commanders who managed to temporarily improve performance did so only with the power of personality and "in their face" discipline. But these valiant attempts never came to address the core problems of role and vision. The Regiment was no longer the same organization which began its "great adventure" in 1968. As a result of events beyond its control, sensational problems coupled with an unbending, even naive attitude, the Regiment slipped toward darkness.

Notes for Chapter Seven

1. Letter to author, 1 July 1998.
2. "The Canadian Airborne Regiment—A Proscribed Elite," 6, *Information Legacy,* Document Control No. 905211, p. 615788. The SSF (which in reality was just another brigade group albeit with an airborne element) contained two infantry battalions, the Canadian Airborne Regiment and 1 RCR, which was garrisoned in London, Ontario. 1 RCR eventually moved to Petawawa in the summer of 1992.
3. The Regiment deployed to Cyprus in March 1981, March 1987, and was scheduled for another tour in 1990-1991, however, this was cancelled because of OP Python. In addition, 3 Commando was placed "Under Command" 2 RCHA for a tour in Cyprus in September 1986. The "flip-flop" in thinking in regard to maintaining the Regiment as a strategic reserve or maintaining the ability to fulfill its mandated purpose, led Major-Gaudreau to lament that commanders and staffs began to "play" the Regiment as it suited them. In other words, when it was deemed expedient not to use the Regiment, the need to keep it as a ready force was presented. When circumstances dictated its use, this was forgotten and it was launched on conventional rotations. Letter to author, 18 September 1998. This duplicity would lead to further problems. This issue is discussed in Chapter Eight.
4. "CFOO 3.21.5, The Canadian Airborne Regiment," dated 23 March 1977, *Information Legacy,* Document Control No. 905320, p. 627634.
5. Ibid.
6. "Handover Notes," July 1977, 42. Fraser Papers. This task became known as MAJAID (Major Air Disaster).
7. "CFOO 3.21.5, The Canadian Airborne Regiment," dated 25 April 1968, *Information Legacy,* Document Control No. 905191, p. 614785. Italics are my own.
8. "CFOO 3.21.5, The Canadian Airborne Regiment," dated 23 March 1977.
9. Lieutenant-General J.J. Paradis, Commander FMC, "Parachute Training—Canadian Airborne Training," 27 April 1997. DHist—NDHQ files on Canadian Airborne Regiment, not yet filed at time of use.
10. "SSF Restructuring Brief" for Commander FMC and CDS, 25 January and 2 February 1977 respectively. CAFM; and DLO comments, dated 13 May 1979. DHist—NDHQ files on Canadian Airborne Regiment, not yet filed at time of use.
11. Ibid.
12. Lieutenant-General J.J. Paradis, letter FM 1901-7723 (Comd), dated 5 December 1980, Annex B, CFOO 3.21.5, "Functions and Capabilities of the Canadian Airborne Regiment." DHist—NDHQ files on Canadian Airborne Regiment, not yet filed at time of use. The contradictory nature of the tasks was also noted by a DG Policy & Plans, memorandum, dated 12 July 1979. It specifically noted that the Regiment's "two primary and incompatible wartime tasks were DCO & CAST." Lieutenant-General Foster, as Regimental Commander during this period, remarked, "I was part of the CAST Brigade Group that would deploy to North Norway under the NATO umbrella. I was less comfortable about that because we are talking about a high intensity combat situation and possibly war in Europe. I was responsible for sovereignty operations which meant deployment in Canada's north and domestic operations, whatever, they might be." Somalia Commission, Transcript of Evidentiary Hearing, Vol 3, 5 October 1995, 401.
13. "CFOO 3.21.5, The Canadian Airborne Regiment," dated 1 March 1985, *Information Legacy,* Document Control No. 905321, p. 627708. Italics are my own.
14. The evolution of the Regiment to battalion status was not necessarily considered a bad thing, as long as it remained a pure airborne organization. Some promoted the idea, others indicated that in reality, since 1977, the "Regiment" was in fact nothing more than a battalion with vestiges in name only of a Regiment. The prime concern, however, was that the continual erosion of the Regiment's strength and uniqueness would make it more vulnerable to disbandment. The perception was the closer it resembled and was seen as a normal infantry unit, the more precarious was its existence. After all, why keep an infantry unit with limited mobility (vehicles) and costly special requirements (related parachuting activities and equipment)? Specific individuals have been and will be quoted throughout.

15. Beno, "The Way Ahead," 7. Beno Papers. Beno actually recommended that the Regiment be organized "the very same as any other infantry battalion." His paper was in response to the problems experienced in Somalia. See Chapters Eight and Nine. Beno also reflected on the problem created by the multiple assigned tasks, many of which were mutually exclusive. He stated in the early years of the SSF they had a tasking for the Arctic, CAST and AMF(L) and the UN. He stated, "how do you develop a coherent plan? What equipment do you get?" He asserted that conflicting foci and tasks are detrimental to a small organization. He explained that it "chips away at the cohesiveness of a unit or formation." Interview with author, 20 May 1998.

16. Interview with author, 5 November 1998. Colonel Mark Skidmore, the Regimental Major (RM) from 1989-1991, recalled that there was a continual fight over the necessity to maintain a strong airborne capability. He explained the debate revolved around the cost of infrastructure, training, and operations & maintenance expenses of keeping aircrew current. Skidmore recollected that during a 1989 Airborne Advisory Board, chaired by Brigadier-General Douglas, the SSF Commander, and attended by the regimental commander, commander of CABC, PMD and a representative of Air Transport Group, a figure of $1 billion was floated as the cost for maintaining the airborne capability. This however, was cast in the widest sense (inclusive of the Regiment, CABC, aircraft, aircrew, special allowances, night LAPES requirement, etc). This figure, he cautioned was misleading as it included costs which would exist regardless if there was a parachute capability or not. For example aircraft would continue to fly just as many hours, only assigned to different missions. It was because of the constant attack that Skidmore stressed the importance of convincing politicians that they needed the capability. Interview with author, 13 February and 25 April 1997.

17. Interview with author, 4 June 1998.

18. Ibid.

19. Interview with author, 16 December 1998. He stated that during his tour they repainted their helmets [olive drab to UN blue and back] so many times that it actually gained weight. Colonel Hatton served in 2 Commando as a platoon commander and intelligence officer from 1977-1979; and as the FMC SSO3 Infantry-Airborne in 1983.

20. Interview with author, 8 December 1997. Colonel Cowling also believed that the absence of a "Special Emergency Reaction Team" (SERT) for anti-terrorist scenarios probably meant that the requirement to mount a response would fall on the Regiment. As a result, he arranged for individuals to take some specialist training at Fort Benning to ensure some expertise was available.

21. Interview with author. Bragdon served in 2 Commando as a platoon commander and company commander from 1973-1976, as CO from 1984-1986, and as the FMC staff officer Infantry-Airborne from 1979-1981. Bragdon also believed that a SERT role was suitable for the Airborne Regiment and he formulated proposals along this line.

22. Interview with author, 6 October 1998. Pentney served as operations officer and DCO of 2 Commando from 1982-1985; and as CO from 1988-1990.

23. Ibid. Brigadier-General Douglas was another who supported an element of Special Forces capability. He insisted that the Airborne gave the SSF and the CF the ability to interact with the American SF. Interview with author. Conversely, Colonel Mark Skidmore reflected that "what ruined it [Regiment] was that we tried to be Special Forces instead of good solid infantry." Interview with author, 13 February 1997.

24. Interview with author, 5 November 1998.

25. Interview with author, 18 August 1998.

26. See Chapter Four, text and accompanying endnotes 60-63 & 68.

27. Canadian Airborne Regiment, "1 Commando," *Maroon Beret,* November 1986, 33. General Allard later explained to Dr. Doug Bland during a May 1992 interview that he viewed the Canadian Airborne Regiment as a special training tool, in which individuals would serve two years and then return to their parent units and thus spread the skills to the rest of the Army.

28. Patrick Sullivan, "Deaths of Nine Paratroopers Throw Rare Spotlight on Unit," *The Globe and Mail,* 1 February 1989.

29. Interview with author, 16 December 1998.
30. Director General Policy memorandum, "CANUS Int Estimate 1979," 12 July 1979. DHist—NDHQ files on Canadian Airborne Regiment, not yet filed at time of use.
31. Proceedings of the Special Committee of the Senate on National Defence (hereafter Senate Defence Committee), 31 October 1989, 4:180; and Colonel J.M.R. Gaudreau, Letter, 3120-1 (R Comd), dated 17 March 1986, "Operational Concept For the Canadian Airborne Regiment to Defeat the Wartime Land Threat to CDA," 4-5. The appreciation astutely noted, "Based on the historical experience of the Second World War, the Canadian government or the Canadian people will be most unwilling to allow our ground forces to deploy out of country—Europe—until we have satisfactorily dealt with an enemy presence on our sovereign territory." However, threat must be balanced against enemy intention and probability of occurrence.
32. Senate Defence Committee, 26 January 1988, 12:30.
33. Senate Defence Committee, 31 October 1989, 4:178; and *Canada's Land Forces*, 71.
34. Senate Defence Committee, 31 October 1989, 4:182.
35. Interview with author, 18 March 1998. Douglas added that DCO was a bit of a smoke screen.
36. Interview with author, 8 December 1997.
37. Senate Defence Committee, 31 October 1989, 4:181-82; *Canada's Land Forces*, 72-73; Gaudreau, "Operational Concept For the Canadian Airborne Regiment to Defeat the Wartime Land Threat to CDA," 2; M.J. Goodspeed, "SPETSNAZ: Soviet Diversionary Forces Checkmate in Two Moves?" *CDQ,*, Vol 18, No.1, Summer 1988, 44; and William Baxter, "The Soviet Threat from the Sky," *Army*, Vol 31, No. 4, April 1981, 42-43.
38. Senate Defence Committee, 31 October 1989, 4:182.
39. Canada, *Minister's Statement—Defence Estimates 1984/85* (Ottawa: SCEAND, 1984), 7.
40. Senate Defence Committee, 20 February 1986, 13:24. Colonel Cuppens, then the Director of Military Plans Coordination stated that "owing to the size of our country and the limited resources of the CF, mobility is the key factor in the conduct of these [DCO] operations." The Senate Committee then expanded on his sentiment. They concluded that "in practise, this means that the units conducting defence of Canada operations must have an airborne capability." Senate Defence Committee, 31 October 1989, 4:182; and *Canada's Land Forces*, 73. However, they did not define the required size of the capability, nor how it should be organized.
41. Senate Defence Committee, 17 April 1984, 8A:6.
42. Interview with author, 15 April 1998. The perennial complaint over mobility in the North raises the question of commitment to DCO. The lack of adequate over-snow vehicles was raised in the late forties and early fifties as a factor detrimentally affecting the employment of an airborne company group. (Appreciation on the Employment of the Active Force Brigade Group in Defence of Canada, 7 November 1949, Dhist File 112.3M2 (D400); and "Factors Affecting the Employment of An Airborne Company Group," 8 June 1950.) The necessity of the special vehicles, as well as their absence was also raised in Parliament. See *Debates,* 17 March & 8 June 1950, 854 and 3359 respectively. The problem was never fully rectified. As late as 1986, the lack of an adequate over-snow vehicle for the North was still an issue. It was reported that "one of the SSF's serious limitations was the lack of sufficient over-snow vehicles to provide mobility." One paratroop officer explained, "Once we hit the ground all we have for mobility are 'bangey-boards [military skis] and snowshoes." The continuing problem prompted the SSF Commander to confirm that "something must be done to increase the winter mobility of Canadian soldiers." Captain Tony Keene, "Exercise Lightning Strike," *Sentinel,* 1986 / 3, 6-7. See also Gaudreau, "Operational Concept For the Canadian Airborne Regiment to Defeat the Wartime Land Threat to CDA," 6.
43. Interview with author, 18 March 1998.
44. R.B. Byers, and M. Slack, eds., *The Canadian Strategic Review, 1985-1986* (Toronto: CISS, 1988), 126-128; Sokolsky, 13; and J.T. Jockel, *Security to the North. Canada-US Defence Relationships in the 1990s* (East Lansing: Michigan State University Press, 1991), 30-31.

45. Byers, *Strategic Review 1985-1986,* 130. Melvin Conant linked the US Coast Guard cutter *Polar Sea* moving through Canadian waters to the "political receptivity of an increased defense effort." M.A. Conant, "The Long Polar Watch: An American Perspective on Canada's Defence of Its Arctic," *American Review of Canadian Studies,* Vol 18, No. 3, Autumn 1988, 373. Once again the government tried to play down the effect of the American challenge. Joe Clark, the Minister of External Affairs, stated, *"Polar* Sea has left no trace on Canada's Arctic waters and no mark on Canada's Arctic sovereignty. It is behind us and our concern must be for what lies ahead." *Debates,* 10 September 1985, 6463.

46. Canada, *Challenge and Commitment—A Defence Policy for Canada* (Ottawa: DND, June 1987), II.

47. Ibid, 23. This echoes the earlier sentiments of Joe Clark (which is also reminiscent of others). He stated, "Only with full sovereignty can we protect the entire range of Canadian interests. Full sovereignty is vital to Canada's security...And is vital to Canada's national identity." *Debates,* 10 September 1985, 6463.

48. *Challenge and Commitment*, 55-56. Erik Nielsen (MND 1985) stated, "I want to emphasize the importance of fully exercising sovereignty in our north. The DEW Line has served Canada well, but Canadians do not control it...The North Warning System will be a Canadian-controlled system-operated, maintained and manned by Canadians. Sovereignty in our north will be strengthened and assured for the future." *Debates,* 13 March 1985.

50. Beatty claimed the FOLs would "enhance the Canadian Armed Forces ability to ensure Canada's northern sovereignty." DND News Release, 11 March 1987 as quoted in Byers, *Review 1987,* 106.

51. Ibid, 193. He also noted, "the emphasis on sovereignty protection can pose two long term future problems for the United States. First, Canada can devote its very scarce military resources to presence rather than military mission, knowing that the United States can be counted on, in the final analysis, for defence."

52. Canada, *1994 Defence White Paper* (Ottawa: DND, 1994), 15.

53. This theme has remained consistent. *Defence Planning Guidance 1998 (DPG 1998),* stated that "while Canada faces no direct military threat at present...Canada must have the ability to protect its sovereignty." Canada, *Defence Planning Guidance 1998* (Ottawa: DND, 1997), 1-1.

54. Interview with author, 23 November 1996. Lieutenant-Colonel Peter Bradley recalled that the first flood of untrained soldiers arrived the summer prior to the move. He noted they came right from the battle school and with absolutely no experience or training beyond the basic infantry level. Interview with author, 15 September 1997. See also Bercuson, *Significant Incident,* 204-208.

55. Letter to author, 31 March 1997.

56. Interview with author.

57. Interview with Colonel Dick Cowling, 8 December 1997. Cowling explained that as a result of the arrival of inexperienced soldiers the organization now had to run individual training instead of collective [unit level] or advanced skills training. The Hewson Report also noted the commencement of accepting personnel directly from basic training started in 1978. The Report explained that this was done only in exceptional circumstances to maintain acceptable manning levels. Lieutenant-General Kent Foster outlined the shortages that existed in 1977. Foster recalled that on his arrival, as Regimental Commander, 1 Commando "numbered 180, 188, something like that. It was supposed to be in the neighbourhood of 350." *Somalia Commission,* Transcript of Evidentiary Hearing, Vol 3, 5 October 1995, 400.

58. Letter to author, 1 July 1998.

59. "Manning: Canadian Airborne Regiment," 9 October 1985, *Information Legacy,* Evidentiary Exhibits.

60. Ibid. Certain steps were already in place to assist with the manpower shortages. Firstly, any volunteer for the basic parachutist course was required to sign a waiver stating that he would serve in the Airborne Regiment if called to do so. Failure to fulfill this contract could, and did, result in the loss of the right to wear the distinctive parachutist qualification badge (commonly referred to as "wings"). Secondly, the parent regiments and their battalions often directed posted individuals to the Airborne whether they volunteered or not. As will be discussed, often the Airborne was used to discard those individuals who were viewed as undesirable. Colonel Rick Hatton candidly asserted that an ongoing

fallacy is the notion that everyone who served in the Airborne volunteered to do so. Interview with author, 16 December 1998.

61. See Chapter Six, text and accompanying endnote 28.

62. See Chapter Six, text and accompanying endnotes 56-59. See also CAFM, Research Paper, Part 1,1E Doc 1—*The Canadian Airborne Regiment and the Special Service Force*, 2-3. During the initial period the paratroopers were allowed to stay in their current commando, regardless of their parent regiment affiliation, until attrition and postings eventually created relatively "pure" affiliated commandos.

63. *Somalia Commission*, Transcript of Policy Hearing, Vol 4, 21 June 1995, 620 and 5 October 1995, 409; and the Canadian Forces Board of Inquiry—Canadian Airborne Regiment Battle Group, Phase I, Vol XI, H-1/6 (hereafter referred to as BOI—Cdn AB Regt BG).

64. Interview with author, 19 August 1996. One humorous anecdote was the case of Colonel Strome Galloway, a distinguished RCR World War II veteran and former "RCR Colonel of the Regiment" who telephoned 3 Commando (RCR). When he did not recognize the name of the officer he was talking to, the individual (3 Commando 2IC) promptly replied, "That's probably because I'm a PPCLI officer." There was a short pause and Colonel Galloway questioned "Are there any real officers from 3 Commando available?" The individual replied, "Not of RCR background; can I help you?" at which point Galloway said, "No thank you, I will call back later." Interview with Major Peter Bartlett, 15 May 1996.

65. *Somalia Commission*, Transcript of Evidentiary Hearing, Vol 3, 5 October 1995, 408.

66. Mobile Command (FMC), *Mobile Command Study—Report on Disciplinary Infractions and Antisocial Behaviour with particular reference to the SSF and the Canadian Airborne Regiment* (hereafter referred to as the Hewson Report), September 1985, 45; and BOI Cnd AB Regt BG, Phase I, Vol XI, p. H-1/6. Former Regimental Commanders Ian Douglas, Michael Houghton, Walt Holmes and Peter Kenward all commented on the problems which arose directly from affiliated commandos and the resultant interference of the feeder regiments.

67. Beno, "The Way Ahead," 8/14. Beno Papers. Brigadier-General Beno added that "offsetting weaknesses in one subunit by moving personnel to another is generally not done because of current regimental affiliations."

68. See Chapter Three, text and accompanying endnotes 66 and 68.

69. Interview with author, 23 November 1996. Blanchette added, "as the Old Guard left, the New Guard received no [PPCLI] support."

70. Interview with author, 15 April 1998. Colonel Hatton also recalled the concern felt by Regimental officers during the evolution to affiliated commandos. He stated that it became known that some "cowboys" were arriving in the next posting cycle. Hatton explained that "the old [regimentally mixed] 2 Commando could have handled it, but the new [pure PPCLI] organization could not." Interview with author, 16 December 1998.

71. Interview with author, 18 March 1998.

72. BOI, Cdn AB Regt BG, Phase I, Vol XI, H-1/6 and Vol XI, 16-30.

73. Hewson Report, 46.

74. BOI, Cdn AB Regt BG, Phase I, Vol XI, K-2/9; and Beno, "The Way Ahead," 3 & 5, Beno papers. There is overwhelming consensus on this issue by former Airborne personnel who served in leadership positions (ie, regimental commanders, commanding officers, officers commanding, regimental sergeant-majors (RSM), commando sergeant-majors (CSM). All conceded that there were numerous, and very blatant, instances of weak personnel being posted in. In the same vein, it was noted that the calibre of replacements was often directly related to the COs and RSMs of the dispatching units. Not surprisingly, there was agreement from those interviewed that those COs and RSMs without Airborne experience were more likely to unload weak or "problem" personnel. Colonel Michael Houghton asserted that "many COs were concerned when good soldiers wanted to serve in the Airborne Regiment. They saw it as a threat to their own units." Interview with author, 5 November 1998.

75. Interview with author, 7 October 1998. Major-General Hewson testified, "we [FMC study and *Report on Disciplinary Infractions and Antisocial Behaviour with particular reference to the SSF and the Canadian*

Airborne Regiment] did hear expressions of concern that there might have been some sloughing off of less than fully competent soldiers to the Airborne Regiment. Because of that, we felt that other regiments should be reminded of their responsibility in this regard. *Somalia Commission*, Transcript of Evidentiary Hearing, Vol 2, 3 October 1995, 353.

76. Interview with author, 16 January 1997.
77. *Somalia Commission,* Transcript of Policy Hearings, Vol 4, 21 June 1995, 627.
78. Letter to author, 31 March 1997.
79. Interview with author, 20 May 1998; and Beno, "The Way Ahead," 5/14. Beno Papers.
80. Interview with author, 23 January 1998. Colonel Mitchell served in the Airborne Regiment from 1979-1982 as the Regimental Adjutant and DCO of 3 Commando; and from 1986-1988 as the Regimental Major.
81. The detrimental effect of the "airborne offers" (promotions used to fill vacancies in the Canadian Airborne Regiment), was specifically commented on by the Somalia Commission. *Somalia Commission,* Final Report—Executive Summary, "Personnel Selection and Screening," 2.
82. Interview with author, 15 September 1997. Ernie Beno observed that some officers and NCOs were given subsequent tours because they received a "'reputation' of being the 'airborne type,' or because of an 'only the airborne can handle them' attitude." Beno, "The Way Ahead," 3. Beno Papers.
83. Interview with author, 4 June 1998.
84. Interview with author, 7 October 1998. Another possible contributing factor to the problem was the inexperience of the junior NCO corps and an increasing number of sergeants (Sgt). Manpower shortages in the mid to late eighties necessitated the promotion of many to the rank of master-corporal (MCpl) and Sgt who were not yet ready. For example, it was common for an infantry battalion to dispatch its promising young privates to the Infantry Section Commanders Course (ISSC) after only a year of service. Due to the manning shortfalls these individuals were "DAPSed" (accelerated promotion) to MCpl. They were then employed as an infantry section second in command (2IC). However, taskings and shortages at the Sgt rank normally meant that these individuals would become acting section commanders. Reality quickly showed that a good follower (private) did not always make a good leader. Furthermore, the inexperience of the "DAPSed" MCpls created problems in training, supervising and establishing the appropriate role model for their subordinates. This problem was exacerbated when a newly promoted inexperienced, and often immature young MCpl was posted to the Airborne Regiment. It is not hard to comprehend that these individuals, who wanted to fit in and be accepted, could easily be manipulated and controlled by long serving paratroopers within their platoon or section. The issue extends to the rank of Sgt as well. During this period the previous norm of a newly promoted Sgt with an average of 10-12 years of experience was replaced with individuals with only 5-8 years. Once again the lack of breadth and depth of experience had a telling effect.
85. Interview with Colonel D.B. McGibbon, 24 November 1998. McGibbon was a principal staff officer in DLO at NDHQ and worked closely with Major-General Pitts on the issue of the Airborne Regiment's move to Petawawa. He recalled that Pitts predicted that the move would result in disaster for the Regiment.
86. Interview with author, 6 June 1998.
87. Interview with author, 18 March 1998. Major-General Bob Stewart concurred that the manpower shortage led to a situation where "some individuals became permanent fixtures in the Regiment and were not returned to their parent Regiments as was initially intended." Letter to author, 1 July 1998.
88. Rochester, "Birth of a Regiment," 34.
89. Interview with author, 15 April 1998.
90. Interview with author, 14 April 1997.
91. Interview with author, 4 October 1996.
92. The definition of leadership becomes controversial. There is a direct correlation between blame and who is speaking. For instance senior officers tend to blame junior officers for lax discipline and being overly concerned with being "one of the boys." Officers in general blame the senior NCOs and the per-

sonnel and recruiting system (for not screening individuals with criminal records prior to enlistment). NCOs tend to point the finger at the Charter of Rights, which is perceived as limiting their ability to act. In addition, NCOs also complain of lack of support from their superiors when they actually attempted to discipline individuals. In reality, all shared a degree of the blame. Discipline begins with self-discipline and the enforcement of pertinent rules and regulations falls on all within the chain of command. To state that poor discipline existed because the lower echelons failed to do their job does not explain why the action of those deficient was not corrected. Some examples: Colonel Ian Douglas, the Regimental Commander from 1982-1985, attributed the erosion of discipline in the unit to failures in the manpower selection system and to a growing tendency among junior officers to be too lax. Major-General Bob Gaudreau observed that many leaders took discipline and proper behaviour for granted and required constant reminding to keep a firm grip on things. Colonel Kenward mentioned the fact that 2 Commando senior NCOs spoke of a failure of support from their chain of command prior to his arrival. Interviews with author, and Bercuson, *Significant Incident*, 204-210.

93. Interview with Lieutenant-Colonels Watkin and Bradley, 4 June 1998 and 15 September 1997 respectively. The derogatory term LEG originates from the Second World War. Regular infantry wore canvas leggings as part of their uniform. The elite paratroopers were spared this ordeal. They were issued with high cut jump boots into which the uniform trouser could be tucked. Needless to say, the paratroopers quickly christened their brethren with the contemptuous label "LEGs." A more contemporary version translates the meaning to "Lacking Enough Guts." This is not surprisingly a peacetime mutation. Beyond the obvious fact that leggings are no longer worn, the act of parachuting is seen as a test of individual courage. It has taken on an importance of far greater proportion than it did during the war. Since virtually all infanteers saw combat, and those in the regular line infantry for longer periods than the airborne units, the question of individual courage was rather moot.

94. Brigadier-General Ian Douglas acknowledged, "We knew from the SIU [Special Investigations Unit, military] and the OPP [Ontario Provincial Police] that they [Para Nomads] were tied to the Hell's Angels." Douglas's attempts at eradicating the club were largely frustrated. The 1 Commando CO at the time insisted that it was just a R22eR club and that the members had a legal "right" to participate. Douglas stated that the problem was eventually solved by a combination of making it difficult for the motorcyclists to come onto the base and slowly posting the participating members back to their parent regiments. Interview with author, 18 March 1998. Beno, Gaudreau and Stewart all asserted that the weapon thefts were "inside jobs" and were linked to the motorcycle club. Interviews/letters to author.

95. Confidential interview. Specific incidents include the booby-trapping of an officer's office with an artillery simulator wrapped with nails, as well as the later well-known burning of an officer's car on the parade square in 1990 and that of a senior NCO in 1992.

96. R.I. Stewart, "Discipline, Soldierly Behaviour and Leaders' Responsibilities," 7 May 1984. Accessed from Major-General Stewart's personal papers, hereafter referred to as Stewart Papers. 0a. Letter to author, 1 July 1998. Stewart acknowledged that part of the problem was the "convoluted / organizational structure [CO status, as well as affiliation, of the commandos] and in part to a failure to take tough action when it was required." See also Peter Cheney, "Canada's Rebel Soldiers, The Airborne Regiment in Somalia," *The Edmonton Sunday Journal,* 30 January 1994, D1, 2 & 7; and Peter Cheney, "The Airborne Story," *The Montreal Gazette,* 22 January 1994, B1-2.

98. Interview with (and letter from) Major-General Gaudreau, 18 August 1998; and *Information Legacy,* Hearing Transcripts, Vol 3, 5 October 1995, 537. General C.E. Therriault, the CDS, was an Air Force officer. Major-General de Chastelain was an infantry officer (PPCLI). Lieutenant-General Belzile (R22eR) was the actual FMC Commander during this period.

99. Hewson Report, 1 & E-10; Interview with (and letter from) Major-General Gaudreau, 18 August and 18 September 1998 respectively; and *Information Legacy,* Hearing Transcripts, Vol 3, 5 October 1995, 537.

100. Hewson Report, Covering Letter, 2; and interview with Major-General Gaudreau, 18 August 1998.

101. Hewson Report, 51-54.

102. Ibid., 52. The effects of lower experience and qualification levels, in the aftermath of the move from Edmonton to Petawawa, was now making itself felt. The report specifically concluded that "there is a lower incidence of anti-social behaviour amongst soldiers who have spent some time with an infantry

battalion than amongst those newly arrived from infantry battle schools." As a result the study team recommended that, "Only mature, trained infantry soldiers who have served with a regular infantry battalion for one or two years should be considered for service with the Canadian Airborne Regiment. Battalions and career managers must continue to cooperate in ensuring that only suitable personnel are sent."

103. Hewson Report, Covering memo, 26 September 1985, 2. Major-General Hewson added, "This is a touchy subject and I believe the regiments are, in most cases, doing their best." The report recommended that the practice of assigning infantry personnel to a commando based on regimental affiliation should continue.

104. Ibid., Executive Summary, 1. This one line underscored the importance of the study; namely, prevent the disbandment of the Regiment.

105. Ibid., 51.

106. The report warned that "unless the matter of taskings, turbulence and absentee junior leadership is addressed now, there is a real danger that present cases of antisocial behaviour will escalate both in frequency and severity." Hewson Report, 31. A cynic would query whether the "vehicle" had been hijacked in an attempt to return the Regiment to its former privileged existence of preferred manning and no taskings. After all, taskings are the bane of *any* unit's existence.

107. Interview with Lieutenant-Colonel Ken Watkin, 4 June 1998. He was the SSF legal advisor from 1983-1986.

108. Interview with Lieutenant-Colonel Richard Dick, 15 April 1998.

109. *Somalia Commission,* Transcript of Evidentiary Hearings, Vol 2, 3 October 1995, 361. The report's findings were later questioned by Commissioner Desbarats during the Somalia Inquiry. He stated, "I was struck by...the communique from Brigadier-General Stewart [see text and endnote 96, this chapter]...and it seems to contrast with your overall findings... that concluded there is no cause for alarm or requirement for precipitive [sic] action." Transcript of Evidentiary Hearing, Vol 2, 3 October 1995, 362-264. A perception that the study team may have downplayed the problem in a misconstrued sense of "loyalty" to the Regiment and/or the Army does arise. Major-General Gaudreau testified in front of the Somalia Commission that "the Hewson Report had created a lot of staff action and navel-gazing across the Army." Quoted in Bercuson, *Significant Incident,* 210.

110. *Information Legacy,* Hearings Transcripts, Vol 17, 16 November 1995, 3104. Quote belongs to Colonel John Joly. However, similar comments and other complimentary remarks in regard to Major-General Gaudreau's leadership were consistently given by those interviewed.

111. *Information Legacy,* Hearings Transcripts, Vol 3, 5 October 1995, 417.

112. Letter to author, 18 September 1998. This issue will be further explored in Chapter Nine.

113. Letter to author, 1 July 1998. Specifically Stewart recalled in addition to himself, the brigade major, base administration officer, brigade RSM, CO 2 RCHA, as well as a host of other more junior staff officers were all ex-members of the Regiment.

114. Ibid. Stewart wrote a letter to David Bercuson which stated that the Regiment was often a "pain in the ass, ill disciplined," and "possessed an unhealthy attitude fostered by their officers which made the life of the SSF Commander more difficult than it needed to be." Stewart, "Thoughts, Opinions and Observations," 5, Stewart Papers. A newspaper account reported that "some airborne officers are unhappy at the loss of autonomy and view the new force with disdain and refer to it as the Special Service Farce." McNutty, 24.

115. Interview with author, 20 May 1998. Beno agreed that the Regiment definitely received special treatment. He insisted that the rank of the regimental commander was the first reason. However, he discounted the presence of an "old boys airborne club," as a factor. Beno stated, "if you whine enough and make enough noise you often get what you want."

116. Interview with author, 15 April 1998. He bears out Major-General Stewart's comment that the Airborne received preferential treatment in the SSF. He said "we felt like favoured sons." Dick also believed the ability to act independently was largely influenced by the rank level of the regimental commander.

117. Fraser, "Handover Notes," 3, Fraser Papers.//

118. Interview with author, 8 December 1997.

119. The attitude was not only a function of those within the Regiment. Colonel Houghton recalled his turmoil as he was caught in the middle of a tug-of-war between his Brigade Commander (Brigadier-General Ian Douglas) and the Deputy Army Commander (Major-General Kent Foster). Both claimed control of the Regiment. As a result, Houghton stated he was put in the awkward position of taking direction on administration and training from the SSF Commander, but was tasked directly from Army HQ for operational purposes. Houghton confessed, "I didn't know who I was under command." Interview with author, 5 November 1998. This approach was in line with Foster's belief that one characteristic of airborne forces is the need for a direct line to the senior commander. *Somalia Commission,* Transcript of Evidentiary Hearing, Vol 3, 5 October 1995, 384. During the post-Somalia period a move was made to restore the Regiment's independent status and remove it from the SSF's chain of command. Chapter Nine deals with this issue in greater detail.

CHAPTER EIGHT

ON THE EDGE OF THE ABYSS
The Canadian Airborne Regiment and Somalia, 1990-1993

I guess what I'm getting at is whether there is a pattern here over really a quarter of a century of the regiment's existence of a long-standing recurrent problem of trying to find something for this highly-trained regiment to do.

Somalia Commissioner Peter Desbarats.[1]

As the 1990s approached, the Canadian Airborne Regiment entered its third decade of service unsure of its future. As we have seen, serious corrosive forces were working relentlessly both within and outside the Regiment. Although its success at maintaining a reputation for challenging and extremely tough training was unrivalled, it met with no such fortune in regard to convincing others of its unquestioned importance within the military family. The paratroopers were still seen by many as aberrants.

The Airborne's existence remained turbulent, buffeted by the competing efforts of those who attempted to marginalize the Regiment and those who tried, at any cost, to show its importance. As a direct result, the Canadian mission to Somalia in 1993, and the sad events surrounding it, became the prevailing snapshot of the country's airborne experience. It demonstrated the best, as well as the worst, of Canada's airborne forces. More importantly it underlined the continuing, and at times invidious, struggle within the military to determine the place of the paratrooper in the nation's Armed Forces.

The Canadian Airborne Regiment also entered the 1990s as a very disgruntled organization. Despite the historic rhetoric of being the nation's "fire-brigade" and the designated UN stand-by force, the reality was much different. With the exception of the emergency deployment to Cyprus in 1974, it had never been employed in an operational capacity other than normal Cyprus rotation tours. Of great distress to Canada's premier warriors was the reality that rather than deploying to hot spots throughout the globe, they were instead used to train others to proceed overseas on actual operations. The paratroopers stood on the sidelines and assisted in the preparation to deploy communication and service support units for Iran/Iraq and Namibia in 1988 and 1989.

They watched as elements of 1 RCR and 2 Field Ambulance left for the Gulf War in 1990/1991. To add insult to injury, the paratroopers, who were tasked to train the medical staff, were incessantly inundated by complaints from the medical personnel who did not want to go.[2]

The Oka Crisis of 1990 cast a further shadow. That August, after a month-long standoff between Mohawks and the police, the Quebec government asked the Canadian Forces to replace the provincial police (SQ) at the barricades at Oka. Ten days later the army received a further request to dismantle the Mohawk barriers.[3] During this period, the Commander of the Army, Lieutenant-General Kent Foster, gave the Airborne Regiment the mandate to prepare for possible deployment to Oka. Six weeks of diligent training was undertaken. The paratroopers constructed mock-ups of the barricades and they exercised every conceivable contingency. Foster explained that the Regiment's role was kept secret because they were his "ace in the hole."[4]

The paratroopers, however, saw it differently. Colonel Skidmore, then the Regimental Major, recalled that as a result of the warning order to deploy, the Airborne had formed two large riot squads who trained "away from the public eye." He believed that the paratroopers were not deployed because it would have been "seen as a large escalation of force." Skidmore felt that there was a prevalent fear that "bringing in the Maroon Berets" meant that it was time "to crack skulls." He quickly noted that the Regiment desperately wanted to deploy specifically to dispel that myth. But, when the crisis ended on 26 September 1990, the Regiment had never even left Petawawa.[5] And so their morale dropped again.

Then a year later another glimmer of hope helped despoil some of the despondency within the Regiment. In mid July 1991, Marcel Masse, the Minister of National Defence, announced that Canada was contributing 740 troops to participate in the United Nations Mission for the Referendum in Western Sahara.[6] More importantly the contribution for the new mission, designated Operation (OP) Python, was to involve the Canadian Airborne Regiment. Once again the Regiment thought it was finally going on operations.

The Regiment's supposed role in the Sahara was to monitor a cease-fire and ensure that troop reductions and the prisoners of war (PoW) exchange, which were mutually agreed to by the Popular Front for the Liberation of Saguel et Hamra on the one hand and Rio de Cros (POLISARIO) guerilas and the Moroccan Army on the other, were honoured.[7] Training for the deployment began on 1 September and the Regiment was to be in position in the Western Sahara by the start of the next month. In Petawawa, the Regiment enthusiastically completed its preparatory work-ups. Vehicles were painted and packed. Equipment was readied and crated. As a result of the operation, an upcoming exercise in Jamaica and a rotation to Cyprus were cancelled. But, ominously, dates began to slip. Postponements were followed by further delays. Not surprisingly, on again/off again direction increased in frequency and the paratroopers quickly dubbed the operation OP "Monty" Python. By December 1991, even the die-hard optimists realized the mission was a bust.

The failure of the Sahara operation to happen for the Airborne was due to an inability on the part of the two African antagonists to resolve the issue of who was qualified to vote. Consequently the UN mission collapsed and its purpose became one of sustaining the existing observers in place. On 19 February 1992, NDHQ ordered the Special Service Force to cancel OP Python and direct the Canadian Airborne Regiment to revert to UN stand-by status, with the ability to move on thirty days' notice. Two days later, the SSF commander stood down the now dejected Canadian Airborne Regiment.[8]

The latest disappointment stoked the already seething level of disillusionment. The SSF commander was very concerned about what he called the "frustration factor." He further acknowledged that the CDS, General de Chastelain, was "very much aware of this."[9] Other senior Army officers with airborne service were equally worried about the bad effect in the ranks. It was "a real bone of contention for all...who were on 'stand-by' for everything, yet saw conventional units getting the tasks."[10] There was a morale problem and it "certainly undermined the faith of subordinates in the senior army leaders."[11]

The absence of a mission was not the Regiment's only pressing concern in the early nineties. Larger events profoundly affected the unit. The end of the Cold War saw Canadians wanting their "peace dividend." As elsewhere in the world military systems were being dismantled and budgets cut. When the financial screws began to effect the Regiment all the old opposition arguments re-emerged. The most difficult to answer was why maintain an expensive unit that has no specific role and has not been deployed on an operational mission? Scalpels were drawn once again as another reorganization was imposed on the Airborne. Falling hard on the futile preparations for the Sahara operation was the Army's announcement that the Airborne Regiment was to be officially reduced from regimental to battalion status. The Army once again looked for savings by cutting the Airborne's structure.

Trying to be "master of his own destiny" as he later wrote, Walt Holmes, the Regimental Commander at the time, struggled to preempt this latest attack by countering with a proposed organizational structure which was deemed workable from the Regiment's perspective. Holmes felt strongly that the Airborne had to protect itself if it hoped to survive. Like many other airborne supporters, Holmes believed that the threat of disbandment would be intensified now that the Regiment was to be reduced to an airborne battalion structure more in line with the line infantry units.[12]

All through 1992, the Regiment, with the active support of the SSF, worked diligently at convincing higher headquarters of their operational concept for the proposed airborne battalion. Despite the considerable staff effort and numerous discussions in regard to appropriate missions and tasks, the problem of reconciling the gap between the Airborne's assigned roles and the Regiment's actual capabilities was never resolved.[13] Brigadier-General Ray Crabbe, the SSF Commander pointedly declared that the "airborne battalion is incapable of executing most of the assigned or implied tasks without significant augmentation of firepower, mobility / counter-mobility forces, security, etc." He concluded, "the tasks essentially call for a battle group."[14] A former Director of Infantry agreed with Crabbe. He thought that the standing capability of the Regiment, after restructuring, was inadequate to undertake the full range of missions that it could reasonably expect to be given either in a domestic or international context.[15]

Amazingly, despite the further reduction in strength and resources, authorities in the Army and at NDHQ forced the Regiment, or more accurately now the airborne battalion, to maintain its all inclusive mission statement. The new restructured airborne battalion retained the identical role and tasks as given in the 1977 and 1985 CFOOs (3.21.5), namely, to "provide rapid deployment airborne/air-transportable forces capable of responding to any emergency situation in support of national security or international peacekeeping."[16] The incessant warnings, from both the SSF and Airborne commanders as well as other staff officers, that the assigned taskings across such a broad spectrum of conflict required an organization greater than that of an airborne battalion, fell on deaf ears.

Such pressure from above only further widened the cracks in the unit's faulty original substructure. The same powers were constantly driving home the old complaint that the Airborne was a luxury that the Army could ill afford. And the Battalion seemed to have few friends at Army Headquarters in 1992, all which added further to the unit's woes. An internal Army study at the time reported that an airborne/airmobile capability was required, but its likelihood of employment would be "rare." The analysis envisaged the airborne role primarily for territorial or domestic operations in remote locations. It also stressed the perceived limitations of paratroops, namely the fact that airborne forces lacked general purpose combat capability; were expensive; and possessed limited combat power, tactical mobility and sustainability.[17]

Further resistance came from Land Forces Central Area (LFCA) Headquarters. Brigadier-General G.S. Thomson, the Acting Commander, invoked an ageless criticism of specialist forces. "In this time of financial and fiscal restraint," he wrote, "this headquarters can not support the concept of an infantry battalion being specifically equipped for one role. The Airborne Battalion should receive similar equipment and be capable of performing the general purpose combat role."[18] Thomson concluded that only once this had been achieved could consideration be given to the "light-scale air-droppable requirement."[19]

In the end, Army HQ imposed yet another even smaller structure on the Airborne. The reorganization occurred on 24 June 1992, and coincided with the change of command from Colonel W.M. Holmes to Lieutenant-Colonel P.R. Morneault. The Regiment was once again reduced. Its strength dropped twenty percent, from 754 members to 601 all ranks.[20] Holmes later summarized the deleterious effect of the new change. He stated that prior to the reorganization, the Airborne Regiment was in effect a small brigade. Holmes further explained that previously it had five unit commanders who were commanding officers; it had a headquarters staff comparable to that of a brigade; and it was designed to be expandable, so that in times of tension, it could be enlarged to a brigade-size organization if needed. He also pointed out that after the last reorganization, the Airborne no longer had this flexibility, nor were the support and services that permitted expansion any longer in place. The Regiment, he noted, was now similar to the other line infantry battalions in the Army. It could not operate independently and had to work under a brigade headquarters in terms of command and control. Furthermore, it now had to rely on other units of a brigade for combat support and combat service support.[21] It seemed that the Regiment's opponents at Army HQ had won.

Nonetheless, the imposed reorganization was not conceived as part of a carefully thought out strategy. There seemed little doubt that other financially hard pressed Army leaders were quite prepared to dwell on both the perception and the reality that the Airborne Regiment was an expensive luxury, an irreverent organization with no pervasive role. As a result, it was a tantalizing target for the required budget cuts. Even Holmes himself conceded that the reorganization was simply "a numbers game" with the further motive of restructuring the Regiment so that it would conform fundamentally, in size and organization, with that of a normal rifle battalion. Holmes proffered that "those of us in the Regiment had a vision of how it should be organized and those outside had a different vision, and we lost." Significantly, the three-man Army HQ study team designated to complete the Regiment's final "Table of Organization and Equipment," consisted of individuals with no airborne experience. The final decision, said Holmes, was simply "forced down our throats."[22]

The tug-of-war which ensued demonstrated the continuing conflict between the competing camps on the issue of airborne capability. Unfortunately, this latest reorganization in June of 1992 did nothing but further erode the structure of the Regiment. It was merely another example of "shaving the proverbial ice cube." None of the systemic flaws in the foundation of the Airborne were corrected, much less addressed. Downsizing seemingly became the accepted compromise between the pro- and anti-airborne camps. The quagmire associated with the unit's missions and tasks, as well as its actual role in the Army, was left unresolved. The quandary of leadership, manning, and support from the parent regiments was ignored. The Report of the Commission of Inquiry into Somalia, several years later, declared that "the downsizing that took place during the 1992 restructuring of the CAR occurred without first determining the appropriate 'concept of employment' for the Regiment. What emerged was poorly conceived."[23] It further noted that similar to the Regiment's experience in 1977, the current downsizing "occurred without sufficient consideration being given to the appropriate mission, roles, and tasks of the CAR."[24] Until these issues were resolved the Airborne would, and quite rightly so, remain a target for its opponents.

In spite of the June 1992 cuts, the Regiment managed to save one vestige of its former self. A recommendation by the SSF commander to retain the title Canadian Airborne Regiment, despite its battalion status, was accepted. This was a small but significant victory. The motive for the retention of the title, however, lies more in economy than concern over tradition. As Brigadier-General Crabbe explained, "the naming of the Airborne battalion has significant implications. The Airborne Regiment has considerable investment in Regimental accoutrements, clothing etc." Or, in laymen's terms, it can be described as "kept the name because it was too expensive to change the letterhead." Nevertheless, Crabbe also felt that aside from minimizing costs and the disruption in terms of things regimental, such as associations, kit shops, messes, and museums, the term "Regiment" was extremely important to clearly indicate that the organization was in fact unique (due to its parachute role).[25]

The significance of the latest assault on the Airborne Regiment did not go unnoticed. The advocates who supported a robust airborne capability within the military wanted to do something to demonstrate the Regiment's relevance. The absence of a credible and pervasive role, compounded by the decision to downgrade the Regiment's status and numbers continued to seriously weaken the argument for the retention of a strong airborne organization. The failure to be allowed to participate in many of the recent operations such as at Oka or the Gulf War exacerbated the predicament. Esoteric notions of insertions into the remote corners of the tundra, or the necessity for a quick-reaction force, capable of deploying on a moment's notice, were no longer valid. The Regiment had existed for almost a quarter of a century. During this time it was never required to execute a task that a conventional unit could not have performed within relatively the same time frame. It became evident, even to the staunchest airborne supporter, that they were losing ground. The question—why exactly do we need an expensive airborne organization?—simply would not go away. After all, it was a legitimate question. However, the airborne fraternity gave very little thought to the validity of their detractors' arguments. Instead of attempting to carve out and articulate a pervasive role for an airborne force in Canada and develop constituencies to support it, the airborne advocates maintained an arrogant and naive belief that airborne forces were simply a "given" in any modern Army structure.

Assaults against the stubborn paratroopers and uncomplimentary rumours only caused them to dig in. They now looked to their benefactors for support. They did not look in vain. Not surprisingly, a special bond existed between the Regiment and many of those elsewhere in the military who had had former airborne service. It was this link with its very sympathetic extended "airborne family" to which the Regiment now turned. The paratroopers counted on those friends in positions of influence to assist their quest for operational employment. And they had some success.

While we have already seen that the Canadian Airborne Regiment was selected for the Sahara operation in 1991 which eventually fell through, this story is worth revisiting to demonstrate how the extended airborne family worked outside to protect the Regiment. It was these airborne friends and family who had actually lobbied for and ensured that the Regiment was designated as the unit for OP Python in the Western Sahara. At the time the Army headquarters staff did not pick the Airborne Regiment as their first choice. However, the prevailing pressure from the airborne family to give the task to the Regiment was obvious. In recommending the original choice, the Army staff had advised Lieutenant-General Kent Foster, the Commander of Land Force Command (LFC, formerly FMC), that with a "purely factual" analysis, the 2 R22eR was the obvious choice for some solid reasons: the anticipated language of operation in theatre was French, the unit was equipped with the Grizzly Armoured Vehicle General Purpose (AVGP) and as a result, required less preparatory training, and finally the unit had no NATO commitment.

Brigadier-General Michel Matte, the Chief of Staff Army Operations, admitted that the appreciation conducted by his staff did not take into consideration such factors as "morale and / or spreading of the 'goodies' amongst the Command units."[26] However, he specifically stressed that the disadvantages of sending the Airborne Regiment could not be ignored. Particularly, his analysis noted that the Regiment did not have enough vehicles for the task, nor were they of the right type. Therefore, it concluded that a redistribution would be necessary and that this would affect the entire command for the full duration of the mission, as scarce equipment was taken from other units for the Airborne Regiment. Furthermore, this also necessitated a considerable effort in regard to driver training and vehicle familiarization. Finally, a pro-Airborne decision also necessitated the cancelling of an exercise in Jamaica and the requirement to find a replacement unit to take the Airborne Regiment's upcoming rotation to Cyprus in February 1992.

Matte had concluded matter-of-factly that the "neat solution appears to send the 2 R22eR on this mission." He also made it clear that if the Airborne Regiment was selected, "we must be ready to pay a price as some decisions must be made without the insurance that the mission will occur."[27] But, in the end, perhaps predictably, Matte's boss, Kent Foster, was not convinced of his subordinate's cool logic. Foster was a long-standing paratrooper and former regimental commander, and he gave the paratroopers the nod to go to West Africa. Brigadier-General Matte conceded that "the entire staff and I knew the decision was already made [before commencing the estimate]. I prepared the memo [to the Army Commander] knowing full well that Foster had already decided on the Airborne."[28] Brigadier-General M. Caron, the LFC Operations Officer (G3) agreed. "When the estimate came back," he declared, "it was obvious that the decision was already made." Caron recalled that the brief and simple note from the Army commander commended the staff for a very good appreciation; however, it directed that the Airborne be given the tasking.[29]

Foster later testified before the Somalia Commission that "it weighed heavily with me that I had an organization like that [Airborne Regiment] that wasn't being used to provide some relief to the rest of my army who were being tasked and double tasked and triple tasked. I couldn't afford the luxury of an organization like that that wasn't carrying its fair share of the load."[30] The statement is somewhat disingenuous. By tasking the Airborne, another unit was required to pick up the Regiment's rotation to Cyprus. In addition, both 1 RCR and the RCD were required to transfer equipment and personnel to the Regiment, as well as conduct vehicle training for the paratroopers. The tasking of the Regiment became extremely disruptive to those two units, each of which were available for the mission. In short, what Foster wanted was to give his old regiment a preferred operational job.

The intervention of the airborne family hurt everyone including the Airborne whose morale took another hit when the mission fell through. Moreover, the decision only heightened the resentment of the line regiments because they saw the Canadian Airborne Regiment receive special treatment in an illogical way; to boot they had all their vehicles "stolen." For them it seemed another case of pandering to the "prima donna paratroopers."[31]

Despite the eventual and very disappointing cancellation of the Sahara mission, the Airborne's supporters did not abandon them. In the summer of 1992, the UN secretary-general recommended that an enlarged UN presence, including both military observers, as well as an armed security force, was required throughout Somalia. The Security Council unanimously accepted his request. Subsequently, on 27 July UN Security Council Resolution 767 was passed. It called for the secretary-general and the international community to provide urgent humanitarian assistance to Somalia.[32] Two weeks later the prime minister advised the UN of Canada's willingness to provide transport aircraft to deliver humanitarian relief supplies. He also informed the secretary-general that Canada was prepared to consider the contribution of military security forces of battalion strength within the context of a larger UN force.

Expectantly, on 25 August the UN informally approached Canada with a request to provide a self-contained battalion to participate in the mission in the Horn of Africa. Eight days later, the MND announced that Canada was deploying 750 peacekeepers as part of the UN Operation in Somalia (UNOSOM). The new commitment, designated OP Cordon, was a classical UN peacekeeping operation mandated under Chapter VI of the UN Charter.[33]

As part of UNOSOM, the principal mission of the Canadian battalion was to provide security for the distribution of humanitarian relief, as well as participate in limited local humanitarian projects. The unit would be stationed in the area of Bossasso, in northern Somalia. There were three distinct phases of the proposed operation. The first priority was to get aid to those in need. Next was the necessity to encourage reconciliation between the belligerents and population at large, and finally there was the requirement to assist with rehabilitation.[34]

Later that summer of 1992, when the Canadian government announced the choice of the Canadian Airborne Regiment, it automatically rekindled the old resentments. The airborne lobby was once again accused of interference and for obvious reason. The paratroopers' opponents saw this as just another attempt to placate the Airborne's repeated pleas for an operational task. Major Mark Lilienthal, a staff officer working in the Directorate of Land Force Requirements in NDHQ, recalled "prior to Somalia the emphasis was on getting them [Airborne] a mission, anything." He explained that the reason was quite simply to "justify their existence."[35] Colonel Houghton, a former Regimental Commander and the Director of Peacekeeping Operations (DPKO) at the time conceded, "there is no doubt the 'airborne family' had a lot to say about it."[36]

Much of the enmity was derived from a perception that the Airborne Regiment was selected prior to any decision being made to participate in the mission, much less the result of a formal analytical process. There was some substance to this notion. During the Daily Executive Meeting (DEM) at NDHQ on 28 July 1992, the day following the passage of UN Resolution 767, General de Chastelain, the CDS and former paratrooper from the Defence of Canada Force era, agreed with the acting VCDS, Lieutenant-General Foster, that "the Canadian Airborne Regiment would be well suited for such a task [UNOSOM security battalion]."[37] Once again, the "hidden hand" of the Airborne's extended family seemed to be taking care of its own.

Interestingly, several years later when he testified before the Somalia Commission, General de Chastelain played down the importance of his statement on that day in July 1992. Before the Somalia Commission he acknowledged, "I concurred in that idea, but that was conversation at the table. The recommendation would have to come from Land Forces Command of which unit they felt appropriate when the time came should we reach that stage."[38] Nevertheless, the official record shows a different account. DEM notes for 28 July indicate that the CDS not only concurred with the recommendation of the Airborne Regiment but also thought "that this could become a contingency plan once the costs and ramifications had been fleshed out and the concept approved by the DM and himself [CDS]."[39] Three days later the CDS received a completed estimate, prepared especially for him by NDHQ J3 Plans, not the LFC (Army) staff. The estimate coming from this source suggests that the decision of who was to be chosen was not strictly an Army decision as the CDS had claimed. The analysis confirmed the mission was supportable, but did not identify any one particular unit. It included a possibility of four major units being available, namely, the RCD, 12 RBC, the Canadian Airborne Regiment, and 5 RALC.[40]

Less than a week later Beno, the newly appointed Special Service Force Commander was informally briefed by the out-going Brigadier-General Ray Crabbe, who was also a former paratrooper. Crabbe confided that the Airborne Regiment had been selected for human relief operations in Somalia.[41] This was almost a month prior to any official government announcement on participation. The perceived personal involvement of General de Chastelain intensified during his participation in the Airborne's "Jump Bivouac" in Petawawa during the final week in August 1992. He was continually assailed by frustrated paratroopers who were tired of watching other units deploy overseas. The CDS responded with the cryptic, "keep your powder dry, gentlemen, there may be something coming up."[42] It appeared the fix was in.

The extended Airborne family's role in ensuring that the Airborne Regiment was sent to Somalia, despite the denials by senior commanders, was well recognized within the Army. "When Op Cordon came about," revealed Brigadier-General Matte, "their [Foster and Brian Vernon, the new LFC COS] attitude was that they [Airborne] missed the last one [mission to Western Sahara] so they're now going on this one for sure."[43] Brigadier-General Caron agreed. The former LFC operations officer conceded that the entire staff knew the decision was made before the estimate had even been started.[44]

The direction to send the Airborne Regiment, however, was not endorsed by everyone, particularly Beno, the new SSF Commander. Beno asserted that "the Airborne Regiment was selected for emotional, not rational reasons."[45] He further acknowledged that "this direction came from the CDS."[46] Later, Beno's "After Action Report" for the Somalia mission emphasized the political nature of the decision. He wrote, "It is understood that the Cdn AB Regt was tasked for OP Cordon/Deliverance for reasons of morale—largely because this unit had been frequently stood down on ops for many years. Given that it had to be totally re-equipped (eg, with AVGP), re-roled (mechanized vice para), re-trained (eg, drivers, crew commanders, mechanized operations) and restructured (eg, vehicle technicians, [equipment] scaling), it would have been more expedient to task another unit—either 1 RCR or the RCD."[47] "Tasking the Cdn AB Regt," Beno added, "also had an impact on the morale of 1 RCR, who lost not only their AVGP but had to, along with the RCD, train and prepare the Cdn AB Regt." The SSF commander candidly concluded that the selection "was not the most rational decision based on facts available at the time the decision was made."[48] Again this part of the story points out how well intentioned "friends" do not always act wisely and often contribute to harm.

The selection of the Airborne raised additional concern, especially once the time frame was discovered. The short fuse dictated that the designated unit had only twenty-one days to get ready to deploy. This meant that little time was available for anything but mission specific training. Lieutenant-Colonel John Turner, the SSF Operations Officer during this period remembered the resulting confusion and especially that "it was a bit surprising because what we were tasked to do was take away the vehicles that 1 RCR was using to give them to the Canadian Airborne

Regiment. Based on the initial time lines...it was slightly surprising at my level that we were taking vehicles away from one unit, a mechanized infantry unit, to give to another."[49] Even Colonel Holmes, the previous Regimental Commander, admitted later that although the Airborne was a suitable unit, its selection was not necessarily the best decision at that particular time.[50] Whatever these officers thought before or after the decision to send the Airborne to Somalia in late 1992, the point was they were chosen and they were going.

But before one looks at the Airborne's performance in Somalia and the very tragic and sad events, it is necessary to assess important issues that transpired between the time the Cdn AB Regt was chosen and the time they finally deployed. These critical months go a long way in explaining that the fate of the Regiment was both the accumulation of its flawed past fused with its current and continuing problems.

Many systemic problems within the Airborne became evident prior to the Regiment's deployment in December 1992. A rash of disciplinary incidents, particularly in relation to 2 Commando, brought back to the fore the long-standing difficulties that had not been adequately dealt with since the Hewson Report. Incidents included the destruction of an officer's personal property during an exercise, the illegal use of pyrotechnics, the discharge of weapons in a provincial park, excessive alcohol consumption and the burning of a duty-NCO's vehicle which was parked on the Airborne Parade Square. None of these incidents were sufficiently resolved.[51]

Likewise, the Regiment's pre-deployment training left a great deal to be desired in both senior leadership and actual preparation. Brigadier-General Beno, the SSF Commander who was later credited as the only leader in the chain of command who provided adequate supervision of the training preparation of the Regiment, was considerably distressed at the unit's obvious shortcomings.[52] He was concerned at the lack of focus behind the unit's haphazard training approach and he was highly critical of the Regimental Commander's abilities. Beno charged that the Commanding Officer, Lieutenant-Colonel Paul Morneault, "failed to grasp the scope and scale of the requirement" and continually failed to observe the actual training that was taking place.[53]

Despite Beno's intervention little improvement was made. He lamented that the attitude of the Airborne's senior leadership seemed "lax and disbelieving."[54] Apparently, the paratroopers felt that they were already adequately trained and little else was required. Certainly it seems that Morneault did as well. In addition, Brigadier-General Beno felt that far too much time was spent on individual skills instead of collective activities. He was absolutely right. During Exercise Stalwart Providence in October 1992, the brigade-controlled evaluation of the Airborne Regiment's operational readiness to deploy to Somalia revealed that the unit had no regimental standard operating procedures (SOPs). The evaluators also identified a disturbing impression that there were three distinct and autonomous entities participating in the exercise instead of one single unit. Lieutenant-Colonel Jim Ferron, an exercise controller, commented, "one major observation was the lack of consistency within the Regiment; no one followed SOPs or doctrine."[55]

In addition, a tendency, particularly in the case of 2 Commando, to be overly aggressive created a sense of unease in both the assessors and the commander of the SSF. Ferron felt that there was an "airborne mind set" apparent throughout the exercise. He described this as an attitude which exuded the sentiment that "they were the best and toughest unit in the Canadian Army."[56] While esprit de corps is a powerful motivator for any military body, in the case of the Airborne the consistent preference for the use of overwhelming might, instead of minimum force, when confronted with exercise scenarios brought out its more disturbing side. At the same time Beno himself saw some very disquieting things in the Regiment and he openly condemned the emphasis placed on recurring concepts such as "butt strokes, use of gas, baton/shields, attack and defence."[57] This sense of unease was made even more disturbing because the focus for the Airborne at this stage was peacekeeping.

Even the Airborne CO himself conceded the need to council the Officer Commanding (OC) 2 Commando. Morneault quipped, "he [Major Anthony Seward, OC 2 Commando] has been reading the wrong chapter—counter-insurgency instead of peacekeeping."[58] Notwithstanding the CO's assurances, any subsequent discussion toward rectification of this problem seemed to go nowhere with Morneault or Seward. In the privacy of his diary Beno wrote, "Seward and gang too high strung—will get people shot."[59] The Special Service Force Commander was clearly worried, and equally he understood the remedy to this dilemma was simply the need for good leaders at all levels of command. But not everybody in the Canadian Airborne Regiment or elsewhere was listening to him.

Given that Beno could not get Morneault to understand and cure the problems, he took what would be considered under any circumstances to be drastic action. After the brigade evaluation in October, Beno refused to declare the Regiment operationally ready. Instead he ordered supplementary training, expressly to overcome the problems of regimental standardization and the passage of information. Additionally, Beno directed the paratroopers to conduct more mission-specific tasks to ensure proficiency was attained at meeting standard SOPs in regard to humanitarian assignments.[60] His ultimate reform was to sack the Airborne CO, citing his inability to adequately prepare the Regiment for deployment. Beno specifically singled out Morneault's penchant for micro-managing and his subsequent inability to develop or supervise the necessary unit training requirements. Furthermore, Beno believed that Morneault was unable to solve the disciplinary and leadership dilemma festering in the Regiment.[61]

The drastic measures seemed to work. The apparent efforts of the new Commanding Officer, Lieutenant-Colonel Carol Mathieu, combined with additional training, resulted in the Airborne Regiment being declared operationally ready by mid November 1992. However, once again the systemic predicament was cured with a bandaid. The problem was greater than just a weak CO who was himself symptomatic of the problem, as was his replacement. So too was the root cause of their difficulties. It was not an inherent "airborne thing," but rather indicative of the quality of leader and soldier that had been sent to the Regiment in recent years. It is no secret that poor leadership at the NCO and officer level is conducive to poor discipline and unprofessional behaviour. This unfavourable situation was further compounded by the fact that many of those individuals who were drawn to, or were sent to the Regiment, tended to be those who were perceived as overly action-oriented, aggressive, and "gung-ho." Mixed with a false sense of elitism, the end product was nothing short of a time-bomb, especially once it was placed in a critical situation such as Somalia.

But this was not a new revelation. Many of these problems had been identified as early as the late seventies and had not been corrected over the years. Once again the quality of personnel sent to the Regiment became a major concern, especially in 2 Commando. The parent "feeder" regiments were continuing to use the commandos as an expedient disposal system for officers and soldiers who were considered troublesome or exceptionally aggressive.[62] Several years later, Dr. Charles Cotton articulated the idea clearly before the Somalia Commission when he commented that the Airborne Regiment not only became a dumping ground for the problem children, it was also seen as a type of reform school.[63]

The PPCLI, responsible for manning 2 Commando, was particularly criticized by both those inside and outside the military establishment. It became evident that the Patricias failed to send their best members to the Airborne, nor did they willingly take back their more troublesome individuals.[64] The quandary was so acute that Beno, as the SSF Commander, felt compelled to write to the Patricia Godfather (the senior serving Patricia) to formally register an observation that there was a problem with the type of soldiers provided by the PPCLI: "man for man, 2 Commando has had the highest incidence of ill-disciplined, unmilitary, criminal and anti-social behaviour" within the Regiment.[65] The situation was such that it was later revealed by witnesses appearing before the Somalia Commission that for some time some NCOs in 2 Commando were afraid of their soldiers and as a result were less likely to take vigorous disciplinary measures against troublemakers. The commission concluded that a parallel chain of command existed which exercised an informal leadership over the members of the commando. The commission further reported that this informal command net sometimes opposed the official leadership.[66]

The impact of these flaws was greatest at the leadership level. Careful scrutiny of the issue demonstrated that the "chain of command repeatedly ignored warnings that candidates being chosen for important jobs were inappropriate selections."[67] Many airborne officers knew, as one wrote, that it was important that the Regiment consistently receive "its fair share of high flyers and not just the tough 'airborne' sort or those who didn't quite make it in their parent Regiment."[68]

A large part of the problem was rooted in the Army's proclivity to readily acquiesce to the will of the parent regiments on the issue of selecting the commander of the Airborne Regiment. As a result, individuals outside the Airborne's chain of command, and largely unaccountable—specifically the representatives of the regimental councils (Regimental Godfathers)—had incredible influence in the process. Their nominees were basically appointed as a fait accompli. It made little difference if stronger candidates were available. The rotational command principle granted a virtual monopoly to the regiment whose turn it was to supply the new commander. Brigadier-General Matte, the Chief of Staff of Army Operations at the time, acknowledged that the Army failed as a corporate entity. "Bad decisions," he stated, "were made in an attempt not to antagonize the regiments [RCR, R22eR, and PPCLI]." Matte conceded that "we allowed selection of Commanding Officers to be done knowing full well that some individuals were not and would not be accepted by our own regiments as COs."[69] Paradoxically, the choice was made by the parent feeder regiments, yet it was the Airborne that paid the price for the consequences of a poor selection.[70]

By the time Morneault received command of the Airborne in the early 1990s the proof was readily available. Neither he nor his successor were the preferred candidates for the job. However, it was the R22eR's turn to provide the commander and no one questioned their choice. When Morneault was dismissed, the requirement to save regimental face was paramount.[71] Therefore, the R22eR provided his replacement despite the availability of better, more experienced individuals. Brigadier-General Beno lamented, "I offered three names to replace Morneault; Kenward (PPCLI), Mitchell (RCR), and MacDonough (PPCLI), and specified that they should have had command experience as well as UN experience."[72] However, the end result was an individual who had not been selected to command in his own parent regiment. The explanation lay in the concern over appearances. The senior leadership in the Army deemed it impossible to fire a "Vandoo" and replace him with a "Patricia."[73] As a result, the Regiment was denied the best possible candidate for the upcoming operation. In the end, with these serious leadership and disciplinary problems apparently endemic, delay and indecision in the fall of 1992 added their own little twists for the Regiment.

Much like OP Python to the Sahara the previous year, the contentious argument concerning which unit should have been selected to go to Somalia became academic. Delays in receiving an actual deployment date soon clouded the issue. The mission that was to be launched by the end of September 1992, had now dragged well into November. Ominously, by the end of the month, with the rapidly deteriorating conditions in Somalia the UN secretary-general entreated the Security Council to contemplate new alternatives for dealing with the crisis there. Five days later, the Security Council unanimously adopted an option which called for enforcement action rather than peacekeeping under Chapter VII of the UN Charter. This decision changed the entire scope of the mission. It evolved from peacekeeping to peacemaking. The paratroopers would not be tasked with trying to maintain the peace, but rather would be responsible for imposing it on the antagonists, by the use of force if necessary. Such would test the fibre of any unit.

On 3 December 1992, Security Council Resolution 794 created an American led enforcement operation entitled the Unified Task Force (UNITAF). UNITAF was authorized to use all means necessary to "establish as soon as possible a secure environment for humanitarian relief operations in Somalia."[74] As a result, OP Cordon, the original mission to northern Somalia, was suspended on 2 December. Two days later NDHQ formally cancelled it. On 5 December NDHQ issued a new warning order to the Special Service Force. The Canadian involvement in the UNITAF mission to Somalia was subsequently designated OP Deliverance. The paratroopers were now participants in the newly evolved UN *peacemaking* mission.[75]

In Canada, General John de Chastelain announced that the new mission was a "peace enforcement action to ease the suffering of the Somalian people." Furthermore, he added, "the contingent was authorized terms of engagement to take all steps to ensure that the job gets done."[76] The specific mission assigned to the Canadian Airborne Battle Group was to provide a secure environment for the distribution of humanitarian relief supplies in the Canadian Humanitarian Relief Sector (HRS), an area covering approximately 30,000 square kilometres. Their specific tasks included: the security of airports; the protection of food convoys; the protection of food distribution centres; the rebuilding of infrastructure which included roads, bridges and schools; the re-establishment of a local police force in Belet Huen; and numerous other humanitarian projects.[77]

Once in Somalia, many of the concerns about the quality and suitability of the Airborne, already manifest in the pre-deployment, quickly reappeared. Again, the flaws were attributable to poor leadership at the NCO and officer level. This was a direct outgrowth of the problems that had been identified earlier but not corrected. The consequences were not slow in coming. Some commandos undertook unconventional as well as unnecessary covert patrol operations. It also became evident that elements within the Airborne Battle Group were mistreating Somalis who had been captured while illegally entering the Airborne compounds to steal.[78] Major Seward's own admission highlights the complete bankruptcy of this officer. In a personal letter he wrote:

> Just now I am in the Command post. Five Somali teenagers have been caught stealing from Service Commando. They have been passed to me for security and transfer to the Somali police. The troops are, however, taking advantage of the situation to put on a demonstration. They're pretending that their intentions are to cut off the hands of these kids with machetes. It sounds awful, but if you were sitting here, you'd be laughing too. Soldier humour is infectious.[79]

The need for effective leadership was critical in Somalia. The Canadian paratroopers' tolerance was often stretched to the limit. The Somali population was not always appreciative of the soldiers' efforts on their behalf. The paratroopers were exposed to rock throwing, shootings, protests, spitting and constant thievery. The Airborne Battle Group compounds became natural targets; night after night, looters and thieves would slip through the razor wire barrier and steal anything and everything. The frustration was immense. Those thieves who were apprehended were turned over to local authorities, only to be released without sanction. For the paratroopers the incessant ingratitude and hostility, from the very people they were there to assist, was difficult to understand and accept.[80]

Predictably if unacceptably, the patience and tolerance of the Canadian paratroopers, as well as that of the Somalis sometimes snapped. Through the course of the whole operation Canadians killed four Somali nationals and wounded numerous others. Some of the deaths were unquestionably avoidable. One such killing occurred on 4 March 1993. Increased security at the engineer compound and neighbouring helipad, undertaken by the reconnaissance platoon, resulted in gunfire as two would-be thieves attempted to escape. Initially, the shooting was termed justifiable within the Rules of Engagement by a unit-controlled investigation. However, continuing allegations by one of the contingent's medical officers, who professed that the death of one of the interlopers was the result of a deliberate execution-style killing eventually raised some disturbing questions.[81] Although these allegations have never been conclusively proven or refuted, the shootings themselves have been declared unjustifiable. The carefully planned ambush operation obviously was "designed to send a strong message to would-be infiltrators that any attempt to penetrate the perimeter of Canadian installations would be met with gunfire."[82]

As disturbing as these allegations are, they are not the only ones. Mixed messages reverberated through the Airborne compounds in Somalia. Not only was a questionable shooting very quickly dismissed and the participants praised, but there existed a perception that abusive behaviour was ignored and not punished. This outlook became prevalent in some elements of the Airborne Battle Group. This was due in part to the fact that mistreatment of prisoners was condoned by some officers and NCOs within the Canadian contingent. In sum this laid the groundwork for the defining moment of the Somalia mission, if not for the very existence of the Canadian Airborne Regiment itself.

On the night of 16 March 1993, an apprehended looter, Shidane Arone, was systematically beaten to death while in the custody of 2 Commando. What made this tragedy even harder to understand is the fact that throughout the beating, numerous soldiers, senior NCOs and officers either heard the cries or actually dropped by the bunker and witnessed the beating in progress; yet, no one stopped it until it was too late.[83] Seven days later, Major Seward wrote in his diary, "it is my intention to openly and readily state that I did order Somali intruders to be abused during the conduct of apprehension and arrest."[84] But Seward's attempt at delayed self-martyrdom was only posturing. Besides it was too late by years for those paratroopers, both officers and men, who had already crossed any acceptable moral boundary.

The tragic killing changed the manner in which the mission was ultimately assessed. Although some had questioned the rationale for sending the paratroopers to Somalia in the fall of 1992, the issue at the time was largely one of apparent favouritism. Very few, with the exception of Brigadier-General Beno, raised leadership concerns. Moreover, the discourse quickly dissipated because the Regiment's powerful supporters wanted the Airborne to undertake the mission. However, after the Shidane Arone killing the post-Somalia debate over "who should have been selected" became an issue in itself. It became a hunt for a "smoking gun." The search for evidence of negligence or incompetence on the part of senior commanders, in regard to the selection of the Airborne Regiment for duty in Somalia, completely altered the nature of the central and immediate issue of the killings. Those examining the "Somalia Affair" were now trying to roll back the guilt in an attempt to ensnare more than just a number of errant paratroopers. Not surprisingly, their targets proved to be elusive. Like children caught pilfering cookies, those who originally had worked hard at ensuring the paratroopers received the mission, now tried to distance themselves from their actions.

It is evident that the Canadian Airborne Regiment was selected for partisan reasons. Numerous military estimates had judged that the most efficient response would have been to send a mechanized unit instead of re-equipping and re-training a light infantry organization. The fact that the Airborne continually won out, is testimony to the influence of its patrons. However, this represented a pyrrhic victory. First, the campaign fuelled the ever-boiling cauldron of resentment against the Airborne. Second, and more importantly, it strengthened a recurring legitimate criticism. If airborne forces are simply employed as regular infantry, particularly at the expense of existing mechanized infantry units, why continue the costly existence of a specialized airborne unit?

Despite the incestuous interference of the extended airborne family, lost in the acrimonious post-Somalia debate is the fact that whether selected for partisan reasons or not, the Airborne was totally competent to perform the Somalia task. Undeniably, the Regiment was often saddled with questionable leaders and soldiers. But, it also contained many more of sterling character.[85] While not trying to excuse those responsible for the killings, uneven behaviour caused by the very few cannot be allowed to destroy the worth of the many in the same unit. This was no different from any other unit in the Army. Inappropriate behaviours and their resultant scandals have occurred on virtually all missions and in all theatres of operations in which Canadians have participated.[86]

As for the suitability of the Airborne Regiment as a whole for the deployment to Somalia, Colonel Peter Kenward, a senior staff officer in the Joint Peacekeeping Directorate in NDHQ at the time, was one of many who asserted that the Regiment was an appropriate unit for the mission. He explained that the Airborne's experience in dealing with varied environments, harsh conditions and lack of infrastructure made it an excellent choice.[87] Even Brigadier-General Beno, who questioned the choice originally, conceded that "by the time they [Airborne Regiment] deployed, and given the warlike scenario they were hastily sent into, they were the best unit Canada had for OP Deliverance."[88]

When objectively examined, the performance of the unit in-theatre tends to support these statements. The Airborne Battle Group's overall performance was quite laudable. The paratroopers landed in Somalia during the hottest time of the year in conditions that were later acknowledged "as extreme as Canadian troops have ever encountered."[89] Aside from the temperature, the soldiers were faced with the threat of diseases such as malaria, cholera, hepatitis, typhoid, tuberculosis and numerous others. Venomous insects and snakes were widespread and tenacious parasites were virtually unavoidable. In addition, all local water, even when boiled was undrinkable.[90]

The climatic and environmental conditions were accentuated by further difficulties unique to the Canadian area of responsibility, which was also known as the Belet Huen Humanitarian Relief Sector (HRS). Specifically, the Canadian zone encompassed an area which housed major militia formations of the three most powerful faction leaders in Somalia. Furthermore, the Canadian area of responsibility was also in close proximity to the turbulent Ethiopian border."[91]

Despite these challenges the Airborne Battle Group actively proceeded to fulfill their mandate. Success was achieved through a combination of dialogue and firm military operations. Joint committees with local authorities and clan chiefs were reinforced by dismounted and vehicle patrols throughout the sector. This unremitting physical presence soon created an atmosphere of control, dominance, and security.[92]

The Airborne Battle Group was exceptionally successful in its efforts. The aggressive patrolling and confiscation of weapons quickly stabilized the entire region. Village sweeps and roadblocks were highly productive. The Airborne Regiment Battle Group projected such control and dominance over the area that the local militia commanders acquiesced to placing their heavy weapons in compounds, thus taking them out of circulation. As a result of the Airborne Regiment's hard work UNITAF Headquarters declared the Belet Huen HRS "secure" in less than three months after the arrival of the Canadian paratroopers.[93]

As remarkable as the Airborne Battle Group's pacification program was, its humanitarian effort was even more praiseworthy. Hugh Tremblay, the Director of Humanitarian Relief and Rehabilitation in Somalia, used the paratroopers as a model for others. His simple advice revolved around the theme, "If you want to know and to see what you should do while you are here in Somalia, go to Belet Huen, talk to the Canadians and do what they have done, emulate the Canadians and you will have success in your humanitarian relief sector."[94] Robert Press, a writer for the *Christian Science Monitor* wrote, "Belet Huen appears to be a model in Somalia for restoring peace and effectively using foreign troops during this country's transition from anarchy to a national government."[95]

The chaos that existed in Somalia had originally prevented the humanitarian relief agencies from distributing the required aid, particularly to the outlying villages in the more remote areas. The arrival of the Airborne Battle Group radically changed this state of affairs. UN organizations and non-governmental agencies (NGOs) were now capable of expanding their operations not only in the settled areas, but also into the hinterland. However, the success of the Canadian effort was not based solely on the security they provided.

The key to the Airborne's success was the cooperation and close coordination with both the local population and the humanitarian agencies. The head of the African Department of the British Foreign & Commonwealth Office wrote, "the visitors were struck by the rapport the Canadian forces have developed with both the local Somali community and aid agency representatives in Belet Huen, whilst at the same time carrying out their security duties in a highly effective and professional manner."[96] This sentiment was echoed in a letter written to the CDS by the coordinator for Oxfam-Quebec. It stated, "mais ce qui a surtout mérité l'admiration de la population somalienne est le fait qu'ils [Airborne Battle Group] ne se sont pas contentes de bien realiser leur mandat de 'peace makers' mais on les a vus travailler coté a coté avec les Somaliens pour realiser des projets communautaires."[97]

Even the Somalis themselves praised the Canadian paratroopers. General Mohammed Ahmed Hubero, a United Somali Congress official from Belet Huen, stated, "the Canadians have done more for this region in five months than the two previous regimes did in thirty years."[98] The Somali clan chieftains were also "effusive in their praise" of the paratroopers during the visit of the LFCA Commander, Major-General Brian Vernon.[99] Comparably, Major-General Lewis Mackenzie, Vernon's predecessor, also publicly acknowledged that during two visits to Belet Huen, he was repeatedly told by the elders and local police chief that they all wanted the Canadian paratroopers back. The Somalis asserted that the Regiment had done far more for Belet Huen than their Italian, German and Malaysian successors.[100]

The laudatory comments were justly deserved. In total, the Airborne Battle Group's achievements included: the formation of five local committees to restore local government; the conduct of approximately sixty humanitarian convoys that provided aid to ninety-six villages; the construction of four schools attended by 5,400 students at the end of the Canadians' tour; the instruction and training of 272 school teachers; the supervision and training of local doctors and nurses; the training of 150 policeman in Belet Huen, 20 in Matabaan and 15 in St. Emily; the provision of potable water to local refugees; the repair of approximately twenty wells; the repair of village generators; the repair of the Belet Huen and Matabaan hospitals; the construction of a bridge; and the repair of over 200 kilometres of road.[101]

The overall efforts of the Airborne Battle Group won them the unqualified accolades particularly of those who actually witnessed the incredible accomplishments. Jonathan T. Howe, the special representative to the UN secretary-general stated, "the outstanding work of your unit in its area of operations in both military and humanitarian aspects of the mission has been outstanding."[102] The American UNITAF commander, Lieutenant-General R.B. Johnston, similarly commented, "The Canadian Airborne Regiment has performed with great distinction and the Canadian people should view its role in this historic humanitarian mission with enormous pride."[103]

In addition, Robert Oakley, the Special Envoy to Somalia, wrote, "in six months, with only 1,200 soldiers operating in a nightmare of violence, heat, disease and conflict, the Canadians have secured and supported all relief operations, organized local schools and medical clinics, and negotiated cease-fires among warring factions. The tragedy has been suspended and a real foothold of peace has been established in the region as a result of Canadian efforts."[104] He extended his admiration with the comments that "there is no question but that their [Airborne Battle Group] discipline, operational readiness, immediate responsiveness to assigned tasks, care and use of equipment, and ability to operate effectively in difficult climatic conditions were considered to be at the very top of all Unified Task Force units."[105]

Tribute from Canadian diplomats was initially equally as generous. The Minister of State for External Affairs, Barbara McDougall, professed that Canadian paratroopers could hold "their heads high." She called their work a "modern miracle."[106] The Canadian High Commissioner to Somalia, Her Excellency, Lucie Edwards, also applauded the paratroopers. She declared, "They [Battle Group] went the extra mile and found imaginative solutions. They have only added lustre to their reputation as peacekeepers."[107]

The praise, however, was fleeting and of far less interest than scandal to a voracious press.[108] Quite simply, it was from the Airborne Regiment that some officers and soldiers crossed the line in Somalia. It would be naive to think that the press or the Canadian public would react in any other way. Nonetheless, in what would amount to a tragedy of its own, the act of killing Shidane Arone became the defining image of the Airborne's operation in Africa to the exclusion of all that was good. The documented success of the Airborne Battle Group was quickly ignored, even dismissed. The commander of Land Forces Central Area lamented that the significant and positive results of the Airborne Battle Group were "sullied by a combination of politically-driven criticisms and domestic media speculation."[109] The mission was now increasingly defined by the media as a complete failure. This redefinition was neither corrected nor challenged by DND. It was too dangerous politically. There was a conscious fear that to do so would somehow appear to condone the wrongdoings that had transpired. An impression soon emerged that it was more acceptable to allow the honour and service of hundreds of soldiers to be tarnished rather than risk potential embarrassment of senior leaders should they attempt to correct the record.

As the Canadian news media started to reveal the events in Somalia and the Regiment returned to Canada in the spring/summer of 1993 support for it weakened considerably. The paratroopers were increasingly seen as pariahs by a large segment of both the military and public, but especially by the media. The Regiment could expect little public support from its previous backers. It had become evident that any pro-airborne sentiment was quickly dismissed as the rantings of "airborne apologists" and those attempting to preserve an archaic "boys will be boys" club. Conversely, the Airborne's detractors now had a field day pointing out how Somalia was a manifestation of what they had been warning about for years. The way the story unfolded rattled up the military and political chain well beyond the Airborne. While the murder would never be displaced as the centre of the scandal, the scandal itself became one which infected the top military leadership and was influenced by hard political reality.

Notes for Chapter Eight

1. *Information Legacy,* Hearings Transcripts, Vol 3, 5 October 1995, 442.
2. The issue of frustration was a recurring theme. It was raised in interviews at all levels. The soldiers, NCOs and junior officers were frustrated that their high levels of readiness and training were not being utilized and angry that other less prepared units were sent. Corporal Ford captured the essence of the prevailing sentiment. His comment on the Oka Crisis and the Gulf War was a terse, "we watched on TV while remaining Stand-By." Interview with author, April 1995. Senior officers focussed on both the morale issue, as well as the danger of becoming irrelevant. If the unit is a "stand-by" force but never utilized, why retain it?
3. Major Gerald Baril, "Mission Accomplished," *Sentinel,* April/May 1994, 40.
4. Interview with author, 6 June 1998. Lieutenant-General Foster stated, "I slept a little easier knowing I had that contingency covered."
5. Interview with author, 11 June 1997.
6. *Information Legacy,* "OP Python Synopsis," Document book 120, tab 3, DND 039091. The United Nations mandate was to establish the conditions for a referendum on the future of the Western Sahara by identifying and registering qualified voters and by supervising the repatriation of refugees and non-residents before the vote.
7. Ibid. See also Colonel John Gardam, *The Canadian Peacekeeper* (Burnstown: The General Store Publishing House Ltd., 1992), 68-69; and Captain Brett Boudreau, "The Great Berm of Western Sahara," *Sentinel,* December 1992-January 1993, 5. The Canadian contribution was the largest contingent of the proposed 1,700 military personnel, and 900 civilian staff.
8. *Somalia Commission*, Transcript of Evidentiary Hearing, Vol 4, 10 October 1995, 604-605; and *Information Legacy,* "OP Python Synopsis," Document book 120, tab 3, DND 039091.
9. Beno, "Attitude and Values," 2, Beno Papers.
10. Major-General Gaudreau letter to author, 18 September 1998.
11. Ibid.
12. Colonel W.M. Holmes, "Proposed Organization of Canadian Parachute Battalion," 8 May 1991, 1. His concern was shared by Major-General Bob Stewart. Stewart lamented, "the Regiment from its very first year of existence has been threatened with disbandment and this threat will be intensified now that the Regiment is reduced to an airborne battalion structure." Letter, R.I. Stewart to W.M. Holmes, 5 March 1992, Beno Papers.
13. *Somalia Commission*, "First Draft, Concept of Employment of the Canadian Airborne Regiment", 7 May 1992, Document Book 7, tab 18; "Second Draft: Concept of Employment of the Canadian Airborne Regiment", 12 May 1992, Document Book 7, tab 15; "Concept of Employment of the Canadian Airborne Regiment", 4 November 1992, Document Book 29, tab 19.
14. *Somalia Commission,* "Concept of Employment of the Canadian Airborne Regiment," 28 May 1992, Document Book 7.
15. *Information Legacy,* "Hearing Transcripts," Vol 16, 15 November 1995, testimony of Colonel John Joly, 2938.
16. Colonel W.M. Holmes (RComd), Letter 1901-2 (RComd), 19 May 1992, "The Canadian Airborne Regiment Transition Plan," Annex A, CFOO; and CFOO 3.21.5, 23 March 1977 and 1 March 1985,

Information Legacy, Document Control No. 905321, p. 627,708 and Document Control No. 905320, p. 627,634 respectively. The continuing struggle to come to grips with nebulous tasks continued. The Regimental Commander wrote to his superiors, "This idea [MAJAID] should be quashed before someone actually tries it and we fail miserably." *Somalia Commission,* "First Draft. Concept of Employment of the Canadian Airborne Regiment," 7 May 1992, Document Book 7.

17. "Operational Concept, Airborne Battalion. Review Comments," 2 April 1992. DHist NDHQ files not processed at time of use. The continuing institutional belief of the relevance of the parachute capability remained constant. It was seen by many as merely a tool to access remote regions in Canada. See Chapter Four, endnote 59. Brigadier-General Holmes argued that the "cost" issue was a red herring. He noted that no one has ever placed a dollar figure on the cost of airborne capability. He asserted it is a false argument. "For example, a parachute is far cheaper than an Armoured Personnel Carrier. Furthermore, if aircraft are not flying paratroops they will be employed on other missions." Holmes declared that aircraft hours flown are as great now as when the Regiment existed. Interview with author, 17 July 1997. Holmes's argument was reinforced by an LFC study. The subsequent report noted that "the maintenance of the CF parachute capability comprises less than 2% of the Air Transport Group budget to conduct tactical airlift exercises and support parachute training." The analysis also concluded that "the annual recurring operations and maintenance costs of the Canadian Airborne Regiment with its light scales, are considerably less than the comparable costs of a mechanized infantry battalion." LFCHQ, "The Requirement For An Operational Parachute Capability In the Canadian Forces Structure," 21 February 1994, 2 & 4; and Letter, Commander of the Army to the CDS, "The Canadian Airborne Regiment Recommendations for Consideration," 19 April 1994, Annex A, A-1 & A-4.

18. *Somalia Commission,* "Concept of Employment of the Canadian Airborne Regiment," 28 May 1992, Document Book 7.

19. Ibid. Colonel Mark Skidmore, the Regimental Major at the time, reinforced this motive behind the downsizing. He explained that cost was the issue. Skidmore asserted that in light of the cuts in the budget the airborne became seen as a luxury. Therefore, the Army scaled it down as a stop-gap measure. Interview with author, 25 April 1997. The downsizing of the Airborne Regiment to Battalion status was also cited as an example of "directed reductions" during Lieutenant-General P.J. O'Donnell's (VCDS) brief to the Special Joint Committee on Canada's Defence Policy, 25 April 1994. DHist (unprocessed at time of use) NDHQ files (Presentation Slide Deck) on the Canadian Airborne Regiment.

20. *Somalia Commission,* "Canadian Airborne Regiment Structure," 4 June 1993, Document Book 7; "Canadian Airborne Regiment, Regimental Secretariat Manning," 25 May 1992; and Holmes, "The Canadian Airborne Regiment Transition Plan."

21. *Information Legacy,* "Hearing Transcripts," Vol 4, 10 October 1995, testimony of Colonel Holmes, 643–644. The actual re-organization of the Regiment, although significant, had no real or perceived effect on the individual paratroopers in the commandos. Most soldiers stated they didn't notice any real change as far as they were concerned. Warrant Officer Miller summed up the general consensus. He stated, "the troops really didn't care...we lost some people in administrative support but it didn't effect the troops, it didn't change our training." Lieutenant-Colonel Skidmore agreed. He observed, "the guys didn't care much." Skidmore himself acknowledged, "the downgrade from unit to company status didn't effect anything...in essence the Commando was never anything other than a company. It had operational autonomy on exercise but in reality I didn't have the responsibilities or powers of a CO." Major Collin Magee, the new OC (vice CO), arriving after the reorganization echoed these sentiments. He commented, "the impact on the Commando was negligible, it didn't seem any different from when I was the DCO of the Commando years ago." The integration of commandos into a battalion structure, however, was easier said then done. Although the commandos lost their official unit status, they still maintained distinct differences in attitudes, operating procedures and standards. The commandos were a direct representation of their parent regiments, and although proud of their membership in the Airborne Regiment, they still made every effort to maintain their independence. Substantial progress in integrating the commandos into a true battalion organization, with common standards, training plans and operating procedures was not effectively put into place until the arrival of Lieutenant-Colonel Kenward, in September 1993.

23. *Information Legacy,* Executive Summary, "Suitability and Cohesion," record 147/13628.
24. Ibid.
25. *Somalia Commission,* "Regimental Considerations: Reorganization of the Canadian Airborne Regiment," 27 August 1991, Document Book 7. Henceforth, the term "unit" will be used in the text, in addition to "Regiment" and "Airborne" to describe the Canadian Airborne Regiment. The term "formation" will no longer be used as a replacement for the title Canadian Airborne Regiment. Furthermore, the use of the term Canadian Airborne Battle Group or derivatives thereof, refers to the Regiment with additional supporting elements attached, such as its affiliated artillery battery or engineer squadron.
26. *Information Legacy,* "Selection of Unit for Minurso OP Python," 2 May 1991, Document Control No. 030012 (DND032547).
27. Ibid.
28. Interview with author, 10 August 1999.
29. Interview with author, 12 August 1999. Brigadier-General Caron acknowledged that his staff questioned why they had to do the estimate since they all knew the Army Commander was intent on sending the Airborne. Caron insisted that "the staff would still provide an accurate assessment to keep the record straight." Caron stoically affirmed, "staffs recommend, commanders decide."
30. *Information Legacy,* "Hearing Transcripts," Vol 3, 5 October 1995, testimony of Lieutenant-General Foster, 424.
31. What inflamed matters even more was the deployment of the Regiment to Camp Lejeune, North Carolina, after the mission was cancelled. Disappointment was not exclusive to the Airborne. Other personnel and units who, similar to the Airborne Regiment, had not recently deployed on operational tasks were not given a consolation prize consisting of a southern deployment. Discussions and interviews with numerous officers serving at the time in NDHQ and SSF Headquarters, as well as 1 RCR and the RCD.
32. *Somalia Commission,* "Transcript of Policy Hearing," Vol 2, 19 June 1995, 265-267; Letter, DM and CDS to the MND, *Information Legacy,* Document Control No. 111798, p. 107551; and ibid., "Option Analysis for a Security Battalion in Support of UN Humanitarian Assistance Operations in Somalia As Requested by CDS," 31 July 1992, Document Book 9, Tab 28; and Dan Loomis, *The Somalia Affair* (Ottawa: DGC Publishing, 1996), 115-116.
33. *Information Legacy,* "DND Press Announcement. Canadian Airborne Regiment Going to Somalia," 2 September 1992, DND Document Control No. 111796, p. 107509. UNOSOM was created on 24 April 1992, through UN Resolution 751, in response to the continuing deterioration of the situation in Somalia. The military/civilian operation was envisioned as a multi-national force of over 4,000 personnel. The military was assigned the task of monitoring the cease-fire in Mogadishu, securing humanitarian aid and ensuring its safe delivery to distribution centres as well as protecting UN personnel. UNOSOM was overtaken by the US-led UNITAF on 4 December 1992.
34. *Somalia Commission,* "Transcript of Policy Hearing," Vol 2, 19 June 1995, 266-267; *Information Legacy,* "FMC Contingency Plan OP Cordon," 3 September 1992, Document Control No. 000099 (DND 000042); and Loomis, *The Somalia Affair,* 111-113.
35. Interview with author, 29 November 1997. Lilienthal also remembered the malevolent debate that surrounded the airborne question leading up to the 1994 White Paper within LFC. He asserted that the "Black Hatters" (Armoured Corps) in DGLFR in Ottawa, were adamant that the Airborne Regiment was not required. The recurring questions were: "Why retain them? What do we need them for? [and] What have they actually done?" It was the power centre in LFC HQ in Montreal which dismissed this group and decided on the Airborne's retention.
36. Interview with author, 5 November 1998. Houghton maintained that the airborne organization was the only one capable of going in rapidly and surviving.
37. *Somalia Commission,* Document Book No. 32.1, Pre-Deployment, DEM 28/07/92.
38. *Information Legacy,* Hearing Transcripts, Vol 49, 20 February 1996, testimony of General de Chastelain, 9920-21. Colonel Houghton, DPKO, confessed that he was constantly briefing General de

Chastelain during this period and he "kept whispering in his [CDS's] ear that the Airborne Regiment were the ones to go." Interview with author, 5 November 1998.

39. *Somalia Commission*, Document Book No. 32.1, Pre-Deployment, DEM 28/07/92.

40. *Information Legacy,* "Option Analysis for a Security Battalion in Support of UN Humanitarian Assistance Operations in Somalia As Requested by CDS," 31 July 1992, Document Book 9, Tab 28. Although no specific unit was recommended, certain "red-lined" comments conveyed the impression that the Airborne Regiment was not considered a solid choice. For example, under "Forces Available" four units were identified. However, a highlighted entry noted that "The Cdn AB Regt is in the Process of converting to an AB Bn with 3 AB Coys, a Log Coy and a Bn HQ. Present unit strength is 659 pers reducing to 601 pers next year. There are few AVGP qualified drivers in the Cdn AB Regt."

41. Brigadier-General E.B. Beno, "Day Book," 5 August 1992, Beno Papers. The entry noted," Discussions with BGen Crabbe. He mentioned that Cdn AB Regt warned off for human relief operations in Somalia and to assist in cease fire control." The reference to being warned off must refer to an informal brief. The official warning order for OP Cordon was not received by the SSF until 5 September.

42. *Information Legacy,* Hearing Transcripts, Vol 49, 20 February 1996, testimony of General de Chastelain, 9931. General de Chastelain never served in the Regiment, however, he did have airborne service in the DCF, specifically, in 2 PPCLI from 1960-1962. In addition, he maintained a strong link with the Regiment by retaining his jump currency and attending 'Jump Bivouacs' in Petawawa from the mid eighties up until this period.

43. Interview with author, 10 August 1999.

44. Interview with author, 12 August 1999.

45. Interview with author, 20 May 1998; Beno, "The Somalia Affair, Personal Reflections," 1; Beno, "Personal Estimate of Somalia Affair, 6 Jan 1997"; and Beno, "Day Book," 4 September 1992, Beno Papers. The entry for 4 September read, "I pointed out to the staff at LFCA and FMC that we were sending the wrong unit for the wrong reasons."

46. Beno, "The Somalia Affair, Personal Reflections," 1; and Beno, "Personal Estimate of Somalia Affair, 6 January 1997." Beno Papers. Lieutenant-Colonel Peter Atkinson, a staff officer at FMC Headquarters at the time conceded the decision of "who should go had nothing to do with the military estimate." He maintained it was dictated by Lieutenant-General Foster. Interview with author, 14 April 1997.

47. *Information Legacy,* "Operation Cordon/Deliverance After Action Report," 2 February 1993, Evidentiary Exhibits, Book 24, tab 1.

48. Ibid. Lieutenant-Colonel Bill Peters, the CO of 1 RCR at the time, acknowledged that Beno's preference at the time was 1 RCR. However, Peters recalled that Beno told him the decision may be "political." Both Beno and Peters saw no reason why 1 RCR could not be ready. Interview with author, 3 February 1998. Beno's notes for the period stated, "1 RCR could just as easily have been assigned the task of Somalia." However, he did acknowledge certain disadvantages such as the increased need for Militia augmentation. Beno, "Training Comparison: 1 RCR/Cdn AB Regt," Beno Papers.

49. *Somalia Commission,* Transcript of Evidentiary Hearing, Vol 18, 20 November 1995, 3409; and "Operation Cordon: Guidance," 8 September 1992, D1-4, SILT Control No. 0392. Major James Rettie, another SSF staff officer recalled that the sentiment at the time was one of amazement within the headquarters. He stated "it was incredible. The Airborne were chosen even though the task was for a mechanized unit. The result was that two other units, 1 RCR and the RCD, were fundamentally disrupted." Interview with author, 14 April 1997.

50. Bercuson, *Significant Incident,* 222.

51. *Information Legacy,* Report of the Commission of Inquiry, Vol 2, Record 3804. The Commission noted, "we received evidence showing that during Col Holmes' tenure as CO, the types of misconduct which triggered BGen Stewart's condemnation on May 7, 1984, were again evident within the CAR." See also *Somalia Commission*, Transcript of Evidentiary Hearing, Vol 4, 10 October 1995, testimony of Colonel Holmes, 605-606; BOI—Cdn AB Regt BG, Phase I, Vol XI, D-1/7-3/7; Beno, "The Somalia Affair—Personal Reflections," 2, Beno Papers; David Pugliese, "Somalia: What Went Wrong?" *Ottawa Citizen,* 10 October 1995; and Bercuson, *Significant Incident,* 223-224.

52. *Information Legacy,* Executive Summary—Training. The Commission stated, "Leaders at all levels of the chain of command, with the notable exception of the Brigade Commander during initial stages, failed to provide adequate supervision of the training preparations undertaken by the CAR for Operation Cordon."
53. Beno, "The Somalia Affair—Notes from Day Book, Recollections and Comments," 3-5, Beno Papers. Beno's distress over training, and particularly the fitness of the CO to prepare the Regiment, commenced 7 September 1992. Concern was evidenced on a daily basis from this date until he informed Lieutenant-Colonel Morneault that he was to be dismissed on 21 October.
54. Beno Diary Extracts, 12 & 24 September 1992, Beno Papers.
55. Interview with author, 8 April 1998. At the time, Ferron was OC B Sqd, RCD. The RCD CO, Lieutenant-Colonel Matthew MacDonald, also noted the independent/autonomous operating procedure of the "three independent commandos." MacDonald further observed that the apparent autonomy of commandos also led to a failure to pass on or share key information within the entire unit. He did note, however, that "My overall assessment was that the Airborne Regiment had come a long way in a very short period of time on tasks that were not familiar to them. For the most part they showed improvement." *Somalia Commission,* Transcript of Evidentiary Hearing, Vol 27, 13 December 1995, 5051 & 5080-5081. A diary entry for Brigadier-General Beno, on 20 October 1992, stated that Lieutenant-Colonel Morneault, CO Cdn AB Regt, "agrees there is no regimental standard." Beno Diary Extracts, Beno Papers.
56. Interview with author, 8 April 1998.
57. Beno Diary Extracts, 16 September 1992. See also *Information Legacy,* Report of the Commission of Inquiry, Vol 2, Findings; and Pugliese, "What went so wrong?" This account quotes criticism from officers who complained that 2 Commando was too "quick off the mark to use force to handle potential problems." Interviews with evaluators from the RCD reinforced these sentiments. It was noted that quick attacks were regularly conducted upon arriving at road blocks. Similarly, the presence of crowds inevitably led to a violent response.
58. Beno Diary Extracts, 16 September 1992, Beno Papers.
59. Ibid., 1 December 1992, Beno Papers. 2 Commando created another acrimonious debate as a result of its action prior to deployment and later in theatre. A popular myth was established, by media, and to a degree the BOI—Cdn AB Regt BG, that Lieutenant-Colonel Morneault had tried to prevent 2 Commando from participating in OP Cordon/Deliverance because of the disciplinary problems experienced. The myth alleges that Morneault was stymied in this attempt by Brigadier-General Beno. The reality is somewhat less sensational. Morneault approached Beno on 5 October with the intention of using "non-deployment" of 2 Commando as a "threat" to break "the wall of silence" in regard to the burning of the Duty NCO's vehicle. However, Beno, after careful deliberation informed Morneault later that afternoon that "group punishment" was not acceptable. The Airborne CO was then told to sort out the problem at his level. The reality is that Morneault never recommended that 2 Commando not deploy because he deemed them unfit as a collective group for deployment to Somalia. *Information Legacy,* Hearing Transcripts, Vol 36, 22 January 1996, testimony of Lieutenant-Colonel Morneault, 6973-6976; Beno Diary Extracts, 5 October 1992; Letter, E.B. Beno to David Bercuson, 1 September 1996, Beno Papers; and "For the Record," *esprit de corps,* Vol 4, No. 2, 13.
60. Beno, " The Somalia Incident," 12-13. Beno Papers.
61. Letter, Brigadier-General E.B. Beno to Major-General L.W. MacKenzie (Commander LFCA), 19 October 1992, "Replacement of Commanding Officer Canadian Airborne Regiment." SILT Document Control No. 0424; Beno, "The Somalia Drama—A Soldier's Point of View," 2. Beno Papers. See also *Information Legacy,* Hearing Transcripts, Vol. 43, testimony of Major-General MacKenzie, 8337, 8351 & 8533; Evidentiary Exhibits—Exhibit P-64, Document book 15, tab 18, 2 and Exhibit P-78, Document book 29, tab 7; *Information Legacy,* Report of the Commission of Inquiry, Vol 2, Record 3906.
62. BOI Cdn AB Regt BG, Phase I, Vol XI, Annex H, H-1/6; and *Information Legacy,* Report of the Commission of Inquiry, Vol 2, reference 3850. See also, *Information Legacy,* Hearing Transcripts, Vol 3, testimony of Major-General (retd) Gaudreau, 552–554; Ibid., Vol 24, testimony of CWO (retd) Jardine, 4557–4558; Ibid., Vol 34, testimony of MWO R.A. Murphy, 6592.

63. Donna Winslow, *The Canadian Airborne Regiment in Somalia. A Socio-cultural Inquiry* (Ottawa: Commission of Inquiry into the Deployment of Canadian Forces to Somalia, 1997), 67.

67. *Information Legacy,* Executive Summary, Selection of Personnel and Selection, Record 156.

68. Letter, R.I. Stewart, to W.H. Holmes (RComd), 5 March 1992, Stewart Papers.

69. Interview with author, 10 August 1999.

70. *Information Legacy,* Executive Summary, Selection of Personnel and Selection, Record 156.

71. *Information Legacy,* Hearing Transcripts, Vol 43, 1 February 1996, testimony of Major-General (retd) MacKenzie, 8392; Ibid., Vol 36, 22 January 1996, testimony of Lieutenant-Colonel Morneault, 6884; and Bercuson, *Significant Incident,* 219-220.

72. Beno, "The Somalia Affair," 3C, Beno Papers.

73. *Information Legacy,* Hearing Transcripts, Vol 43, 1 February 1996, testimony of Major-General (retd) MacKenzie, 8392; Beno Diary Extracts, 19 & 20 October 1992; and Beno, "The Somalia Incident," 13, Beno Papers.

74. UN Department of Information, *The UN and the Situation in Somalia,* Reference Paper, 15 December 1992, 4-7; BOI—Cdn AB Regt BG, Phase I, Vol XI, A-1/33; and Loomis, *The Somalia Affair,* 115. The UNITAF operational concept was based on a four phase scheme designed to restore stability to Somalia. Phase One was the initial landing by American forces to secure the port and airport at Mogadishu and the airfields at Baledogle and Baidoa. Phase Two was the securing of the port and airfield at Kismayu, and airfields at Hoddur, Bardera, Gialalassi and Belet Huen. The final objective of this phase was the securing of the port of Marka. Phase Three envisioned the expansion of security and relief operations throughout the Humanitarian Relief Sectors (HRS) and Phase Four was the transition of command and control from UNITAF to UNOSOM II.

75. *Somalia Commission,* Transcript of Policy Hearing, Vol 2, 19 June 1995, 269-272.

76. Loomis, *The Somalia Affair,* 293. This aspect of the mission has been totally lost in the post-Somalia sequence of events. The Somalia Commission's final report noted, "The mission called for troops who were well led, highly disciplined, and able to respond flexibly to a range of tasks that demanded patience, understanding, and sensitivity to the plight of the Somali people. Instead they arrived in the desert trained and mentally conditioned to fight." *Information Legacy,* Executive Summary—Training. The first phase is required of all UN missions or operations. The second was specifically required by this mission based on the mandate of UNITAF.

77. *Somalia Commission,* Transcript of Policy Hearing, Vol 2, 19 June 1995, 273; and Canadian Joint Task Force (CJTF), *In the Line of Duty* (Ottawa: DND, 1994), 16. To accomplish their assigned mission the Airborne Battle Group divided the Canadian HRS, also known as the Belet Huen HRS, into four security sectors, which in turn were assigned to the sub-units of the Battle Group. The town of Belet Huen was designated as Zone 2 and was the responsibility of the dismounted 2 Commando (reinforced by the 1 RCR Mortar Platoon). The southeastern section of the HRS was designated as Zone 1, and the southwestern portion Zone 3. The Shabelle River separated the two sectors which were the responsibilities of 1 and 3 Commandos respectively. Both of these sub-units were mounted in the "Grizzly" Armoured Vehicle General Purpose (AVGP). The northeastern area was designated Zone 4. This area was considered the most complex of the four zones because it contained two hostile Somali factions, the Ethiopian border and an exposed flank to the still unstable central regions of Somalia. This sector was the responsibility of A Squadron, the RCD, which operated out of the town of Matabaan, located approximately eighty kilometres northeast of Belet Huen.

78. Letter, Brigadier-General E.B. Beno to Colonel J.S. Labbé (Commander Canadian Joint Task Force Somalia), 8 April 1993. Beno wrote as a result of being shown "trophy photographs" depicting paratroopers with captured Somalis. He was concerned that these callous pictures represented excessive and reprehensible behaviour. See also, "General Urged Troops to Lighten Up." *The Globe & Mail,* A6; Allan Thompson, "Wider Airborne Violence Revealed," *Toronto Star,* 6 October 1996, A1; and Beno, "Treatment of Somalis in the Custody of the Canadian Airborne Battle Group," Beno Papers.

79. *Information Legacy,* Report of the Commission of Inquiry, Vol 1, Incidents and Disciplinary Measures, Record 2798. The letter was written on 27 January 1993.

80. *Somalia Commission,* Transcript of Evidentiary Hearing, Vol 7, 23 October 1995, testimony of Dr. Menkaus (academic specialist on the Horn of Africa), 1266-1352; and Peter Worthington, "Private Brown," *Saturday Night,* September 1994, 34. Mistreatment of Somalis by other military international contingents later caused scandal in countries such as Belgium, Germany and Italy. Allegations included mental and physical abuse, beatings, and the killing of captured thieves. See Andrew Duffy, "Now its Belgian Soldiers," *Ottawa Citizen,* 12 April 1997, 1; Raf Casert, "Somalia scandal sparks Belgian review," *Ottawa Citizen,* 18 April 1997, A10; "Now Belgium rocked by Somali scandal," *Toronto Star,* 12 April 1997, A18;"Burns, shocks given Somalis Italian says," *Toronto Star,* 7 June 1997, A21; and Vera Haller, "Italy's Somalia scandal grows," *Ottawa Citizen,* 15 June 1997, A5. See also Jocelyn Coulon, *Soldiers of Diplomacy: The United Nations, Peacekeeping, and the New World Order* (Toronto: University of Toronto Press, 1994), 98-99.

81. According to the report of Major Armstrong, "the deceased had been first shot in the back and subsequently 'dispatched' with a pair of shots to the head and neck area. Major Armstrong considered that the wounds were consistent with the Somali being shot as he lay wounded on the ground." *Information Legacy,* Report of the Commission of Inquiry, Executive Summary—Mission Aftermath, Record 2874. Master-Corporal Petersen testified that he observed that "the dead Somali's neck was blown out, his head was gaping open at the back of the skull and his face was sagging to one side." Ibid., Report of the Commission of Inquiry, Vol 1—March 4 Shooting, Record 2871. The officer in charge of the operation was Captain Rainville. His posting to the Regiment, as well as deployment to Somalia was questioned by the SSF commander because of Rainville's existing "Rambo" reputation.

82. *Information Legacy,* Report of the Commission of Inquiry, Vol 5, 4 March—Findings, Record 9569. The commission was scathing in its comments of the handling of the incident. It asserted that actions both within theatre and by the command structure in Canada were negligent in ensuring a proper investigation was conducted. See also Coulon, 97.

83. Peter Worthington, *Scapegoat. How the Army Betrayed Kyle Brown* (Toronto: Seal Books, 1997), 116-135; Peter Worthington, "Private Brown," 35-36; Brian Bergman, "A Night of Terror," *Macleans's,* 28 March 1994, 26-28; and "Brutal Allegations," *Macleans's,* 7 March 1994, 13.

84. *Information Legacy,* Report of the Commission of Inquiry, Vol 1, Record 3026. Seward did question the link between his instruction and the death. He wrote, "To what extent this order caused MCpl Matchee and Tpr Brown to beat to death a Somali intruder will be a matter for litigation. I may not be found criminally responsible but my military career is certainly finished."

85. The issue of whether or not the Airborne Regiment was representative of the Army at large will be dealt with in detail in Chapter Nine.

86. Taylor and Nolan, *Tarnished Brass* and *Tested Mettle*; Barry Came, "Shamed In Bosnia," *Maclean's,* 29 July 1996, 10-12; Worthington, *Scapegoat,* 314-315; Desbarats, 4-5; and Winslow, 72-74. *Esprit de Corps* magazine also ran a running critique of any and all foibles present in the CF in virtually every issue of its publication from 1993 to the present.

87. Interview with author, 16 December 1998.

88. Letter, E.B. Beno to Ian Douglas, 4 April 1997, Beno Papers. Lieutenant-Colonel Matthew MacDonald, the RCD CO tasked with conducting the confirmatory exercise concluded, "The Airborne Battle Group will have a successful tour in Somalia because they have good officers, NCOs and soldiers. I have pointed out some weaknesses as I saw them during Ex Stalwart Providence. None of these problem areas are insurmountable and the battalion, in fact, came a long way in a very short period of time considering that mounted operations of this type take a long time to master. I am sure that they have learned some valuable lessons from the exercise and will profit from them." *Somalia Commission,* Transcript of Evidentiary Hearing, Vol 27, 13 December 1995, 5066. The De Faye Commission concluded that the selection of the Canadian Airborne Regiment for service in Somalia was appropriate. BOI—Cdn AB Regt BG, Phase I, Vol XI, Annex H, 19 July 1993, H-2/6. Similarly, General de Chastelain sent a minute to the DCDS on 11 April 1994, which supported the position of the Airborne as a CF UN force. His feisty note stated, "We should not apologize in anyway for the Cdn AB Regt being a UN force." The written direction was indicative of the period. One, it was sent to the "DCDS (thru JAG) [Judge Advocate General, military legal chief]. Second, the strong support of the decision was not made in public. *Information Legacy,* Evidentiary Exhibits, Document Control No. 001873, Document No. DND018961.

89. BOI, Cdn AB Regt BG, Phase I, Vol XI, A-4/33. The Airborne Battle Group consisted of Regimental Headquarters based on HQ commando (and included a reconnaissance platoon and a direct fire support platoon; 1 and 3 Commando mounted in Grizzly AVGPs; 2 Commando as a dismounted infantry company reinforced by mortar platoon from 1 RCR; 'A' Squadron RCD mounted in Cougar (armed with a 76mm gun) AVGPs; a close support engineer squadron from 2 CER; and service commando reinforced by surgical and dental teams.

90. BOI, Cdn AB Regt BG, Phase I, Vol XI, A-3/33. The living conditions were particularly primitive as the paratroopers had only the most basic of necessities. Soldiers were given six litres of water a day per man for consumption, and it was only after three weeks that a five gallon jerry can of water was made available per section for washing of oneself or one's laundry. Corporal Ed Ormond captured the attitude when he stated, "You had to be an airborne paratrooper to survive the harsh conditions we endured while there...no showers or any way to get clean at all, living in trenches and eating dirt for two months." (Submission to author, April 1995). Sergeant Mark Godfrey testified at the Somalia Commission, "we were living in a hole and every night it would fill up with various insects...we were limited to one jerry can of water per man per day. So you had to either eat with it, drink with it or wash with it. It was harsh conditions." (*Somalia Commission,* Hearing Transcripts, 3 April 1996, 10823).

91. Letter, Lieutenant-General R.B. Johnston, Commander UNITAF to Admiral J.R. Anderson, CDS, 1 May 1993, 1.

92. Ibid, 2-3; and BOI, Cdn AB Regt BG, Phase I, Vol XI, A-11/33 to A-16/33. The incessant patrolling and continuous presence of paratroopers in Belet Huen earned them the nickname the "Clan who never sleeps" from the Somalis. CJTF, *In the Line of Duty* (Ottawa: DND, 1994), 18.

93. Letter, Robert B. Oakley, (Special Envoy to Somalia), to the MND, dated 11 May 1993, 2; and BOI, Cdn AB Regt BG, Phase I, Vol XI, A-2/3. The Canadian HRS was declared secure 28 March 1993.

94. Loomis, *The Somalia Affair,* 410.

95. Ibid., 439.

96. Letter, T.G. Harris (Head, African Department, Foreign & Commonwealth Office—UK), to High Commissioner for Canada, dated 9 March 1993. The Canadian High Commissioner to Kenya, with accreditation to Somalia, Her Excellency Lucie Edwards quoted one of her staff who had worked closely with the Canadian soldiers in Somalia. She stated, "You know, those Canadian military, they've got the Somalis figured out. It takes a long time for people to do that, but they've done it." Loomis, *The Somalia Affair,* 431; and BOI—Cdn AB Regt—Phase I, Vol XI, K-4/9.

97. Letter, Guy Naud (Program Coordinator Oxfam-Quebec), to CDS, dated 10 May 1993. The International Medical Corps was another organization which sent a letter of gratitude (9 May 1993) which echoed the sentiments of many others. Specifically it stated, "The CF sought the input of the humanitarian relief organizations in Belet Weyne [Huen]. They responded by working closely with us to establish greater security in our relief work....The CF went beyond their mandate in bringing about change and positively influencing our health programs." The supervisor of the Save the Children Fund for the Hiran Region, in April 1993, reported, "since the arrival of the Canadians, the malnutrition in the sector dropped from more than 50% to less than 15% among the children under five years old." Canadian Airborne Regiment Battle Group. *Operation Deliverance—Somalia December 1992-June 1993 (operation souvenir yearbook),* 11. The Battle Group's efforts were such that Lieutenant-General Johnston, the Commander of UNITAF commented, "One of the very striking successes of the Canadian Airborne Regiment has been the Regiment's focus on civic action programs designed to improve conditions for the Somali communities with the Belet Uen [Huen] HRS. I gave HRS commanders no specific civic action responsibilities and simply relied on the commanders to take the initiative and pursue programs within their capabilities." Letter, Johnston to CDS, 1 May 1993, 2.

98. *Somalia Commission*, Transcript of Policy Hearing, Vol 2, 19 June 1995, 284.

99. Letter, W.B. Vernon (Commander LFCA) to DCDS, 13 May 1993, 2, Beno Papers.

100. Major-General (retd) Lewis Mackenzie, "In Defence of Matieu and the Airborne," *Toronto Star,* 22 July 1994, A21.

101. *Information Legacy,* Hearing Transcripts, Vol 52, 1 April 1996, testimony of Captain Jacques Poitras, CJFS Public Affairs Officer in Somalia, record 88361-88374.
102. *Somalia Commission,* Transcript of Policy Hearing, Vol 2, 19 June 1995, 284.
103. Letter, Johnston to CDS, 1 May 1993, 4.
104. Colonel Serge Labbé, *Canadians in Somalia: Setting the Record Straight or Somalia Cover-Up* (Private Printing, 1994), 363. Colonel Labbé's well-written book is a comprehensive catalogue of the humanitarian effort conducted in Somalia. However, it is completely uncritical of the mission. Furthermore, there is a painful absence of clarification or even mention of the controversial aspects of the tour. Despite the book's 556 pages, there is only a single paragraph which mentions the "unfortunate deaths" of Somalis under Canadian custody. Likewise, there is the briefest of remarks on subjects such as ROE and no reference of the confusion following the March killings. The unbalanced account detracts from the credibility of an otherwise insightful look into the Somalia mission.
105. Letter, Oakley to the MND, 11 May 1993, 4.
106. "Canadians Praised for Success in Somalia," *The Globe & Mail,* 10 May 1993, A8.
107. BOI, Cdn AB Regt BG, Phase I, Vol XI, K-4/9.
108. Peter Worthington, himself a journalist and writer, commented, "the media are basically only interested in a provocative story and don't much care who gets hurt. That's a harsh assessment, and doesn't apply to all individuals in the media, but collectively I think that tends to be the case." Letter, Peter Worthington to Mia Beno, 5 July 1996. Beno Papers. Decades earlier, Brooke Claxton, the MND, commented, "newspapers never explain, never correct, never withdraw. Newspapers are the most irresponsible of all the agencies having to do with public affairs." Bercuson, *True Patriot,* 171.
109. Letter, Major-General W.B. Vernon to DCDS, 13 May 1993. Beno Papers.

Top: Members of 3 Commando march off parade during D-Day 50th Anniversary ceremonies in Gosport, UK, 4 June 1994. (Courtesy of Canadian Airborne Forces Museum.)

Bottom: The mayor of Petawawa inspects the Regiment during freedom of the city ceremonies, June 1994. (Courtesy of P. Kenward.)

Top: HRH Prince Andrew talks with an unidentified sniper from Pathfinder Platoon during the Regiment's 25th Anniversary ceremonies, September 1994. (Courtesy of P. Kenward.)

HRH Prince Andrew inspects 2 Cdo during the Regiment's 25th Anniversary ceremonies, September 1994. He is accompanied by Major James Hammond, OC 2 Cdo (left), and Lieutenant-Colonel Peter Kenward and Colonel Fraser Eadie (rear).
(Courtesy of P. Kenward.)

The Cdn AB Regt, on parade during the Special Service Forces Farewell to the Canadian Airborne Regiment ceremony, 1 March 1995. (Courtesy of R. Prouse.)

The Cdn AB Regt ceremoniously marches off the square symbolizing its departure from the Brigade, during the SSF Farewell to the Canadian Airborne Regiment parade, 1 March 1995. (Courtesy of R. Prouse.)

Left to right, Colonel Fraser Eadie, Brigadier James Hill, Colonel Peter Kenward, at the Regiment's final Mess Dinner, 3 March 1995. (Courtesy of the 1 Cdn Para Bn Association Archives.)

Top: The CO, Lieutenant-Colonel Peter Kenward, signs the disbandment document, Nicklin Parade Square, CFB Petawawa, 4 March 1995. (Courtesy of R. Prouse.)

Bottom: Disbandment Parade, 4 March 1995. (Courtesy of D. Halcrow.)

Top: The Regiment marches past the "Into Action" statue located at the main gate of CFB Petawawa, as part of the final Regimental activity, Laying Up the Colours, 5 March 1995.   (Courtesy of the Canadian Airborne Forces Museum.)

Bottom: Laying Up the Colours, The Royal Canadian Regiment Drill Hall, Building Y101, CFB Petawawa, 5 March 1995.   (Courtesy of P. Kenward.)

Twinning Ceremony of the Canadian Airborne Regiment and the US 75th Ranger Regiment, March 1994, Fort Benning, Georgia. (Courtesy of P. Kenward.)

CHAPTER NINE

AN ABSENCE OF HONOUR
The Disbandment of the Canadian Airborne Regiment, 1993-1995

Political and CF leadership involvement in Ottawa starting in March 1993 dragged the Canadian Army into a morass. Rather than take decisive and effective action they allowed the situation to fester and grow. Media hype and political-military mishandling of the issues has made a national scandal out of a localized crime.

Brigadier-General Ernie B. Beno, 1996.[1]

In January 1995 the Canadian Airborne Regiment was suddenly and unexpectedly disbanded by the prime minister. The political and military leadership tied the demise of the Regiment to its disciplinary problems and the tragic, brutal killing of the Somali teenager Shidane Arone by some of the Regiment's members. The defence minister labelled the Regiment's problems systemic and clearly stated that the loss in public confidence in the Canadian Airborne Regiment left no other option but disbandment. But the answer was not so simple—because the root problem was never examined. The Regiment's troubles in Somalia were merely manifestations of long term chronic problems which had plagued the Airborne and its predecessors from their inception almost fifty-three years earlier. Therefore, it is important to examine the events from the Regiment's return from Somalia up until the actual disbandment announcement to fully comprehend the impact that personalities in power, as well as the continuing debate in regard to the relevancy of paratroopers, had on the decision to cut the Canadian Airborne Regiment from the Canadian Forces order of battle.

Undeniably, since the Airborne's return to Canada in the spring/summer of 1993 it could not shake the focus on its disciplinary problems or the murder of Arone. The extent of the damage caused to the Regiment's reputation was not fully realized until the troops had returned home. Sergeant Mark Godfrey described the disheartening reality of the homecoming:

> When my plane landed in Ottawa there was a guy at the front of the plane who said, simply get off the plane, don't look around, head straight for the hanger in a single file and we'll brief you when you get in the hanger. And we got in the hanger

and he explained to us, okay, when you step out of the building there's going to be a thousand media there, and we were anything but heroes. But we weren't allowed to talk to anyone. We moved from the plane through Ottawa to Petawawa without seeing a soul and then we got to Petawawa we saw our families and then the real scope of what was going on in Canada came to light. I mean, we heard bad press and stuff, but we didn't imagine the scale that it was at.[2]

Another Somali veteran, Master-Corporal Whynot, recalled the disappointment of his reception in Canada. He lamented, "I felt that I had accomplished a lot, that I had learned about myself and other people, but I couldn't even talk about being over there. Here we were all seen as evil, the scum of the earth."[3]

The effect on the families was similarly incalculable. Daily battering of the Regiment in the press failed to differentiate between the guilty and innocent. In the final analysis all of the paratroopers were portrayed as guilty by association. Editorial cartoons depicting the Airborne Regiment as Nazis and members of the Ku Klux Klan had a telling effect on dependents and the public at large. The hard-earned accomplishments of the tour were quickly erased and the mission's successes were now defined by a single event. One frustrated spouse stated, "It sounds like my husband has spent five and one half months away from home and accomplished nothing."[4]

The media onslaught both surprised and chagrined the members of the Airborne Regiment and their families. Their reaction may have been naive, but it was symptomatic of people who subscribe to an idealistic belief or goal. The real world had caught up with them.

The effect of the Arone killing and the resultant bad press was so powerful that it actually caused direct action against the paratroopers' next of kin. There were episodes where family members wearing distinctive Airborne Regiment apparel were harassed and scorned in public. Sometimes children in school, whose fathers were known to be in the Regiment, were likewise bullied and tormented.[5] Some senior military personnel in Ottawa were well aware of the adverse press and its detrimental effect on both the soldiers and their families; however, they did nothing to alleviate the problem.[6] It appeared as if the chain of command within the Defence Department did not want to clarify the events that transpired in Somalia, or refute erroneous stories in the press. Moreover, no campaign medal was issued as a public endorsement, if not reward, for the Canadian contingent's efforts in Somalia.

The senior leadership's attempt at letting the entire matter blow over backfired. The incensed media would not let it go. But then why should they? They were not getting any answers. As a result, any sense of accomplishment or validation sought by the paratroopers to justify their time spent in-theatre became lost in the sandstorm of Somalia. Months of deprivation, frustration, stress, and sacrifice were incredulously redefined. What made matters worse was that no one in the military hierarchy made any attempt to correct the many inaccuracies and wide-ranging stereotypes.[7]

There was also very little help from the civilian defence community in Canada. One reason for this silence was the lack of detailed information being allowed out by DND on what really happened. The second reason, and one that highlights a chronic problem in this country, is that the informed defence community has always been small and thereby is hardly ever able to educate the public on highly emotional issues such as the Airborne's performance in Somalia. As a result, the only people who could comment were those inside the government or military and they seemed content to remain tight-lipped. Predictably, the serving Somali mission veterans, as well as their families, experienced a feeling of bitterness and injustice. Sergeant Greg Janes lamented, "why were we left to defend ourselves?"[8]

The continuing high volume of criticism of the Regiment's performance in Somalia, even after its return to Canada, finally led the CDS, Admiral John Anderson, to formally establish the *Board of Inquiry (BOI)—Canadian Airborne Regiment Battle Group* (informally named the de Faye Commission after its Chairman, Major-General Tom de Faye), on 28 April 1993. The CDS gave the BOI the mandate "to investigate the leadership, discipline, operations, actions and procedures of the Airborne Battle Group."[9] The Board began hearings in Ottawa on 11 May and four days later travelled to Somalia to continue its investigation in-theatre. Interviews were resumed in Ottawa less than a month later and the entire BOI was suspended shortly thereafter pending the completion of a number of judicial proceedings. The BOI never resumed its investigation and it was later eclipsed by the Somalia Commission established by the government.[10] The message was unmistakable. The government felt it had no choice but to appoint a separate independent commission to determine the truth. Politicians and many in the public domain no longer trusted the military to investigate itself. Even though the BOI was eventually superceded, its brief history is worth exploring for what it reveals.

The government's lack of faith in the judgement of the military may have been rooted in the Board of Inquiry's initial work. The Board presented its Phase I Report in late summer 1993. The CDS was pleased with the results. Admiral Anderson wrote, "I am heartened by the overriding conclusions of the report which state that the 'efforts and accomplishments of the Canadian Forces personnel in Somalia, in general, and the Canadian Airborne Regiment (CAR) in particular, were truly outstanding and that there has been no evidence presented to the Board that would indicate any systemic problem within the Canadian Airborne Regiment which should, in any way, limit its usefulness or employability.'"[11]

The CDS's comments were hardly reassuring. The disciplinary and leadership problems evident in the Airborne in the early 1990s, specifically during the pre-deployment period and during the unit's time in Somalia from October 1992 to May 1993, were reminiscent of problems identified as early as the beginning of the 1980s. In addition, the same contentious debate over the role and relevancy of paratroopers still created bitter dissension in the Army.

Furthermore, Admiral Anderson's naive opinion neglected the de Faye Committee's list of deficiencies. This specifically advocated a review of the organization and staffing of the Canadian Airborne Regiment by the commander LFC to address the problem of inadequate manning policies. The Board particularly targeted the quality of replacements sent to the Regiment and the ability of the Airborne CO to allocate personnel within his unit as he felt necessary, regardless of feeder regiment affiliation. It also advised the LFC commander to take the necessary measures to ensure that "2 Commando and the Airborne Regiment are provided the high calibre [personnel] and stability they require." It also believed that the Commander of the Army should "examine the manning of the Regiment and improve the mechanisms with a view to giving more flexibility to its Commanding Officer."[12] All of this did indeed suggest that Admiral Anderson's comments were not well thought out.

The BOI further recommended that the "practise of having an officially sanctioned Airborne Indoctrination Course (AIC) continue." It recognized that a challenging AIC would sufficiently suppress "any informal drives to create independent rites of passage" and would provide the leadership with full control of the values being inculcated.[13] The Board's findings also went well beyond the Regiment. They provided recommendations for improvements to Canadian Forces doctrine and policies in areas such as rules of engagement, screening processes for deployments, logistic support, and the handling of detainees, in an attempt to ensure that problems experienced in Somalia would not be repeated.[14]

The Board of Inquiry, unlike the Hewson Report, did not placate the critics in or out of the military. An internal DND review considered the final report as flawed. Major-General Jean Boyle, then the Associate Assistant Deputy Minister (Policy and Communications) and Chairman of the NDHQ "Somalia Working Group" conducted an assessment of the study which pointed out in July 1994 that "a close reading of the de Faye board's report, comparing it with information from courts-martial testimony, would reveal that there were weaknesses and, more important, significant discrepancies in the de Faye board's findings and recommendations, on which the CDS was basing a number of reforms."[15] He further noted that certain conclusions did not appear to be borne out by the actual testimony heard. Moreover, Boyle felt that there had been enough evidence before the de Faye board to suggest that leadership problems reached up the chain of command right to the Canadian Joint Force Somalia Command. In addition, Boyle then also acknowledged that there were documents that indicated direct attempts to cover up facts behind the 4 and 16 March 1993 incidents. He finished by concluding that the most pressing issue regarding the Canadian Airborne Regiment was leadership.[16]

The criticism of the BOI raises a disturbing question. How could such an esteemed investigative team have been so naive or inefficient? Apparently, the traditional reluctance to criticize other senior leaders, regimental practises, or the Army's decisions and actions in general, was deep-rooted. As such, a misconstrued "loyalty" to the military institution became a systemic weakness rather than a strength. The Army demonstrated another example of its historic inability to be critical of itself. As a direct result, it left the door wide open for others to do the job for them.

As for the Airborne Regiment, it weathered the Board's report, the subsequent analysis and the ongoing media scrutiny. A series of courtsmartial for those charged with wrongdoing or misconduct during OP Deliverance, began in the fall of 1993. Their prolonged high-profile deliberations ensured that the Regiment remained a source of public embarrassment to DND and the government. Although overt endorsement of the Regiment by its well-placed supporters was not forthcoming, an active campaign to redeem the Airborne in the public eye was in fact actively, if furtively, underway. An NDHQ assessment of airborne capability candidly acknowledged that the "AB [airborne] lobby is interested in raising the profile of the CAR."[17]

In doing so the Airborne's sponsors utilized a multi-faceted approach. As we know, the redemption campaign in fact was begun well before the sad events in Somalia. It had started during the 1992 reorganisation with an initiative to strip the Cdn AB Regt from the Special Service Force and restore it as an independent entity. This was tenaciously pursued. The extended airborne family believed that a halt to the erosion of the Regiment's status was fundamental to the survival of the Airborne Regiment. What the Airborne's supporters attempted to do was to exploit the nostalgia of the "glory days" of the Airborne's early years—if they had ever existed.

This plan to re-establish an independent Cdn AB Regt was being strongly pushed by Airborne patrons. Brigadier-General Beno, then newly assigned Commander of the Special Service Force, wrote in his diary on 18 August 1993, "Spoke to Brian Vernon (COS at FMCHQ) [Chief of Staff at Army Headquarters]. Hinted that I better sign on to the mech plan [conversion of SSF to 2 Canadian Mechanized Brigade Group with an independent Airborne Regiment]." Beno later confided that at the time he was still preoccupied with Somalia and the preparation of the Airborne Battle Group. But for the moment he entered into his diary a telling comment which showed the emotional nature of decisions being made in regard to the Airborne. Beno wrote, "Airborne Regiment being 'independent reporting to who, I don't know and configuration to be resolved.'"[18] It was apparent that compelling analysis and articulation of a meaningful role for the Regiment was still absent. Rather, members of the airborne lobby attempted to use their positions and rank to force their desired outcome on the Army rather than employ force of informed argument. Their confidence in their power to gain these goals was so high that the incumbent regimental commander included the fact that the Airborne was to be split from the SSF in his "1992 Transition Plan."[19]

The issue was eventually decided at Army Council in April 1993. The Canadian Airborne Regiment was to fall under command of Land Forces Central Area (LFCA). The Regiment was once again to become an independent entity with the CO reporting directly to a "two-star" position effective 1 October 1993.[20] Indeed, it looked like the extended airborne family had won. But had it? The required Ministerial Organization Order submitted to change the command relationships and the title designation was never signed. The senior serving paratrooper at the time attributed the delay to a fundamental review of major defence issues *(1994 Defence White Paper)* currently being undertaken by the MND.[21] Furthermore, the revelation of the events in Somalia, and the turmoil which followed, burned the Airborne Regiment's recent unfortunate record into the consciousness of the political and military leadership. As a result, the extended airborne family now found even its influence substantially decreased, and even suspect.

Nevertheless, in the fall of 1993 the Airborne's supporters spared no effort to rebuild the Regiment's image. Another key element of the campaign to restore the paratroopers' stature was afforded when OP Deliverance, the Airborne's 1992/1993 mission to Somalia, claimed yet another victim. On 15 September, the Airborne Regiment's CO, Lieutenant-Colonel D.C.A. Mathieu, was relieved of command. The LFC Commander, Lieutenant-General Reay, quickly denied that the CO was being dismissed for any shortcoming. He tried to offset the rumours that there were failings by saying publicly that Mathieu's reassignment was not a disciplinary measure, "but rather an administrative procedure designed to ensure the transparency of the legal and disciplinary process."[22] No matter how it was packaged, it now allowed for the appointment of the officer who had been the preferred choice to replace Morneault in the fall of 1992.[23] This was Lieutenant-Colonel Peter Kenward. Nobody should have been fooled by Reay's face-saving words: Mathieu had been fired.

A mere two days after Mathieu was dismissed Kenward took command. The effect of the change quickly made itself felt, as the decentralized, laissez-faire attitude of the former CO was replaced by a highly structured approach with strong centralized control. Kenward had a reputation as a strict no-nonsense disciplinarian and an exceptionally fine field soldier. This fuelled the perception, within the Regiment and the Army at large, that the senior military leadership hoped to redeem the image of the Airborne under his iron tutelage.

Kenward made no secret of his personal mission. He affirmed that he had received no specific directive. However, Kenward acknowledged that he "didn't need a lecture specifying the need to 'clean house.'" He clearly "understood what was required."[24]

Kenward's unwritten mandate was no surprise to the paratroopers. After all, the CO himself quickly announced to the entire Regiment that his intention was to ensure nothing short of the Airborne's survival. He explained that the only way to achieve this was by demonstrating that the unit was the most operationally ready battalion in the Canadian Forces. Only in this manner would others see its worth. Words were no longer enough.

Kenward used his trademark authoritarian style and provided directives that ensured a universal standard for the entire battalion. He accepted no commando "quiffs" or diluted allegiance in his regiment. The new CO reigned in everyone and reminded them that regardless of the infantry regiment of origin, they were now part of the Canadian Airborne Regiment. Furthermore, Kenward strictly controlled all unit activities from morning parades and physical training, to individual and collective training. In addition, he ensured the development of a demanding training plan, the revision of Regimental SOPs, and the establishment of a new emphasis on administrative soundness.

Kenward's leadership represented the "line in the sand." The new commanding officer was an experienced infantry officer and paratrooper. He would tolerate no nonsense. As for the "family," they hoped to use Kenward as the embodiment of a new revitalized Airborne Regiment. They understood that strong leadership was a central tenet in the reformation of the unit's stature in the eyes of others. However, they also realized that this was not enough. The recurring question of the relevance of airborne forces had to be answered. As a result, a renewed effort was made to patch the Regiment's cracked foundation.

This would not be easy. A number of initiatives were undertaken to address the concept of operations, role and tasks of the Regiment. This was critical, particularly in light of the unit's proposed independent status. LFC HQ instructed the Regiment to maintain all assigned tasks, specifically the UN stand-by force and the defence of Canada role, until yet another analysis of the Regiment had been completed.[25] However, elements within the Army leadership deemed the situation serious enough to warrant the implementation of a series of immediate actions.

First, the Army Commander, Lieutenant-General Reay, directed the immediate transfer of the NATO ACE Mobile Force (Land) task, namely the reinforcement of Norway, to the Airborne. Once again, the paratroopers' benefactors believed that an operational focus would solidify the Regiment's place in the Army organization.[26] The rationale was explained in an internal NDHQ analysis. A study undertaken by the Director General Force Development bluntly reported that the subject task "provides the opportunity to secure an elevated status for the CAR [Canadian Airborne Regiment] with Total Forces and the possible leverage to restructure the CAR with increased manpower and equipment."[27] However, the latest tasking was nothing more than hanging labels on a group to give it an operational mission.

But as the public exposure of events in Somalia intensified the airborne lobby was challenged by staff officers and military analysts at National Defence Headquarters. They noted that "deterrence is no longer the Cold War imperative it once was. The sustainment of combat power is now paramount."[28] In this respect, the NDHQ study team concluded that the Airborne Regiment did not possess the necessary capability to meet the mission requirement. More importantly, the newly assigned AMF(L) task had been performed by regular mechanized infantry units for years. The airborne lobby which had pushed hard to gain the operational role for the Regiment fell into a trap of their own making. In fact, their parochial interest was exacerbating the problem. In the desperate attempt to prove the Regiment's worth, the Airborne's supporters, in spite of their attempts to revive the Regiment, were in fact aggravating and exposing its flaws. In the end, these "champions" failed to show the unit's distinctive value.[29] Once again the Regiment could not demonstrate that it did anything more than displace a normal infantry unit.

The effort to ensure an operational role for the Regiment was not the only method by which the airborne family attempted to convince the Army that there was a definite need for an airborne structure within the institution. The systemic problem related to the Airborne's expansive, all-inclusive role was addressed by an attempt to rationalize the unit's existence, not on the basis of a particular mission or task, but rather on its unique capability. To provide a clear aim and focus, the Regiment now articulated a specific mandate for which they were responsible,

This requirement was defined as "the parachute delivery of 540 personnel, 12 vehicles and over 50 tons of combat supplies, at night, from 650 feet AGL [above ground level], onto one or more Drop Zones, with the complete force on the ground in less than 10 minutes."[30] The challenge was daunting and the CO continually stressed the importance of the message both verbally and through posters prominently displayed throughout the Regimental lines. The "unofficial" mission statement seemed to give purpose to paratroopers who grabbed in vain at any indication that they were indeed viewed as indispensable by their Army brethren. But such a claim was still a self-contrived one and had little validity outside of the airborne group.

As already suggested, unfortunately, this attempt to sell the Airborne Regiment was flawed. It never became clear what level of the hierarchy actually endorsed this mission statement. Furthermore, not everyone in the Army, much less the Canadian Forces, agreed with the stated job for the force. Even some of the more prescient officers within the Regiment itself knew that it was a wrong tactic. Major Jamie Hammond, the Officer Commanding 2 Commando at the time queried, "where does this fit into the present Canadian Government policy?"[31] Hammond also insisted that the Airborne's role was never adequately translated into a coherent training plan. He was very much afraid that the failure to adequately review and tailor the airborne mission and tasks, to fit relevant and realistic requirements, resulted in the inability to build the constituencies within the military and government that were needed to support the airborne organization as it existed.[32] But there were not enough such officers inside or outside the unit who could, or perhaps even wanted to dissuade those on the wrong track.

To further exacerbate this shortcoming, the revisionist view that Canadian airborne forces were fundamentally for DOC operations, strictly within the nation's frontiers, again became dominant within the military. The public embarrassment to both the government and the CF, caused by the Airborne in Somalia, allowed critics of the Regiment to push their viewpoint. Their assessment was predicated on a belief that in the Canadian context, there was low threat, minimal risk, and questionable actual employment for airborne forces. Not surprisingly, they claimed that there was a need for only a very small airborne organization at best. The paratroopers' bad public image ensured that this school of thought was no longer automatically dismissed.

For the public, politicians, and NDHQ, the ongoing courts martial over Somalia continued to conjure up awful images of the Airborne's tour there. Not surprisingly numerous studies were commissioned to examine the question of the Canadian Airborne Regiment's future. As the more sensational information unfolded in Ottawa and in the nation's newspapers throughout 1993 and 1994, the survival of the Regiment was no longer a sure thing. Colonel Kenward himself felt the chill of the change in attitude when he recalled, "the Army was not united vis-a-vis the Airborne and its requirement to exist. Certain key individuals were against it, and quite frankly were elated at the turn of events."[33] Kenward felt that the motives for now attacking the Regiment were numerous. Selfish corps interests were at play, he insisted, as were personal shortcomings. He believed that some opponents hid behind the old arguments of operational relevance, such as "paratroopers were not required," they were "too expensive," and they were a "luxury," to cloak their own inadequacies.[34] The acrimonious debate was eventually overcome by events; meanwhile, the Regiment was subjected to one meticulous review after another. Its fate was such that the Director of Infantry penned a quick minute to the Airborne CO stating, "I honestly don't know where we are headed. Only time will tell."[35] It was a *cri de coeur* full of alarm.

The scrutiny of the Airborne Regiment intensified throughout 1994. A new series of studies were undertaken at both Army HQ and NDHQ. Interestingly, as each came out the tone was conspicuously different. The first one in June 1994 was the LFC report signed by Lieutenant-General Reay and endorsed by the Chief of Defence Staff. It was an eloquent ten-page defence of the airborne capability. It recommended the retention of the status quo. As CDS, General de Chastelain, in his covering letter to the MND concluded, "I recommend that you [MND] agree to the continuation of the parachute role as an important part of the combat capability of the Canadian Forces, and that the Canadian Airborne Regiment continue to provide it."[36]

The CDS's strong endorsement was somewhat surprising because the second report, an NDHQ analysis was distinctly different from that of the Army. Its tone was less laudatory and more critical. Significantly, the aim the Ottawa study team was given was also an important indicator. The Chief of Force Development (CFD) specifically directed the researchers to "identify the *minimum* requirement for an airborne capability."[37] The key word here was "minimum." In the end, the team concluded that the Canadian Forces needed airborne forces to address domestic tasks in remote areas. However, the report clearly acknowledged that a thorough analysis of the most effective and efficient means of projecting a presence into these inaccessible areas had not been done. Specifically, they had not examined which method of air delivery, namely parachute or long-range helicopter with an air refuelling capability, would be the optimum solution for the Canadian Forces.[38] The study team's final conclusion reflected its unemotional tie toward the issue. It neglected to promote a specific option and stated simply, "a structure that provides three airborne companies is adequate to meet any reasonable range of possibilities."[39]

During these new investigations no final decisions were reached and the defence review in preparation for the *1994 White Paper* ploughed on. Nevertheless, the ground had been set. The recurring question in regard to the Airborne's relevance, compounded by persistent resentment, and exacerbated by the embarrassment it represented to the political and military leadership made the Canadian Airborne Regiment progressively an even more vulnerable target. As we know, several studies had been commissioned to explore its future. Ominously, the direction included the mandate to determine the minimum requirement. Efforts of the well-placed members of the extended airborne family were sidetracked, even negated. The Regiment which had just recently completed a reduction to battalion status was once again under the butcher's eye.

Still the Regiment's patrons continued to lobby even though their numbers were dwindling and their arguments were becoming less effective. Time was of the essence. In light of the worsening public controversy that persistently engulfed the paratroopers, concrete action was necessary to rebuild the image of the Canadian Airborne Regiment. As already noted, the first step the friends of the Regiment tried to take was to empower the unit with a visible operational mission and a distinct status. The second step was an internal reorganization that would improve its viability. By the end of September 1993, the Regiment was increased from a strength of 601 to 665 all ranks.[40] This expansion was due to the addition of an air defence platoon and an airborne engineer platoon to the combat support commando. The additional combat components were to give the Airborne Regiment Battle Group more organic combat capability.

Another critical program begun in 1993/1994 was the attempt to institute reform through stringent manning requirements for those individuals posted to the Regiment. The time members spent in the Airborne was to be carefully monitored and their terms restricted. Individual soldiers were required to satisfy a specific selection criteria that screened out administrative or disciplinary burdens. More importantly, leadership ranks were to have command experience prior to service with the Airborne Regiment.[41] This initiative failed to materialize. Elements within the senior leadership, especially in the feeder infantry regiments and at NDHQ, apparently sensed the Airborne was a lost cause and as a result, little effort at approving the initiative was made. In any case, the reform issues were ultimately overtaken by events.

The Canadian Airborne Regiment also tried to contribute to its own redemption. Under the firm hand of its CO the unit made substantial headway. In addition to a challenging and gruelling training schedule, the Regiment won the 1994 Canadian Forces Small Arms Competition, including the Queen's Medalist (top scoring individual marksman in the CF). As well, the Airborne won the vaunted Hamilton Gault Trophy (highest aggregate score for a unit's annual marksmanship results and timings for the "2 by 10 mile" fitness march). Furthermore, the Regimental team, representing Canada, won the prestigious North European Command Infantry Competition (NECIC) with the most commanding Canadian performance in the competition's history.[42] One will never know if these accomplishments meant anything. Perhaps they came too late.

Yet, for its part, the extended airborne family positioned at NDHQ and Army HQ also played its trump card; namely, finding high profile operational taskings. In the summer of 1994, the Regiment received direction to support two separate missions deploying to Rwanda, Africa. Within a week of notification, the first of two platoons from 3 Commando was dispatched. This platoon accompanied 2 Field Ambulance from August to October, as the security element, on OP Passage, which was a Canadian sponsored humanitarian mission. The second platoon deployed from August to January as the security platoon for 1 Canadian Division Headquarters and Signals Regiment (1 CDHSR) as part of OP Lance, the Canadian designation for its participation in the UN Assistance Mission in Rwanda (UNAMIR).[43]

Both platoons did very well in these missions. Indeed, the efforts of the paratroopers were quietly applauded by the commanding officers of the supported units. However, both of these commanders would not repeat their glowing tribute openly. It was a signal perhaps that associations with the Airborne could be dangerous to careers or that other units were rejecting them. But whatever the motives the sole publicity the Regiment received was the notoriety it could not afford: it was the public exposure of two disciplinary incidents. The first involved two drunken paratroopers inflicting injury to themselves during a "blood-brother" ritual. The second entailed the discharge of weapons into a stone structure a group of airborne soldiers were securing. In both cases, the commanding officers of the supported units quickly pointed out that the individuals were members of the Canadian Airborne Regiment.[44] Again, it was another unexpected hard knock for the Regiment.

Nevertheless, the paratroopers made positive impressions in their overseas duties. After approximately a month in-theatre, there were reports of mass killings in the southeast region of Rwanda, in the area designated Sector "2 Bravo." The task to provide a presence to increase the confidence of the population and determine the verity of the rumours fell singularly to the Airborne platoon attached to 1 CDHSR. The airborne platoon solved the problem quickly and quietly. Their subsequent success was such that Major-General Tousignant, then the Commander of UNAMIR II, wrote to the CDS:

> The local government and military commanders were convinced that the Canadians had deployed at least one and perhaps two companies into the sector. Most of the villages in the sector were deserted at the beginning. After constant patrolling of all villages, the people gained confidence in the level of security afforded them and started to return.[45]

Three weeks after the mission's commencement, the tired and filthy platoon of paratroopers, who numbered less than forty, passed responsibilities for the sector to an entire Nigerian infantry battalion, which had arrived to conduct a relief in place. The effectiveness of the paratroopers was clear. The Force Commander wrote,"If I had been given a full battalion of Airborne troops, I could have secured the four corners of Rwanda in half the time."[46] But few back in Canada listened to such praise.

Despite the efforts taken to raise the public image in Canada of the Airborne Regiment, by both the paratroopers and their supporters, absolutely no headway was made. It remained under unprecedented public scrutiny; moreover, there was now also little support from the chain of command. As for the Regiment it toiled hard to prove that it was not an ill-disciplined, rogue unit, as portrayed in the press. The efforts actually improved morale and confidence for a while. The Airborne's high standards of fitness and training were always self-evident to the members of the Regiment, but now by virtue of the string of victories, in the national and international military competitions during 1993/1994, and its performance on another operational tour, members hoped that their worthiness and prowess would be evident to others. However, the lack of positive press or public acknowledgements by the senior miliary leadership eventually led the paratroopers to believe that no one outside the Airborne really wanted to know or even cared. Strangely, success was muted. Increasingly all through these post Somalia years it seemed that there was an element in the Department of National Defence that wanted to simply rid itself of the Regiment.

The undercurrent of enmity toward the paratroopers was not surprising. In fact it was naive to expect otherwise. The Airborne Regiment was a public and in many ways an institutional pariah. The events in Somalia unleashed a chain of events which engulfed the senior leadership of DND well beyond the Regiment and embarrassed the government. Moreover, the revelations about the Airborne and how the attending events were handled in Ottawa showed plenty of other problems at NDHQ and elsewhere. To careerist bureaucrats and political sycophants, both in and out of uniform, the fact that their discomfort originated from actions attributed to the Airborne Regiment was not easily forgotten.

And rightly so. The death cries of Shidane Arone continued to haunt one and all well beyond the night of his sadistic killing. That single event was numbing, and the failure of so many to do anything to stop the beating remains inexplicable. Incredibly, the tragedy magnified. The appearance of an attempt to cover up the incident outside as well as inside the Regiment spoke volumes about serious failures in the military and political chain of command at DND. A better movie script could not have been written. A brutal killing, an evident breakdown of military leadership, a cover-up, and a minister of defence who was the acknowledged front-runner in the Progressive Conservative leadership race. It was all there.

The sad truth is that the Regiment now found itself embroiled in the political arena in an utterly hopeless position created both by its own failings and the separate agenda of those around it. Given the expected general election in the summer of 1993 the events in Somalia, and the controversy that preceded it, were an embarrassment to the candidate, Kim Campbell, then the Minister of Defence, who was touted as the next prime minister of Canada. The Airborne Regiment now became an effective tool for the opposition parties and media to attack the governing party prior to an upcoming election. To aggravate an already simmering problem, elements of the civilian and military leadership of DND tried to "fix" the problem. A fiasco of monumental proportions ensued. One has to retrace these terrible events to understand what happened.

When the killings took place in March 1993, the Canadian Joint Headquarters in Somalia reported the incidents promptly to NDHQ. In Ottawa, Colonel Haswell, then a staff officer in the

Director General of Public Affairs (DGPA), later testified that "we recommended that we should get this information out as quickly and completely as possible because the Public Affairs branch felt that early disclosure would reduce the negative impact on DND." He also conceded that the overriding concern at the moment "at very high levels in the Department [was] that nothing be done to interfere with the leadership run" and that this viewpoint affected the release of information.[47] And so a conscious decision was made to control any political damage rather than see public justice done.[48] Something had to give. Something expendable. Such a distorted interpretation was cataclysmic for the public, the Canadian Forces, and for the majority of competent and honourable members of the Canadian Airborne Regiment.

Both civilian and military leadership embarked on this perverted course and much has been printed on the influence of key personalities such as the Deputy Minister, Bob Fowler, and numerous senior flag rank officers.[49] Despite the often confusing, convoluted and always bitter debates over who was to blame it has generally been acknowledged that attempts to cover up the incidents that transpired in Somalia, and the subsequent mishandling by the chain of command, did indeed occur.[50]

More obvious still was the realization that the paratroopers could not count on any support from anyone. Internal discourse within DND bore this out. Brigadier-General Beno was appalled by the DGPA strategy. "In regards to PAFF [Public Affairs] matters," he wrote his superiors, "we are being allowed to 'proceed down the road and develop the situation.' We are doing so without a concept of operations, objectives, boundaries or intelligence and no maps of minefields." "This leaves us wide open," he warned, "to ambushes, snipers, obstacles and dissipation of energy."[51]

Beno's voice was not alone. Major-General Vernon, the Commander of LFCA also felt that there was a "sense of betrayal" in that the soldiers felt that DND neglected to effectively defend its troops abroad.[52] Vernon further charged that assurances that NDHQ would correct misleading facts and stories published by the media, were not being honoured.[53] Even Dr. Daniel Bon, the Director General of Policy Planning at DND later conceded that the "force [Airborne Regiment Battle Group] was not dealt with fairly by the press and public, and some of our leaders."[54]

But for the fate of the entire Airborne Regiment, it was the events after the actual killings that transformed the issue from one of a series of local criminal acts, compounded by poor leadership, to one of national scandal centred primarily on the Regiment. The brutality of a number of paratroopers became eclipsed by the mishandling and "political" interference of an alleged cover-up. Peter Worthington opined that the "Somalia incidents that provoked the inquiry have almost become irrelevant."[55]

In all of it there was a distinct lack of honour. On one level, the behaviour of a number of airborne officers and soldiers sullied the reputation of the nation's military. On a separate plane, lapses of integrity and professionalism at NDHQ further tarnished the institution's standing in the public eye. Not surprisingly, the senior military leadership ordered yet another examination of the requirement for an airborne capability as part of the defence review leading up to the *1994 White Paper*. More ominous was the fact that the drafters of the new white paper were working feverishly to cut all references to the Canadian Airborne Regiment and all things airborne. Dr. Bon admitted later that there was a feeling that the Airborne was causing the government so much grief that something drastic would probably be done with it. As a result, in anticipation of such a governmental action, the word "airborne" or any inference to it, was neatly excised. "In fact the only reference to airborne in the *1994 White Paper*," quipped Bon, "was 'Airborne Early Warning,' I know because we word checked it."[56]

The climate was such that nothing the paratroopers had accomplished mattered. Indeed, the very presence of some success only muddied the water. As a result, good performance and reforms were quietly applauded by those who supported the Regiment and ignored by those who did not. Major Anthony Balasevicius, a long-standing paratrooper stated that the Airborne never cultivated friends and as a result, when it came time to ask for help, no one was there to provide it. The irony was not lost on Balasevicius. "Those we laughed at," he reflected, "now watched us die."[57] This corrosive environment spawned what would become one desperate last attempt to redeem the stature of the Regiment.

Again some influential members of the airborne family at LFC HQ had enough clout to have the Canadian Airborne Regiment slated to replace 1 RCR in Sector South, in Croatia and it was so announced in early January 1995. Colonel Semianiw, then the Operations Officer (G3) at LFCA HQ admitted that the decision was made because of an understanding that there was a need to "put the Airborne into the breach."[58] Colonel Kenward affirmed that "no one stated this is an opportunity to save yourself, to make-up for the debacle in Somalia, but it was recognized that this was a possibility to send a message to the chain of command and the public at large."[59] Kenward conceded that there were private conversations in Land Forces Command outlining the fact that "these guys need this, they're under a lot of heat so let's do this," but he quickly added, "I'd like to believe the analysis was done on who was best capable to do this."[60] Notwithstanding the process, or lack thereof, the point is that the Army Commander made a conscious decision to give the Regiment an opportunity to redeem itself on an operation.

Whether or not this final intervention by the airborne benefactors would have solved the Regiment's perceived villainy is a mute point because unexpectedly, one more public revelation did crushing damage. The unit's substructure finally gave way. On 15 January 1995, the CTV television network broadcast excerpts from a homemade video, made by soldiers of 2 Commando during their tour in Somalia, on the nightly news. Several members were shown making racial slurs and behaving in an unprofessional manner. Media reaction was sharp, as was the subsequent political furor. Once again, the recurrent Somalia issue catapulted the Airborne Regiment into the public and political spotlight. The mortal blow, however, came three days later when another amateur video depicting a 1992 1 Commando "initiation party" was aired. The tape exhibited 1 Commando paratroopers involved in behaviour that was degrading, disgusting, and racist in nature.[61] Its release embarrassed the government and the Canadian Forces. It also completely destroyed whatever was left of the Airborne Regiment's image. The question of public trust evaporated. The enormity of the crisis was clear. The disgusting spectacle alienated any remaining support and opened the way for the destruction of the Canadian Airborne Regiment.

If individuals in public, defence and political circles did not have their minds made up against the Regiment in 1993, these new revelations two years later did the trick. No one wanted to be associated with the publicized depravity that was beamed into millions of homes. Clearly, the day of reckoning had arrived. For years there had been a large constituency which had argued against any viable parachute capability because of economic and parochial interests. Furthermore, behind all of this was the fundamental flaw that the airborne role and its relevance to current defence needs had never been resolved. Now driven by the disgusting television scenes and earlier crimes in Somalia, the critics pounced on the old flaw. To disband the Regiment would be easy for these opponents. After all, they had often attacked the various forms of the airborne for years. Other skeptics of the airborne concept had as frequently thought of the unit as "rogue" and irreverent. Once again the two videos only proved to them that the Canadian Airborne Regiment was an embarrassment to the Canadian Forces and the government.[62]

After the repugnant video revelations the Liberal government took speedy action. While the defence minister demanded a report on the new Airborne episodes within a week, it was just a formality. An Army assessment prior to the broadcast of the videos had already noted that the "extreme scrutiny" of the Regiment as a result of Somalia, "may encourage a decision to eliminate the Cdn AB Regt from the CF Order of Battle."[63] After the exposure of the two films the prevailing perception of staff officers at the various regional and national headquarters was that a decision to disband the Airborne was already made. Confirmation was all but affirmed when Prime Minister Jean Chrétien, interviewed while vacationing in the Caribbean, stated, "If we have to dismantle it [Canadian Airborne Regiment], we'll dismantle it. I have no problem with that at all."[64] In his heart, Peter Kenward, the Airborne Commander, knew that the prime minister's televised remarks were a definite signal that the "train was in motion."[65]

The execution of the investigation fell to Land Forces Central Area, commanded by Major-General Vernon. But even his clear preferences for his old unit could not save the Regiment and he likely knew it. Nevertheless, the LFCA investigation went on. Time was short so the approach was kept as simple as possible.[66] The CFB Petawawa military police were tasked to examine the videos to determine what criminal or military charges, if any, were warranted. In addition, an investigation team, led by the LFCA G3, then Lieutenant-Colonel Semianiw, and assisted by Major Jim Ferron, the SSF representative, were tasked to report their findings to a set of questions that were designed to evaluate the level of reform that the Regiment had achieved since Somalia. The commanding officer recalled that the Regiment and investigation team were hard-pressed to answer the queries in such a short time span, particularly since the nature of the questions kept changing. Nevertheless, the fate of the Airborne seemingly hinged on the following inquiries:

1. Are there sanctioned initiation rites in the Canadian Airborne Regiment; if so what are they. Since this incident, have other unsanctioned rites of a similar nature or any other incident of hazing occurred and does it, in any form, still occur in the Canadian Airborne Regiment. Additionally, have the De Faye recommendations on hazing been implemented.

2. Regarding the specific incident which was alleged to have occurred in the summer of 1992; what date did the event occur and where did it happen.

3. Have racist activities been eliminated in the Canadian Airborne Regiment. In particular, what orders, regulation or policies are in place to ensure that any incidence of racism is dealt with.

4. If the Canadian Airborne Regiment should continue to be considered suitable for operational deployment on UN duty to Croatia on OP Harmony Roto 6.

5. What personnel and policy changes have occurred in the Canadian Airborne Regiment since the specific incident in question.[67]

The final LFCA report to the Chief of Defence Staff and Minister of National Defence stated that an objective analysis of the facts demonstrated that the current Airborne Regiment was distinctly different from the Airborne Regiment in Somalia. Colonel Semianiw's assessment indicated that the Airborne should not be disbanded and that a "line in the sand" had truly been drawn. For his part, Major-General Vernon, the LFCA Commander, was also convinced of the strides in reform. "New leadership, more effective control, and a vigorous and exacting training regime," he declared, "have, in concert, produced a marked change in the Regiment." He went on to say that "there has been a 'sea change' within the Canadian Airborne Regiment since Sep 93. The regiment is the best trained and led unit within LFCA and, probably, within the Army."[68] However, during the course of the investigation, the sudden disclosure of a third video depicting yet another 1 Commando initiation ceremony, from the summer of 1994, shattered these good reports. Although the activity depicted in the most recent tape was not as revolting as its predecessor, the fact that the forbidden activities were still occurring merely confirmed latent suspicions.[69]

The report was presented to the minister on 23 January 1995. The paratroopers did not have long to wait to discover their fate.[70] The MND scheduled a press release for that same afternoon, at which time he announced, "although our senior military officers believe the Regiment as constituted should continue, the government believes it cannot. Therefore, today under the authority of the National Defence Act, I have ordered the disbandment of the Canadian Airborne Regiment."[71]

Despite the fact that many anticipated the outcome, many others still could not believe it. Brigadier-General Bruce Jeffries, the SSF Commander, was stunned by the announcement. During a news conference he stated, "my recommendation was clearly to retain the Regiment and to give it the opportunity to prove itself in Croatia. Obviously, I do not feel there is a blot there that could not be removed."[72] Major-General (retired) Lewis MacKenzie endorsed this belief with a terse, "I don't think this was justified in any way."[73] The sentiments of most were aptly expressed by Paul Cane, who was a former member of the Airborne. "It's sad," he said, "when we live in a world when the actions of a few can out number the actions of a thousand members like myself, past and present, that achieved great things."[74]

More than anything else a feeling of betrayal slowly permeated the entire Regiment. Much like the authorities who had ensured its survival, opposite yet just as powerful individuals now assured its death. Major-General Vernon, like many others, believed that the decision to disband was made before the investigation into the videos was even completed.[75] This is no surprise. It was long evident even to the lowest ranking paratrooper that the Regiment's existence had become highly politicized. The MND's admission that the four days allocated to the CDS to investigate the entire matter was not sufficient only supported the suspicions of the Airborne supporters. Likewise, the candid affirmation of the prime minister that "I am told that a lot of it [disciplinary and behavioural problems] had already been rectified because these video tapes are coming from two, three years ago" only confirmed the misgivings of the paratroopers.[76] But, more disturbing was the apparent influence of some of the defence minister's advisors, particularly the rapidly rising Major-General Jean Boyle who in 1993 after the murder of Shidane Arone had carefully attempted to control the damage seeping out of Somalia on behalf of his military and civilian superiors.[77] The whisperings of these individuals were perceived as damning to the Regiment.[78]

The sense of betrayal was augmented by various political statements trying to justify the actual disbandment. David Collenette, the Minister of National Defence, for instance, claimed that the conduct of some members of the Airborne Regiment over the past few years had seriously impugned the reputation of all members, past and present, and brought into question the trust others bestowed in all of the Canadian Forces. He maintained that there was something "radically wrong" with the Regiment and that its problems were "systemic." Finally, he concluded that the "cumulative effect on the public's confidence in the Regiment led me to conclude that the Regiment had to be disbanded."[79] However, opinion polls failed to substantiate the rationale. A Gallup survey conducted on 27 January 1995, demonstrated that of all those questioned, exactly half disagreed with the decision to disband the Regiment. Only thirty-two percent actually supported the disbandment order.[80]

In essence the airborne's fate was once again settled by virtue of key personalities in power and political expediency, rather than sound military advice based on an uncompromising analysis of the operational requirement. Unfortunately, much of the opinion on the Airborne, which led to a series of bad decisions over the years was often hurried and based on half truths and misperceptions. The airborne in itself was not the fundamental problem. It was simply a symptom of a larger illness. The quick fix was not the cure for the greater malaise that permeated the entire Canadian military institution.

In the period after the killing of Shidane Arone in the spring of 1993 the problem was consistently and narrowly defined in terms of the paratroopers and the Airborne Regiment itself. The disciplinary difficulties of the eighties were marched out as proof, as was the run of incidents prior to deployment in the fall of 1992. The accepted theme was that the nature of airborne soldiers inherently creates this type of problem. The conduct of the paratroopers was defined as a clear aberration of the behaviour normally found in Canada's "Combat Arms" soldiers.[81] General John de Chastelain, the CDS, who himself was previously seen by the airborne family as an extremely well-placed supporter, later retorted that the Regiment "was responsible for its own demise."[82]

Having pinned the problem on a bad perception of airborne troops in general, many within the higher military command quickly seized on the *idée fixe* that the actions committed by a number of paratroopers were in fact an aberration. Responsibility for the perceived abhorrent behaviour, they said, could be attributed to the influence of the American and French airborne forces. The on-going unit exchanges, they now argued, exposed the Canadian paratroopers to attitudes and practices that were alien and detrimental.[83] The emergence of racism and the introduction of the "Rebel Flag" were seen as unmistakable indicators. Furthermore, they charged that there was a disturbing elitist mentality in the Airborne Regiment. In the post Somalia / post disbandment period it became faddish, if not politically essential, to disavow any admission to fostering a personal attitude that the Airborne was somehow considered special or elite.

Equally as damaging for the Canadian Airborne Regiment was the blatant reshaping of events. The media's redefinition of the Somalia mission was never challenged. With time it became publicly accepted that the operation was a debacle and a wholesale failure. Evidence suggests such was not the case. Nonetheless, the conventional wisdom was soon repeated by the civilian and military leadership itself. The impact was such that even Lieutenant-Colonel Mathieu, the Airborne Battle Group's commanding officer during OP Deliverance, later lashed out and stated that "heads higher than his will roll because the Airborne wasn't ready."[84] Even the Somalia Commission, established by the government in March 1995, frustrated more with events that transpired after the mission, and specifically with personalities in NDHQ, lent credence to the myth in their final report. Their dramatic, but not necessarily accurate, introductory preamble stated:

> From its earliest moments the operation went awry. The soldiers, with some notable exceptions, did their best. But ill-prepared and rudderless, they fell inevitably into the mire that became the Somalia debacle. As a result, a proud legacy was dishonoured.[85]

The Airborne's troubles were conveniently labelled "systemic." This buzzword was neither defined, nor explained. Its vagueness was its strength. It was left to the audience to draw their own conclusions. But, the "systemic" problem was framed in terms of the inherent difficulties associated with paratroopers and airborne organizations. The issues of role, relevancy, relationship to the Army at large and manning practises were not included. Disciplinary problems, allegations of wanton violence, racist innuendo, elitist attitudes, ties to US paratroopers in the American Deep South, and connections to the "paras" of the notorious French Foreign Legion, were all presented as clear manifestations of the claim. The myth conveyed the message that the troubles and the embarrassment caused to the nation's government and military institution were inherent and inescapable, and were a result of the "costly" airborne organization's existence. Paratroopers, one was led to believe, were simply unsavoury characters if not born killers.[86]

Such prevailing ideas, however, were erroneous. They were exceptionally convenient and enormously effective for absorbing culpability, but they were not accurate. The Airborne's demise was a reflection of the larger long-term failure of the Army; specifically, its inability or reluctance to make hard decisions and to take the necessary steps to ensure the stability of the institution. The Army placed a higher priority on acquiescence than on critical thought, on a tolerance for the secretive machinations of Regimental Councils which were largely not accountable, and on providing for the government politically acceptable solutions instead of sound military advice. All of these factors led to a collective abrogation of responsibility in regard to correcting the problems that were evident in the Airborne long before Somalia. Peter Desbarats, one of the Somalia commissioners, noted that the "Airborne was only the most brutal manifestation of the disease. Amputating it did nothing to resolve the real problems except to allow the leadership to pretend that they had cured it." He summarized: "this was more dangerous than doing nothing."[87]

Lieutenant-General Foster, a former Regimental and Army Commander, also thought that the Airborne Regiment's problems were really a manifestation of a malaise running throughout the Canadian Forces. Moreover, he blamed the Army for failing to deal with the flaws at the root of the Airborne's demise.[88] Similarly, Lieutenant-Colonel Lorne O'Brien, a long-serving Army officer and former paratroop commander, finally said what many were too frightened to admit. He declared that there was an inherent irony in disbandment. If in fact there was a problem in the Airborne, he said, then there was also a problem in the entire Regimental System. O'Brien pointed out that by its very nature the airborne was the sum of the component parts of the line infantry regiments.[89]

The real reasons for the ultimate fate of the Airborne were forgotten in the sensationalized killing of Arone and the later vulgar videos. As already mentioned the Airborne became a "reform school" for the discarded troublemakers of other units. It was not the fact that an individual was a paratrooper that created the disciplinary quandary, but rather that he was a troublemaker from another regiment who imported his nefarious behaviour. A Special Service Force assessment pointed out that the demise of the Canadian Airborne Regiment was "due not to operational deficiencies but to a failure in application of the personnel system" over the long run.[90] Years before the disbandment of the Airborne, in the fall of 1993, Lieutenant-General Gordon Reay, the Commander of the Army, had conceded as much when he wrote his official response to the recommendations which were proffered by the de Faye Commission. Reay confessed, "these incidents [disciplinary problems during pre-deployment to Somalia and in-theatre] are directly attributable to the personnel establishment of the Regiment not being manned as deliberately as it should have been in the past two years."[91]

The long-term bad manning practices and outright "dumping" were unquestionably key problems. But amid the wreckage caused by murder and bestial initiation revelations in the mid nineties the fundamental flaws were ignored. The "rogue regiment" continued to remain a convenient target. Colonel Hatton, a former paratrooper commented, "[historically] we became the whipping boys." He recalled that if someone got into trouble it was always alleged to have been a member of the Regiment. He observed that it seemed "to fulfill people's impression of us, what they expected."[92] Brigadier-General Beno also held the same view. A reputation, he felt, could be quickly developed, and in turn, fuelled by further incidents. He went on to say that the reputation becomes further magnified as a direct result of undue attention that is consequently focussed on the subject organization. In regard to the Airborne, Beno concluded, "because of the high visibility of this unit, and because some believe it is different from other infantry and Combat Arms units, when things go wrong they tend to be exaggerated."[93]

This became the Regiment's predicament all through the eighties and nineties. It could not shake perceptions or its past. Nor could it depend on the assistance of its masters. A graphic example is that of the Army Commander himself. During a telephone interview with the editor of *esprit de corps* magazine, Lieutenant-General Reay made reference to the Regiment's poor disciplinary record. The editor quickly challenged him for singling out the Airborne Regiment. As a result, Reay had to concede that if any of the other Army "regiments were held up to the same microscopic scrutiny it would produce the same damning results."[94]

This was the element that was ignored. Quite simply, the Airborne Regiment was not an aberration. It was not different. It was representative of other Army units in regard to discipline. During the Somalia mission the SSF commander reported that "historical records and comparative records of disciplinary problems showed no disturbing trends, certainly nothing worse than other Infantry and Combat Arms units."[95] In the summer of 1993 the de Faye Commission also concluded that "in terms of numbers of disciplinary infractions, the state of discipline in the Canadian Airborne Regiment was similar to that of other infantry units."[96] Colonel Wells, a former Director General of Security at NDHQ indicated that the number of incidents reflected in military police reports "compared favourably to those of its [Airborne Regiment] sister infantry battalions in the Special Service Force, and that its disciplinary rate was consistent with the other infantry battalions in the Army."[97] Moreover, Colonel Semianiw acknowledged that the Commander's Investigation, initiated as a result of the hazing videos in January 1995, similarly documented that the Regiment's record was "normal, no worse than any other unit."[98]

Furthermore, Major-General Gaudreau testified before the Somalia Commission in October 1995 that the problems faced by the Airborne Regiment were in fact typical of those faced across the entire military structure of Canada.[99] This in turn was reinforced by an internal LFC report which acknowledged that "every regiment has at least one serious incident in its history that has discredited the honour of the [respective] regiment." It affirmed that such incidents were inevitable, if not "unavoidable manifestations of human failing."[100]

Statistical analysis also challenged the myth that all airborne units are more poorly behaved than others. An examination of the *Record of Summary Trials* for numerous National Defence Act (NDA) offences, for all LFC infantry units, from 1988 to 1993, revealed that the Regiment was never the unit with the highest number of trials/offences. In fact, it was well within the average for each given year.[101] Similarly, the accusations of rampant racism were equally unfounded. A 1993 investigation by the military's Special Investigations Unit (SIU) noted that the number of alleged or suspected white supremacists in Petawawa numbered twelve. Of those approximately a third were members of the Airborne Regiment and another third belonged to 1 RCR.[102] Ironically, there were more visible minorities serving in the Regiment than in the Regular Forces as a whole (2.8% compared to 2.2%).[103]

The hazing videos exposed in 1995 were also a distortion of the reality of what went on in the Regiment as a whole. They did not represent accepted airborne behaviour, initiation practices or rituals. The military police investigation of the incident, so graphically depicted on TV, disclosed that "from the interviews conducted thus far (25) it appears that the initiation ceremony was sanctioned within 1 CDO [Commando] but not necessarily the Cdn AB Regt."[104] The military police report also revealed that "it appears that events of a similar nature may have occurred elsewhere in the Royal 22nd Regiment."

The very specific and troublesome images exemplified the diversity of the parent infantry regiments. Individuals from the three distinct feeder regiments brought with them the strengths, as well as the weaknesses, of their parent organizations. Brigadier-General Walter Holmes believed that the personalities of the three parent infantry regiments were very different. When these distinct cultures came together in the Airborne, he admitted, "inevitably it creates problems for you."[105]

Holmes's observation was reinforced by academic analysis. Donna Winslow concluded in her socio-cultural study prepared for the Somalia Commission that within the Airborne there were distinct "regimental sub-cultures [RCR, PPCLI, R22eR]" that represented the different unit cultures.[106] The "regimental quiffs" and practices, as well as the hard-to-break sub-unit independence, about which so many had warned since the late seventies now came home to roost in the nineties.[107] With society's much changed values, such practices could no longer be ignored. But after the Arone tragedy and the videos no one in politics, the public, media, or even the military itself, wanted to acknowledge these long-term explanations. After all that would entail the admission of a mistake, and more importantly the concession that perhaps this was not an isolated problem with paratroopers.[108]

A comparison of the Airborne's troubles with those of Canada's other military units deployed on overseas missions was also conveniently ignored. Many of the Canadian contingents that deployed to the Former Yugoslavia experienced disciplinary difficulties, particularly in relation to drunkenness. Examples abound: 2 Service Battalion had the CO, RSM and several soldiers returned home during their tour in Yugoslavia for proven malfeasance or alleged misconduct; soldiers in the RCD gave their unit the nickname "ChargeBat" due to the high number of charges that had been laid against soldiers for disciplinary infractions; elsewhere serious questions were raised about lost equipment and vehicles during R22eR tours; and another national scandal erupted in 1994 as the result of the questionable behaviour of sixty Canadian peacekeepers at the Bosnian Bakovici mental hospital. Missions to Cambodia and Haiti were equally fraught with incidents of scandalous and unprofessional behaviour that included corruption, drunkenness, and prostitution. This brief overview is not comprehensive by any stretch of the imagination. Neither is it designed to be a condemnation, nor exoneration, of the military or its personnel. It is, however, testimony to the inherent fallibility of mortals. It is also a reminder that the Airborne was not an aberration.[109]

Nevertheless, the concept of the "rogue unit" was not only perpetuated, but actively promoted. The "Rebel Flag" of 2 Commando fame became another diabolical and sinister symbol. It was purported to represent blatant racism within the Regiment. Undeniably, the flag embodies many connotations such as racism. However, the confederate battle flag is also perceived by many to represent ideas such as the "underdog," pursuit of a "lost cause," and status as "outsiders/rebels to the existing system /status quo." Clearly, those individuals who held racist beliefs gravitated toward the dark interpretation of the symbol. But, in reality, although the flag evolved to represent a challenge to authority, it was not meant to symbolize or depict collective or widespread racist beliefs, any more than the fleur-de-lis of 1 Commando represented a wholesale separatist intention within that francophone sub-unit.

The origin of the Confederate or rebel flag, as a distinct symbol of 2 Commando, is difficult to pinpoint. According to Lieutenant-Colonel Ron Bragdon, a former CO of 2 Commando, the banner was always part of 2 PPCLI. For instance, he recalls that while the battalion was in Germany, during the early eighties, the battalion's hockey team which had been named the "Rebels" and had been associated with the flag for more than twenty years, did the unheard of: it actually bested the "Vandoo" team for the first time in memory. Bragdon stated it was only natural that members of this battalion, when posted to the Airborne, would bring their symbol with them, particularly to incense their rivals in 1 Commando.[110]

This explanation, however naive it might be is not widely accepted. The most consistent explanation for the origin of the rebel flag centres around the belief that it was adopted in the early 1980s as a "rallying symbol" for the paratroopers of 2 Commando who wished to carve out a distinct identity for themselves. The de Faye Commission heard testimony that actually linked the origins of the flag to a presentation by an American officer to 2 Commando following an arduous joint exercise in the United States. The performance of the PPCLI paratroopers was apparently deemed exceptional by their allies. Moreover, the Americans characterized the Commando as having a "rebel" attitude.[111] Ostensibly, the Confederate flag and the appellation "rebels" were quickly adopted. But more important, the 2 Commando soldiers seemed to have had official sanction, if not outright encouragement. For instance, the flag was regularly paraded at various competitions to rally support. To most, the banner had no racist overtones.[112]

Nonetheless, the chain of command eventually became concerned about the use of the rebel flag in 2 Commando. With time it became clear to the senior officers within the Regiment that there was a direct linkage between an internal discipline problem and the adopted symbol. The rebel flag was flown publicly on some occasions when commanders disciplined or attempted to impose unpopular directives on soldiers of 2 Commando. As a result, the flag quickly evolved to symbolize a challenge to authority. Colonel Walter Holmes was one of many regimental commanders who banned the public display of the flag because it signified a "unit seeking a separate identity." "The flag," he recalled, "was often taken out after punishment was imposed on members of 2 Commando [and] in our view, it signalled a form of rebellion against constituted authority."[113] All the same, in the post Somalia period the prevailing image, which was not corrected, was that the flag was the rallying point for a nest of white supremacists active within the Regiment. As already mentioned, although a very few may have seen the flag in this manner, the vast majority in the Airborne did not.

The rebel flag, however, was not the root of the problem but rather a symptom. The disciplinary difficulties within the Regiment were not uniquely airborne. They were simply a failure of leadership. Former Regimental Commanders, Major-Generals Gaudreau and Pitts have both made the point that this was the root of the Airborne's demise.[114] Gaudreau was sure that the Regiment's problems were a result of the negligence of officers and senior NCOs in regard to discipline.[115]

The dilemma of inadequate guidance and supervision was, once again, not an inherent 'airborne thing,' but a result of a failing in the Army leadership. Major Hammond observed that the major systemic problem was the fact that the Airborne "relied on other regiments with their own self-interest at heart for manning."[116] Brigadier-General Beno thought that the Regiment was "not well served by those who select personnel, particularly for command positions, for service in the unit."[117] These assessments were reinforced by a former Commander of the Army,

Lieutenant-General Gordon Reay. He conceded that the "selection of some of the officers and NCOs posted to the Canadian Airborne Regiment in recent years, has not been as deliberate as it should have been in this high readiness unit." Reay believed that this "ultimately resulted in leadership shortcomings, ill-discipline, and the emergence of a small lawless element whose challenges to authority and intolerable actions in operations, disproportionately overshadowed and discredited the achievements of the remainder of the Regiment."[118]

Notwithstanding this admission to his internal DND audience, the Army commander seemingly did little to alter the public perception of the Airborne as an ill-disciplined and out-of-control unit. Journalist Peter Worthington has made a poignant observation: "what has been overlooked is that the Airborne's performance in Somalia verged on the spectacular until the prisoner incident."[119] Furthermore, the Regiment was almost completely transformed for the better after the unit's return from Somalia. Colonel Semianiw has noted that the wholesale house clearing during the summer of 1993, resulted in a seventy percent replacement of the leadership ranks.[120] Colonel John Joly, the Director of Infantry at the time reported "the problems that were evident in the Cdn AB Regt as a result of the Somalia experience have been redressed."[121] Even Reay believed that the significant change in the manning of the Regiment during this period represented a rejuvenation that "restored the leadership, discipline and obedience."[122]

But in the end, and in spite of these reforms over the intervening three years between the death in Somalia and the disbandment of the Airborne the facts no longer seemed to matter. Frustratingly, to the paratroopers there was an appearance that nothing was being done to correct the erroneous perception of the Airborne as an ill-disciplined "rogue regiment." To make matters worse, NDHQ imposed a "gag order" on all members of the Regiment. This only exacerbated the suspicions of the airborne soldiers. Although regulations controlling the dissemination of information, particularly criticism, were always in force, special direction passed through the chain of command in the aftermath of the disbandment announcement in January 1995, apparently from the CDS's office, were now directed specifically at the paratroopers. Quite simply, they were ordered to say absolutely nothing, to anybody, in regard to the controversies that engulfed the Regiment.[123]

These orders limiting the information flow to the public remained a sore point with the paratroopers from the spring of 1993 to disbandment in 1995. Beginning in mid 1992, NDHQ promulgated a series of directives which increasingly tightened the control of public statements that could be made by service members.[124] Reassurances given by senior leaders, and the Director General of Public Affairs, that the tight control was merely to ensure the most accurate, efficient and effective response to on-going media scrutiny was met by skepticism from the airborne soldiers. Their suspicions were apparently well-founded. General Boyle later testified to the Somalia commissioners as to the intent of the "national authority" overseeing the release of information: "we wanted to restrict Land Forces Command, Land Forces Central Area and Petawawa from commenting openly about what was happening, about what was to evolve." He conceded that the motive for these restrictions was largely determined by "command influence" but also grew out of fear of prejudicing on-going courts martial.[125] Nevertheless, officers and soldiers were repeatedly assured that the chain of command would not allow damaging or erroneous stories to go unchallenged.

Unfortunately, few from NDHQ or the Army sprang to the defence of the Canadian Airborne Regiment in public. Brigadier-General Beno angrily decried the fact that "the senior leadership in the Department and the Armed Forces have never challenged the inaccurate and misleading media allegations, nor have they permitted individuals to defend themselves publicly."[126] The frustration became such that Major-General Vernon asked the rhetorical question, "who defends the soldiers?" Events finally convinced Vernon that the "system," especially at National Headquarters, would not protect its own. He charged that "we were rather restrictive in allowing people to speak...and we gave our own troops the impression that, in fact, we were hiding with our heads buried in the sand hoping this whole business would blow over and disappear."[127] The frustration for the dwindling numbers of Airborne supporters in Ottawa and elsewhere was so acute it provoked such former soldiers as Major-General Pitts to complain later that "the treatment of the Airborne Regiment, leading to its disbandment in a climate of rancour and resentment is without precedent in Canada and indeed is almost unheard of in any military circles."[128]

Once back from Somalia the Regiment did reform itself. However, the image of a new and vibrant Airborne had little or no effect and might even have muddied the waters. On one side the critics continued to argue that airborne forces were of marginal value in an operational context, particularly in the case of Canada. On the other side, the patrons of the airborne concept were no longer in a position to carry the day. More importantly, the tempest was no longer centred on the events in Somalia, but rather on the fallibility of the entire military institution, especially those with their hands on the controls. As a result, the perpetuation of inaccurate and misleading myths served a useful purpose. By targeting the Airborne Regiment, the personalities in power used Canada's paratroopers for political purposes as whipping boys for the failure of military leadership. Conveniently the airborne troubles shifted the blame. It was hoped that sacrificing the Canadian Airborne Regiment would disarm the continuing criticism and scrutiny of the Canadian Forces and government. The sacrifice of the Airborne was intended to symbolize the purge of all the Army's apparent problems.

And so, the Airborne Regiment was formally shut down in official ceremonies on the weekend of 4-5 March 1995. By that time and for at least two years prior no one seemed concerned about inaccuracies or halftruths. The disbandment parades were elaborate and very well attended. The emotional address by the commanding officer captured the sentiment of most of those on and off the parade square. Lieutenant-Colonel Kenward summed it all up on behalf of the Regiment:

> Let the message be clear. Those of us who serve the Regiment today are not moving on in disgrace. We have loyally and very credibly carried the standard of soldiering excellence passed to us from those paratroopers who came before. We need not look down but continue to hold our heads high and stare straight ahead, knowing we stood in the door and were always ready to do our duty.[129]

In the end, no matter how it was packaged the reality was that Canada's airborne capability was extinguished, or at best had embarked on a lengthy hiatus. It was the end of an era, the end of the "great adventure." Yet, the words of a former member captured the essence of the surviving paratroopers. He avowed, "you can take away my regiment, but you can never take away my pride in it."[130] In Ottawa, no doubt some soldiers and politicians thought the demise of the Airborne was a good thing, while others smugly believed that the leadership crisis in the military had gone away. They were wrong.

Notes for Chapter Nine

1. E.B. Beno, "The Somalia Affair—Personal Reflections," Beno Papers.
2. *Somalia Commission,* Hearing Transcripts, Vol 54, 3 April 1996, 10834.

3. Interview with author, 24 February 1997.
4. Dianne Collier, *Hurry Up and Wait* (Carp: Creative Bound Inc., 1994), 146.
5. Ibid., 147; Ian Macleod, "Trained for war, sent for peace," *Ottawa Citizen,* 3 May 1993, A1; and Robert Stewart, "The Effect of the Media Frenzy over Somalia on Military Families," [article online], accessed 15 January 1999; available from www.globalserve.net/vertigo/somalia.html.
6. BOI Cdn AB BG—Phase I, Volume XI, A-21/33.
7. Peter T. Haydon, a senior research fellow with the Canadian Institute of Strategic Studies reported that "many members of the press corps are themselves not without bias and, more significantly, far too few of them have adequate knowledge of military structures and procedures." CISS Strategic Datalink No. 62, February 1997, "The Somalia Inquiry: Can it Solve Anything?"
8. Worthington, *Scapegoat,* 175. To make matters worse a blanket gag order took even this option away from those who served. This issue will be dealt with later in the chapter.
9. BOI Cdn AB BG—Phase I, Volume XI, Appendix 3 to Annex A, 1/5.
10. *Somalia Commission*, Transcript of Policy Hearing, Vol 2, 19 June 1995, 281-282.
11. BOI Cdn AB Regt—Phase I, Vol XII, CDS Comments, 15/30.
12. BOI Cdn AB BG—Phase I, Vol XII, 16/30, & 27/30. The latter recommendation was an attempt to stop the parent infantry regiments from sending whomever they chose, without the Cdn AB Regt CO being able to refuse a nominee and receive an alternate in lieu. The BOI recognized that the best candidates were not always sent to the Airborne by the feeder infantry regiments. This is reminiscent of similar remarks made by the Hewson Report almost ten years earlier. Amazingly, the recommendation was made once again to keep regimental affiliations of commandos.
13. Ibid., 29/30. The BOI advised that the "content be thoroughly reviewed to ensure it is sufficiently challenging to suppress any informal drives to create independent rites of passage."
14. Ibid., Summary of Recommendations.
15. *Information Legacy,* Report of the Commission of Inquiry, Vol 1, "Major-General Boyle's Analysis of the De Faye Report, Record 3160. Brigadier-General Beno raised the issue as well, quoting even one of the Board members, Clive Addy, as being unable to explain how certain conclusions were made without the accompanying evidence (example—the myth that Morneault recommended 2 Cdo not deploy because of concerns in regards to their suitability.) Beno reflected that the BOI's focus on incidents rather than issues led to recommendations that were narrow in scope and depth. Letter, Beno to Bercuson, 1 September 1996; and Beno personal notes. Beno Papers.
16. Ibid. Major-General Boyle pointed out "that several issues remained unresolved," and he recommended that the Minister of National Defence, as advised by the CDS, "establish an independent board of inquiry to evaluate the role of the 'chain of command' in the preparation and dispatch of the CAR for its mission to Somalia, and to evaluate NDHQ's performance in the management of the Somalia events, with particular attention to its handling of five incidents (the incident at the Bailey bridge, the March 4th shootings, Mr. Arone's death, the incident at the Red Cross compound on March 17th, and the attempted suicide of MCpl Matchee)." Ironically, he would get caught in his own net.
17. Assessment done by DGFD, "Airborne Capability—Structure Options," 28 April 1993, 4. DHist—NDHQ files on Cdn AB Regt, not filed at time of use.
18. Beno Diary Extracts, 18 August 1992. Beno Papers.
19. Colonel W.M. Holmes, "The Canadian Airborne Regiment Transition," 19 May 1992, 7.
20. Colonel B.M. Archibald (COS LFCA), Letter 1901-7723 (COS), "Command and Control Concept—Canadian Airborne Regiment," 10 September 1993; Letter, LFC Commander to the CDS, 19 April 1994, "The Canadian Airborne Regiment—Recommendations For Consideration," 28 June 1994, 2; Letter, Beno to Major-General MacKenzie (Commander LFCA), 19 January 1993. Beno Papers. Under the new concept the Regiment was still to be available for employment as the Area Immediate Response Unit. However, if a requirement for the unit at the national level occurred the Area IRU task was to be tasked to another unit. As part of the reorganization, SSF was re-designated 2 Canadian Mechanized Brigade Group (2 CMBG). A comment must be made on the individuals in power. At the time the CDS,

LFC commander, COS LFC, and commander LFCA were all PPCLI, and virtually all were viewed as staunch Airborne supporters. All served as paratroopers in one capacity or other in their careers.

21. Message, SSFHQ UNCLAS G3 1825, 02 291640Z Nov 93, "Org Structure of SSF, Cdn AB Regt and 2 RCR." Brigadier-General Beno recalled that Major-General Vernon "kept insisting that the Airborne would become an independent unit and actually ordered that the Regiment take down the SSF patch. However, the executive never arrived." Interview with author, 20 May 1998. The proposed move to independent status sparked another initiative. A proposal for a distinctive shoulder patch consisting of Pegasus was submitted to the Chain of Command. Two problems arose immediately. The first was the question whether a separate patch was warranted and the second was the fact that the Pegasus patch was unacceptable because it only acknowledged the ancestral ties to the 1st Canadian Parachute Battalion but not to the First Special Service Force. A new design was proposed and submitted to the SSF Commander, who subsequently endorsed it. However, the next level of command did not approve it. LFCA HQ stated they did not support the initiative and the issue eventually became a mute point and was buried by the larger concern of survival of the Regiment. Minutes of a Regular Meeting of the Canadian Airborne Regiment—Regimental Executive Meeting (REC) held 26 September 1993, 5/6 and 09 April 1994, 5/7. Major-General J.M.R. Gaudreau stated that he was not surprised by the lack of support due to the "Regiment's uncertain place in the chain of command." He further noted that, "this uncertainty should end after the defence review." Gaudreau's comments were made at the Canadian Airborne Regiment, Regimental Executive Meeting (REC) held 09 April 1994.

22. John Ward, "Top Somali Officer Relieved of Command." *Ottawa Citizen*, 16 September 1993, A3. Lieutenant-Colonel Carol Mathieu was later charged for negligent performance of duty for his command in Somalia. The courtmartial acquitted Mathieu, as did a subsequent re-trial.

23. See Chapter Eight, text and accompanying footnotes 71-73.

24. Interview with author, 16 December 1998. Brigadier-General Greg Mitchell was more blunt. He categorically asserted that Kenward was sent to "clean-up the Regiment, overcome the problems that had built-up over the years, bring back the morale, and salvage the Regiment's pride." Interview with author, 23 January 1998. Mitchell stated that Kenward was a perfect candidate for the job. He noted that the newly appointed CO was not only a tough field soldier but also had insight and was able to see the 'big picture.'

25. Colonel B.M. Archibald (COS LFCA), Letter 1901-7723 (COS), "Command and Control Concept—Canadian Airborne Regiment," 10 September 1993.

26. Ibid.

27. DGFD, "Airborne Capability—Structure Options," 28 April 1993, 4. The report noted that "it appears that an AB option was the original intention of the CDS and central staff when the Immediate Reaction Force (Land) option was first examined."

28. Ibid.

29. The idea of assigning the AMF(L) role was raised as early as the summer of 1992. The regimental commander at the time seems to have sensed the desperation. He wrote, "I have heard a strong rumour that the Regiment will inherit the AMF(L) role in the near future. If this is true then the org of the Regiment will be driven by this fact and we could see considerable changes. I firmly believe that it may be a nugatory effort to launch off on another staff exercise before the future of the Regiment is determined one way or another." W.M. Holmes, "Transition—Cdn AB Regt," 22 June 1992, 1.

30. A bulletin locally produced by the unit, entitled "The Requirement," was widely distributed and posted. It was also embedded in the Regiment's Annual Training Plan. However, it was never officially included in any other DND publications.

31. Interview with author, 16 December 1998. Hammond reinforced a recurring theme. He stated, "we were at the whim of the CO." He compared this to his experience with the American airborne forces. During his visits he noted that their role was clear, as were their exercises. Everything was about supporting national policy. Major Hammond recalled the Canadian aversion to this way of thinking. He had suggested an exercise scenario which entailed "oil drums on the runway at Frobisher Bay" requiring a parachute insertion. Hammond noted that no one was interested. He commiserated that "operations behind enemy lines" and "raids" attracted greater interest and focus.

32. Ibid.
33. Interview with author, 16 December 1998.
34. The argument in regard to the relevance of airborne forces is an emotional one. As with most complex issues it is not as black and white as supporters or detractors may wish others to believe. In the Canadian context airborne forces are not required to fulfill the mandate as given by the government. That is one reason there is no specific mention of airborne or parachute troops in the *1994 White Paper*. However, they are essential for the Army as a training vehicle, unifying tool, and link to allies.
35. Minute sheet accompanying director of infantry, LFC HQ, "Estimate of the Impact to Re-Establish 1 Canadian Parachute Battalion (1 Can Para)," 28 February 1994.
36. Letter, CDS to the MND, "The Parachute Role and the Canadian Airborne Regiment—Recommendations Regarding the Future," 28 June 1994. *Information Legacy,* Evidentiary Exhibits, Document Control Number 001877, p. 24093. The report was required as a result of direction given to the previous CDS by the MND "to make recommendations as to the future of the Canadian Airborne Regiment." The CDS also endorsed Lieutenant-General Reay's recommendation that the Regiment in its present configuration be separated from the brigade group structure, and be put under the command of the LFCA Commander.
37. DGFD, "Airborne Capability—Structure Options," 28 April 1993, 1. Italics are my own.
38. Ibid., 5.
39. Ibid., 5. The report opined that either a battalion or single airborne companies within three separate regular infantry battalions would suffice noting that there were advantages and disadvantages to both. The team's unemotional tack towards the issue underlined the absence of former paratroopers in its company. Their ambivalence was also underlined in their unsubstantiated observation that "the speed with which other NATO countries have contributed AB forces may be a false precedent and have more to do with a post cold war need to rationalize their continued existence than any legitimate mission analysis."
40. *Regimental Standing Orders for The Canadian Airborne Regiment—1994*, 6/75 & 10/75; "Regimental TOE," 26 October 1993; Cdn AB Regt, "Increased Manning Level Canadian Airborne Regiment," 13 December 1993; and Lieutenant-Colonel Peter Kenward, "The Last 27 Years," *Maroon Beret*—Final Edition.
41. Commander SSF, "Manning of Cdn AB Regt," 2 May 1994. The SSF commander noted a central weakness with the proposed policy. Although endorsing the need for quality personnel in the Airborne, he wrote, "This is a command and leadership issue, which cannot be solved by writing more rules."
42. Lieutenant-Colonel Peter Kenward, "Regimental Commander," *Maroon Beret*—Final Edition, 5. The unit also overwhelmingly dominated the brigade level Skill at Arms and Sports competitions as well as the Area Biathlon championships.
43. Message, LFCHQ, Unclas G3 537, 29 2000Z June 1994, "Operation Order No. 1"; and "3 Commando—3 Cdo Back in Africa," *The Connecting File—1994,* 22-23. OP Passage was the Canadian sponsored humanitarian initiative intended as an immediate emergency response to the cholera epidemic that was ravaging the overcrowded refugee camps, as well as the transient Rwandan population that was attempting to return to their homes at the cessation of hostilities. This mission was of two months' duration. OP Lance, which was a standard six month mission, was the Canadian contribution to the UN Assistance Mission In Rwanda II (UNAMIR II). 1 CDHSR was responsible for the provision of communications for the UN Mission Headquarters, as well as for the infantry battalions of the five contributing African countries that made up the military element of UNAMIR II.
44. This created great resentment. Throughout the preparation and actual tour the units were quick to tell the Airborne CO and staff that the respective platoons were "Under Command," and as a result the Regiment had no say in regard to employment or in-theatre policy. However, when the incidents occurred the same officers quickly pointed out how the errant individuals did not belong to them but were in fact members of the Regiment. Undeniably, the incidents which transpired were unnecessary and demonstrated poor judgement. The first event happened on OP Passage as a result of the foolishness of two off-duty paratroopers who became drunk in their quarters and decided to become "blood

brothers." The resultant cuts to their palms required stitches and despite the fact that the individuals were fit to report for duty at their next scheduled shift, the incident raised a furor making the national news as yet another case of secret airborne rituals in the night. The two individuals were repatriated immediately, as a clear indication to all, that no stupidity or act that would reflect badly on the Airborne Regiment or Commando would be tolerated. The event became frustrating to everyone in-theatre and back in Petawawa, as accuracy of reporting was lost in the media frenzy. Lou Nodelman, an editorial columnist reported the two paratroopers "almost killed themselves in drunken blood rituals where cuts were so severe they were airlifted to Canada for medical treatment." The second, and more serious lack of judgement transpired in the platoon on OP Lance. A Section second-in-command, while tasked to provide security for a local building, allowed several soldiers not on duty, to consume beer and discharge shotgun blasts at the large stone structure. The master-corporal in charge was quickly and severely disciplined by the 1 CDHSR CO, who sentenced him, in a summary trial, to ninety days in the CF Detention Barracks. Not surprisingly, this incident as well quickly exploded in the media and brought renewed criticism of the Airborne Regiment. The Platoon Commander, Captain James Price, commented, "We've felt the weight of the Regiment on our shoulders, and we knew that every little mistake would be magnified by ten." DND News Release, NR-94,039, "Negligent Performance of Duty in Rwanda," 16 September, 1994; Bruce Wallace, "Fighting a Reputation," *Maclean's*, 30 January 1995, 17; Interviews with Captains James Price, Dave Simpkin, Warrant Officer Hartnel, Master-Corporal Domini, and Corporals Howett and Rattray.

45. Letter, Major-General G.C. Tousignant, to CDS, 21 October 1994, "Performance of Composite Canadian Platoon." The Force Commander further noted, "a small contingent of Canadian soldiers [8 Platoon] made a significant impact on UNAMIR operations by deploying quickly; conducting detailed and thorough patrols; taking the time and effort to win the confidence of the local government, military and citizens; providing accurate and timely information back to my HQ; and constantly displaying a 'can do' attitude. It is a distinct pleasure to have these fine soldiers under my operational command." The 1 CDSHR Sitreps sent back to Canada (information copy received by the Airborne Regiment) described the patrols as "Signal Regiment Patrols." Oddly enough, no effort was made to point out that the stellar performance was that of paratroopers from the Airborne Regiment.

46. Wallace, "Fighting a Reputation," 17.

47. In the matter of the Arone killing, most observers agree that top officials in DND learned of the death within 48 hours of the event, yet it appeared that a decision at containment rather than disclosure was taken. Even Major-General Boyle reached this conclusion. See *Information Legacy,* Report of the Commission of Inquiry, Vol 1, "MGen Boyle's Analysis of the De Faye Report, Record 3160; and Hearing Transcripts, Vol 95, testimony of Colonel Haswell 18480-18555. Kim Campbell's own chief of staff (at the time) acknowledged that he was informed of the death only hours after it occurred and Campbell herself stated she was briefed around 17 March. See Luke Fisher, "On the Defence," *Maclean's,* 26 July 1993, 16; David Pugliese, "HQ in Somalia Coverup," *Ottawa Citizen,* 14 June 1997, A1; D'Arcy Jenish, "What did He Know?" *Maclean's,* 15 April 1996, 17-18; "Colonel cites politics in delay over Somalia," *The Globe & Mail,* 14 September 1996, A1; and David Pugliese, "Military hid murder to shield Kim Campbell, inquiry told," *Ottawa Citizen,* 14 September 1996, A1/2. As early as 22 January 1993, and again on 1 March 1993, due to the expected leadership candidacy of the Minister of National Defence, Kim Campbell, the Deputy Minister, Robert Fowler, had reminded members attending DEM that it was necessary to exercise "extreme sensitivity in all matters relating to public statements, speeches, press releases." *Information Legacy,* Report of the Commission of Inquiry, Vol 1, Passage of Information about the March 4th Incident, Record 2888. The tendency for the military to try and anticipate the "politically preferred" option prompted Major-General Stewart to lament, "too many of the officers filling the senior appointments at these headquarters [NDHQ & FMC] were too much in tune with the bureaucrats and politicians." As a result, he concluded that "the political authorities were never faced with straight forward military advice." Letter, Stewart to Professor David Bercuson, 15 January 1996, 3. Stewart Papers. After a lengthy study of the Somalia Inquiry and related issues, Peter Haydon, a senior research fellow at the Canadian Institute of Strategic Studies, concluded that "military leaders must not attempt to be political or to construct their advice in politically acceptable terms. Their responsibility is to provide sound military advice." "The Somalia Inquiry: Can It Solve Anything?" Strategic Datalink No. 62, February 1997, 4.

48. A decision not to award a campaign medal caused enormous bitterness. The failure to provide this well deserved award painted the entire Canadian contingent as somehow guilty and undeserving. The question of a campaign medal was continually raised with the military and political leadership. The response given was constantly that the medal would "be issued in the near future," or that it was just "awaiting ministerial approval." The fact remained that the leadership, both military and civilian, refused to publicly recognize the accomplishments of deserving service personnel due to the potential "optics" of awarding a medal for a mission that was now wrapped in controversy in the press. The Board of Inquiry—The Canadian Airborne Battle Group, included in its recommendations, released on 31 August 1993, that "the CF formally recognize, at an appropriate scale, time and place, the exceptional contribution by members of CJFS and the Battle Group to the operation in Somalia, recognizing that this operation was carried out under some of the most arduous climatic and cultural challenges to which Canadian soldiers have been subjected in years." On 13 November 1996, Doug Young, the newly appointed MND, finally announced that the government would award a campaign medal to those who served with honour in Somalia. On 17 June 1997, well over four years after the mission, the first awards ceremony was conducted in Ottawa for approximately fifty personnel who received their medals from His Excellency the Right Honourable Romeo LeBlanc, Governor General of Canada. His Excellency stated, "We as a country admit our mistakes, but let us also have the generosity to praise the great majority of our Forces in Somalia who did their duty and more, with discipline, dedication and compassion." DND News Release Communique, "Governor General Presents Somalia Medal to Members of the Canadian Forces," 17 June 1997; and Jim Bronskill, "Troops who served with honour decorated for Somalia service," *Ottawa Citizen,* 18 June 1997, A1.

49. See *Information Legacy,* Report of the Commission of Inquiry, Vol 3, General Jean Boyle, Record 9550; Vol 5, Findings, Record 10043; and Vol 5, Allegations of Cover-up, Record 12635. See also Peter Desbarats, *Somalia Cover-Up. A Commissioner's Journal* (Toronto: McCelland & Stewart, 1997),157 & 277; Peter Worthington, *Scapegoat,* 155; Scott Taylor and Brian Nolan, *Tarnished Brass* (Lester Publishing Ltd, 1996); and Scott Taylor and Brian Nolan, *Tested Mettle* (Ottawa: Esprit de Corps Books, 1998), 36-37, 73-74, 81-83, 98, and 197.

50. *Information Legacy,* Report of the Commission of Inquiry, Vol 1, "MGen Boyle's Analysis of the De Faye Report, Record 3160; and Vol 5, Findings, Record 10043, and Vol 5, Allegations of Cover-up, Record 12635. The Commission Report noted, "We have considered, in detail, evidence relating to the response of the chain of command to allegations of cover-up in relation to the March 4th incident. Regrettably, we have concluded that efforts were made, in various ways, to cover up or conceal information about that incident." See also, Dale Grant, "The Demise of Canada's Military?" *Military Technology,* Vol 20, No. 6, 1996, 11; and Coulon, 97-98.

51. Letter, E.B. Beno, Commander SSF, to Commander LFCA, 5 May 1993, "PAFF Strategy—Somalia Investigation and Inquiry." Beno Papers.

52. Letter, Commander LFCA to DCDS, 2. Beno Papers.

53. E-mail Commander LFCA to Commander SSF, 14 April 1994. Beno Papers.

54. Presentation by Dr. Daniel Bon, "Current Issues in Defence Policy," at Queens University, 22 September 1997. Brigadier-General Ian Douglas was more blunt. He angrily argued that "the Airborne Regiment was hung out to dry!" Speech given by Ian Douglas at the Canadian Airborne Museum Fund Raising Dinner, Ottawa, 4 June 1999.

55. Letter, Worthington to Beno, 5 July 1996. On 20 March 1995, under an Order in Council, P.C. 1995-442 a three member commission was established to examine the 'Somalia Affair' in detail. The scope of any public inquiry was determined by its terms of reference which were divided into two parts. The first part charged the commission to inquire into and report generally on the chain of command system, leadership, discipline, operations, actions, and decisions of the Canadian Forces, and on the actions and decisions of the Department of National Defence in respect of the Somalia operation. The second part of the terms of reference required the commission to examine specific matters relating to the pre-deployment, in-theatre, and post-theatre phases of the Somalia operation. In January 1997, the MND announced that Cabinet had decided that the Inquiry had gone on long enough and that all hearings would end on or about March 31, 1997. The final report with recommendations was required by June 30, 1997. *Information Legacy,* Report of the Commission of Inquiry, Vol 1, Terms of Reference;

and "Briefing Note for the Minister of National Defence—Commission of Inquiry into the Deployment of the Canadian Forces to Somalia (Somalia Commission), prepared 5 October 1996.

56. Presentation by Dr. Daniel Bon, "Current Issues in Defence Policy," at Queens University, 22 September 1997.

57. Interview with author, 10 March 1997.

58. Interview with author, 1 December 1997.

59. Interview with author, 16 December 1998.

60. Ibid.

61. The video depicted a black member of 1 Commando tied to a tree, and later being led around with the message "I love the KKK" written on his back. Other scenes depicted urine and faeces being spread on individuals, as well as the passage of regurgitated food from one individual to another. The video's impact was such that the CDS apparently offered his resignation to the MND because the video represented a breakdown of leadership and discipline. The MND refused it. CBC and CTV Nightly News, 18-21 January 1995; *Somalia Commission,* Transcript of Evidentiary Hearing, Vol 49, 20 February 1996, testimony of General De Chastelain, 9917-18; Taylor and Nolan, *Tested Mettle,* 207; Luke Fisher, "Canada's Shame," *Maclean's,* 30 January 1995, 14; and Dave Rider, "Video Outrage," *Ottawa Sun,* 19 January 1995, 4.

62. Major-General (retd) Terry Liston stated that the Airborne Regiment, "represented a type of macho undisciplined culture that senior officers have been concerned about ever since the Airborne was formed." Dave Rider, "Veterans stunned by news," *Ottawa Sun,* 24 January 1995, 2. The economic motive was also one that cannot be ignored. Many analysts, based on this rationale and the continuing embarrassment caused by the Regiment predicted its demise. Gwynn Dyer stated, "and for a federal government determined to cut defence spending, the scandal-plagued Canadian Airborne may look like one luxury it could live without." Luke Fisher, "We are Soldiering On," *Maclean's,* 28 March 1994, 29. See also Peter Worthington, "Armed Forces Fall Guys," *Toronto Sun,* 5 April 1994, 11 and "Few Good Men," *Ottawa Sun,* 12 April 1994, 11. The pressure was obvious by the level of cuts required at the time of the downsizing of the Regiment. The MND commented, "Since 1991-92, operational activities have been reduced by about 25% because of cumulative reductions in operations and maintenance funding. This reduced level of activity will need to be continued." Unfortunately the Regiment was very effective at drawing unwanted attention. *National Defence—Budget Impact*, February 1994, 2.

63. LFCHQ, "Estimate of the Impact to Re-establish 1 Canadian Parachute Battalion," 28 February 1994, 5.

64. CBC and CTV Nightly News, 20 & 21 January 1995; and Fisher, "Canada's Shame," 14.

65. Interview with author, 16 December 1998.

66. The efforts and energy of the Regiment during this period were focussed on providing information for its defence. The Regimental and Commando leadership conducted their own inquiry to determine whether similar events had occurred since the 1992 video, as well as, to assemble a defence that was centred on highlighting the accomplishments and changes since the return of the Regiment from Somalia. Despite disagreement and warning from some of his "War Cabinet" Lieutenant-Colonel Kenward decided on a "line in the sand" strategy, that basically rested on the fact that his arrival marked a new era and that he personally had put an end to any objectionable practises and behaviour in the Regiment. However, this stratagem was short-lived. The floor collapsed on the CO's plan when it became known that another video, taken in August 1994, depicting another 1 Commando "initiation party" existed. The argument that the new CO represented a new era simply imploded. Although the 1994 video was not as controversial as the 1992 tape, it still contained objectionable behaviour. At this point a fatal mistake was made. Throughout the week of investigation, no one viewed the tape. Its content was assessed only through the questioning of the OC of 1 Commando, who steadfastly maintained that it was a "beer call" with a few drinking games. Kenward testified in front of the Somalia Commission that "I had Major Juneau confirm on no less than three occasions between 18-20 January that his description of the '94 Beer Call was accurate." An atmosphere of desperation was evident. The Regiment's strategy hinged on the proclaimed "line in the sand" and no one wanted to admit that perhaps it had been crossed. On 22 January, the CO conducted a final confirmation meeting with his "War Cabinet" prior to delivering the completed investigation to the Commanders of LFCA and

the SSF. The group was instructed to remain in place to ensure all were available in the event that there was clarification or action required. At this point, the 1994 tape was viewed by some of the members present. It quickly became evident that the tape was another time bomb and although not on the same level as the 1992 video, it did contain unacceptable behaviour. Regimental credibility was now further strained. The CO, who had just completed his briefing to the commanders of LFCA and the SSF, was now required to return and explain to his superiors that the results of the investigation he submitted just minutes ago were not accurate, that in fact, the 1994 video did contain objectionable behaviour. The description of the behaviour in the tape as innocuous, later led to the firing of the LFCA commander as the result of allegations that he knowingly misled the Commander of the Army, CDS and MND, as to its contents. Author's Diary; Interview with Colonel Semianiw, 1 December 1997; Loomis, *Somalia Affair*, 601; *Debates,* 8 February 1995, 9326, and 9 February 1995, 9417-18, 10 February 1995, 9466; and Jeff Sallot, "General Punished for Staff's Failing," *The Globe and Mail,* 9 September 1996.

67. Letter, Commander LFCA, 1080-7723 (Comd), 19 January 1995. Both members of the investigation team, Colonel Semianiw and Major Jim Ferron, the SSF G4 at the time, were carefully scrutinized. Neither of the two had ever served in the Regiment. Semianiw's choice was made because of his reputation as an "efficient and sharp" staff officer. Brigadier-General Mitchell stated that "Vernon had faith that Semianiw could cut through and get to the core of the problem in the short time frame." Interviews with Mitchell and Semianiw, 23 January 1998 and 1 December 1998. See also *Information Legacy,* Letter Commander LFCA to the CDS / MND, "Report Fact Finding Mission Into the Canadian Airborne Regiment," 22 January 1995.

68. *Information Legacy,* Letter Commander LFCA to the CDS / MND, "Report Fact Finding Mission Into the Canadian Airborne Regiment," 22 January 1995, 3.

69. Ibid., Annex B—Military Police Investigation Concerning Initiation Rites in the Cdn AB Regt (Sitrep—Airborne Initiation Video Investigation). The report stated, "during the investigation yet another video has been turned over to the MP by Cdn AB Regt authorities. This tape, taken following the 1994 airborne indoctrination course, has been reviewed by Petawawa MP and is judged to be relatively benign. Co Cdn AB Regt has requested CO 2 MP Pl to conduct an investigation into this recent tape to answer the same questions as are being sought in the case of the initiation tape."

70. The CO was assured that he would be told of the decision prior to the airing of the MND's address on national television. Meanwhile, in Petawawa, the demoralized Regiment drew itself up in the early afternoon on the wind-swept Nicklin Parade Square in numbing cold to hear the MND's decision. At 1450 hours, the CO appeared and stated that he had received no call in regard to the fate of the paratroopers. He then dismissed the Regiment to their respective quarters to watch the announcement on television. Several minutes later a deathly silence intertwined with utter disbelief and shock permeated the Airborne lines. The apparent disdain of the paratroopers held by elements of the senior leadership now made itself felt. The respect associated with being told their fate via the chain-of-command was absent. Instead they were briefed by the CBC. Although the CDS could not save the Airborne this time, it was decided that the disbandment would not be a silent passage into the night. The ceremony was to be conducted with dignity. The SSF Commander relayed the following direction, "The acts of a few individuals which led to the Regiment's disbandment are not in any way reflective of the standards of performance or behaviour exhibited by the vast majority of officers, NCOs, and soldiers who have filled its ranks. Accordingly, the Regiment's disbandment must be reflective of the high standards established by that majority and should therefore be characterized by dignity and professionalism." Brigadier-General N.B. Jeffries, Letter 1901-7723 (Comd), 16 February 1995, "Disbandment of the Canadian Airborne Regiment—Implementation Order," 1/13. The disbandment was structured to occur in three phases: Phase 1—Ceremonial Activities (completed by 5 March 1995); Phase 2—Re-Organization (to be in effect at 31 0730 March 1995); and Phase 3—Technical Closure (to be complete NLT 01 October 1995).

71. Speaking Notes For the Honourable David Collenette, P.C., M.P., Minister of National Defence Press Conference, 23 January 1995, 11-12; MND Press Conference, telecast on the CBC, 1500 hours, 23 January 1995; Dave Rider, "End of an Era," *Ottawa Sun,* 24 January 1995, 16; and *Debates,* 9 February 1995, 9418. The CO was warned of the decision five minutes prior the statement by SSF HQ which itself had just received word of the announcement. The Commander of the Army sent a message the same

day that clearly stated, "This was a decision that was made solely by the Minister despite the advice of the Chain of Command." Message, Comd 014, "Disbandment of Cdn AB Regt," 232240Z Jan 95.

72. Laura Bobak, *Ottawa Sun,* 27 January 1995.

73. Brenda Branswell, "Airborne Jumps into history with spirit unbroken," *Ottawa Citizen*, 5 March 1995.

74. Ibid.

75. Interview with Colonel Semianiw, 1 December 1997. See also endnotes 64-67 this chapter.

76. Rider, "End of an Era," 16.

77. *Information Legacy,* The Report of the Commission of Inquiry, Vol 3, "Factors in Decision Making—General Jean Boyle," Record 6694-9550.

78. It was well known that Boyle had the ear and trust of both the DM and the MND. One staff officer who worked in the Director NDHQ Secretariat office noted that Boyle "let it be known that he had influence with the MND" and "he didn't mind dropping the MND's name." The officer also recounted that there was a distinct impression that the decisions taken by the MND were influenced by a very small group to which Boyle belonged. Confidential Interview, February 1998; Peter Worthington, "Two Generals, one leader," *The Toronto Sun*, 17 September, 1996, 11; and "Memorandum for Record," March 1995, Beno Papers. See also Winslow, 37.

79. MND Speaking Notes, 23 January 1995, 9-11; *Debates,* 9 February 1995, 9418; and Letter, MND to Brigadier-General Beno, 6 April 1995. Beno Papers. The "systemic" problem was framed in terms of the inherent difficulties associated with paratroopers and airborne organizations. The issues of role, relevancy, relationship to the Army at large and manning practises were not included in the terms "definition."

80. DGPA, *Canadians on Defence 1994-1995 Yearbook* (Ottawa: DND, 1995), 14-18.

81. Winslow, 138-141; Letter Commander LFC to CDS, "The Canadian Airborne Regiment—Recommendations for Consideration," 19 April 1994, 1; Letter MND to E. Beno, 6 April 1995; Peter Cheney, "The Airborne Story," *The Gazette,* 22 January 1994, B1 and "Canada's Rebel Soldiers," *The Edmonton Sunday Journal,* 30 January 1994, D1.

82. "A Soldier's Viewpoint," *esprit de corps,* Vol 6, Issue 12, April 1999, 6.

83. Interviews with Brigadier-Generals Theriault and Douglas, 28 April 1998 and 18 March 1998. See also Bercuson, *Significant Incident,* 205. Bercuson quotes Major-General Pitts, Brigadier-General Cox and Colonel Fraser discussing the issue. It was apparently overlooked that continual UN tours in the former Yugoslavia exposed Canadian soldiers to brutality, corruption, genocide, institutional drunkenness and racism, yet these behaviours were not absorbed or accepted. Exposure is not the problem. How you deal with it, is. It is a question of leadership and education.

84. CBC-TV Current Affairs, " the 5th Estate—SOMALIA" (unofficial transcript of subject episode), 17 October 1995, 1. Mathieu further claimed that "it's my superiors who are responsible."

85. *Information Legacy,* Report of the Commission of Inquiry, Executive Summary, 1.

86. Cotton, "Military Mystique"; Winslow, 138-141; Peter Cheney, "The Airborne Story," *The Gazette,* 22 January 1994, B1 and "Canada's Rebel Soldiers," *The Edmonton Sunday Journal,* 30 January 1994, D1.

87. Desbarats, 3. See also Bercuson, *Significant Incident,* 242; and Winslow, 8.

88. Interview with author, 6 June 1998. Another former paratrooper, Colonel Rick Hatton, concurred. He acknowledged that the "problems were of our own making." He further conceded that the "Army failed badly to sort out the Airborne Regiment." Interview with author, 16 December 1998. Major-General Gaudreau concluded that the disbandment of the Regiment was "in the end a self-inflicted wound [by the Army]." Letter to author, 18 September 1998.

89. Interview with author, 14 April 1997.

90. Brigadier-General N.B. Jeffries, "Future Airborne Capability," SSF Staff paper, 30 January 1995, 3.

91. Letter, Commander of the Army, to the CDS, "Response to Leadership and Discipline Issues—Canadian Airborne Regiment Board of Inquiry," 28 October 1993. He further admitted that the problem was also compounded by the fact that "superiors, on occasion, excused the conduct of the Regiment because of

a certain mystique surrounding the 'maroon beret.'" See also Chapter 7, text and accompanying footnotes 113 & 114.

92. Interview with author, 16 December 1998. Donna Winslow conceded, "when I started my study [sociocultural study as commissioned by the Somalia Inquiry] I had a negative image of airborne soldiers, much like most civilians, based on Hollywood stereotypes, but I was constantly surprised." She further noted her amazement at the depth of reflection Airborne soldiers were capable of. Winslow presentation at the Canadian Council for International Peace and Security Seminar, Novotel Conference Centre, Ottawa, 11 December 1997.

93. Beno, "The Way Ahead," 8 & 13. Beno Papers.

94. Editorial, *esprit de corps*, Vol 4, No. 2, 9. See also Peter Worthington, "A blind eye to a regiment's sins," *Ottawa Sun,* 1 August 1996, 11.

95. Beno, "The Somali Affair," 2. Beno Papers.

96. Cdn AB Regt BG—BOI, Phase I, Vol XI, Annex C, C-5/8.

97. Canadian Airborne Forces Association (CAFA) Written Submission Number 2 to the Commission of Inquiry into the Deployment of Canadian Forces to Somalia, Februay 1997. Beno Papers.

98. Interview with author, 1 December 1997. Lieutenant-Colonel Ferron also attested that the Regiment did not have a reputation worse than anyone else in the Brigade prior to the hazing video. Interview with author, 8 April 1998. See also *Information Legacy,* Letter Commander LFCA to the CDS / MND, "Report Fact Finding Mission Into the Canadian Airborne Regiment," 22 January 1995, 2.

99. *Information Legacy,* Hearing Transcripts, Vol 3, 5 October 1995, testimony of Major-General Gaudreau, 560.

100. LFC, "Estimate of the Impact to Re-Establish 1 Canadian Parachute Battalion," 28 February 1994, 2-3.

101. *Information Legacy,* Evidentiary Exhibits, "Summary of Court Martial Offences, Period 1 January 1988-31 December 1992," Document Control No. 000226, DND Document No. 200146. As with all statistical data, there is a degree of unreliability due to interpretation. For instance, the data given contains an inherent danger. Often a high number of trials is viewed as a sign of ill-discipline and a unit out of control. However, the converse is likely. It could be demonstrative of good control and a no-tolerance approach. Conversely, a low number of charges could be indicative of a lax, laissé-faire approach where the leadership is weak and reticent to alienate its subordinates. The use of this data must be weighed in conjunction with the other evidence. Further indications of the scope of problem was evidenced in a former SSF commander's observation during the period 1992-1993. He observed that in regard to drug problems, the soldiers returning from Germany were the prevalent concern in Petawawa. Beno, "Attitudes and Values," 2, Beno Papers.

102. *Somalia Commission,* Document Book 8, Racism, "Right-Wing Extremism at CFB Petawawa, SII 026 / 93," 6 May 1993; and Beno, "Attitudes and Values," 2, Beno Papers. The SIU report also noted that the allegations / evidence against the individuals was in most cases both dated and very weak. Lieutenant-Colonel Ron Bragdon emphasized the injustice of the allegations against the Airborne Regiment. He recalled that in the mid eighties a 2 PPCLI CO, who had never served in the Airborne, and who was seen as a protégé of the incumbent regimental colonel, who also loathed the Airborne, rid himself of those soldiers who were suspected of adhering to white supremacist ideology by posting them to the Regiment. Interview with author, 7 October 1998. The issue of the use of derogatory racial terms is also disingenuous. J.A. Barber's studies led him to conclude that "beyond the well known fact that servicemen serving abroad almost invariably adopt derogatory slang terms to describe any foreigners with whom they come in regular contact, there is also scholarly evidence to the effect that foreign service is more likely to reinforce parochialism than it is to broaden understanding." Winslow, 256.

103. Winslow, 39.

104. *Information Legacy,* Letter Commander LFCA to the CDS / MND, "Report Fact Finding Mission Into the Canadian Airborne Regiment," 22 January 1995.

105. Interview with author, 17 July 1997.

106. Presentation by Donna Winslow, "Culture in the Army," to the Combined Land Staff at NDHQ, Ottawa, 3 April 1997. Winslow defined culture as the behavioural patterns that new members are encouraged to follow. She noted that "culture is not the end but how we do things." Winslow emphasized the problem of affiliated commandos. She stated that regimental affiliation heightened the belief that each commando had its own distinct regimental sub-culture that fostered a "we don't do it that way in our regiment" approach. The danger she pointed out was that this also fostered a mentality that the misdeeds or problems of one commando or regiment would not be corrected by members from another regiment for fear of meddling in someone else's business, as well as a diffident, "it's not my problem." See also Winslow's "Socio-Cultural Inquiry" for the Commission of Inquiry, 68-75 and 96-101.

107. See text and accompanying endnotes, Chapter Seven, 64-67. Brigadier-General Mitchell recalled the absolute disbelief, horror, and shock by those former paratroopers, including Vernon, who were at LFCA Headquarters at the time of the hazing video. He stated that there was a collective sentiment that this was not "our Regiment" and that none of those present had ever heard or seen anything remotely like it in their day. This feeling was shared with those serving in the Regiment at the time as well. The only recognized or sanctioned airborne initiation activity had always been the Airborne Indoctrination Course begun in 1975 by Colonel Fraser. The AIC was a gruelling seven to ten day training course that provided a refresher of infantry and parachuting skills. At the end of the course the participants were awarded their coins and Maroon Berets. The only other activity was the "camming-up" of a new member's face during his first jump with the Regiment. This activity usually entailed military issue camouflage being liberally applied to a paratrooper's face and hands while waiting to board the aircraft for the drop. See also Worthington, *Scapegoat,* 56 & 244.

108. It is difficult to discuss this issue without fear of being labelled anti-francophone. But, the fact of the matter is that the R22eR, as a regiment, have seven murders to their record since the early eighties. Furthermore, the machete killing of the Fort Colonge civilian in 1985, which prompted the Hewson Report, was also committed by a member who had been recently posted to 1 Commando. The point to be made is not one of race or culture, but rather that the Airborne or more specifically, the "paratrooper," was not the problem. They both individually and collectively were representative of the Army and CF. The problem was an institutional one. See Worthington, *Scapegoat*, 314-317; Peter Worthington "Armed Forces Fall Guys?" *Toronto Sun,* 5 April 1994, 11 and Worthington, "A Blind Eye to a Regiment's Sins," *Ottawa Sun,* 1 August 1996, 11.

109. See endnote 86, Chapter Eight.

110. Interview with author, 7 October 1998.

111. *Information Legacy,* Document Control No. 902569; and interview with Anthony Balasavecius, 1 June 1999; See also Peter Cheney, "The Airborne Story," *Montreal Gazette,* 22 January 1994, B1; Bercuson, 211; and Winslow, 206-209.

112. *Information Legacy,* Document Control No. 901874; Document Control No. 000196, "Annex A—Commander SSF Comments—Canadian Airborne Regiment—Preparations and Activities Related to OP CORDON," 22 October 1992; Document Control No. 900520, DND No.16124, DND Project Pegasus, Major Seward, 25 May 1993; and Document Control No. 000321, DND No. 011724, "Review of Controversial Items," BOI, 11 July 1993. See also endnote 113 this chapter. Major Seward testified, "these guys are nineteen, twenty years and it's, they're looking for an identity, Okay? To set them apart, and that's why they latched on to the rebel mentality and the rebel flag."

113. *Information Legacy,* Hearing Transcripts, Vol 4, testimony of Colonel Homes, 595-97. Lieutenant-Colonel Morneault commented, "I believe this whole Rebel flag thing has been blown out of proportion. That is my personal opinion, that is has been blown out of proportion from the outset and I thought I told the military Board of Inquiry two years ago the same thing." Ibid., Hearing Transcripts, Vol 36, January 1996, testimony of Lieutenant-Colonel Morneault, 6942. See also Bercuson, 211.

114. *Somalia Commission,* Transcript of Policy Hearing, Vol 4, 21 June 1995, 627.

115. Letter to author, 18 September 1998.

116. Interview with author, 16 December 1998.

117. Beno, personal correspondence, 10 February 1994. Beno Papers.

118. Letter, Reay to CDS, "Responses to de Faye BOI," 28 October 1993, 2.

119. Letter, Worthington to Beno, 5 July 1996. Beno Papers.

120. Interview with author, 1 December 1997; *Information Legacy,* Document Control No. 900234, DND No. 388174, "[LFCA] Report—Fact Finding Mission into the Canadian Airborne Regiment," Annex F: Personnel and Policy changes within the Cdn AB Regt, 22 January 1995. There was a 66% turnover in the personnel of the Cdn AB Regt as of January 1995. Rotation out of unit (all ranks) for 1992-94 was based on a unit strength of 594 pers and represented an approximate 48% changeover of personnel in the Airborne Regiment.

121. LFCHQ, "Estimate of the Impact to Re-Establish 1 Canadian Parachute Battalion (1 Can Para)," 28 February 1994, 5.

122. Letter, Reay to CDS, "Responses to de Faye BOI," 28 October 1993, 3. Major Hammond, OC 2 Commando noted the change in his sub-unit. Of the 38 commanders, from the rank of master-corporal to major, only two were with the Commando in Somalia. James Hammond, "How about a little respect for the Canadian Airborne," *The Globe and Mail,* 31 January 1995, A19; and Geoffrey York, "Military Targets Airborne Rogues," *The Globe and Mail,* 28 March 1994, A1. At time of disbandment 3 Commando's position was similar. The analysis conducted in response to the hazing video investigation revealed that since APS 1993, 83% of the officers and 67% of the senior NCOs were newly posted in to the Commando.

123. Direction was explicit and was passed during the weekly Commanding Officer Orders Groups. Officers and soldiers of the Regiment were under no circumstances to comment on any aspect of the on-going inquiries or courts martial. Moreover, they were not authorized to comment or speak to the media, regardless of how offensive or erroneous they felt a story may be. The CO explained that the Army would centrally control the dissemination and correction of information.

124. George Orsyk (pseudonym), "The Canadian Military Gag Order. A Brief History," *esprit de corps,* Vol 6, Issue 4, February 1998, 4-5.

125. *Information Legacy,* Hearing Transcripts, Vol 88, 14 August 1996, testimony of General Boyle, 17152.

126. Beno, "The Somalia Drama," 4. Beno Papers.

127. *Information Legacy,* Hearing Transcripts, Vol 80, 18 June 1996, testimony of Major-General Vernon, 15535; and personnel correspondence, Beno / Vernon, 18 October 1995. Beno Papers. Their views are not simply "bitter grapes." They represent the sentiments of those who served in the Regiment during the period. See also Winslow, 53-54; Taylor and Nolan, *Tarnished Brass* and *Tested Mettle*; Desbarats, 4-5; and Worthington, *Scapegoat,* 111.

128. *Somalia Commission,* Transcript of Policy Hearing, Vol 4, 21 June 1995, 612.

129. "CO's Farewell Message," *Final Parade Program.* During the parade the CO addressed his soldiers and asserted, "I have nothing but the deepest respect for the soldiers who served with me who are on parade here today. I do not accept and I will not accept under any conditions that this regiment is disbanded with disgrace. It is not!" The technical date of the disbandment is actually 5 March 1995, in accordance with the CDS decree that the Regiment be struck from the CF ORBAT with an effective date of 05 March 1995 in accordance with Ministerial Order 95003. LFCA HQ message UNCLAS COS 030, dated 032145Z Mar 95, 4. As of 6 March 1995, the remnants of the Regiment were designated the Canadian Airborne Holding Unit. The distinctive parachute smock was no longer authorized wear and the Airborne cap badge was removed. The maroon beret was retained; however, members now wore the cap badge of their parent infantry Regiment.

130. Ron Corbett, "Petawawa will never get over it," *The Ottawa Sun,* 5 March 1995, 5.

CHAPTER TEN

A QUESTION OF SURVIVAL
Canada's Airborne Capability After Disbandment, 1995-1999

The Regiment has defined the concept of teamwork and has given each of us a better understanding of our potential. Since arriving in Petawawa in 1977, it [Canadian Airborne Regiment] has set the pace—and the Brigade and Base have had to change gears to keep up. This example will be sorely missed.

Brigadier-General N.B. Jeffries, SSF Commander, March 1995[1]

While the Airborne Regiment disappeared officially in early 1995, the airborne concept did not, because it was too well rooted in its past. But so too were all the controversial questions, particularly the fundamental one of relevance which in one way or another had been there since the Second World War. During the Canadian Airborne Regiment's existence after 1968, it had weathered many budget cuts, force reductions, and calls for disbandment. The difference after 1995 lay in the fact that its supporters were seemingly powerless to protect it in light of the magnitude of the embarrassment and political scandal it had caused. Its demise offered a possible solution to the problems that many perceived had been created by the paratroopers in the first place. Disbelievers now pointed out that airborne forces were an anachronism, and a costly one at that. The critics quickly emphasized the view that an airborne organization, reliant on slow moving transport aircraft, was no longer relevant in the current combat environment bloated with high-tech surface-to-air missiles (SAMs). The spoilation of the Regiment was thus easily couched in a manner that avoided being seen as an attack on the nation's defence or Canada's military capability. In short, the consequences of disbandment were both militarily and politically seen as minimal.

As with the spoilation of most controversial things, passion for and against the Canadian Airborne Regiment was intense. And there were claims of costs to be paid. The validity of the cost arguments is hard to determine and is very subjective. All costs are relative to the value placed on palpable, as well as intangible, concepts and capability. The human cost was one that was not apparently calculated. The decision to disband the Regiment, ostensibly in disgrace, seared the very souls of those who served with dedication, dignity and honour. What was ignored was the fact that most who answered their nation's "call-to-arms" in the airborne did so for reasons other than self aggrandisement. Moreover, service in the Airborne Regiment, the Army's vanguard—with its constant challenge, hardship, and high readiness status—was further evidence of an individual's willingness to subjugate self to the institution.[2] For the advocates of an airborne force disbandment broke the faith. Unquestionably, the bitter truth is that most Canadians did not care. But to the soldiers it was a bitter pill to swallow. It only added to the belief that their senior leadership failed to support them.

The break-up of the Airborne Regiment had a profound effect on the paratroopers and their families. Throughout the final ceremonies in March 1995, the parade square bore witness to tough soldiers who had accustomed themselves to withstand fear, hardship, and pain, rather than show any sign of weakness, but now sobbed shamelessly in the arms of their loved ones. One spouse noted, "I watched my husband be destroyed overnight. He put a lot of time and energy into his 19 year career. Now he has no enthusiasm."[3]

The calculation of cost also failed to account for the level of perceived betrayal among the airborne soldiers, as well as those veterans of the Regiment. Master-Corporal Winston Rattray dejectedly commented, "I devoted my life to the Army, and these days they're not giving it back." The decision to disband the Regiment, he added, "crushed my whole belief in the Canadian political system. Up until that point I dedicated my life to the defence of Canada."[4]

Similarly, Master-Corporal R.J. Howett expressed a similar pain. "When they disbanded the Regiment," he lamented, "they took away my family. I lost a whole bunch of brothers and I'm still a little bitter over that."[5] Corporal L.A. Lamoureaux echoed the sentiment of loss. He commiserated, "it was a big family and now its like something was taken away, as if someone robbed me."[6] However, Master-Corporal Leadbeater captured the essence of most of the paratroopers. He stated, "it was the biggest kick in the nuts I've ever had. The most horrible day of my life was the final parade."[7]

The cost went well beyond the effect on the personnel and their families. It was also measured in the loss of training value to the Army. A 1982 Special Service Force document claimed that the removal of the Airborne from the Order of Battle would undoubtably speed up the "slide to military mediocrity in the Canadian Army."[8] General Allard's original intent of providing the soldier with a unit in which he could be challenged as he had never been challenged before, came to fruition with the establishment of the Canadian Airborne Regiment. It became renowned as the best training unit in the Canadian Forces. Several veteran regimental commanders believed that the Regiment became a "beacon" for those with a sense of adventure and a desire to test themselves,[9] and that the Airborne offered "another peak, another ledge, another challenge, to those who were really seeking something more."[10]

The Regiment's last commander, Colonel Kenward, recognized that in a peacetime army the necessity of an airborne unit was acute. He explained that, beyond its operational capability, it provided a valuable test for soldiers; it allowed them to confront fear and conquer it. Kenward admitted that it was difficult to convince "business planning minds" of this reality, but he insisted its value was incontestable. He declared that the Regiment gave its soldiers a "war story." In the process, it developed their leadership, pride, self-confidence, and individual skills. One could, Kenward went on, "never, ever, put a dollar sign to that."[11] The trouble with these viewpoints is they are difficult to quantify and validate. Like higher education in the humanities, one cannot easily corroborate their value.

The Airborne put a premium on motivation, skill and self-reliance, particularly at the lowest levels. Major Philip Bury, one of the Regiment's first officers, recalled that the paratroopers operated on the "ragged outer-edge," which heightened the dependence on themselves and their comrades.[12] Psychologist and former paratroop officer Lieutenant-Colonel Peter Bradley felt that the autonomy and self-reliance inherent in the paratroopers transcended the boundaries normally found in the regular infantry regiments. For him individuals in the Airborne "didn't feel constrained by where you were in the organization." There was, Bradley said, a central tenet that everyone, regardless of rank, was responsible "to do something if things went astray."[13]

The airborne experience provided more training value than just the enshrinement of virtues such as a can-do attitude, special spirit, and toughness. It also developed unrivalled light infantry skills. Major-General Stewart recalled the arrival of the Regiment at Petawawa in 1977. He insisted that the paratroopers brought to the SSF "a high standard of soldiering and infantry skill including physical fitness...[which] had a very positive effect on the other units of the SSF and encouraged them to pick up their standards of soldiering and fitness."[14]

The experience gathered in the Regiment also served a critical cross-pollination function. The individual fieldcraft, leadership, navigation, and patrolling skills developed and honed in the Airborne provided the mechanized infantry battalions with a vital infusion of needed expertise. Brigadier-General Holmes, who commanded both paratrooprs and line infantry thought that this transfer of skill made "mechanized soldiers better soldiers."[15] "As a Commanding Officer of a [line] battalion," he went on, "I valued the soldiers I got from the Airborne Regiment; they are all first class, they did training in the Airborne Regiment that we couldn't accomplish in the normal line battalion and they brought experience back with them and it rubbed off on the soldiers and it was a positive thing...so, and I think I speak for all my colleagues who have commanded battalions over the years that that was the case in most instances."[16]

As a result of disbandment, the Army lost a valuable leadership nursery. The Airborne was an incubator for the officer and NCO leadership for the infantry. Many former line battalion COs and RSMs maintained that individuals with airborne service were the ones you could invariably trust for the "hard tasks."[17] The nature of the training and the personal growth that resulted was unparalleled. Colonel Skidmore, the former Executive Assistant to the Commander of the Army, opined that Lieutenant-General (now General and CDS) Maurice Baril would have closed the airborne capability down, had he not realized its critical importance to the Army for the training it provides as well as its function as a testing ground for individuals. Baril was a former parachute instructor and jumpmaster at Rivers, Manitoba, and he understood firsthand the need within the Combat Arms for the challenge inherent in parachuting and airborne operations.[18]

For the Army, the loss of the Airborne also extended to the more concrete. It represented the forfeiture of the capability to rapidly project national power, whether for domestic or international crises. A 1994 Land Forces Command estimate concluded that "within the Land Force the only high readiness force that is capable of conducting land operations expeditiously into any condition of climate and terrain is the Canadian Airborne Regiment."[19] The report noted that the Regiment was ideally suited to conduct expeditionary, contingency and vanguard operations which ensured a military presence, by parachute if necessary, which in turn would enable the follow-on deployment of slower, less mobile conventional forces. It further declared that "the Regiment, in conjunction with the required tactical airlift, constituted the national strategic reserve that underpins the credibility of Canadian sovereignty operations."[20]

And so it seemed that disbandment had effectively erased Canada's airborne capability. As we have read, the Defence Department's carefully crafted *1994 White Paper* erased all references to airborne or parachute forces. This ensured that no embarrassment would arise from apparent inconsistencies between word and deed if the Airborne Regiment was abolished.[21] It also suggests that DND was preparing itself and the public for the disbandment a year before it happened. But the Canadian airborne experience was not fated to end, at least not yet. When the axe fell in early 1995, an effort by those who strongly believed in the utility of airborne forces, and who were determined to keep it alive, quickly put forward the airborne's traditional default position, defence of Canada. Ironically, in the past such a role had been largely discounted and it had ensured the marginalization of Canada's paratroopers for many years. After 1995, it once again became the saviour of the nation's airborne forces.

The continuing existence of a national airborne capability appeared to be fragile. It certainly was small. After the order to disband on 23 January 1995, no direction was promulgated in regard to the fulfilment of the airborne role in either the short or long term. It was only during the ensuing turmoil and confusion of closing down the Regiment, literally a scant few days prior to the actual disbandment ceremonies on 4-5 March, that Petawawa received a signal from Land Forces Command Headquarters which said "there are some outstanding operational tasks for which an element of the Regiment must be prepared to execute. For these reasons, Commander LFC has directed that the CO Canadian Airborne Holding Unit[22] develop a company size group, (based primarily on RCR members) with appropriate command and control and elements of Airborne Service Commando not to exceed 300 members to provide contingency troops in the event of short notice operations."[23] A more detailed directive ten days later, on 13 March 1995, emphasized the need for a parachute force. It concluded simply, "Canadians will not accept the contention that we cannot put troops on the ground anywhere in this country at anytime."[24] This all goes to suggest that the decision to abolish the Regiment was based on sociopolitical ideas rather than the invalidity of the airborne concept.

In March 1995, a very small "phoenix" was borne out of the ashes of the Canadian Airborne Regiment. The former 3 Commando, now re-designated 3 Commando Group, was brought back to life and authorized to have a strength of 187 personnel.[25] Individual and sub-unit equipment that had been cleaned and packed away was now re-issued. In addition, a training plan was quickly resurrected. The establishment of 3 Commando Group, which represented Canada's interim airborne capability, officially took effect on 6 March 1995.[26]

In the span of a few short days, Canada's provisional parachute force went from the brink of oblivion to a state of continual high readiness, albeit hardly a regiment or even a battalion. The new LFC mandate required 3 Commando Group to be capable of deploying on operations within forty-eight hours of notification. The interim parachute force was designated as an Army vanguard force. As such, its tasks as the official documents show were: to conduct territorial and continental defence operations; conduct domestic and regional tasks; conduct surveillance and reconnaissance of the Canadian land mass to demonstrate a national presence; and to act as an immediate reaction force vanguard for domestic operations, for employment in areas where conventional forces could not be deployed in a timely fashion.[27]

As a result of the new mission, airborne training, which had ceased with the Defence Minister's disbandment order in January, now quickly returned to its previous hectic pace for a small segment of the former Airborne Regiment. Nonetheless, this was but an interim solution. And almost immediately the old questions and the vociferous debate began anew. What role did paratroopers have in the Army? More importantly, how would they be organized? The answer to the paratroopers' future lay in their past. As in the past, political expediency and dominant personalities in power once again determined the fate of Canada's much reduced airborne warriors.

Even though the airborne idea managed to survive the Regiment's destruction the situation and environment were different. There was a definite shift in support in some elements of the Army. Many who had promoted, or at least were not averse to paratroopers in earlier times now seemingly began to distance themselves from the airborne soldiers. This phenomenon was in fact well in train even before the Regiment was officially axed. For instance, the Commander of the Army, Lieutenant-General Reay, appeared to be one such individual who seemed to sniff the wind before the chop. Despite his admission in October 1993 that he had "seriously contemplated the dissolution of the Canadian Airborne Regiment," his public posture was just the opposite and exceptionally reassuring to the paratroopers.[28] When asked a month later, in November 1993, during a gathering of Army officers in Ottawa, if the upcoming White Paper included a mention of the Airborne Regiment, he responded that the first twelve drafts did, but the most recent had exchanged "Airborne Regiment" with the term "parachute capability." Nonetheless, he boldly proclaimed that as commander of the Army it was for him to decide how parachute capability was defined. Reay concluded with the soothing prediction that "there will be at least two berets hung up" if the Airborne were to be disbanded.[29] Everyone present understood the implied reference to the second beret, namely, that of the CDS, General de Chastelain.

The Army Commander also gave further reassurances to the paratroopers in the Airborne Regiment's Officers Mess in December 1994. Once again, he insisted that he would resign if the minister dared dismantle the Regiment. However, the disbandment order prompted no such action on his part. In fact, subsequent events raised the suspicions of many. Lieutenant-Colonel Ron Bragdon accompanied Major-General Keevinar, the NATO ACE Mobile Force (Land) Commander, on a visit to LFC a few days after the disbandment announcement in January 1995. He recalled with alacrity Reay's contentment with the prospect of using the Airborne's manning credits to bring back the third battalions of the three regular infantry regiments. Reay's satisfied demeanour was so apparent that Keevinar was prompted to comment later to Bragdon that "the General was not acting like someone who has lost a member of the family." Keevinar also pointed out that Reay had that smug look, not of mourning but rather he was behaving as if a plan had come together.[30] The Commander of the Army appeared to be quite capable of playing all threads at once.

Lieutenant-General Kent Foster was another who many felt had abandoned the Regiment. Foster, a longtime staunch supporter of the airborne cause was now in the unenviable position of being both the Honorary Colonel of the Regiment, and as a retired soldier, the deputy minister of the Department of Health and Welfare. His visits to the Regiment during the period from late January to March 1995 were often preceded with a caution to the officers that he did not wish his presence to be publicly known because he did not want to deal with the media. As a result, an impression that Foster's liaison with the paratroopers was much like an affair between a prominent politician and his illicit mistress soon became prevalent.

The conflict of interest seemingly extended beyond the question of public association. During one of the final meetings of the regimental executive committee, Brigadier-General Douglas, a former regimental commander, raised the issue of commencing a more proactive and vocal campaign to ensure the continued existence of some form of viable airborne capability. He warned of the likelihood that the CDS and Commander of the Army might sell out the option of a new centralized airborne unit. Moreover, he asserted that prominent retired individuals such as Fraser Eadie, Herb Pitts, and Douglas himself should speak out publicly in an effort to prevent this.[31]

But Foster who as the Honorary Colonel was at the same meeting dissuaded those present from such a course of action. He assured those assembled that he still maintained a privileged access to and good relations with the CDS and others. Foster insisted that he could best assist behind the scenes. There was no need, he counselled, to have a public campaign because it would only lead to a harmful backlash. Foster's motives are difficult to unravel as subsequent events and his own apparent inactivity in support of the airborne concept, seem to indicate.[32]

Once the ministerial disbandment came in January 1995, it seemed that no one in the entire military pyramid wanted anything to do with either a tainted and dying Airborne Regiment, or a reborn paratroop concept. Colonel Semianiw, then the LFCA Operations Officer (G3), recalled that "we felt we were very much alone. I personally felt like a leper." Absolutely no one wanted to support the Regiment in its preparations for its final disbandment ceremonies. Semianiw remembered it was a "political hot-potato." The Air Force offered up only one aircraft for the final farewell parachute drop. Despite the continual telephone calls and desperate pleas for assistance, he recalled, no answer was forthcoming from the Air Force. The wall of silence continued right up to the week prior to the parade when the log jam was finally broken. It took Canada's steadfast ally, the Americans, with a promise to provide two Starlifter aircraft for the farewell ceremonies, to seemingly embarrass their Canadian counterparts into action. At the last minute, the Canadian Air Force confirmed that six aircraft would be made available after all.[33]

The prevailing institutional enmity to those things "maroon" lingered in the aftermath of disbandment. This became all too clear when the various former airborne soldiers returned to their parent regiments. Lieutenant-Colonel Dan Mitchell, a former Commandant of the Canadian Parachute Centre, recalled, "airborne was a dirty word. People were scared to say it."[34] The Commanding Officer of 1 R22eR during the period, Lieutenant-Colonel Garth von Einsiedel, also recollected the open hostility that the former 1 Commando (R22eR) soldiers faced on arrival back in Valcartier. He said there was a distinct aversion to any symbol associated with the airborne. Indeed, all items depicting the Airborne Regiment logo were forbidden by order of NDHQ. Soon, the purge extended to any maroon item. There was, Von Einsiedel noted, even an unsuccessful attempt made to remove the entitlement to wear the maroon beret itself.[35]

A similar expurgation swept through Petawawa as it did at Valcartier. Increasing pressure to erase any link with Pegasus became prevalent. As a result, the summer of 1995 was punctuated with the purge of any vestiges of the past. Maroon T-shirts were banned by HQ for what remained of the SSF paratroopers and in their stead the CF issue green V-neck garment was worn. Not surprisingly, the small band of paratroops realized that they, as well as the capability they represented, were once again being pushed to the periphery of the Army.

The purge of any vestiges of the Airborne Regiment and the airborne concept at large was just one manifestation of the efforts made to marginalize Canada's parachute capability. The other was a very deliberate and cloaked decision making process surrounding the disbandment. On 31 January 1995, Army Headquarters tasked LFCA, under the command of Major-General Vernon, to study the means by which an airborne capability could be maintained in the wake of the Airborne Regiment's disbandment. Army Council direction explicitly included the necessity to base any recommendation for a continued airborne capability solely on the official defence policy as expressed in the *1994 White Paper*. The Council also specified that suggestions must include measures to mitigate against a repetition of the events that led to the Airborne's demise.[36]

LFCA HQ examined four options. Each one entailed a centralized parachute capability housed in a single unit. Vernon recommended that the maintenance of the airborne capability be in the form of a parachute capable light infantry battalion.[37] Colonel Semianiw recalled that the LFCA study and proposal essentially called for a return of 1 Canadian Parachute Battalion. But he also vividly remembers that higher authorities were not interested. The Army Commander bluntly denounced the LFCA recommendation as "a wolf in sheep's clothing."[38]

A disturbing trend became evident. Reay, the Commander of the Army, who less than a year before had presented a similar strong argument to the Chief of the Defence Staff and Minister of National Defence, now categorically reversed himself.[39] The rumour quickly surfaced that the decision was to return to the decentralized parachute companies of the Mobile Striking Force era. The story received real credence when a local Petawawa radio station announced on 1 March 1995 that David Collenette, the MND, had announced that the airborne capability would be decentralized outside of Petawawa.[40]

Lieutenant-General Reay quickly denied that any decision had been made. While addressing the assemblage at the Airborne farewell Mess dinner on the night of 3 March, he stated that a decision was close, but not yet ready. An announcement, he promised, would be made in less than three weeks, once political approval had been obtained. He gave no clue as to the favoured option. Nonetheless, most in his audience had already come to suspect that the decision was to return to Jump Companies. However, the serving paratroopers, as well as the extended airborne family, believed that the decision was not promulgated prior to the highly-charged and emotional disbandment ceremonies for fear of provoking public criticism from the large number of airborne supporters gathered for the Regiment's farewell activities with its attending hordes of curious reporters and news cameras.

In spite of Reay's highly agile utterances, it seems that a decision on what was going to happen had been made well before the general appeared at the farewell Mess dinner. A former staff officer at NDHQ recalled that the CDS was confronted with the issue some weeks earlier at the commanders' video-conference, where Reay raised the matter of the parachute company. The Chief of the Defence Staff, General de Chastelain, quickly interrupted and stated that they could discuss the matter later. The staff officer also confided that the CDS had become quite agitated, even paranoid, about leaks and would not discuss policy at meetings. Evidently, decisions were made only behind closed doors in private gatherings.[41]

Finally, the truth came out and indeed a decision had been made. On 12 April, the commander of the Army arrived in Petawawa to brief the paratroopers on the future of airborne forces in Canada. The decision, Reay said, was to maintain parachute capable forces in Canada, as a decentralized capability. "The Land Force will initially maintain its parachute capability by establishing three independent Parachute Company Groups," he explained, "reporting to their respective Brigade Headquarters." "These Independent Parachute Company Groups," Reay added, "will be the lead elements of what will eventually be three Light Infantry Battalions, to be located at CFB Edmonton, Petawawa, and Valcartier."[42] Despite Reay's earlier strong proclamations that he, as Commander of the Army, would determine how parachute capability in the Army was defined, he now rationalized his announcement by saying that he had no choice in the matter since he was obligated to react to the *1994 White Paper*.[43]

In reality, Reay had long before committed himself to the decentralized option. On 13 March 1995, a month before he came to Petawawa with the "decentralization scheme," he had written, "what is different today is Canada's new Defence Policy. Careful reading of the White Paper reveals that Canada is not committed to an airborne (warfighting) contingency commitment in any explicit manner."[44] Reay assiduously emphasized the absence in the document of the words "parachute" and "airborne."[45] However, he did maintain, as did the CDS and MND, that the White Paper, envisioned an *implied* parachute requirement, "primarily in a domestic context."[46]

In spite of the Army Commander's pitch, the new decentralized interpretation was not readily accepted by all; in fact Reay convinced very few. Lieutenant-Colonel Dave Pentney, a staff officer in the Army's Land Forces Requirement cell, examined the requirement for an airborne capability as part of the formulation process of the *1994 White Paper*. His analysis, much like the other estimates completed on the same issue, emphasized the need for an airborne battalion group, centralized in one location, to fulfill the requirement to reach inaccessible areas. Pentney briefed the CDS, but acknowledged that it did not matter. He declared "they had already made the decision to go back to the Mobile Striking Force [idea]."[47]

Not surprisingly, by March 1995, Reay recommended the decentralized option, professing that it "clearly best conforms to defence policy, although it is more expensive than the simple recreation of an Airborne Regiment."[48] The reversal was stunning. Less than a year earlier, Reay had clearly deemed this option the worst possible route. Entitled, "Option 4—Mobile Strike Force," it had the fewest advantages and on the whole, the most disadvantages among the five possible alternatives.[49] At that time, in April 1994, Reay had explicitly proclaimed that the optimal decision was to retain the status quo, namely the Airborne Regiment. Failing this, the Army Commander advocated the establishment of a new unit, specifically, a return to 1 Canadian Parachute Battalion.[50]

The decision regarding Canada's airborne capability was once again hostage to personalities in power and political expedients of the day. The decision, regardless of how the Army Commander attempted to package it, was blatantly political. It did not represent sound military advice. Nevertheless, it did send a clear message to those in the chain of command: the distinct perception that political correctness and the provision of such answers as the senior commanders *felt* were desired by their political mandarins, were the order of the day. Perhaps to expect anything else was naive.

This hard reality escaped very few. Brigadier-General Walt Holmes, in his capacity as Director General Land Force Requirements in NDHQ, flatly declared that a "parachute company is all that is politically acceptable."[51] He further acknowledged that no effort would be made to reconstitute a battalion in the near future. Holmes conceded "we're just basically keeping the art alive."[52]

The commandant of the Canadian Parachute Centre agreed. He professed, "right now we're in the maintenance of capability mode."[53] The SSF commander was of the same opinion. "The present way ahead for the army's parachute capability," he wrote, "represents a 'minimum viable' approach that is seen to be consistent with both operational and financial realities. It permits basic levels of skill and expertise to be retained, but results in an extremely limited operational capability."[54]

It was the destruction of the operational capability that raised concern. Major A.J. Bibeau, another NDHQ staff officer who worked on a 1993 rationalization of the airborne capability, avowed that the real usefulness of the parachute capability existed in an integral entity.[55] An SSF study also endorsed the concept that the "critical mass" for parachute operations was "battalion size." It clearly declared that the "battalion is the minimum size element in which the necessary combat functions are integrated to produce effective combat power."[56]

Similarly, the lessons learned from the Mobile Striking Force experience of the 1950s, although brought forward, were ignored. In 1966, General Allard had eloquently defended the need to have a single centralized parachute unit. This too was conveniently forgotten. It appeared that 30 years later the Canadian Army had "returned to the future," and seemed prepared to discover hard truths all over again. Not surprisingly, the small rump of the airborne force in existence after 1995 was marginalized just as it predecessors had been. Parachute activities took on a low priority in both the Air Force and the parachute units themselves. Much like Allard's complaint three decades earlier, that large periods elapsed where only one parachute company was available for operations because of rotations to Europe, tours to Bosnia-Herzegovina and Haiti crippled the availability and readiness of the contemporary jump companies.[57]

Parachuting, the basic skill of any airborne force, became dependent on the commanding officers of the Light Infantry Battalions and their immediate superiors. Lieutenant-Colonel Mike Jorgenson, the Commanding Officer of 3 RCR, confessed that "jumping is a real problem now." The Parachute Company, he claimed, if lucky, would conduct a drop every three months. This created immense training problems. He acknowledged that "now if you want to jump people hesitate." Jorgenson also added that there is often uncertainty in regard to the requirements, capabilities and skills. He lamented that we have gone from an "anything is possible, to an unsure, hesitant, 'maybe,' attitude."[58] In order to be a good and confident parachutist one must constantly practise the craft. This was not being done.

The parachute decentralization announcement had other crippling spin-offs. The Air Force quickly comprehended after 1995 that parachute capability was not a priority for the Army. Predictably therefore, support for airborne training became even less of a concern for the Air Force. Both the Canadian Parachute Centre (CPC) in Trenton, Ontario and the paratroopers themselves have commented that very little effort, or priority, was placed on making aircraft available. Major Dave Gallea, the Officer Commanding the Training Wing at CPC, remarked that parachute training and continuation parachuting is "Priority 8" on the Air Force's tasking list. He explained that the delivery of routine baggage to other Air Force bases is of a higher priority and could result in the loss of training aircraft for the paratroopers. Beyond the loss of training, it also imposes horrendous delay costs on the Army.[59]

Army's low priority for its own parachute forces was further revealed in April 1999. At that time the Army Council decided that it was no longer necessary for the Army to maintain a battalion-level parachute capability. As a result, 159 "jump" positions were removed from the Light Infantry Battalion establishments and the CPC was cut from eight annual basic parachutist course serials to six.[60] The savings amounted to approximately $120,000.00.[61] The rationale for the further degradation of the parachute capability was very simple. "We've been too busy and too short of resources," explained Major-General Bruce Jeffries, the Deputy Chief of the Land Staff. "We made a pragmatic decision to economize in an area which is not a 'must-do' for us," he added, "it is desirable—desirable in terms of maintaining the capability, desirable from the soldier's point of view because of the extra challenge it provides. But we can't afford desirables." Jeffries concluded, "we have to focus on the 'must-dos'."[62]

The other important consideration to Major-General Jeffries and the other members of Army Council was the fact that the *1994 White Paper* made no mention of the requirement for a parachute capability.[63] That carefully worded document, with all words relating to "airborne" conveniently excised, that was drafted at the height of the scandals embroiling the Airborne Regiment, once again became the justification to further erode Canada's airborne forces.

The sum total of all the events both before and after Defence Minister Collenette's decision to decentralize the airborne forces indicates that the wheel had gone one full turn. The airborne was again marginalized. The paratroopers are once more operating in the shadow. As disappointing as this is to the airborne's supporters, it should not be a surprise. The absence of a credible role for paratroopers in Canada has always been their undoing. The fire-brigade task, with the ability to rapidly project power may be essential to some nations, but it has never been important to Canada. The nation's politicians have never shown a proclivity to dispatch troops on a moment's notice—and such a slow approach is not entirely wrong. There is a degree of wisdom in the "sober second look." To commit too quickly, or to possess the capability to become involved precipitously, can embroil a nation in events which in clearer light might be better ignored.

Furthermore, airborne forces and their accompanying image have never been popular with conventionally minded Canadians, in or out of the military. Specialized troops are often resented in the military institution. For an armed force like Canada's, already predicated on a multi-purpose combat role, airborne ideas are unlikely to win much enthusiasm. In addition, the current political and organizational climate within the Armed Forces and DND are equally hostile to airborne forces. Wracked with internal debate and parochial struggles, and still clinging to the vestiges of a NATO European-oriented mechanized heavy force, paratroopers become just another competitor for ever-dwindling resources.

Alas, in the late 1990s the raison d'etre for the paratroopers became once again the defence of Canada. However, as already stated, one cannot expect much emphasis or support for a role some have no faith in and others hold in contempt as expensive adventurism. Major-General Bruce Jeffries acknowledged that the decision to revert to a "minimum viable" parachute force was based on the "risk that the Government and the Department were prepared to take, given the assessed likelihood of tasks that will demand substantial parachute or airborne capabilities."[64] The continual assessment that Canada faced no direct military threat underpinned the marginal requirement for paratroopers in the defence of Canada role.[65] Other reasons for this nation to have an airborne force are doubtful. For instance, aid to the civil power was always a concern, but in a developed country such as Canada, the likelihood of a crisis erupting in an area not accessible by other means than the parachute, was minimal. As a result, the cheapest insurance policy was once again deemed sufficient. Thus, for the airborne idea it becomes once again a simple question of survival.

Notes for Chapter Ten

1. Brigadier-General N.B. Jeffries' address at the "SSF Farewell to the Airborne Regiment" ceremony at CFB Petawawa, 1 March 1995.

2. Major Jamie Hammond stated that the Airborne represented a group of people who accepted that the job was the number one priority. He further commented that the more the CF emphasizes quality of life issues the more it will "lose the ability to pick-up a unit and deploy on short notice without being constrained by those very issues." Hammond maintained that the paratroopers were unquestionably imbued with the necessary sense of commitment that provided the country with the necessary rapid reaction force.

3. "The Final Parade," *Maroon Beret—Final Edition*, 26.

4. Interview with author, 23 May 1997.

5. Interview with author, 29 August 1996.

6. Interview with author, 29 July 1996. See also Ron Corbett, "Petawawa will never get over it," *Ottawa Sunday Sun,* 5 March 1995, 5 and 16-17; Rosie DiManno, "Airborne dies with tears, rage," and Jim Rankin, "'Airborne Forever!' Vet Cries," *The Toronto Star,* 5 March 1995, A1 & A11.

7. Interview with author, 23 May 1997.

8. *Information Legacy,* "A Proscribed Elite," 8.

9. Interview with Colonel Houghton, 5 November 1998. See also Canadian Airborne Forces Association, "Written Submission Number 1 to the Commission of Inquiry into the Deployment of Canadian Forces to Somalia," 13 June 1995, 5.

10. Interview with Colonel Kenward, 16 December 1998.
11. Ibid.
12. Interview with author, 14 December 1998.
13. Interview with author, 26 June 1998.
14. Letter to author, 1 July 1998. Stewart also wrote that the Regiment "gave the SSF a special spirit." He noted that he had served in other brigades but none had the "special spirit that I witnessed in Petawawa." See endnote 1.
15. Interview with Brigadier-General Holmes, 17 July 1997.
16. *Somalia Commission*, Transcript of Evidentiary Hearing, Vol 4, 10 October 1995, testimony of Colonel Holmes, 664-665. A witness at the De Faye BOI commented, "Airborne training just makes a good soldier that much better." BOI—Cdn AB Regt BG, Phase I, Vol XI, K-2/9.
17. Interview with Colonel Rick Hatton, 16 December 1998. Hatton recalled that as a CO of 3 RCR, his RSM stated that the first thing troops look at in regard to an officer is whether he has his "white wings" denoting service in the Regiment.
18. Interview with author, 3 February 1998. Skidmore also noted that with the demise of the Regiment the CF "lost a useful tool, if not for national unity, then for Army unity." Interview with author, 13 February 1997.
19. LFC, "Justification for an Airborne Capability in the Canadian Forces," 19 April 1994, 4. The report also maintained that the Regiment's light scales and high mobility greatly simplified the problems related to its intercontinental deployment and sustainment from Canada to the Allied Command Europe (ACE) area, as well as providing flexible and expeditious response to the wide range of potential UN operations which could be assigned to the CF. Major-General Gaudreau commented that the existence of the Regiment meant that "for once the CF had a real quick reaction force capable of deployment in the remote areas of Canada, for either DCO, MAJAID and ALCANUS." Letter to author, 18 September 1998.
20. Ibid., 4. See also "The Requirement for an Operational Parachute Capability in the Canadian Forces Structure," 21 February 1994, 4-11.
21. See Chapter Nine, text and accompanying endnote 56.
22. Designation given to the remaining elements of the Canadian Airborne Regiment, effective 6 March 1995 (the day following official disbandment). The Canadian Airborne Holding Unit ceased to exist as of 1 September 1995 when it was absorbed by 3 RCR upon its move from CFB Borden to CFB Petawawa.
23. Message—LFCHQ COS 030, dated 032145Z Mar 95, "Disbandment Cdn AB Regt."
24. LFCHQ, "Operational Enhancement of the Land Field Forces and Maintenance of a Parachute Capability," 13 March 1995, 2 & 5.
25. SSFHQ, "Maintenance of an Interim Airborne Capability," 5 April 1995, 2.
26. Ibid.
27. Commander SSF, Letter 1901-7723 (Comd), 18 March 1995, "Maintenance of a Continuing Airborne Capability—Interim Planning Guidance." The Commando Group was also given the task of maintaining a MAJAID (Major Air Disaster) Airborne Support Group response capability in the alternate role. The primary group was tasked to CABC.
28. LFCHQ, "Response to Leadership and Discipline Issues—Canadian Airborne Regiment BOI," 28 October 1993, 2. Reay apparently forgot his stirling endorsement of the Regiment when he wrote a foreword for the official OP Deliverance publication, *In the Line of Duty* (Ottawa: DND, 1994). He stated, "The difficult mission revealed, once more, how important proper training, professionalism and leadership are. I can assure you that I never had any doubts about your ability to carry out this assignment in the finest traditions of the Army, and you have proved me right."
29. Author's diary, November 1999.
30. Interview with Lieutenant-Colonel (retired) Ron Bragdon, 7 October 1998.

31. Author's diary, 3 March 1995.
32. One motive for Foster's actions, or inaction, may be found in his personal beliefs. He observed that airborne forces have come and gone in Canada several times. Foster affirmed that the "destiny is there," implying that there will always be airborne forces in Canada because of its inherent capability, regardless of personal feelings, prejudices and animosities. He acknowledged that some people insisted that "we, as a collective group, should be more active." However, Foster maintained that some things take time. He remarked that "for individuals time is fleeting, for an organization time is infinite." Foster concluded that a centralized airborne unit will surface again. Interview with author, 6 June 1998.
33. Interview with author, 1 December 1997.
34. Interview with author, 21 May 1998.
35. Interview with author, 14 March 1997.
36. LFCAHQ, "Maintenance of an Airborne Capability in the Canadian Forces," 13 February 1995, 1.
37. Ibid., 1.
38. Interview with author, 1 December 1997.
39. See Chapter Nine, text and accompanying endnote 36. General Sir Richard Gale, former GOC 6th Br Airborne Div, warned that "the military commander must never allow his military judgement to be warped by political expediency." Gale cautioned, "the task of the military man is to view all problems in terms of fighting efficiency. The moment he finds himself being forced off this clear line on to the vagaries of political argument he will be in danger." R. Gale, "The Impact of Political Factors on Military Judgement," *RUSI,* Vol 99, No. 593, February 1954, 37.
40. Author's Diary, 1 March 1995.
41. Confidential interview, February 1998.
42. Message, LFC Comd 049, dated 120945Z April 1995, "Establishment of a Decentralized Parachute Capability."
43. Author's Diary, 12 April 1995.
44. LFC Commander, "Operational Enhancement of the Land Field Forces and Maintenance of a Parachute Capability," 13 March 1995, 1.
45. LFC Commander, "Retention of a Parachute Capability," 13 April 1995, 1.
46. Ibid, 2. The "implied parachute requirement" is cloaked under the all-inclusive generic multi-purpose combat capability, that can conveniently include or exclude virtually anything. Peter Kasurak, of the Office of the Auditor General observed that DND has never fully described what "multi-purpose combat forces" are. His personal belief was that the Department did not want to. One must admit, there is a certain degree of security in vagaries. Presentation to the Defence Resources Management Course, in Ottawa, 16 May 1997.
47. Interview with author, 6 October 1998.
48. LFC Commander, "Operational Enhancement of the Land Field Forces and Maintenance of a Parachute Capability," 13 March 1995, 2.
49. LFCHQ, "The Canadian Airborne Regiment Recommendation For Consideration," 19 April 1994, Annex B, "Estimate of the Options Open to Maintain an Airborne Capability in the Canadian Forces," B 1-10.
50. Ibid., 1.
51. Interview with author, 17 July 1997. Initially, much emphasis was placed on the ability to combine the three parachute companies to form a single parachute battalion in the event of an emergency requiring such a large force. The RCR Light Infantry Battalion was therefore given the additional role of maintaining the capacity to provide a parachute tactical battalion headquarters. However, no effort has ever been made to exercise this option, nor has any direction, or SOPs been issued to accommodate this professed capability. Sharon Hobson, "Canadian Army Reacts to Life After the Paras," *Jane's International Defense Review,* 12/1996, 23; LFC Commander, "Operational Enhancement of the Land Field Forces and Maintenance of a Parachute Capability," 13 March 1995, 1; and interviews with Lieutenant-Colonels Dave Pitfield, Mike Jorgenson (former COs 3 RCR), and Dan Mitchell (Commandant CPC).

52. Hobson, 25.
53. Interview with Lieutenant-Colonel Dan Mitchell, 21 May 1998.
54. Brigadier-General N.B. Jeffries, "Airborne Engineer Capability," 28 November 1995, 1. The emphasis on "minimum" became evident in later years. From September 1996 to March 1997, Major Tony Balasavecious, the RCR Parachute Company OC, fought a desperate battle to safeguard DZ Anzio in Petawawa. The Brigade decided to open it up as a mechanized "battle-run" and general training area. The paratroopers' concern that the inevitable ruts, caused by the heavy combat vehicles, would become a serious safety hazard was completely ignored. It was not until the paratroopers mobilized the assistance of the base environmental officer, who pointed out that the DZ was in fact a protected environmental area, that the Brigade backed down. Interview with Major Balasavecious, 29 January 1998.
55. Interview with author, 17 July 1997. He was a member of a DGFD study team. Bibeau also conceded that "because of the scandal they didn't wish to stay with that [centralized capability in one unit], so they went with one of the other options."
56. SSFHQ, "The Re-establishment of a Rapid Reaction Capability Within Canada's Land Force," 30 January 1995, 2.
57. See Chapter Four, text and accompanying endnotes 63-66. Lieutenant-Colonel Mitchell, Commandant CPC, noted that the parachute capability goes up and down with operational deployments. This is similar to General Allard's experience that on average only one parachute company is actually operationally effective. Interview with author, 21 May 1998.
58. Interview with author, 14 February 1998. The commandant of the CPC reinforced this theme. He stated that at present the state of capability is largely CO dependent. Mitchell observed, "when you get a CO who is keen, then we see an increase in parachute operations and support. If the CO is less inclined we see an almost neglect of capability." Interview with author, 21 May 1998. A general theme, emanating from those serving in parachute companies and the light infantry battalions, has emerged that indicates that the previous mentality and parachute expertise is quickly disappearing. Warrant Officer Mark Miller noted, "The thought is still there but the heart is no longer there. It's [para company] filled with good intentions, but it's unsure if they will maintain the standard." Master-Corporal Leadbeater added, "we're losing the experience base...we're trying to keep it but it's hard." Corporal Howett lamented, "the level of PT and soldiering has dropped. We don't have the experienced personnel we use to have. We no longer have a basic indoctrination on rigging or drills. All we have left is the maroon beret, yet some of the individuals who wear it now can't even uphold the airborne standard." Captain R.J. Martin substantiated the sentiments when he asserted, "There are lots of things that are being lost quickly, especially matters of rigging. In addition, there is resentment in the Battalion. It's hard to have both para and non-para together. There are lots of guys wearing green berets who have bags more experience than the guys now wearing the maroon beret." Major Tony Balesavecious, a former OC of the RCR Para Company, added a different element to the co-existence. He stated, "Our ability to survive depends on our ability to get along with the unit. Once we are perceived as being a threat to their objectives or the cohesiveness of the unit, our ability to maintain the maroon beret, jumping, etc, becomes in doubt." Interviews with author.
59. Interview with author, 21 May 1998. Galea stated that a one day "no jump" delay due to weather or aircraft shortages cost the CPC $1400.00 in rations alone for a double serial course.
60. Paul Mooney, "Battalion-level parachute capability cancelled," The Maple Leaf, Vol 2, No. 7, 15 April 1999, 16. The concept of a battalion level capability was based on the premise that all three decentralized parachute companies (from the respective light infantry battalions) could be brought together under the umbrella of a composite battalion headquarters. For this reason additional jump positions were established within the different LIBs to allow for the necessary battalion headquarters personnel (i.e., CO, Adjutant, RSM, Operations Officer). Following disbandment and upon the announcement of the stand-up of the LIBs, LFC tasked 3 RCR to provide the commanding officer and battalion headquarters staff, on order. The concept was never actioned or even practised.
61. Interview with Colonel Walter Semianiw, Director Land Force Requirements, 2 June 1999.
62. Mooney, 16.

63. Interview with Colonel Semianiw, 2 June 1999.
64. Jeffries, "Airborne Engineer Capability," 28 November 1995, 1.
65. Canada, *Defence Planning Guidance 1998* (Ottawa: DND, 1997), 1-1; Interviews with Anne Bradfield, Director General Operational Research, 27 June 1997 and Gary Christopher, Defence Analyst—DDA, 15 July 1997.

CHAPTER ELEVEN

CONCLUSION

My fondest memory was that the soldiers, as a group and regardless of rank, were just the best soldiers (and men for that matter) with whom I have ever worked in the Army. They were selfless and self-effacing, fit to a standard that I have never seen emulated elsewhere, hard working and brave. I don't mean brave in a self-serving or rhetorical way; they simply would do anything, anywhere, any time.

Lieutenant-Colonel J.P. Sweetnam, Letter to author, 1992[1]

The Canadian airborne experience has always been a paradox. The paratroopers, who for the greatest part of their existence represented the best of the nation's warriors, were largely disliked within the military and virtually ignored in civilian circles, at least until the horrific killings in Somalia in 1993. Similarly, the parachute organizations that embodied aggressiveness and an offensive spirit were shunned. Incongruously, despite their unquestionable martial prowess, airborne forces were never fully accepted by Canadian military or political institutions.

Paratroopers were the nation's bastard sons. Conceived in times of grave danger and always with the best of intentions, they were never fully integrated into the larger family because they had to be different by definition. Thus they were tolerated but never embraced by the conventional military establishment. Airborne forces were perceived as inordinately privileged and extremely costly. Moreover, some said they were a luxury, an opulence that a small budget-starved force, such as Canada's, could ill afford.

An examination of the evolution of the country's airborne organizations over the past 50 years has demonstrated that national political and military leaders consistently took an irresolute and confused approach to the requirement for airborne forces. During the early years of the Second World War the decision to establish a Canadian parachute capability was initially rejected because no clear role for these special troops was visualized. The concept was later accepted but only with the caveat it be kept at a very low and decentralized level. The growing

American and British interest in airborne forces during the war provided the catalyst for the establishment of a Canadian parachute battalion that served with distinction throughout the rest of the conflict but was quickly disbanded at the end of the war.

In 1946, the postwar planners failed to see a place for paratroopers in Canada's dramatically scaled down peacetime army. Traditional anti-military sentiments within the government, compounded by the enormous war debt, fuelled a drive for economy instead of the creation of the comprehensive military operational capability that some of the soldiers wanted. Moreover, the Canadian Government was responding to voters' preference for social programs and their desire to return to ordinary pursuits after six long years of war. As a consequence, the Liberal administration approved only a skeletal military force designed to provide the framework for mobilization of a citizen's army in time of crisis and little else.

However, the onset of the Cold War in the late 1940s sensitised North Americans, particularly Canada's southern neighbour and ally, to the concept of an open and exposed flank to their North. To the Americans, the Canadian North represented a gateway to invasion. The rapid evolution of technology, particularly jet aircraft and weapons of mass destruction, exacerbated this concern in the 1950s. With the spectre of Pearl Harbor still fresh in their national consciousness, Americans would not allow Canadians to dismiss the northern approach, regardless of the actual threat probability.

The perceived vulnerability of the northern gateway as viewed by Canada's seemingly paranoid southern neighbour was not dismissed lightly in Ottawa. The memory of having to assert national control and sovereignty over the Canadian North during the war was still fresh in the mind of Prime Minister King and his government after their wartime experiences with the United States. Canada's political and military leadership were now very aware how quickly and unilaterally the Americans would act when they felt their security was jeopardized. Whether the Canadians liked it or not the defence of the United States had become continental defence. As a result, to maintain sovereignty over the North, Canada was required to demonstrate the capability of its defence.

And so in the late 1940s, the North, paradoxically, became both the pretence for the re-emergence of paratroopers and ultimately their Achilles heel. Under the 1946 joint Basic Security Plan for the defence of North America with the United States, Canada was required to provide troops capable of destroying enemy lodgements in the North. However, Canadian threat assessments continually disagreed with Washington about the likelihood of such a contingency. For Canadian planners the Arctic itself was seen as its best defence. The tight-fisted Liberal government was averse to tossing money into the ice in response to an eventuality which they adamantly said would not happen. While all of this was occurring, Canada's military became focussed on a potential European battlefield and the NATO alliance structure there.

In light of all of these mutually competitive forces paratroopers became the ideal political solution. They were high-readiness troops with great strategic mobility. Furthermore, they represented a credible force to meet Canada's northern commitment. But more importantly, airborne forces were seen by the government and military as cost effective, particularly if they were maintained only as "paper tigers." In short, paratroopers became a politically expedient solution. They represented the nation's northern defence and land force commitment to the joint Canadian / US Basic Security Plan.

But it was all largely a façade. The parachute forces' capability was directly correlated to the perceived likelihood of their employment. The defence of Canada role, as the northern focus was called, was largely dismissed as a hollow task satisfying politics and diplomacy rather than real military threat. Enemy capability and intentions were repeatedly shown to repudiate any probability of a hostile attack on land from the North. As a result, in the 1950s the nation's airborne forces were automatically marginalized. They were starved of equipment and personnel, and assigned other tasks that detracted from their supposed primary role. The operational capability of the Mobile Striking Force and Defence of Canada Force became largely a token effort. In the late fifties the reassessment of the potential peril to North America as primarily an air threat, further diminished the perceived relevance of airborne forces. By the mid sixties, the nation's airborne organizations represented nothing more than a hollow shell. They embodied nothing more than an effort to keep a special skill alive.

Paradoxically however, this period also held the conditions which could have raised the fortunes of the country's airborne warriors. Until then, paratroopers were associated exclusively with the defence of Canada, a role that was largely bankrupt and of little real military concern. Airborne forces represented nothing more than the cheapest possible insurance premium available. Yet, by the mid sixties a faddish belief in strategic mobility, "Special Forces" to fight guerilla insurgencies, and a need for "Light Forces" capable of responding swiftly to brush-fire wars springing up throughout the Third World, came to the rescue. This scenario now provided another possible role for airborne soldiers.

And so by 1964, under the tutelage of the strong-willed Minister of Defence, Paul Hellyer, and his new and equally determined Army Commander, Lieutenant-General Jean Victor Allard, dramatic changes were implemented to the structure of the Canadian Armed Forces. Central to their vision was a Land Force that was tactically and strategically mobile. Key to this tenet was the inclusion of an airborne regiment, centralized in one location and under one command.

Lieutenant-General Allard's outlook on the paratroop organization was one that went well beyond the narrow defence of Canada role. He envisioned that the airborne force would be utilized as a strategic reserve, capable of rapid response to a wide array of world crises. Allard postulated that they could buy time for the deployment of larger mechanized forces in NATO. They could also respond to international flashpoints in a UN context. In addition, a key motive was the conviction that his new airborne regiment would provide adventure and challenge for soldiers who wished to test themselves. A natural spin-off, he hoped, was that this new force would act as a model and eventually raise the standards of the Army as a whole.

Despite open resistance from within his own establishment, in 1968 Allard forced his creation, the Canadian Airborne Regiment, onto the Army which at that time and for many years after was mesmerized by heavy mechanized conventional forces designed only for war in Europe. In spite of the Army's inflexibility, Allard's rise to the position of Chief of Defence Staff ensured that his wishes were carried out.

The emergence of the Canadian Airborne Regiment as the manifestation of airborne force at a time when overall military strength was falling was an impressive accomplishment. Predictably, this fact, compounded by the manner in which the Regiment was brought forward, created much resentment in other military circles. Of greater concern, however, was the weak foundation upon which the Regiment had been built. The role of the new Canadian Airborne Regiment was wide-ranging and all inclusive. It was given no clear, credible or pervasive role. Allard's contention that the Regiment provided a unique contribution, one that could not be performed by existing organizations, was never clearly accepted by the military establishment at large. Ominously then, there was no widely embraced rationale for the Airborne's existence.

Even though the Airborne Regiment was designated the national UN stand-by force, with the exception of its deployment to Cyprus in 1974, it was never used as such. It was also labelled as the nation's strategic reserve, but its light scales of equipment, particularly its shortage of vehicles, caused many to dismiss it as unemployable for anything other than a domestic context. Without much employment and no credible role the Canadian Airborne Regiment got a reputation very quickly as an expensive and pampered formation.

To exacerbate the problem, the more the Airborne's benefactors tried to demonstrate its worth, the more they highlighted its fundamental flaw, namely, the lack of a credible role. Its strength was its speed of deployment and strategic reach. But these capabilities were not required, nor arguably even wanted. For many in and out of military circles such characteristics were not useful. For them there is great wisdom in sober second thought. Speed of action and strategic deployment have rarely been demanded by Canadian governments for many reasons. The need for time to ready one's forces is an excellent means to allow a potentially explosive situation to crystallize, if not dissipate. In addition, following is almost always less resource intensive than leading. Besides, as a junior partner in large alliances, sometimes there was limited choice and that was not always a bad thing.

Therefore, the only role for the Airborne, that has always been their fallback position, was the defence of Canada. The Arctic's distance and remoteness have always been used to justify the need for the parachute as a means of entry. However, this task held little credibility and the advent of alternative means of delivery, and the growing profusion of northern communities and airstrips, made this claim even more fragile.

As a result, lacking a clear and pervasive role that was widely accepted by the larger military establishment, the Airborne Regiment became hostage to either the derision or support of those in power. Its fortunes began to rise and fall like the waters of a turbulent river. Inevitably, its status was slowly eroded. It was decreased in size. In addition, it was stripped of its formation status and privileged access to the Army Commander. By the late 1970s, it was moved and subordinated to another formation, namely the Special Service Force. Increasingly, it became used as just another infantry unit. The normal rotation tours and taskings of the conventional line regiments became routine in the Cdn AB Regt. Predictably, the quality of its personnel began to slip as well. The Airborne's preferential manning policy had by 1980 become a mere memory. The feeder regiments were now loathe to send their best personnel to an organization that was viewed as just another unit. In fact, the Regiment became a convenient solution for disposing of troublesome individuals. The paratroopers' reputation suffered accordingly.

Nevertheless, those who believed in the Regiment fought to preserve it, but the struggle became a vicious circle. The more it resembled a normal unit the greater were the calls for its destruction. After all, why maintain a costly airborne unit if its relevance to the country is minimal? This in turn fuelled partisan efforts by the extended airborne family, particularly those in positions of influence, to prove the Airborne's worth. Often blinded by their "good" intentions, their efforts however widened the split even further. Time after time, when the Airborne received a mission it meant stripping equipment from other more conventional units. Each effort only reinforced the accusation that the Regiment was an anachronism and a parasite that sapped the declining resources of the remainder of the Army. Rather than attempt to define a pervasive and specific role for the Regiment and build the necessary contingencies to win institutional support, the Regiment and its benefactors continued to cling to an arrogant belief that they were indispensable. Not surprisingly, this fuelled the already overflowing resentment and served only to further alienate the airborne soldiers from the remainder of the military.

The debacle surrounding the events in Somalia rightly exposed the paratroopers and their supporters to public scrutiny but it was often uninformed, unreasoning and unforgiving. The deaths of the Somalis in 1993 were a painful tragedy in themselves; however the events showed what impact the actions of a few could have, in spite of the many real accomplishments of the Airborne Battle Group in that theatre. However, the far wider shame was what Somalia revealed about Canadian military leadership well beyond the Airborne. Nevertheless, the Canadian Airborne Regiment paid most heavily.

The revelations in Somalia caused continuing embarrassment to a very scandal sensitive government. This turn of events intensified the growing debate over the actual need for airborne forces and their relevance in Canadian defence and national security. The 1995 disclosure of repugnant hazing videos pushed the issue over the brink. Again the problem became defined exclusively in terms of the airborne. The solution was rendered in the guise of disbandment.

But the analysis of the Canadian airborne experience cannot simply be explained as solely a function of policy, doctrine, shifting priorities or institutional animosity. There is also a psychological component to the whole airborne drama. Many of those serving in the Airborne Regiment, as well as a large number of their supporters began to consider the Canadian paratroopers as a distinct military elite. Their attitudes toward those outside the select "airborne fraternity" deteriorated accordingly. This self-indulgent pretense of elitism further fuelled the animosity between the paratroopers and the remainder of the Army.

This state of affairs is not unique. The status of airborne forces has always been a contentious one. From their inception in the Second World War they have been cloaked in an aura of invincibility and portrayed as the epitome of the combat soldier. Government and military propaganda popularized this warrior image. The resultant "Airborne Mystique" which still applies today is a distinct product of the time in which it was born. The early years of the Second World War were filled with defeat, humiliation, and withdrawal. Britain and the Commonwealth were pinned to the wall. Survival was tenuous at best and the Axis juggernaut seemed unstoppable. It was a time when the public was thirsty for heroes, a role that the tough, fearless, highly publicized paratroopers aptly filled. In speaking about their airborne forces American Lieutenant-General E.M. Flanagan wrote, "It builds our morale, it stiffens the spine and braces the backbone of the public to hear talk about the independent type airborne operation." For him the stereotype was born from the image of an airborne army storming in "to deal a lethal blow to the enemy, deep in his backyard."[2]

The appeal of the paratrooper was also due to the symbolism which was attached to the image of the parachute warrior. The use of airborne forces, as exemplified by the stunning German victories in the Low Countries in 1940, represented a revolutionary new form of warfare which exemplified an overwhelmingly offensive spirit. It was a weapon which was perceived to transcend the stifling death, futility and lethargy of trench warfare of the First World War. As a result, airborne forces quickly framed the public's conception of modern war. The paratrooper was portrayed as the leading edge, the "tip of the spear." Airborne forces were deigned as special troops with a highly dangerous, and extremely hazardous mission to fulfill. Their task was defined as nothing short of facilitating the general advance of the army by seizing key installations and terrain on the enemy's flanks and in his rear. Furthermore, the paratroopers were responsible for creating "alarm and despondency" and complete confusion in the antagonist's safe areas at the most critical moments of attack. Justified or not, political and military leaders associated paratroopers with the necessary prerequisites for military success.[3]

In addition, the imagery of the warrior dropping out of the heavens to smite the villainous aggressor appealed to all. It was the perfect combination of the sanctity of individual human effort within the larger and often smothering atmosphere of modern technological mass warfare.

Airborne forces became synonymous with offensive spirit and capability. They represented, in the layman's perception, the sword that could slay the enemy in his deepest redoubt. Moreover, airborne forces were accepted by many as the personification of modern warfare. More importantly, the paratroopers themselves were lauded as the epitome of the ultimate warrior.[4]

Over time, the military institution, government propaganda, Hollywood stereotypes, and particularly the airborne soldiers themselves, actively promoted this superman image of the paratrooper. Maintenance of morale and support of the war effort were important factors behind the campaign. This notwithstanding, the paratrooper himself became the primary reason for the perpetuation of the 'mystique.' It was quickly apparent that he was undoubtably a different breed from his more conventional infantry brethren. The airborne soldier was indeed special and he truly epitomized the nation's premier land warrior.[5]

The justification for this assertion is not difficult to identify. Behavioural scientists have tendered the observation that airborne units clearly enshrine military virtues. They explained that paratroopers are self-selected and stress such values as courage and excitement, and are oriented toward action and combat.[6] A sociology professor, Donna Winslow of the University of Ottawa, concluded "the Airborne didn't just espouse traditional institutional values of combat / warrior, it embodied them and in many ways exaggerated them."[7]

Why is this so? The strength of the paratrooper goes beyond individual willingness to join. Despite the voluntary nature of airborne soldiering, the selection and training were rigorous and exceptionally discriminating. The complex and dangerous nature of the operations required what was described as an "elite" type of soldier. Military historian and author, Clay Blair, stated that the aspiring paratrooper had to be in superb physical condition in order to withstand the shock of the jump and the hard landing. Furthermore, he insisted that the airborne warrior required nerves of steel.[8]

But, the selection criterion was not the only factor to explain the paratrooper's esteemed position as the epitome of the modern combat soldier. The airborne reputation grew further as a direct result of their demanding training and hard-earned combat record. The well-respected Brigadier James Hill, Commander of the British 3rd Parachute Brigade during the Second World War, simply described parachute troops as the best fighting material in the world. He felt that "the parachutists have shown themselves magnificent infantry, pre-eminent in physique and steadiness of nerve, born guerilla fighters, mobile and tireless, tremendous marchers, and of an undefeated spirit."[9]

The aura around the airborne soldiers was also rooted in the nature of parachuting itself. It captivated the public because of its daring, hazardous nature. General-Leutnant Bruno Brauer, a paratrooper who participated in the invasion of the Low Countries in 1940 as a member of the German Parachute Regiment, put his finger on the attraction. Parachuting, he said, "compresses into the space of seconds feelings of concentrated energy, tenseness and abandon; it alone demands a continual and unconditional readiness to risk one's life. Therefore the parachutist experiences the most exalted feelings of which human beings are capable, namely that of victory over one's self." Brauer concluded, "for us parachutists, the words of the poet, who said that unless you stake your life you will never win it, is no empty phrase."[10]

Parachuting, as Brauer well knew, demands a continual testing of oneself. It requires the individual to repeatedly overcome the anxiety of jumping and this even before one considers the fear of battle. This recurring necessity, the dangerous parachute descent, fuelled the mystique and provided the major difference between airborne forces and other units. This is not a trivial distinction. In 1940, the nucleus of the British Parachute Regiment was drawn from the renowned No.2 (Army) Commando. Nonetheless, the official history of the British Airborne Forces recorded that "these men were tough, but even so all of them could not manage parachuting."[11] The Canadian experience was similar. Parachute training was the preliminary step in training for the First Special Service Force. This was done to test individuals as to whether they had the nerve to go through the commando-type training that followed. Of the first draft of 450 individuals, representing the "cream of Canada's hard-fighting army youth," approximately 7% froze in the door and were immediately returned to their parent units.[12] Similarly, a postwar report revealed that some men who displayed great bravery during the war could not bring themselves to jump from an aircraft.[13]

For the military, parachuting provided an excellent device for attracting and screening individuals for courage and motivation. It "created elitism through an ordeal that tested a man's courage and earnestness before combat."[14] This was the essence of the paratrooper's strength. Lord (Sir Charles Wilson) Moran in his classic work, *The Anatomy of Courage*, theorized that courage was "a moral quality" and "not a chance gift of nature." He asserted that "it is the cold choice between two alternatives, it is the fixed resolve not to quit, an act of renunciation which must be made not once but many times by the power of will." "Courage," Moran concluded, "is willpower."[15]

It is this courage, the ability to repeatedly overcome fear and carry on with the mission, that provides the paratrooper with enormous pride and self-confidence. He continually bested his apprehension and personal trepidation. As a result, the airborne soldier is confident in his ability to overcome future tests of will. British Lieutenant-General F.A.M. Browning, Commander of the First Airborne Corps during the Second World War commented, "Once a man has parachuted he feels he has done something that few other people do willingly. In some way it gives him a sense of superiority over all other troops."[16]

The transformation of the individual due to this new strength, borne of confidence, has a very tangible effect on the individual. Confidence has been described as perhaps the greatest source of emotional strength that a soldier can rely on.[17] Studies have shown that "the general level of anxiety in combat would tend to be reduced insofar as the men derived from training a high degree of self-confidence about their ability to take care of themselves." It was further concluded that "troops who expressed a high degree of self-confidence before combat were more likely to perform with relatively little fear during battle."[18]

The 1st Canadian Parachute Battalion *War Diary* captured the essence of this evolution. One entry revealed, "the average young parachutist upon graduation from our four week course of the US Parachute School can be aptly described as a 'Bull in a China Shop.'" The account stated that "the psychological transformation of the mind of the introvert to the extrovert is apparent in most of our young chutists after completing their qualifying jumps and the course of Judo. They became fearless and to a degree reckless." The writer further observed that they "feel as though they have been given the key to all physical success and conquered all phases of fear."[19]

These observations were not unique but rather highlighted the importance of parachuting to the military. American Major-General A.S. Newman believed that parachuting proves the "will to dare."[20] He further elaborated:

> Parachute jumping tests and hardens a soldier under stress in a way nothing short of battle can do. You never know about others. But paratroopers will fight. You can bet on that. They repeatedly face danger while jumping and develop self-discipline that conquers fear. Subconsciously every trooper knows this. That's why he has that extra cocky confidence.[21]

Similarly another American, Major-General Willard Pearson declared, "If you want to select a group of people who are willing to fight, well, one of the best criteria I know is whether or not they will jump out of an airplane. Now that is not to say that some of the others won't fight, but sure as hell the airborne will."[22] Ward Just, author and former military correspondent, held similar views; he believed that to be "airborne" is viewed as "prima facie evidence of energy, initiative, and bravery."[23] It is these attitudes and perceptions, compounded by the continual testing and hardening of the individual that nourishes and sustains the Airborne Mystique. By the same token, it is also the reason the paratrooper has developed into the Hollywood stereotype of the exceptionally fit, fearless and aggressive braggart, who is always spoiling for a fight.

By the end of the Second World War the paratrooper personified the elite fighting man. The public and large segments of the military establishment itself perceived the airborne warrior as the epitome of a nation's warrior caste. Peacetime soldiering quickly heightened this notion. Military historian S.L.A. Marshall wrote that until men are severely tried, there is no conclusive test of their discipline, nor proof that their training at arms is satisfying a legitimate military end.[24] During a war, combat becomes the great equalizer; all combat units eventually are tested under fire. However, in peacetime no such army-wide validation exists.

It is for this reason that parachuting and the contrived superiority of airborne units took on importance. The act of jumping from aircraft provided a vehicle to test soldiers in the absence of real action. Gideon Aran, a former Israeli paratrooper and sociologist at the University of Chicago, insisted that parachuting creates and reinforces action-seeking dispositions. This in turn, he concluded, guaranteed a better distribution of manpower within the army, based on the premise that action seekers are better suited for combat than for other roles.[25]

The exaggerated importance and bravado associated with paratroopers, however, are loaded with a potential peril. Physically demanding training and the successful completion of the parachutist qualification nurtures a fearlessness borne of self-confidence. Furthermore, even the newest paratrooper is automatically associated with a legacy of daring deeds and unrivalled feats-of-arms, that were dearly paid for in blood by those who came before. In short, the most novice airborne warrior is instantly cloaked in the mantle of the Airborne Mystique. Therefore, it is not surprising that the individual, as well as the group, quickly see themselves as distinct and special, literally a breed apart.

Inherently, any airborne "band" quickly defines itself, whether publicly or internally, as elite. This definition and perception are further compounded by the treatment bestowed on the group by the institution as a whole. From the airborne's earliest beginnings, the hazardous nature of its role necessitated special perks from the military establishment, if for no other reason than to attract volunteers. Special pay, and distinctive insignia and uniforms reflected their exclusive status.[26] It also contributed to their arrogance. The contemporary Canadian example was no different. Despite emphatic denials, numerous senior commanders gave special consideration to Canada's airborne forces. They were entitled to special orders of dress and distinctive clothing items, permission to wear unique insignia, privileged access to special courses, and a greater number of foreign exchanges for training.[27]

The intense esprit de corps and elitist sentiment which are nurtured by the group, and both promoted and tolerated by the chain of command, has definite value. However, this cult of the elite attitude also has its pitfalls. Major-General Newman drew a more earthy analogy: "being a jumper is like being a virgin; you are or you are not. If you are not, nobody is really interested in your tedious explanation of your unfortunate status."[28] This tongue-in-cheek comment actually underlines the essence of the quandary. Namely, the airborne can quickly devolve into an exclusive club which shuns, and if allowed, abhors outsiders.

The self-transformation of the Canadian paratrooper into a closed warrior tribe of its own is not difficult to understand. The farewell message from Major-General Crabbe, a former paratrooper and SSF commander, on the occasion of the Airborne Regiment's disbandment ceremonies in March 1995, captured the sentiment of the exclusivity of the airborne family. "To have felt the rush of wind in the door—to have experienced the sheer exhilaration that comes each time one exits an aircraft trusting one's life to the professionalism of comrades," he wrote, "binds all jumpers in a special fraternity."[29] Similarly, Lieutenant-General Kent Foster, the last Colonel of the Regiment, the Canadian Airborne Regiment, asserted, "Only those who have dared will understand the call of the jumpmaster, the weight of a winter rucksack, the tap on the shoulder and the cry of 'have a good one'!"[30] The "only I know because only I have dared to do it" attitude may be an old flight of logic but it certainly epitomizes the psyche of the Canadian Airborne Regiment.

It is this special fraternity that is both the greatest strength and weakness of the airborne family. Unique to the paratroops is the fact that all officers and men undergo identical training and are faced with the same tests of courage, endurance and strength. There are no shortcuts and no distinctions for anyone. Colonel Kenward recognized that "it is impossible to hide weakness in the Airborne."[31] As a result of the exacting standards that all must meet, as well as the shared hardships, a bond is created based on group identity, mutual respect and solidarity. Membership in the airborne fraternity cannot be bestowed due to affluence, connections, or rank. It must be earned.

As already noted, this unique shared experience builds group cohesion and solidarity. This is significant. Sociologists have argued that high standards and requirements to enter into a group result in a greater sense of commitment and value placed on membership to that group by successful candidates.[32] In simple terms, the greater the degree of challenge, hardship and danger, the greater is the development of mutual respect and affiliation.[33] This strong bond generates the aggressive attitude, sense of invincibility and cohesiveness that exists within airborne units. Samuel Stouffer's monumental study of battlefield behaviour, *The American Soldier,* indicated that 80% of respondents believed that a strong group integration was the main reason for stamina in combat. This study also observed that motivation is primarily dependent on group cohesion and that group cohesion in turn, is the decisive factor for combat efficiency. The steadfast self-confidence in oneself and in one's fellow soldiers engenders a belief and philosophy that there is no mission that cannot be accomplished.[34]

The strength and value of the inherent airborne family solidarity are evident. However, there are also pitfalls. It has long been known that the more attractive the group, the greater is its power over the individuals within. Simply put, the greater the group cohesiveness, the greater is its ability to bring about acceptance and conformity in regard to its norms and goals.[35] The solidarity of the airborne fraternity is unquestionable. However, a dilemma occurs when the organization's culture, which defines criteria for leadership and behaviour, becomes dysfunctional. If the leadership within, which is self-defined, cannot perceive the functional and dysfunctional elements of its own culture, how can it work toward change and a cultural evolution?[36]

The inherent reluctance to change is at the central criticism of elite groups such as airborne forces.[37] To many on the outside, a perception exists that considers those units distinctly different from the conventional mould—whether defined as "elite," "special," or "unique"—as actually no better than ill-disciplined rogue outfits. Military analyst and author, Roger Beaumont, described elites as "virtually encapsulated delinquency."[38] They are often accused of being a "law onto themselves." Retired CF Lieutenant-Colonel, Dr. Charles Cotton of Queens University, in his studies of military culture, especially Canada's, concluded, "their [elites] cohesive spirit is a threat to the chain of command and wider cohesion."[39]

Cotton based his assessment on a belief that traditional, more conventional military norms and values were discarded in the elite organizations. For example, leadership and discipline were found to be, more often than not, informal within parachute units. Furthermore, the normal protocol and emphasis placed on ceremony and deportment was relaxed. Similarly, Eliot Cohen reported that "an almost universally observed [timeless] characteristic of elite units is their lack of formal discipline—and sometimes a lack of substantive discipline as well. Elite units often disregard spit and polish or orders about saluting."[40] General De La Billiere, the Commander of the British SAS Group from 1979-1983, recalled that as a junior officer in the SAS, "the men, for their part, never called me 'Sir' unless they wanted to be rude."[41] Eric Morris believed, "the Long Range Desert Group and other like units did offer a means of escape from those petty tediums and irritants of everyday life in the British Army. Drills, guards, fatigues and inspections were almost totally absent."[42] A disturbing similarity is discernable in the Canadian example as well.

The stereotype of individuals who volunteer for parachute and specialist units also shows a parallel with the Canadian case. It reflects sentiments expressed earlier in regard to the "airborne type" and the penchant of the parent line regiments for dumping the aggressive, action-oriented individuals, as well as the disciplinary problems into the Canadian Airborne Regiment. Similar historical examples abound. David Stirling reflected that the SAS "originals" were not really "controllable" but rather "harnessable."[43] The American Rangers were acknowledged to consist largely of "mavericks who couldn't make it in conventional units."[44] The US Green Berets were later likewise described as those "who wanted to try something new and challenging, and who chafed at rigid discipline."[45] In addition, General De La Billiere noted "most officers and men here do not really fit in normal units of the Army, and that's why they're here in the SAS, which is not like anything else in the Services."[46] He assumed most of the volunteers, like himself, "were individualists who wanted to break away from the formal drill-machine discipline" which existed in the army as a whole.[47]

The peril inherent in the fostering of a special and extremely tight-knit group becomes evident. Their focus can become dangerously inwardly orientated. Members of these special groups frequently develop an outlook that treats those outside the club as inferior and unworthy of respect. This occurrence was observed by John Talbot in his study of French paratroopers. He warned that their sense of independence from the rest of the army, their lack of respect for traditional forms of discipline, and their clannishness were the more disturbing dimensions of the "esprit para."[48] Cohen further reinforced these sentiments. He asserted that paratroop officers were so close to their men, that the battalions resembled militant clans more than military organizations.[49] Donna Winslow has recently confirmed these observations in her socio-cultural study of the Canadian Airborne Regiment.[50]

This realization, however, does not represent a flaw which cannot be avoided or corrected. Most of those who commanded in the Canadian Airborne Regiment conceded that maintaining discipline in the Regiment was extremely challenging. This is not surprising since the airborne tended to attract the more aggressive, energized, independent, and action-orientated individuals. What most regimental commanders realized was the need for strong, dynamic leadership to properly channel the energy and exuberance of their soldiers. In the presence of tough demanding leaders, the individual paratrooper and the airborne unit as a whole, exemplified the best of the country's combat arms officers and soldiers. Without it, they would easily represent the nation's worst.

Unfortunately, with time many paratroopers, as well as their supporters, began to see themselves as a de facto military elite. Correspondingly, they began to act as such and demand special consideration, which they often received from the chain of command, particularly from those in the extended "airborne family." This situation created aggravations and animosity within the military establishment. After all, there was no consensus on the Airborne's claim to elite status.

The simmering debate was never addressed. Only in the post-Somalia environment did a profusion of senior leaders, including former Airborne Regiment commanders publicly decry ever having encouraged elitist sentiments in the Canadian paratroopers. In many cases, their assertions were, and are, obscuring history to conform with current politically correct themes and personal aspirations for continued advancement.

However, the issue of whether or not the Canadian airborne force was a true "elite" must be examined. The determination of military elite status, as discussed in the introduction to this book, must not be based on self-definition but rather on a set of criteria. The first is selection; specifically, the rigorous screening processes which maintain extremely high standards of mental and physical ability and fitness, professional experience and skill levels, maturity, and motivation. Second is the designation of an exclusive and specific special mission or role (either conventional or unconventional or both) that is actually exercised. Third is a recognized reputation for excellence (based on the level of training, expertise and professionalism of the group or on its success in operations). Only when these components are met can a military unit or organization be considered elite.

The question now becomes, how do this nation's paratroopers rate throughout the Canadian airborne experience? The country's original paratroopers of the 1st Canadian Parachute Battalion during the Second World War clearly represented a military elite. So too arguably did the jumpers of the Canadian SAS Company of the immediate postwar period. Afterwards however the elite status began to wane. The paratroopers of the Mobile Striking Force and Defence of Canada Force era were anything but an elite. This is not meant to be derogatory but rather a simple statement of fact. The airborne role was allocated minor importance. As a result, there was little difference, with the exception of an occasional jump, to differentiate the paratroopers from the other soldiers.

The establishment of the Canadian Airborne Regiment in 1968 is more problematic. At first, the Regiment represented a military elite. Although selection criteria were not necessarily as rigorous as those applied against many special force type units, they were in effect. The Regiment received only volunteers who were qualified to advanced levels. Furthermore, the organization's role as a strategic level military reserve was reinforced by special formation status, as well as the direct access the Regimental CO had to the Army Commander. Additionally, the Airborne was exempt from normal and routine tasking. However, by the mid 1970s the Regiment began to lose its preferential status. The infusion of less-qualified personnel and the erosion of the Regiment's position within the Army slowly changed its make-up. Categorically, in the aftermath of the move from Edmonton to Petawawa in 1977, the Airborne clearly ceased to be an elite. Membership after the move required only that an individual be parachutist-qualified. Furthermore, the unit had no mission or role that could not be, and was not, performed by other conventional units.

Nonetheless, the fact that the Airborne was not an elite does not belittle its importance or its unique disposition. In the mid 1990s it became fashionable to downplay the Airborne's special nature in the aftermath of Somalia and the hazing videos. Dismissive phrases such as 'parachuting is just another way to the battlefield,' became common. Even though pleasing to many in an era of airborne-angst, it belied the lack of understanding of airborne operations and the special demand on its soldiers. Although not necessarily an elite, the Canadian paratrooper, for the most part, has consistently epitomized the best soldiers and units in the military's combat arms.

The assertion that the paratrooper represented the nation's premier warrior caste was a direct result of both the soldier drawn to the airborne and the type of soldier required as a result of the airborne way of war. Parachuting denotes a great deal more than just a means of delivery to the battlefield. Paratroopers normally arrive exhausted. They endured the process of dressing and waiting fully kitted for long periods of time. It is not uncommon for individuals to be weighted down with 100 pounds of equipment.[51]

Once dressed, the ordeal of flight to the destination must be overcome. Bucking, lurching aircraft, that are tossed about in the wash of previous airplanes, create additional stress for the paratrooper. Avoidance of flak and contour flying, a technique of flying low to the ground and closely following its features, add to the misery.[52] Once on the objective the paratrooper is hostage to the drop zone. If he survives the jump, he often starts his mission with numerous abrasions and bruises, if not more serious injuries such as sprains and fractures. The battle on the ground now begins and normally, he is the first to fight. British Colonel Neville Morris Pughe stated, "the realization that wherever they are committed in the world they [airborne units] will be in, more often than not, difficult terrain and climates, anything from snow to jungle and desert—deployed in conditions of logistical austerity. This demands considerable physical fitness, considerable self-reliance on the part of the soldiers, an adaptability, which is not always found in what one might call ordinary infantry or other units in the army."[53]

The element of the unknown and uncertainty often encountered on landing requires paratroopers to be highly adaptable, full of initiative, tough, resilient and above all else self-reliant. Lieutenant-General Foster, a former Canadian Army commander, underpinned the tenuousness of the paratrooper's plight. He explained that the paratrooper more often than not finds himself "in the door of transport plane at 800 feet above the ground, travelling at 130 knots airspeed, at night, jumping on to a piece of terrain that you may have only seen from a map."[54] S.L.A. Marshall observed that paratroops must always reckon on the probability of a bad scramble during the drop and their training seeks to emphasize methods by which men can be hardened against this contingency.[55] This realization was such that official military manuals conceded, "no paratroop operation can be expected to go exactly according to plan."[56]

To further exacerbate the unique airborne realm of combat, once the drone of the aircraft engines disappears, the paratroopers are on their own. As Corporal Dan Hartigan, a veteran of the D-day Normandy drop stated, "jumping is the most irrevocable commitment anyone can make." He quipped, "there is no going back."[57] In this vein, the paratrooper normally jumps into enemy held territory, often with minimal support. American General Matthew Ridgway believed that when an airborne unit hits the ground, its members are individuals, most often completely alone. "You have no communications whatsoever for some little time," he explained, "particularly when you have jumped at night. You don't know where you are. You don't know who's around you, friend or foe."[58] British Lieutenant General Sir Michael Gray best encapsulated the

CONCLUSION

plight of the airborne soldier. "A parachutist fights a lonely battle," Gray insisted, "he has no real front or rear. He often feels he is fighting the battle on his own."[59]

During the Normandy invasion, Brigadier James Hill fully understood the ambiguous environment and the potential confusion that his paratroopers would face. For this reason he briefed his troops to be prepared, despite their excellent training, for the chaos that undoubtedly would reign.[60] His words were prophetic. Drops were widely dispersed and units were faced with the task of completing their missions while under strength and lacking important equipment. However, the fight was taken to the enemy by scattered groups of paratroopers and under-strength units. Their missions were successfully executed despite the turmoil.[61] The secret of their success was analysed by Major-General Richard Gale, Commander of British 6th Airborne Division during World War II. "In the end," he wrote, "it all boils down to the individual and it is he that counts. Be alert, be vigilant and be resourceful. What you get by stealth and by guts you must hold with skill and determination."[62]

The maintenance of this legacy was reinforced by General Carl Stiner, Commander of the American XVIII Airborne Corps during Operation Just Cause in Panama in 1989. "When we find ourselves in combat we are not shaken up by the 'fog of war'," he insisted, "we act rather than react." Stiner added "down in Panama our paratroopers repeatedly said during post-battle interviews that they ignored the confusion and the darkness and moved to the sounds of the guns."[63]

This unique battleground, one where the situation is never clear, where the airborne soldier has no safe starting position and may find himself totally alone, deep in enemy territory, must be recognized. These special circumstances necessitate the provision of a fundamentally unique mentality, which in turn requires a very special type of soldier. Paratroopers realize that to survive in these conditions they must display aggressiveness, courage, and tenacity. They must maintain mental alertness and exercise initiative. Above all else, they must possess exemplary combat skills. These requirements are attained through extremely demanding and realistic training that challenges the individual both mentally and physically. To strengthen the cloak of invincibility and imbue an aggressive attitude, emphasis is placed on the mystique of fearlessness and ability to overcome any obstacle. Lieutenant-Colonel Pat Sweetnam, a former CO of 3 Airborne Commando, recalled, "in the Airborne Regiment we were attackers, we were as aggressive as could be and we were proud of it."[64] This belief underscored the brutal nature of the paratrooper's battlefield. It was also rooted in the airborne outlook that no challenge is too great, no foe an equal.

Brigadier-General Bruce Jeffries, the Commander of the Canadian Special Service Force in the mid nineties, expressed an understanding of the special nature of the paratrooper. "The nature of airborne soldiering," he wrote, "is such that a spiritual bond of great strength is created. To serve the [Airborne] Regiment is to accept physical and demanding challenge, to conquer fear, to commit to excellence and to sacrifice in the course of operational readiness."[65] It is just such a realization that sets the airborne soldier apart from his more conventional brethren.

The unique environment in which the paratrooper operates has cultivated a distinct genre of warrior. Colonel Herb Pitts, as Regimental Commander in 1971, responded to a reporter's ill-informed question by simply stating, "we're paratroopers and that speaks for itself."[66] Inherent in this reply was the understanding that the airborne soldier embodied a can-do attitude that was backed up by a physical toughness and an unwillingness to accept any situation as insurmountable. Paratroopers continually demonstrated that they were more confident, physically fit, motivated and resourceful than other soldiers in the Army. Generally, this was a direct result of their training, the type of individual attracted to airborne soldiering and the culture of the organization.[67]

For these reasons, Canada's airborne soldiers have been described as the "backbone of the Canadian infantry."[68] Even at the dissolution of the Regiment in 1995, all those in the Special Service Force recognized that the level of training and operational readiness of the Airborne Regiment was unsurpassed in the Canadian Forces and ranked well with those of any infantry unit in the world.[69] Finally, The Regiment's Colonel-in-Chief, His Royal Highness Prince Andrew, the Duke of York, proclaimed, "Let there be no doubt, there has never been a more committed and more worthy soldier than the paratrooper. For 27 years those soldiers were the Canadian Airborne Regiment—the spearhead and embodiment of the fighting spirit of the Canadian Army."[70]

In the end the Canadian paratrooper has not always represented a distinct military elite. Nevertheless, the airborne soldiers often acted as if they were an elite, and more importantly, they were treated as such by others, including the chain of command that frequently tolerated the paratroopers' at times aberrant behaviour. Thus, an unhealthy attitude quickly ensued among some members of the airborne community who saw themselves "above the law." In addition, many of the paratroopers also began to "feed" off the glory of the Airborne Mystique without ensuring that their individual and collective behaviour was consistent with the high standards it demanded.

In spite of the shortcomings of some of those members who wore the maroon beret, and the very few who were involved in the Arone murder, they did represent a unique group who were distinct from their more conventional infantry brethren. Although drawn from the affiliated infantry regiments, the individuals who gravitated to the Airborne were the more aggressive, physically fit and motivated soldiers. They were the individuals who sought action, adventure, and challenge. Once they became paratroopers, they enhanced these qualities and developed additional attributes and skills, such as confidence, initiative, leadership and self-reliance. The outgrowth of training individuals to operate in the highly dangerous and often very confused environment associated with airborne operations was the transformation of good solid soldiers into even better ones. As a result, the nation's airborne warriors have indeed epitomized the best of our country's combat soldiers. In the final analysis, the Canadian paratrooper has always personified the proficiency of the Canadian Army.

In all, the continuing animosity between the airborne soldiers and the remainder of the military establishment, often exacerbated by the silent debate on elitism, as well as the larger failure to fully rationalize the role, structure, and relevancy of airborne forces, condemned them to an uncertain future. Their existence was continually challenged. They were consistently the target of acrimonious debate. The lack of acceptance by the military establishment as a whole, in regard to the relevancy of paratroopers in the Canadian context, proved to be a difficult obstacle to overcome. Consequently, the nation's paratroopers represented, for most of their existence, the Army's bastard sons.

Nevertheless, throughout their existence, Canada's airborne troops have epitomized the best of the nation's combat soldiers. The sad events of Somalia were symptoms of long term larger problems rather than causes. In the final analysis, the failure to properly identify a consistent and pervasive role for the nation's airborne forces led to a roller coaster existence dependent on personalities in power and political expedients of the day. This approach ultimately brought the "great adventure" to an ignoble end.

CONCLUSION

Notes for Chapter Eleven

1. Letter to author, 24 May 1996.
2. Lieutenant-Colonel E.M. Flanagan, "Give Airborne Spurs," *Infantry School Quarterly*, Vol 39, No. 2, October 1951, 33.
3. Saunders, 103; and William Cockerham, "Selective Socialization: Airborne Training as Status Passage," *Journal of Political and Military Sociology*, Vol 1, No. 2, Fall 1973, 216.
4. See Chapter One, text and accompanying endnotes 70-75. See also Saunders, 320; W.B. Breuer, *Geronimo* (New York: St. Martin's Press, 1992), 9; John Talbot, "The Myth and Reality of the Paratrooper in the Algerian War," *Armed Forces and Society*, November 1976, 71-72; Roger Beaumont, *Military Elites*, (New York: The Bobbs-Merrill Coy Inc., 1974), 101. Beaumont commented, "Airborne forces established a new image of the combat leader. Even generals had to be flat stomached and young;" Bercuson, *Significant Incident*, 175; and Max Hastings and Simon Jenkins, *The Battle for the Falklands* (London: Pan Books, 1983), 267.
5. See Chapter One, text and accompanying endnotes 77-89. The 82nd Airborne Division was reported to have emerged from Normandy with the reputation of being "a pack of jackals; the toughest, most resourceful and bloodthirsty infantry in the ETO." Clay Blair, *Ridgway's Paratroopers. The American Airborne in World War II* (New York: The Dial Press, 1985), 295. See also endnote 4 this chapter.
6. D.R. Segal, J.J. Harris, J.M. Rothberg, and D.H. Marlowe, "Paratroopers as Peacekeepers," *Armed Forces & Society*, Vol 10, No, 4, Summer 1984, 489; and W.C. Cockerham, "Attitudes Toward Combat Among US Army Paratroopers," *Journal of Political and Military Sociology*, Vol 6, Spring 1978, 11. The superiority in combat associated with paratroopers was seen to emanate from such qualities as courage and the seeking of action, which are closely linked to the jump experience. Gideon Aran, "Parachuting," *American Journal of Sociology*, Vol 80, No. 1, 147.
7. Winslow, 47.
8. Blair, 27. See also Saunders, 317. Larry Gough, a writer for the American *Liberty* magazine, recorded, "In the first place, they [parachutists] are perfect specimens. They have to be because their work is rough tough and full of excellent opportunities to get hurt. Mentally they're quick on the trigger, again because their job demands it, because split seconds can make the difference between instant death or a successfully completed job. Larry Gough, "Parachutists Want it Tough," *Liberty*, 4 December 1943, CAFM files.
9. "3rd Parachute Brigade—Training Instruction No. 3," 23 July 1943, 2 & 6. DHist, File 145.4036 (D1). The renowned reputation for the fighting prowess of paratroopers was also noted in anecdotal combat recollections. One account recalled that as the combat at the Merville Battery in Normandy, developed into hand-to-hand fighting, the German gunners recognized the parachutist badge on the British jump smocks. Once German soldiers realized their opponents were *Fallschirmjägers* they quickly lost heart and surrendered. Saunders, 185.
10. Maurice Newnham, "Parachute Soldiers," *RUSI*, Vol 65, No. 580, November 1950, 592. General-Leutnant Brauer commanded a German parachute regiment during the invasion of the Low Countries in 1940.
11. Dr. Terry White, *The Making of the World's Elite Forces* (London: Sidgwick & Jackson Ltd., 1992), 14. Another reference is made in Capt Newnham's *Prelude to Glory*, where the author stated, "...the majority got to the edge of the hole in the aircraft before refusing. Four men fainted in the aircraft, while a number jumped in a state of collapse having forced themselves to do so by sheer willpower."
12. *War Diary of the 2nd Parachute Battalion with 1 Special Service Force Serial 1354*, NA, RG 24, Vol 15301 & 15302, Vol 9—War Diary SSF Bn, 1 April 1943—30 April 1943, enclosed articles "First Jump 'Disappointing' to Many—'Over too Soon,'" and Don Mason, "Air Commandos' will Strike hard at Axis."
13. Major J.S. Hitsman, "Medical Problems of Paratroop Training," *Canadian Army Journal*, Vol 4, No. 1, April 1950, 17.
14. Beaumont, *Military Elites*, 101.

15. Sir Charles Wilson (Lord) Moran, *The Anatomy of Courage* (New York: Avery Publishing Group Inc, 1987), 61. Lord Moran was a front line medical officer during World War I and the personal physician to British Prime Minister Winston Churchill during World War II. Clearly, the question of courage is not quite so simple. Psychologists, sociologists and military historians have shown that courage is also highly dependent on leadership, training, unit cohesion, fatigue and situational circumstances. These factors are important in determining an individual's ability to summon the "willpower" required to face a specific situation. See endnote 18 this chapter and Terry Copp and Bill McAndrew, *Battle Exhaustion* (Montreal: McGill-Queen's University Press, 1990), 59, 75, 97, 100-104.

16. Lieutenant-General F.A.M. Browning, "Airborne Forces," *RUSI,* Vol 89, No. 556, November 1944, 353. Sir John W. Hackett, a veteran of the "bridge too far" at Arnhem late in World War II, remembered that the act of parachuting provided each member with the knowledge that "he had won a very important victory over himself." Roger A. Beaumont, "Airborne: Life Cycle of a Military Subculture," *Military Review,* Vol 51, No. 6, 53.

17. B.M. Bass, *Leadership and Performance Beyond Expectations* (New York: Free Press, 1985), 69. It was further noted that with confidence a soldier willingly faces the enemy and withstands deprivations, minor setbacks, and extreme stress, knowing he and his unit are capable of succeeding.

18. S.J. Rachman, *Fear and Courage* (San Francisco: W.H. Freeman and Company, 1990) 63-64. Studies have also shown that well-led and cohesive units tended to have fewer stress casualties than units lower in these qualities. J.G. Hunt, and J.D. Blair, *Leadership on the Future Battlefield* (New York: Brassey's, 1986), 215.

19. 1 Canadian Parachute Battalion, *War Diaries,* 15 January 1943. CAFM, File A84.019.01, January 1943, Envelope 2 of 22.

20. Major-General A.S. Newman, *What Are Generals Made Of?* Novato, CA: Presidio, 1987, 197.

21. Ibid., 193. It was said of Maxwell Taylor, a wartime commander of the 82nd Airborne Division and later Chief of the Joint Chiefs of Staff, "he really didn't like to jump out of airplanes, but he liked to be around people who jumped out of airplanes." Blair, 36. Gideon Aran observed that "jumping encourages self-confidence, determination, self-reliance, masterful activity, aggression, courage, and other items symptomatic of the phallic-narcissistic type, all of which are very important in a military setting, especially in paratroop commando units, that rely heavily on individual action and are aggressive in nature. Aran," 147.

22. Ward Just, *Military Men* (New York: Alfred A. Knopf, 1970), 130. Research has indicated that airborne troops were more willing to deploy for combat than personnel in more conventional ground manoeuvre units. Segal, "Paratroopers as Peacekeepers," 489.

23. Just, 130. John Talbot described the "esprit para" as the "rejection of materialism, the exaltation of the asceticism, violence and risk, of action for action's sake." Talbot, 75.

24. S.L.A. Marshall, *The Armed Forces Officer* (Washington D.C.: Department of Defence, 1950), 141.

25. Aran, 148.

26. Cockerham, "Selective Socialization," 216; Beaumont, "Airborne," 53; "Training Paratroops," *CATM,* No. 20, November 1942, 10; and "3rd Parachute Training Instruction No. 3," A1. DHist, File 145.4036 (D1).

27. Winslow, 132. The special treatment of the Airborne was also supported by most of those interviewed.

28. Newman, 190.

29. Message, CCUNPROFOR Commander 095, 041202Z Mar 95, "Canadian Airborne Regiment—Laying Up of Colours."

30. General K. Foster, "Remarks by the Colonel of the Regiment," *Maroon Beret—Final Edition*, November 1995, 4.

31. Interview with author, 4 October 1996. One sergeant-major of the British 2nd Parachute Regiment stated that in airborne units the officers and men rely on one another. He explained that "a special bond was created because of the fact that the men knew that the officers, like them, endured the same difficult training prior to arriving at Regiment." Rory Bridson, *The Making of a Para* (London: Sidgwick &

Jackson Ltd, 1989), 81. Major-General Neuman declared, "There's a close bond between the airborne soldier and his officer, because each knows the other has passed the jump test. And they continue to do so together. Each believes the other will be a good man to have around when things get sweaty." Newman, 193.

32. E. Aronson and J. Mills, "The Effect of Severity of Initiation on Liking for a Group," *Journal of Abnormal & Social Psychology,* 1957, 157-158. Elliot Aronson of Stanford University and Judson Mills of the US Army Leadership and Human Research Unit established this in their 1959 laboratory experiments. They stated, "Subjects who underwent a severe initiation perceived the group as being significantly more attractive than those who underwent a mild or no initiation." See also R.B. Cialdini, *Influence. Science & Practise, 3rd ed.* (Arizona: Harper Collins, 1993), 70 &74; and Major James McCollum, "The Airborne Mystique," *Military Review,* Vol 56, No. 11, November 1976, 16.

33. W.D. Henderson, *Cohesion: The Human Element in Combat* (Washington: National Defence University Press, 1985), 14.

34. Elmar Dinter, *Hero or Coward* (London: Frank Cass, 1985), 41; and Anthony Kellet, *Combat Motivation* (Boston: Nijhoff Publishing, 1982), 45-46.

35. W.R. Lassey and M. Sashkin, eds., *Leadership and Social Change* (San Diego: University Association Inc., 1983), 33 & 35; Irving L. Janis, *Victims of Groupthink* (Boston: Houghton Mifflin Company, 1972), 4, 9, 13, & 41.

36. See E.H. Schein, *Organizational Culture and Leadership, 2nd ed.* (San Francisco: Jossey-Bass Publishing, 1992), 15; and Winslow, 53-82.

37. The terms "elite" or "special units" include airborne units and paratroopers in regard to this segment of the chapter. This is necessary to convey the ideas of other scholars who have researched the given issue and utilized the respective terms to capture a wide range of elite and specialist units. See the introduction for the analysis and discussion of the term "elite."

38. Beaumont, *Military Elites,* 192.

39. Charles A. Cotton, "Military Mystique." (Airborne Forces Museum Files—no publication material available.)

40. Cohen, 74.

41. General Sir Peter De La Billiere, *Looking For Trouble. SAS to Gulf Command* (London: Harper Collins Publishers, 1995), 117.

42. Eric Morris, *Guerillas in Uniform* (London: Hutchinson: 1989), 15.

43. Anthony Kemp, *The SAS at War*, 11.

44. Charles M. Simpson III, *Inside the Green Berets. The First Thirty Years* (Novato, CA: Presidio, 1983), 14.

45. Ibid., 21.

46. De La Billiere, 236. The author noted that the re-born SAS in 1952 won themselves a "bad name through their cavalier approach on operations and their riotous behaviour off-duty in Kuala Lumpur." Ibid., 89.

47. Ibid., 98.

48. Talbot, 75. Major-General Lesley McNair, Commander of US Army Ground Forces, remarked at a press conference in Washington, D.C. in 1942, "They [paratroopers] are our problem children. They make lots of money, and they know they're good. This makes them a little temperamental, but they're great soldiers." Breuer, *Geronimo,* 9.

49. Cohen, 69. See also Winslow, 135-141.

50. Winslow, 126-133.

51. Martin Wolfe, a veteran of the Normandy invasion in 1944, remembered having to push paratroopers laden with up to 125 pounds of gear up the steps into his aircraft. Similarly, Colonel Ivan Hershner recalled, "With our gear the average man weighed about 300 pounds that night [6 June 1944]. Martin Wolfe, "This Is It," *Air Power History,* Vol 41, No. 2, Summer 1994, 32; and Heike Hasenauer, "Airborne's 50th Anniversary," *Soldiers,* Vol 45, No. 9, September 1990, 49.

52. J.A. Easterbrook, *Fatigue in Mobile Striking Force Parachutists, JSORT Memorandum No. 55/8* (Ottawa: DND Joint Services Operational Research Team, 1955), 1-8. The research noted, "airsickness contributes to DZ fatigue in turbulent flying conditions," and that DZ fatigue is "intimately associated with high anxiety and tension," and it is "increased by increased flight time."

53. Major Scott A. McMichael, *Discussions on Training & Employing Light Infantry* (Fort Leavenworth: Combat Studies Institute Report, 1986), 2.

54. *Somalia Commission,* Hearing Transcripts, Vol 3, 5 October 1995, 384. Foster also noted the uncertainty of the drop itself. He stated that "you don't know until you are at the RV who is there and what actions are required (due to accidents, persons hung-up in trees, etc)." Interview with author, 6 June 1998.

55. S.L.A. Marshall, *Men Against Fire* (New York: William Morrow & Company, 1947), 152. Lieutenant-General Gale noted that "the confusion that confronts an airborne man when he is chucked out of his glider or parachute and finds himself facing the gloomy realities of life, is terrific. It is training that counts." R.N. Gale, "Aircraft for Army Uses," *RUSI,* Vol 65, August 1950, No. 579, 434.

56. Canada. *Military Science, Part I and Part II* (Ottawa: DND, 1948/49), 99.

57. Barbara Wickens, "Coming Down From the Sky," *Maclean's,* 6 June 1994, 49.

58. Ridgway, 7. Official training directives ensured that the training of the paratrooper was to bring out qualities of independence to ensure they used their own initiative in whatever numbers they found themselves. "Notes on German Airborne Troops," *CATM,* No. 11, February 1942, 13.

59. Lieutenant-General Michael Gray, "The Birth of A Regiment," *Illustrated London News—Red Berets '44,* 1994, 19.

60. At all his briefings since the war Brigadier Hill stresses this story and its importance in the context of parachute operations. This is also the reason for the airborne practise of detailed briefings to all members of a unit. Full understanding of the mission and plan allows for those who arrive on the objective to carry on regardless of casualties among the leaders. The German paratroopers during World War II had Ten Commandments that had to be memorized by all. The eighth commandment stated, "You must grasp the full intention of every operation, so that if your leader is killed you can fulfill it yourself."

61. The 9th Battalion seized the Merville Battery despite the fact that the attack was launched with only 150 of the 635 men allocated for the task. Saunders, 318. Sergeant Bullock, from the 9th Parachute Battalion, and a handful of others were dropped almost thirty miles inland. They reported to their units four days later with evidence to show that they had killed numerous enemy, including twenty senior German generals of Brigadier rank or higher. Another paratrooper swam twenty miles down the Orne River to reach Pegasus Bridge. Ellis Plaice, "The Lonely War," *Illustrated London News—Red Berets '44,* 1994, 60.

62. Gray, "Birth of a Regiment," 19. No doubt should exist over the question of determination or courage. Airborne casualty rates from World War II provide ample proof. The German paratroopers suffered 58% casualties in the invasion of Crete, a full 25% of the participants being killed. Morris, *Guerillas in Uniform,* 45-46; Brigadier M.A.J. Tugwell, "Day of the Paratroops," *Military Review,* Vol 57, No.3, March 1977, 48; and Centre of Military History, *Airborne Operations—A German Appraisal* (Washington D.C.: US Government Printing Office, 1989), 21-23. Another account reported German casualties at 44% and aircraft losses at 170 out of 530 operational (32%). Blair, 29. The American 82nd Airborne Division incurred 27% casualties in Sicily and 46% in Normandy. Ridgway, 102 & 295; Blair 102 & 295. Approximately 80% of the British 1st Airborne Division was lost during Operation Market Garden. F.H. Hinsley, *British Intelligence in the Second World War, Vol 3, Part II* (NewYork: Cambridge University Press, 1988), 382-389. The Waffen SS Paratroop Battalion suffered 62% casualties in its raid on Tito's headquarters in Yugoslavia in 1944. Kunzmann-Milius, *Fallschirmjäger der Waffen—SS im Bild* (Osnabrück: Munin Verlag GMBH, 1986), 7. In the overall American experience of World War II, over 30% of all airborne personnel became casualties. This compares to only 10% among regular infantry formations. Kurt Gabel, *The Making of a Paratrooper* (Lawrence: University of Kansas Press, 1990), 268.

63. Hasenauer, 49.

64. Letter to author, 24 May 1996. Master-Corporal A.E. Innes declared that the Airborne was a unit that was maintaining an aggressive fighting spirit that had largely died out in the rest of the Army. He also added that it was the only place he had served with a real esprit de corps. Interview with author, April 1995. General Jean Boyle, the former CDS, and hardly an airborne supporter, conceded that, "there is no doubt that the Airborne are the toughest and some of the meanest soldiers. They have tremendous fighting capability." Winslow, 117.

65. Canadian Brigadier-General N.B. Jeffries' address to the Special Service Force on 1 March 1995 during the SSF parade in CFB Petawawa to mark the disbandment and removal of the Canadian Airborne Regiment from the Order of Battle.

66. Peter Walls, "Paratroop commandos are ready to go anywhere," *Herald,* 13 January 1973. CAFM Files.

67. Brigadier-General Douglas commented, "soldiers in this [Airborne] Regiment are not known as complainers and they do not tolerate complaints. They show a great pride in not showing pain and working in spite of it." Rick Brennan, "Injured Soldiers 'lulled' by floating sensation: Colonel," *Ottawa Citizen,* 27 January 1984. Colonel Denis Tabbernor asserted, "No matter how hard it was or much pain there was, they wanted to soldier. It was exhilarating." Letter to author, 31 March 1997. CWO B.C. Robinson recalled that he was absolutely stunned if three men reported for sick parade on any given day during his tenure as 2 Commando RSM. Interview with author, 21 September 1998. Colonel Kenworth stated, "The Regiment attracts those who are looking for a challenge, who are aggressive, who are fit and fully motivated." Interview with author, 4 October 1996. Major-General Neuman said, "You cannot accept quitters in the airborne. In addition to other reasons, paratroopers will not tolerate a quitter among them." Neuman, 77.

68. *Somalia Commission,* Transcript of Policy Hearing, Vol 4, 21 June 1995, 621.

69. SSFHQ, "Public Affairs Plan—Disbandment of the Canadian Airborne Regiment," 21 February 1995, 2.

70. "The Petawawa Years, 1977-1995." CAFM Files, no author or date given.

(Courtesy Canadian Airborne Forces Museum)

ABBREVIATIONS

ACE	Allied Command Europe
AIC	Airborne indoctrination course
AMF(L)	Allied Mobile Force (Land)
APC	Armoured personnel carrier
AVGP	Armoured vehicle general purpose
BSP	Basic Security Plan
CABC	Canadian Airborne Centre
CAFM	Canadian Airborne Forces Museum
CAS	Chief of the Air Staff
CANUS	Canada/United States
CAST	Canadian Air-Sea Transportable Brigade
CATM	Canadian Army training memorandums
1 Cdn Para Bn	1st Canadian Parachute Battalion
CAR	Canadian Airborne Regiment: unofficial but commonly used abbreviation
CDA	Conference of Defence Associates
Cdn AB Regt	Canadian Airborne Regiment
CDN AB Regt BG	Canadian Airborne Regiment Battle Group
CDS	Chief of the Defence Staff
CF	Canadian Forces
CFB	Canadian Forces Base
CFD	Canadian Forces detachment
CFP	Canadian Forces publication
CDHSR	Canadian Division Headquarters and Signals Regiment
Cdo	Commando
CFOO	Canadian Forces Organizational Order
CGS	Chief of the General Staff
CIBG	Canadian Infantry Brigade Group
CJATC	Canadian Joint Air Training Centre
CLS	Combined Land Staff (formerly LFC)
CMBG	Canadian Mechanized Brigade Group
CO	Commanding Officer
COS	Chief of Staff
CPC	Canadian Parachute Centre (formerly CABC)
CSM	Company (or Commando) Sergeant Major
DAD	Director Army Doctrine
DCF	Defence of Canada Force
DCO	Defence of Canada Operations (or Deputy Commanding Officer)
DDA	Director Defence Analysis
DEM	Daily executive meeting
DSR	Defence Structure Review
DGLFR	Director General Land Force Requirements
DGSP	Director General Strategic Planning
DHist	(DND) Directorate of History (now entitled DHH)
DHH	Directorate of History and Heritage (formerly DHist)
DLO	Director of Land Operations
DMO & P	Director Military Operations and Plans
DND	Department of National Defence
DPKO	Directorate of Peacekeeping Operations

FMC	Force Mobile Command	PPCLI	Princess Patricia's Canadian Light Infantry
FOL	Forward operating location	R22eR	Royal 22nd Regiment
GOC	General Officer Commanding	RCAF	Royal Canadian Air Force
GS	General Staff	RCE	Royal Canadian Engineers
HALO	High altitude low opening [military freefall parachuting]	RCIC	Royal Canadian Infantry Corps
HQ	Headquarters	RCL	Royal Canadian Legion
HRS	Humanitarian relief sector [Somalia]	RCR	Royal Canadian Regiment
		RCSI	Royal Canadian School of Infantry
ICBM	Inter-continental ballistic missile	RHQ	Regimental Headquarters
IS	Internal security	RM	Regimental Major
JAS	Joint Air School	RSM	Regimental Sergeant Major
JCS	Joint Chiefs of Staff	SAM	Surface to air missile
LAPES	Low altitude parachute extraction system	SAR	Search and Rescue
		SAS	Special Air Service
LAV	Light armoured vehicle	SCEAND	Standing Committee on External Affairs & National Defence
LFC	Land Force Command (formerly FMC)		
LFCA	Land Forces Central Area	SCONDVA	Standing Committee on National Defence & Veterans Affairs
LIB	Light Infantry Battalion		
MAJAID	Major air disaster		
MND	Minister of National Defence	SF	Special Forces
MSF	Mobile Striking Force	SOF	Special Operations Forces
NAC	National Archives of Canada	SOPs	Standard operating procedures
NCO	Non-commissioned officer	SSF	Special Service Force
NDA	National Defence Act	SUE	Small unit exchange
NDHQ	National Defence Headquarters	UN	United Nations
NGO	Non-governmental organization	UNAMIR	UN Assistance Mission in Rwanda
NORAD	North American Air Defence (later Aerospace) Command	UNFICYP	UN Force in Cyprus
		UNHCR	UN High Commissioner for Refugees
NRMA	National Resources Mobilization Act		
		UNITAF	Unified Task Force (Somalia)
OC	Officer Commanding (normally a company or commando)	UNPROFOR	UN Protection Force (former Yugoslavia)
OPFOR	Opposition Force	VCDS	Vice Chief of the Defence Staff
PJBD	Permanent Joint Board of Defence	VCGS	Vice Chief of the General Staff
PMD	Parachute maintenance depot		

I N D E X

1st Canadian Infantry Division, 28
1st Canadian Parachute Battalion, 15, 32, 34, 77
1 Canadian Division Headquarters and Signals Regiment (*see* Signals Regiment)
1 Commando, 122, 163, 172, 228
2 Combat Engineer Regiment, 151
2 Commando, 124, 163, 169, 193-5, 228
2 Royal Canadian Horse Artillery (RCHA), 151
3 Airborne Commando, 152, 163, 173
3 Commando Group, 252
3 Mechanized Commando, 144
3rd British Parachute Brigade, 268
6th British Airborne Division, 15, 31
82nd Motorized Infantry Division, 33

"E" Battery, 2 RCHA, 151

Active Force Brigade Group, 72, 78, 81
Ad Hoc Committee on Defence Policy, 101
Airborne/Air-transportable Brigade Group, 76
Airborne Battle Group (*see* Canadian Airborne Battle Group)
Airborne Commando Regiment, 120
Airborne Indoctrination Course (AIC), 219
Airborne mystique, 18, 267, 270
Airborne Service Support Unit (ASSU), 152
Alaska (*see also* North), 47, 75

Alaska Defence Command, 49
Alaska Highway, 48-9, 82
Allard, Lieutenant-General Jean Victor, 103-7, 121
Allied Command Europe (ACE), 104, 149
American Special Forces, 109
Anderson, Admiral John, 219
Anderson, Lieutenant-General W.A.B., 105
Armored Vehicle General Purpose (*see* Grizzly)
Aran, Gideon, 270
Arctic (*see* North)
Arone, Shidane, 15, 197
Arril, Lieutenant Ken, 34

Baden-Solingen, 144
Bakovici, 234
Balasevicius, Major Anthony, 228
Barr, Colonel Mike, 113, 120, 124, 127
Basic Security Plan (Canada-US BSP), 51, 73, 75, 77, 264
Belet Huen (Somalia), 199
Belzile, Lieutenant-General Charles, 168
Beno, Brigadier-General Ernie, 153, 192-5
Blanchette, Major Mike, 167
Bland, Douglas, 109, 144
Board of Inquiry (BOI), Canadian Airborne Regiment Battle Group, 219
Bomarc surface-to-air missile, 100
Bon, Dr. Daniel, 227
Bossasso (Somalia), 191
Boyle, Major-General Jean, 220, 230
Bradbrooke, Lieutenant-Colonel G.F.P., 33
Bradley, General Omar, 109

Bradley, Lieutenant-Colonel Dr. Peter, 153, 170
Bragdon, Lieutenant-Colonel Ron, 153, 163
Brauer, Lieutenant-General Bruno, 268
British Airborne Forces, 269
British Expeditionary Force (BEF), 28
British Parachute Corps, 28
British Parachute Regiment, 268
British Special Air Service Regiment (*see* Special Air Service)
British War Office, 30
Brooke, Field-Marshal Sir Alan, 27, 35
Brown, Dr. Harold, 100
Browning, Lieutenant-General Frederick "Boy", 27, 269
Burns, Colonel E.L.M., 27, 29

CF-105 Avro Arrow, 100
Cabinet Defence Committee, 76
Cadieux, Leo, 126
Canadian Active Service Force (CSAF), 32
Canadian Air-Sea Transportable (CAST) Brigade Group, 162
Canadian Airborne Battle Group, 196
Canadian Airborne Holding Unit, 252
Canadian Airborne Regiment (Cdn AB Regt) 15, 17, 120-3, 128, 149, 189, 219, 221, 273
Canadian Army Pacific Force, 35
Canadian Army Training Memorandum (CATM), 34
Canadian Cabinet War Committee, 31
Canadian Expeditionary Force (CEF), 28

Canadian Forces Base (CFB) Edmonton (*see* Edmonton)
Canadian Forces Base (CFB) Petawawa (*see* Petawawa)
Canadian Forces Organizational Order (CFOO), 125, 162-3, 187
Canadian Forces Parachute Maintenance Depot, 151
Canadian Joint Air Training Centre (CJATC), 71, 73
Canadian Joint Task Force Somalia Command, 220, 226
Canadian Mechanized Brigade Group(CMBG), 220
Canadian Military Headquarters (CMHQ), 31
Canadian Parachute Centre (CPC), 256, 257
Canadian Parachute Training Centre (CPTC), 70
Canadian Rangers, 146
Canadian Special Air Service (SAS) Company, 71-3, 77, 122
Cannizzo, Dr. Cynthia, 165
CANOL (Canadian Oil) project, 49
Caron, Brigadier-General M., 190
Chief of Force Development (CFD), 224
Chiefs of Staff Committee, 47
Chretien, Prime Minister Jean, 229
Christie, Colonel Andrew, 144, 151
Churchill, Prime Minister Winston, 26
Claxton, Brooke, 70, 79-81
Cohen, Eliot, 20
Cohen, Maxwell, 126
Collenette, David, 230
Conference of Defence Associates (CDA), 147, 149
Cotton, Dr. Charles, 194

Cowling, Colonel Dick, 163
Crabbe, Brigadier-General Ray, 187
Crerar, Major-General H.D.G., 28-30
Cyprus, 143-4, 162

Danson, Barney, 152
D'Artois, Captain Guy, 73
de Chastelain, Major-General John, 173, 191, 196, 231, 253, 255
de Faye Commission, 219, 235
de Faye, Major-General Tom, 219
de La Billiere, General, 272
Deep Battle, 26
Defence of Canada Force (DCF), 16-17, 100-1, 265
Defence Program (1954), 99
Defence Scheme No. 3: Major War, 79
Defence Structure Review (DSR), 145
Desbarats, Peter, 185
Dextraze, General Jacques, 143-4, 148-9
Dick, Lieutenant-Colonel Richard, 153
Diefenbaker, Prime Minister John, 100
Dillon, Major Pat, 169
Director General of Public Affairs (DGPA), 227
Director of Land Operations (DLO), 162
Directorate of Military Operations and Plans (DMO&P), 31, 83, 99
Directorate of Military Training (DMT), 31
Directorate of Strategic Planning, 126
Director of Weapons and Development, 72
Douglas, Brigadier-General Ian, 123

Eadie, Lieutenant-Colonel Fraser, 32
Eden, Anthony, 27
Edmonton, CFB, 49, 122, 149, 255
Edwards, Her Excellency Lucie, 200
elite status, 18-20, 21, 34, 152, 154, 167, 268, 273
Exercise Bulldog II, 85

Exercise Eagle, 81
Exercise Stalwart Providence, 193
Exercise Sweetbriar, 82
Eyre, Kenneth, 45, 112, 127

FLQ crisis, 143
Falls, Admiral Robert, 144, 165
Fallschirmjäger, 27
Ferron, Lieutenant-Colonel Jim, 193
Firlotte, Lieutenant Bob, 34
First Special Service Force, 40, 73, 269
Force Mobile Command (FMC), 104, 123
Fort Benning, Georgia, 31
Foster, Lieutenant-General Kent, 168, 174, 186, 253
Foulkes, General Charles, 100
Fowler, Deputy Minister Bob, 227
Fraser, Colonel Ian, 127, 146, 148, 162
French Foreign Legion, 163

Gale, Major-General Richard, 275
Gallea, Major Dave, 257
Gaudreau, Major-General J.M.R., 150, 164, 173-4, 178,
Gervais, Lieutenant-Colonel I.N., 173
Godfrey, Sergeant Mark, 217
Gray, Colin, 20, 73
Gray, Lieutenant-General Sir Michael, 274
Graydon, Gordon, 79
Green Berets, 272
Griesbach Barracks, 122
Grizzly, Armored Vehicle General Purpose (AVGP), 190

Hammond, Major Jamie, 223
Haswell, Colonel, 226
Hatton, Colonel Rick, 163
Hellyer, Paul, 100, 103
Hewson, Major-General C.W., 173
Hewson Report, 173
High Altitude Low Opening (HALO), 122
Hill, Brigadier James, 268
Holmes, Brigadier-General Walt, 151, 187

Houghton, Colonel Michael, 155, 191
Howe, Jonathan T., 200
Hubero, General Mohammed Ahmed, 199
Humanitarian Relief Sector (HRS) Somalia, 196, 198

Independent Parachute Company Groups, 255
Inter-Continental Ballistic Missile (ICBM) 16, 98-100

Japanese threat (WWII), 47-8
Jeffries, Brigadier-General Bruce, 230, 257, 275
Johnston, Lieutenant-General R.B., 200
Joint Air School (JAS) (*see also* Canadian Joint Air Training Centre), 71
Joint Basic War Plan, US-British Commonwealth Plan 1 (ABC 1), 51
Joint Canadian-United States Basic Defence Plan 2 (ABC-22), 51
Joint Intelligence Committee, 80
Jorgenson, Lieutenant-Colonel Mike, 257

Kenward, Colonel Peter, 153, 221, 237
King, Prime Minister Mackenzie, 28, 44, 51, 70
Kitching, Brigadier George, 82
Korea, 79

Labbé, Lieutenant-Colonel Serge, 173, 206, 209
Land Forces Central Area (LFCA), 188, 221, 229
Land Force Command (LFC), 190
Land Force Restructuring, Detailed Implementation Plan, 150, 152
Light Infantry Battalion (LIB) 18, 257
Loomis, Major-General Dan, 113
Lynch, Charles, 153

Macdonald, Donald, 127
MacDonald, Malcolm, 50
MacGregor, Colonel E.M.K., 108

Mackenzie, Major-General Lewis, 199
Manhattan, 126
Mann, Major-General Church, 69
Massey, Vincent, 50
Mathieu, Lieutenant-Colonel Carol, 194, 221
Matte, Brigadier-General Michel, 190, 192, 195
McDougall, Barbara, 200
McGibbon, Colonel D.B., 109, 145
McNamara, Robert, 109
McNaughton, Lieutenant-General A.G.L., 25, 28-30
Military Airlift Command, 109
Mitchell, Brigadier-General Greg, 170
Mitchell, Colonel William, 25
Mitchell, Lieutenant-Colonel Dan, 254
Mobile Force (Land), 149
Mobile Striking Force (MSF), 16, 76, 78, 82
Moll, Dr. A.E., 33
Montgomery, Field Marshal Sir Bernard Law, vii
Morneault, Lieutenant-Colonel P.R., 188, 193, 195
Munro, Ross, 81
Murchie, Colonel J.C., 28

NATO, 83, 85
NATO ACE Mobile Force (Land), 222
NORAD, 101
National Resources Mobilization Act (NRMA), 32
Newfoundland, 75
Newman, Major-General A.S., 269
Nicklin, Major Jeff, 32
Non-governmental agencies (NGOs), 199
North (Arctic)
 air defence, 99-100
 defence of, 45-50, 74, 101, 126, 166
 security of, 53, 165
 sovereignty of, 52, 75, 126, 166, 266
 US encroachment, 49-50, 74, 101, 126, 166
North American Air Defence Modernization Program, 166

Northern Region Headquarters (NRHQ), 127
Northwest Passage, 126

Oakley, Robert, 200
O'Brien, Lieutenant-Colonel Lorne, 168
Ogdensburg Agreement, 48
Oka Crisis, 186
Operation Cordon, 191
Operation Deliverance, 192, 196
Operation Essay, 143
Operation Lance, 225
Operation Passage, 225
Operational Plan 100, 125
Operation Python, 186

Paget, General Sir Bernard, 30
Painchaud, Colonel, 20, 152
Para Nomads, 172
Parachute Maintenance Depot, 151
Paradis, Lieutenant-General J.J., 176
Parliamentary Standing Committee on National Defence, 105
Pearl Harbor, 48
Pearson, Lester B., 74, 102
Pearson, Major-General Willard, 270
Pentney, Lieutenant-Colonel Dave, 163, 256
Permanent Joint Board for Defence (PJBD), 47
Petawawa, CFB, 149, 161
Pickersgill, J.W., 50
Pitts, Colonel Herb, 124, 144, 146, 271
Polar Sea (US Coast Guard), 166
Pope, Major-General Maurice, 30, 44
Porch, Douglas, 20
Prince Andrew, HRH Duke of York 276
Princess Patricia's Canadian Light Infantry (PPCLI), 73, 77-8, 84, 105, 169, 194, 235
Pughe, Colonel Neville Morris, 274

Ralston, Honourable J.L., 31
Ready Force (*see* UN Ready Force)
Reay, Lieutenant-General Gordon, 221, 232, 253, 255
Rebel Flag, 231, 234
Richardson, James, 146
Ridgway, General Matthew, 274
Rivers, Manitoba, 81
Robertson, Norman, 74, 80
Robinson, Chief Warrant Officer B.C., 113
Rochester, Colonel D.H., 120
Royal Canadian Air Force (RCAF), 30, 99
Royal Canadian Infantry Corps (RCIC), 107
Royal Canadian Legion, 148
Royal Canadian Regiment (RCR), 73, 78, 105, 173, 192
Royal Canadian School of Infantry, 108
Royal 22nd Regiment (R22eR), 73, 78, 105, 195
Rules of Engagement, 197
Rwanda, 225

Sahara (*see* Western Sahara)
Save the Regiment Committee, 148
Semianiw, Colonel Walter, 228, 238
Sentinel, 125
Seward, Major Anthony, 194, 196-7
Sharp, Lieutenant-General F.R., 116
Sharp, Mitchell, 126
Signals Regiment (1 CDHSR), 225
Simonds, Lieutenant-General G.G., xiv, 103
Skidmore, Colonel Mark, 177, 186
Slessor, Sir John, 26
Somalia, 18 185, 196, 267
Somalia Affair, 197
Somalia Commission, 190, 191, 219, 233
Soviet Union, 75, 79
Soviet Special Purpose Forces (Spetsnaz), 165

Special Air Service (British), 72, 122
Special Operations Executive (SOE), 73
Special Senate Committee on Defence, 165
Special Service Force (SSF), 40, 104, 122, 147-9,
St. Laurent, Prime Minister Louis, 74, 79
Stacey, C.P., 44, 46
Standing Committee of External Affairs and National Defence (SCEAND), 149
Standing Committee on National Defence and Veterans Affairs (SCOND-VA), 104
Steadman, Air Vice Marshal, 31
Stewart, Major-General R.I. (retired), 111, 123, 128, 161, 168, 175
Stiner, General Carl, 275
Strike Command, 109
Student, General Kurt, 26
Suez Crisis of 1956, 17, 102
Suez Emergency Force, 102
Sutherland, R.J., 101
Sweetnam, Lieutenant-Colonel Pat, 275

Tabbernor, Colonel Dennis, 167
Tactical Air Command, 109
Tactical Air Lift School, 151
Taylor, General Maxwell, 109
Theriault, General C.E., 173
Therriault, Brigadier-General, 123, 128
Thomson, Brigadier-General G.S., 188
Tousignant, Major-General G.C., 225, 241
Training, airborne forces, 102, 106, 123-4, 257, 274
Tremblay, Hugh, 199
Trudeau, Prime Minister Pierre, 126-7
Turcot, Lieutenant-General Gilles, 126, 143
Turner, Lieutenant-Colonel John, 192

United Nations (UN), 17, 83
UN Assistance Mission in Rwanda (UNAMIR), 225
UN Force in Cyprus (UNFICYP), 143
UN Operation in Somalia (UNOSOM), 191
UN Ready Force, 17, 103, 108, 125, 162, 265
Unified Task Force (UNITAF), 196, 200
US Army Airborne Center, 122

Valcartier, 122, 254
Vernon, Major-General Brian, 192, 199, 229
vertical envelopment, 26
Vienneau, Chief Warrant Officer Jim, 153
Vokes, Major-General C., 83
von Einsiedel, Lieutenant-Colonel Garth, 254

Waters, Lieutenant-General Stan, 101, 148
Watkin, Lieutenant-Colonel Ken, 163, 170
Wavell, General Archibald, 27
Western Sahara, 186
White Paper (1964), 101, 103
White Paper (1971), *Defence in the 70s*, 126, 146
White Paper (1987), *Challenge and Commitments*, 166
White Paper (1994), 167, 221, 224, 227, 255
Whynot, Master-Corporal, 218
Winnipeg Light Infantry, 69
Winslow, Donna, 234
Withers, Brigadier-General Ramsey, 127
Worthington, Peter, 153

Young, Doug, 242

THE AUTHOR

DR. BERND HORN received his Honours BA in Political Science from the University of Waterloo and his MA and PhD in War Studies from the Royal Military College (RMC), Kingston, Ontario. Lieutenant-Colonel Horn is also a serving officer in the Canadian Forces. He joined in 1983 as an infantry officer and he was assigned to the Royal Canadian Regiment (RCR). His regimental service included operational tours to both Cyprus and Bosnia. He also served in the Canadian Airborne Regiment as the Officer Commanding 3 Commando from 1993-95. In addition, he has held a variety of staff positions at National Defence Headquarters in Ottawa. Lieutenant-Colonel Horn is currently the Commanding Officer of 1 RCR in Petawawa, Ontario. He is also an adjunct professor of history at RMC.